THE ORTHODO

Timothy Ware was born in Bath, Somerset, in 1934 and was educated at Westminster School and Magdalen College, Oxford, where he took a Double First in Classics, as well as reading Theology. After joining the Orthodox Church in 1958, he travelled widely in Greece, staying in particular at the monastery of St John, Patmos, and he is familiar with the life of other Orthodox centres such as Mount Athos and Jerusalem. In 1966 he was ordained priest and became a monk, receiving the new name of Kallistos. From 1966 to 2001 he was Spalding Lecturer in Eastern Orthodox Studies at the University of Oxford. He also has pastoral charge of the Greek parish in Oxford. In 1970 he became a Fellow of Pembroke College, Oxford. In 1982 he was consecrated titular Bishop of Diokleia and appointed assistant Bishop in the Orthodox Archdiocese of Thyateira and Great Britain (under the Ecumenical Patriarchate). His other works include *Eustratios Argenti: A Study of the Greek Church under Turkish Rule* (1964), *The Orthodox Way* (1979) and *The Inner Kingdom* (2000). He is also co-translator of two Orthodox service books, *The Festal Menaion* (1969) and *The Lenten Triodion* (1978), and also of *The Philokalia* (in progress: four volumes, 1979, 1981, 1984, 1995).

THE ORTHODOX CHURCH

TIMOTHY WARE

(Bishop Kallistos of Diokleia)

PENGUIN BOOKS

PENGUIN BOOKS

Published by the Penguin Group
Penguin Books Ltd, 80 Strand, London WC2R 0RL, England
Penguin Putnam Inc., 375 Hudson Street, New York, New York 10014, USA
Penguin Books Australia Ltd, 250 Camberwell Road, Camberwell, Victoria 3124, Australia
Penguin Books Canada Ltd, 10 Alcorn Avenue, Toronto, Ontario, Canada M4V 3B2
Penguin Books India (P) Ltd, 11 Community Centre, Panchsheel Park, New Delhi – 110 017, India
Penguin Books (NZ) Ltd, Cnr Rosedale and Airborne Roads, Albany, Auckland, New Zealand
Penguin Books (South Africa) (Pty) Ltd, 24 Sturdee Avenue, Rosebank 2196, South Africa

Penguin Books Ltd, Registered Offices: 80 Strand, London WC2R 0RL, England

www.penguin.com

First published in Pelican Books 1963
Reprinted with revisions 1964
Reprinted in Penguin Books 1991
Reprinted with revisions 1993, 1997
29

Typeset by Datix International Limited, Bungay, Suffolk
Set in 10/12 pt Monophoto Imprint
Printed in England by Clays Ltd, St Ives plc

ISBN-13: 978–0–140–14656–1

www.greenpenguin.co.uk

Penguin Books is committed to a sustainable future
for our business, our readers and our planet.
The book in your hands is made from paper
certified by the Forest Stewardship Council.

Contents

CONTENTS

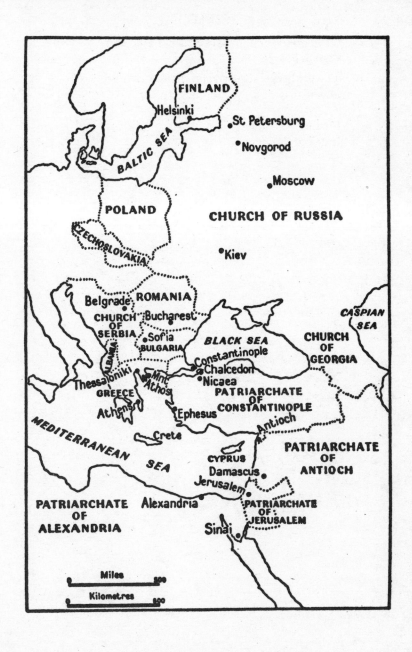

Introduction

Unknown and yet well known.   2 Corinthians vi, 9

'All Protestants are Crypto-Papists,' wrote the Russian theologian Alexis Khomiakov to an English friend in the year 1846. '. . . To use the concise language of algebra, all the West knows but one datum *a*; whether it be preceded by the positive sign + , as with the Romanists, or with the negative – , as with the Protestants, the *a* remains the same. Now a passage to Orthodoxy seems indeed like an apostasy from the past, from its science, creed, and life. It is rushing into a new and unknown world.'[1]

Khomiakov, when he spoke of the datum *a*, had in mind the fact that western Christians, whether Free Churchmen, Anglicans, or Roman Catholics, have a common background in the past. All alike (although they may not always care to admit it) have been profoundly influenced by the same events: by the Papal centralization and the Scholasticism of the Middle Ages, by the Renaissance, by the Reformation and Counter-Reformation. But behind members of the Orthodox Church – Greeks, Russians, and the rest – there lies a very different background. They have known no Middle Ages (in the western sense) and have undergone no Reformations or Counter-Reformations; they have only been affected in an oblique way by the cultural and religious upheaval which transformed western Europe in the sixteenth and seventeenth centuries. Christians in the west, both Roman and Reformed, generally start by asking the same questions, although they may disagree about the answers. In Orthodoxy, however, it is not merely the answers that are different – the questions themselves are not the same as in the west.

Orthodox see history in another perspective. Consider, for example, the Orthodox attitude towards western religious

1. From a letter printed in W. J. Birkbeck, *Russia and the English Church*, p. 67.

I

disputes. In the west it is usual to think of Roman Catholicism and Protestantism as opposite extremes; but to an Orthodox they appear as two sides of the same coin. Khomiakov calls the Pope 'the first Protestant', 'the father of German rationalism'; and by the same token he would doubtless have considered the Christian Scientist an eccentric Roman Catholic.[1] 'How are we to arrest the pernicious effects of Protestantism?' he was asked by a High Church Anglican when visiting Oxford in 1847; to which he replied: 'Shake off your Roman Catholicism.' In the eyes of the Russian theologian, the two things went hand in hand; both alike share the same assumptions, for Protestantism was hatched from the egg which Rome had laid.

'A new and unknown world': Khomiakov was right to speak of Orthodoxy in this way. Orthodoxy is not just a kind of Roman Catholicism without the Pope, but something quite distinct from any religious system in the west. Yet those who look more closely at this 'unknown world' will discover much in it which, while different, is yet curiously familiar. 'But that is what I have always believed!' Such has been the reaction of many, on learning more fully about the Orthodox Church and what it teaches; and they are partly right. For more than nine hundred years the Greek east and the Latin west have been growing steadily apart, each following its own way, yet in the early centuries of Christendom both sides can find common ground. Athanasius and Basil lived in the east, but they belong also to the west; and Orthodox who live in France, Britain, or Ireland can in their turn look upon the national saints of these lands – Alban and Patrick, Cuthbert and Bede, Geneviève of Paris and Augustine of Canterbury – not as strangers but as members of their own Church. All Europe was once as much part of Orthodoxy as Greece and Russia are today.

When Khomiakov wrote his letter in 1846, there were in fact few on either side who knew one another by personal contact. Robert Curzon, travelling through the Levant in the 1830s in search of manuscripts which he could buy at bargain prices, was disconcerted to find that the Patriarch of Constantinople

1. Compare P. Hammond, *The Waters of Marah*, p. 10.

had never heard of the Archbishop of Canterbury. Matters have certainly changed since then. Travel has become incomparably easier, the physical barriers have been broken down. And travel is no longer necessary: a citizen of the western world need no longer leave his own country in order to observe the Orthodox Church at first hand. Greeks journeying westward from choice or economic necessity, and Slavs driven westward by persecution, have brought their Church with them, establishing across all Europe, America and Australia a network of dioceses and parishes, theological colleges and monasteries. Most important of all, in many different communions during the present century there has grown up a compelling and unprecedented desire for the visible unity of all Christians, and this has given rise to a new interest in the Orthodox Church. The Greco-Russian diaspora was scattered over the world at the very moment when western Christians, in their concern for reunion, were becoming conscious of the relevance of Orthodoxy, and anxious to learn more about it. In reunion discussions the contribution of the Orthodox Church has often proved unexpectedly illuminating: precisely because the Orthodox have a different background from the west, they have been able to open up fresh lines of thought, and to suggest long-forgotten solutions to old difficulties.

The west has never lacked persons whose conception of Christendom was not restricted to Canterbury, Geneva and Rome; yet in the past such people were voices crying in the wilderness. It is now no longer so. The effects of an alienation which has lasted for more than nine centuries cannot be quickly undone, but at least a beginning has been made.

What is meant by 'the Orthodox Church'? The divisions which have brought about the present fragmentation of Christendom occurred in three main stages, at intervals of roughly five hundred years. The first stage in the separation came in the fifth and sixth centuries, when what are known today as the Oriental Orthodox Churches became divided from the main body of Christians. These Churches fall into two groups, the *Church of the East* (mainly in what are today Iraq and Iran; sometimes

3

called the 'Assyrian', 'Nestorian', 'Chaldean' or 'East Syrian' Church); and the five *Non-Chalcedonian Churches* (frequently termed 'Monophysite'): the Syrian Church of Antioch (the so-called 'Jacobite' Church), the Syrian Church in India, the Coptic Church in Egypt, the Armenian Church and the Ethiopian Church. The Church of the East today has no more than 550,000 members, although once it was much larger; the Non-Chalcedonians number altogether about 27 million. These two groups are often together styled the 'lesser' or 'separated' Eastern Churches, but such titles are best avoided, implying as they do a value judgement.

This present book, which makes no claim to cover the Christian east in its full complexity, will not be concerned directly with these 'Oriental Orthodox', although we shall be referring to them from time to time. Our subject will be those Christians who are termed not 'Oriental' but *'Eastern Orthodox'*, that is to say, the Christians who are in communion with the Ecumenical Patriarchate of Constantinople; and so when we refer to the 'Orthodox Church', it is the Eastern, not the Oriental, Orthodox that we have in view. Fortunately in our own day there are great hopes of a full reconciliation between these two families of Christians – the Oriental and the Eastern Orthodox.

As a result of this first division, Eastern Orthodoxy became restricted on its eastward side mainly to the Greek-speaking world. Then came the second separation, conventionally dated to the year 1054. The main body of Christians now became divided into two communions: in western Europe, the Roman Catholic Church under the Pope of Rome; in the Byzantine Empire, the Eastern Orthodox Church. Orthodoxy was now limited on its westward side as well. The third separation, between Rome and the Reformers in the sixteenth century, is not here our direct concern.

It is interesting to note how cultural and ecclesiastical divisions tend to coincide. Christianity, while universal in its mission, has been associated in practice with three cultures: Semitic, Greek and Latin. As a result of the first separation the Semitic Christians of Syria, with their flourishing school of theologians and writers, were cut off from the rest of Christendom. Then followed the second separation, which drove a wedge between the Greek and Latin traditions in Christendom. So it has come about that in Eastern Orthodoxy the primary cultural influence has been that of Greece. Yet it must not therefore be thought that the Orthodox Church is exclusively a Greek Church and nothing else, since Syriac and Latin Fathers also have a place in the fullness of Orthodox tradition.

While the Orthodox Church became bounded first on the eastern and then on the western side, it expanded to the north. In 863 St Cyril and St Methodius, the Apostles of the Slavs, travelled northward to undertake missionary work beyond the frontiers of the Byzantine Empire, and their efforts led eventually to the conversion of Bulgaria, Serbia and Russia. As the Byzantine power dwindled, these newer Churches of the north increased in importance, and on the fall of Constantinople to the Turks in 1453 the Principality of Moscow was ready to take Byzantium's place as the protector of the Orthodox world. Within the last two centuries there has been a partial reversal of this situation. Although Constantinople itself still remains in Turkish hands, a pale shadow of its former glory, the Orthodox Christians in Greece began to regain their freedom in 1821; the Russian Church, on the other hand, has in this century suffered for seventy years under the rule of an aggressively anti-Christian government.

Such are the main stages which have determined the external development of the Orthodox Church. Geographically its primary area of distribution lies in eastern Europe, Russia, and along the coasts of the eastern Mediterranean. It is composed at present of the following self-governing or 'autocephalous' Churches:[1]

1. After each church an approximate estimate of size is given. Like all ecclesiastical statistics, these figures should be treated with caution, and they are in any case intended merely as a rough comparative guide. For the most part the figures indicate the number of baptized members rather than those who are actively practising their Orthodoxy.

5

(1) The four ancient Patriarchates:

Constantinople	(6 million)
Alexandria	(350,000)
Antioch	(750,000)
Jerusalem	(60,000)

Though greatly reduced in size, these four Churches for historical reasons occupy a special position in the Orthodox Church, and rank first in honour. The heads of these Churches bear the title *Patriarch*.

(2) Nine other autocephalous Churches:

Russia	(100–150 million)
Serbia	(8 million)
Romania	(23 million)
Bulgaria	(8 million)
Georgia	(5 million)
Cyprus	(450,000)
Greece	(9 million)
Poland	(750,000)
Albania	(160,000)

All except two of these nine Churches – Poland and Albania – are in countries where the Christian population is entirely or predominantly Orthodox. The Churches of Greece and Cyprus are Greek; four of the others – Russia, Serbia, Bulgaria, Poland – are Slav. The heads of the Russian, Romanian, Serbian and Bulgarian Churches are known by the title *Patriarch*; the head of the Georgian Church is called *Catholicos-Patriarch*; the heads of the other churches are called either *Archbishop* or *Metropolitan*.

(3) There are in addition several Churches which, while self-governing in most respects, do not possess full independence. These are termed 'autonomous' but not 'autocephalous':

Czech Republic and Slovakia	(55,000)[1]
Sinai	(900)
Finland	(56,000)
Japan	(25,000)
China	(? 10,000–20,000)

1. Regarded by some of the Orthodox Churches as autocephalous.

(4) There is in addition a large Orthodox 'diaspora' in western Europe, in North and South America, and in Australia. Most of these Orthodox who have been 'scattered abroad' depend jurisdictionally upon one of the Patriarchates or autocephalous Churches, but in some areas there is a move towards self-government. In particular, steps have been taken to form an autocephalous Orthodox Church in America (about 1,000,000), but this has not yet been officially recognized by the majority of other Orthodox Churches.

The Orthodox Church is thus a family of self-governing Churches. It is held together, not by a centralized organization, not by a single prelate wielding power over the whole body, but by the double bond of unity in the faith and communion in the sacraments. Each Patriarchate or autocephalous Church, while independent, is in full agreement with the rest on all matters of doctrine, and between them all there is in principle full sacramental communion. (There are in fact certain breaches in communion, particularly among the Russian and Ukrainian Orthodox, but the situation here is exceptional and, one hopes, temporary in character.) There is in Orthodoxy no one with an equivalent position to the Pope in the Roman Catholic Church. The Patriarch of Constantinople is known as the 'Ecumenical' (or universal) Patriarch, and since the schism between east and west he has enjoyed a position of special honour among all the Orthodox communities; but he does not have the right to interfere in the internal affairs of other Churches. His place resembles that of the Archbishop of Canterbury in the worldwide Anglican communion.

This decentralized system of independent local Churches has the advantage of being highly flexible, and is easily adapted to changing conditions. Local Churches can be created, suppressed, and then restored again, with very little disturbance to the life of the Church as a whole. Many of these local Churches are also national Churches, for during the past in Orthodox countries Church and State have usually been closely linked. But while an independent State often possesses its own autocephalous Church, ecclesiastical divisions do not necessarily coincide with State boundaries. The territories of the four ancient Patriarchates fall politically into several different countries. The Orthodox Church is a federation of *local*, but not in every case *national*, Churches. It does not have as its basis the political principle of the State Church.

Among the various Churches there is, as can be seen, an enormous variation in size, with Russia at one extreme and Sinai at the other. The different Churches also vary in age, some dating back to Apostolic times, while others are little more than a generation old. The Church of Albania, for example, only became autocephalous in 1937.

Orthodoxy claims to be universal – not something exotic and oriental, but simple Christianity. Because of human failings and the accidents of history, the Orthodox Church has been largely restricted in the past to certain geographical areas. Yet to the Orthodox themselves their Church is something more than a group of local bodies. The word 'Orthodoxy' has the double meaning of 'right belief' and 'right glory' (or 'right worship'). The Orthodox, therefore, make what may seem at first a surprising claim: they regard their Church as the Church which guards and teaches the true belief about God and which glorifies Him with right worship, that is, *as nothing less than the Church of Christ on earth*. How this claim is understood, and what the Orthodox think of other Christians who do not belong to their Church, it is part of the aim of this book to explain.

Part One
HISTORY

CHAPTER I

The Beginnings

In the village there is a chapel dug deep beneath the earth, its entrance carefully camouflaged. When a secret priest visits the village, it is here that he celebrates the Liturgy and the other services. If the villagers for once believe themselves safe from police observation, the whole population gathers in the chapel, except for the guards who remain outside to give warning if strangers appear. At other times services take place in shifts . . .

The Easter service was held in an apartment of an official State institution. Entrance was possible only with a special pass, which I obtained for myself and for my small daughter. About thirty people were present, among them some of my acquaintances. An old priest celebrated the service, which I shall never forget. 'Christ is risen' we sang softly, but full of joy . . . The joy that I felt in this service of the Catacomb Church gives me strength to live, even today.

These are two accounts[1] of Church life in Russia shortly before the Second World War. But if a few alterations were made, they could easily be taken for descriptions of Christian worship under Nero or Diocletian. They illustrate the way in which during the course of nineteen centuries Christian history has travelled through a full circle. Christians today stand far closer to the early Church than their grandparents did. Christianity began as the religion of a small minority existing in a predominantly non-Christian society, and such it is becoming once more. The Christian Church in its early days was distinct and separate from the State; and now in one country after another the traditional alliance between Church and State is coming to an end. Christianity was at first a *religio illicita*, a religion forbidden and persecuted by

1. Taken from the periodical *Orthodox Life* (Jordanville, N.Y. 1959), no. 4, pp. 30–1.

the government; today persecution is no longer a fact of the past alone, and it is by no means impossible that in the thirty years between 1918 and 1948 more Christians died for their faith than in the three hundred years that followed Christ's Crucifixion.

Members of the Orthodox Church in particular have been made very much aware of these facts, for the vast majority of them have been living until very recently under the rule of an anti-Christian Communist government. The first period of Christian history, extending from the day of Pentecost to the conversion of Constantine, has a special relevance for contemporary Orthodoxy.

'Suddenly there came from heaven a sound like the rushing of a violent wind, and it filled the whole house where they were sitting. And there appeared to them tongues like flames of fire, divided among them and resting on each one. And they were all filled with the Holy Spirit' (Acts ii, 2–4). So the history of the Christian Church begins, with the descent of the Holy Spirit on the Apostles at Jerusalem during the feast of Pentecost, the first Whit Sunday. On that same day through the preaching of St Peter three thousand men and women were baptized, and the first Christian community at Jerusalem was formed.

Before long the members of the Jerusalem Church were scattered by the persecution which followed the stoning of St Stephen. 'Go forth therefore,' Christ had said, 'and make all nations My disciples' (Matthew xxviii, 19). Obedient to this command they preached wherever they went, at first to Jews, but before long to Gentiles also. Some stories of these Apostolic journeys are recorded by St Luke in the book of Acts; others are preserved in the tradition of the Church. Within an astonishingly short time small Christian communities had sprung up in all the main centres of the Roman Empire and even in places beyond the Roman frontiers.

The Empire through which these first Christian missionaries travelled was, particularly in its eastern part, an empire of cities. This determined the administrative structure of the primitive Church. The basic unit was the community in each city, governed by its own bishop; to assist the bishop there were presbyters or priests, and deacons. The surrounding countryside depended on the Church of the city. This pattern, with the threefold ministry of bishops, priests, and deacons, was already established in some places by the end of the first century. We can see it in the seven short letters which St Ignatius, Bishop of Antioch, wrote about the year 107 as he travelled to Rome to be martyred. Ignatius laid emphasis upon two things in particular, the bishop and the Eucharist; he saw the Church as both hierarchical and sacramental. 'The bishop in each Church,' he wrote, 'presides in place of God.' 'Let no one do any of the things which concern the Church without the bishop . . . Wherever the bishop appears, there let the people be, just as wherever Jesus Christ is, there is the Catholic Church.' And it is the bishop's primary and distinctive task to celebrate the Eucharist, 'the medicine of immortality'.[1]

People today tend to think of the Church as a worldwide organization, in which each local body forms part of a larger and more inclusive whole. Ignatius did not look at the Church in this way. For him the local community *is* the Church. He thought of the Church as a Eucharistic society, which only realizes its true nature when it celebrates the Supper of the Lord, receiving His Body and Blood in the sacrament. But the Eucharist is something that can only happen locally – in each particular community gathered round its bishop; and at every local celebration of the Eucharist it is the *whole* Christ who is present, not just a part of Him. Therefore each local community, as it celebrates the Eucharist Sunday by Sunday, is the Church in its fullness.

The teaching of Ignatius has a permanent place in Orthodox tradition. Orthodoxy still thinks of the Church as a Eucharistic society, whose outward organization, however necessary, is secondary to its inner, sacramental life; and Orthodoxy still

1. *To the Magnesians*, vi, 1; *To the Smyrnaeans*, viii, 1 and 2; *To the Ephesians*, xx, 2.

emphasizes the cardinal importance of the local community in the structure of the Church. To those who attend an Orthodox Pontifical Liturgy,[1] when the bishop stands at the beginning of the service in the middle of the church, surrounded by his flock, Ignatius of Antioch's idea of the bishop as the centre of unity in the local community will occur with particular vividness.

But besides the local community there is also the wider unity of the Church. This second aspect is developed in the writings of another martyr bishop, St Cyprian of Carthage (died 258). Cyprian saw all bishops as sharing in the one episcopate, yet sharing it in such a way that each possesses not a part but the whole. 'The episcopate,' he wrote, 'is a single whole, in which each bishop enjoys full possession. So is the Church a single whole, though it spreads far and wide into a multitude of churches as its fertility increases.'[2] There are many churches but only one Church; many *episcopi* but only one episcopate.

There were many others in the first three centuries of the Church who like Cyprian and Ignatius ended their lives as martyrs. The persecutions, it is true, were often local in character and usually limited in duration. Yet although there were long periods when the Roman authorities extended to Christianity a large measure of toleration, the threat of persecution was always there, and Christians knew that at any time this threat could become a reality. The idea of martyrdom had a central place in the spiritual outlook of the early Christians. They saw their Church as founded upon blood – not only the blood of Christ but the blood of those 'other Christs', the martyrs. In later centuries when the Church became 'established' and no longer suffered persecution, the idea of martyrdom did not disappear, but it took other forms: the monastic life, for example, is often regarded by Greek writers as an equivalent to martyrdom. The same approach is found

1. *The Liturgy*: this is the term normally used by Orthodox to refer to the service of Holy Communion, the Eucharist or Mass.
2. *On the Unity of the Church*, 5.

also in the west: take, for instance, a Celtic text – an Irish homily of the seventh century – which likens the ascetic life to the way of the martyr:

Now there are three kinds of martyrdom which are accounted as a Cross to a man, white martyrdom, green martyrdom, and red martyrdom. White martyrdom consists in a man's abandoning everything he loves for God's sake ... Green martyrdom consists in this, that by means of fasting and labour he frees himself from his evil desires, or suffers toil in penance and repentance. Red martyrdom consists in the endurance of a Cross or death for Christ's sake.[1]

At many periods in Orthodox history the prospect of red martyrdom has been fairly remote, and the green and white forms prevail. Yet there have also been times, above all in this present century, when Orthodox and other Christians have once again been called to undergo martyrdom of blood.

It was only natural that the bishops, who, as Cyprian emphasized, share in the one episcopate, should meet together in a council to discuss their common problems. Orthodoxy has always attached great importance to the place of councils in the life of the Church. It believes that the council is the chief organ whereby God has chosen to guide His people, and it regards the Catholic Church as essentially a *conciliar* Church. (Indeed, in Russian the same adjective *soborny* has the double sense of 'catholic' and 'conciliar', while the corresponding noun, *sobor*, means both 'church' and 'council'.) In the Church there is neither dictatorship nor individualism, but harmony and unanimity; its members remain free but not isolated, for they are united in love, in faith, and in sacramental communion. In a council, this idea of harmony and free unanimity can be seen worked out in practice. In a true council no single member arbitrarily imposes his will upon the rest, but each consults with the others, and in this way they all freely achieve a 'common mind'. A council is a living embodiment of the essential nature of the Church.

The first council in the Church's history is described in Acts xv. Attended by the Apostles, it met at Jerusalem to decide

1. Quoted in J. Ryan, *Irish Monasticism* (London 1931), p. 197.

how far Gentile converts should be subject to the Law of Moses. The Apostles, when they finally reached their decision, spoke in terms which in other circumstances might appear presumptuous: 'It seemed right to the Holy Spirit and to us . . .' (Acts xv, 28). Later councils have ventured to speak with the same confidence. An isolated individual may well hesitate to say, 'It seemed right to the Holy Spirit and to *me*'; but when gathered in council, the members of the Church can together claim an authority which individually none of them possesses.

The Council of Jerusalem, assembling as it did the leaders of the entire Church, was an exceptional gathering, for which there is no parallel until the Council of Nicaea in 325. But by Cyprian's time it had already become usual to hold local councils, attended by all the bishops in a particular civil province of the Roman Empire. A local council of this type normally met in the provincial capital, under the presidency of the bishop of the capital, who was given the title *Metropolitan*. As the third century proceeded, councils widened in scope and began to include bishops not from one but from several civil provinces. These larger gatherings tended to assemble in the chief cities of the Empire, such as Alexandria or Antioch; and so it came about that the bishops of certain great cities began to acquire an importance above the provincial Metropolitans. But for the time being nothing was decided about the precise status of these great sees. Nor during the third century itself did this continual expansion of councils reach its logical conclusion: as yet (apart from the Apostolic Council) there had only been local councils, of lesser or greater extent, but no 'general' council, formed of bishops from the whole Christian world, and claiming to speak in the name of the whole Church.

In 312 an event occurred which utterly transformed the outward situation of the Church. As he was riding through France with his army, the Emperor Constantine looked up into the sky and saw a cross of light in front of the sun. With the cross there was an inscription: *In this sign conquer*. As a result of this vision, Constantine became the first Roman Emperor to embrace the Christian faith. On that day in France a train of events was set in motion which brought the first main period of Church history to an end, and which led to the creation of the Christian Empire of Byzantium.

CHAPTER 2

Byzantium, I:
The Church of the Seven Councils

All profess that there are seven holy and Ecumenical Councils,
and these are the seven pillars of the faith of the Divine Word
on which He erected His holy mansion, the Catholic and
Ecumenical Church.

John II, Metropolitan of Russia (*1080–89*)

THE ESTABLISHMENT OF AN IMPERIAL CHURCH

Constantine stands at a watershed in the history of the Church.
With his conversion, the age of the martyrs and the persecutions drew to an end, and the Church of the Catacombs
became the Church of the Empire. The first great effect of
Constantine's vision was the so-called 'Edict' of Milan, which
he and his fellow Emperor Licinius issued in 313, proclaiming
the official toleration of the Christian faith. And though at first
Constantine granted no more than toleration, he soon made it
clear that he intended to favour Christianity above all the other
tolerated religions in the Roman Empire. Theodosius, within
fifty years of Constantine's death, had carried this policy
through to its conclusion: by his legislation he made Christianity not merely the most highly favoured but the only recognized
religion of the Empire. The Church was now established. 'You
are not allowed to exist,' the Roman authorities had once said
to the Christians. Now it was the turn of paganism to be suppressed.

Constantine's vision of the Cross led also, in his lifetime, to
two further consequences, equally momentous for the later
development of Christendom. First, in 324 he decided to move
the capital of the Roman Empire eastward from Italy to the
shores of the Bosphorus. Here, on the site of the Greek city
of Byzantium, he built a new capital, which he named after

himself, 'Constantinoupolis'. The motives for this move were in part economic and political, but they were also religious: the Old Rome was too deeply stained with pagan associations to form the centre of the Christian Empire which he had in mind. In the New Rome things were to be different: after the solemn inauguration of the city in 330, he laid down that at Constantinople no pagan rites should ever be performed. Constantine's new capital has exercised a decisive influence upon the development of Orthodox history.

Secondly, Constantine summoned the first General or Ecumenical Council of the Christian Church at Nicaea in 325. If the Roman Empire was to be a Christian Empire, then Constantine wished to see it firmly based upon the one Orthodox faith. It was the duty of the Nicene Council to elaborate the content of that faith. Nothing could have symbolized more clearly the new relation between Church and State than the outward circumstances of the gathering at Nicaea. The Emperor himself presided, 'like some heavenly messenger of God', as one of those present, Eusebius, Bishop of Caesarea, expressed it. At the conclusion of the council the bishops dined with the Emperor. 'The circumstances of the banquet,' wrote Eusebius (who was inclined to be impressed by such things), 'were splendid beyond description. Detachments of the bodyguard and other troops surrounded the entrance of the palace with drawn swords, and through the midst of these the men of God proceeded without fear into the innermost of the imperial apartments. Some were the Emperor's own companions at table, others reclined on couches ranged on either side. One might have thought it was a picture of Christ's kingdom, and a dream rather than reality.'[1] Matters had certainly changed since the time when Nero employed Christians as living torches to illuminate his gardens at night. Nicaea was the first of seven general councils; and these, like the city of Constantine, occupy a central position in the history of Orthodoxy.

The three events – the Edict of Milan, the foundation of

---

1. *The Life of Constantine*, iii, 10 and 15.

Constantinople, and the Council of Nicaea – mark the Church's coming of age.

THE FIRST SIX COUNCILS (325–681)

The life of the Church in the earlier Byzantine period is dominated by the seven general councils. These councils fulfilled a double task. First, they clarified and articulated the visible organization of the Church, crystallizing the position of the five great sees or *Patriarchates*, as they came to be known. Secondly, and more important, the councils defined once and for all the Church's teaching upon the fundamental doctrines of the Christian faith – the Trinity and the Incarnation. All Christians agree in regarding these things as 'mysteries' which lie beyond human understanding and language. The bishops, when they drew up definitions at the councils, did not imagine that they had explained the mystery; they merely sought to exclude certain false ways of speaking and thinking about it. To prevent people from deviating into error and heresy, they drew a fence around the mystery; that was all.

The discussions at the councils at times sound abstract and remote, yet they were inspired by a very practical purpose: human salvation. Humanity, so the New Testament teaches, is separated from God by sin, and cannot through its own efforts break down the wall of separation which its sinfulness has created. God has therefore taken the initiative: He has become man, has been crucified, and has risen again from the dead, thereby delivering humanity from the bondage of sin and death. This is the central message of the Christian faith, and it is this message of redemption that the councils were concerned to safeguard. Heresies were dangerous and required condemnation, because they impaired the teaching of the New Testament, setting up a barrier between humans and God, and so making it impossible for humans to attain full salvation.

St Paul expressed this message of redemption in terms of *sharing*. Christ shared our poverty that we might share the riches of His divinity: 'Our Lord Jesus Christ, though He was rich, yet for your sake became poor, that you through His poverty might become rich' (2 Corinthians viii, 9). In St John's Gospel the same idea is found in a slightly different form. Christ states that He has given His disciples a share in the divine glory, and He prays that they may achieve union with God: 'The glory which You, Father, gave Me I have given to them, that they may be one, just as We are one; I in them, and You in Me, that they may be perfectly one' (John xvii, 22–3). The Greek Fathers took these and similar texts in their literal sense, and dared to speak of humanity's 'deification' (in Greek, *theosis*). If humans are to share in God's glory, they argued, if they are to be 'perfectly one' with God, this means in effect that humans must be 'deified': they are called to become by grace what God is by nature. Accordingly St Athanasius summed up the purpose of the Incarnation by saying, 'God became human that we might be made god.'[1]

Now if this 'being made god', this *theosis*, is to be possible, Christ the Saviour must be both fully God and fully human. No one less than God can save humanity; therefore if Christ is to save, He must be God. But only if He is truly human, as we are, can we humans participate in what He has done for us. A bridge is formed between God and humanity by the Incarnate Christ who is divine and human at once. 'Here-after you shall see the heaven open,' our Lord promised, 'and the angels of God ascending and descending upon the Son of Man' (John i, 51). Not only angels use that ladder, but the human race.

Christ must be fully God and fully human. Each heresy in turn undermined some part of this vital affirmation. Either Christ was made less than God (Arianism); or His humanity was so divided from His Godhead that He became two persons instead of one (Nestorianism); or He was not presented as truly human (Monophysitism, Monothelitism). Each council defended this affirmation. The first two, held in the fourth century, concentrated upon the earlier part (that Christ must

1. *On the Incarnation*, 54.

21

be fully God) and formulated the doctrine of the Trinity. The next four, during the fifth, sixth and seventh centuries, turned to the second part (the fullness of Christ's humanity) and also sought to explain how humanity and Godhead could be united in a single person. The seventh council, in defence of the Holy Icons, seems at first to stand somewhat apart, but like the first six it was ultimately concerned with the Incarnation and with human salvation.

The main work of the Council of Nicaea in 325 was the condemnation of Arianism. Arius, a priest in Alexandria, maintained that the Son was inferior to the Father, and, in drawing a dividing line between God and creation, he placed the Son among created things: a superior creature, it is true, but a creature none the less. His motive, no doubt, was to protect the uniqueness and the transcendence of God, but the effect of his teaching, in making Christ less than God, was to render impossible our human deification. Only if Christ is truly God, the council answered, can He unite us to God, for none but God Himself can open to humans the way of union. Christ is 'one in essence' (*homoousios*) with the Father. He is no demigod or superior creature, but God in the same sense that the Father is God: 'true God from true God,' the council proclaimed in the Creed which it drew up, 'begotten not made, *one in essence* with the Father'.

The Council of Nicaea dealt also with the visible organization of the Church. It singled out for mention three great centres: Rome, Alexandria, and Antioch (Canon VI). It also laid down that the see of Jerusalem, while remaining subject to the Metropolitan of Caesarea, should be given the next place in honour after these three (Canon VII). Constantinople naturally was not mentioned, since it was not officially inaugurated as the new capital until five years later; it continued to be subject, as before, to the Metropolitan of Heraclea.

The work of Nicaea was taken up by the second Ecumenical Council, held at Constantinople in 381. This council expanded and adapted the Nicene Creed, developing in particular the teaching upon the Holy Spirit, whom it affirmed to be God even as the Father and Son are God: 'who proceeds from the

22

Father, who with the Father and the Son together is worshipped and together glorified'. The council also altered the
provisions of the Sixth Canon of Nicaea. The position of Constantinople, now the capital of the Empire, could no longer be
ignored, and it was assigned the second place, after Rome and
above Alexandria. 'The Bishop of Constantinople shall have
the prerogatives of honour after the Bishop of Rome, because
Constantinople is New Rome' (Canon III).

Behind the definitions of the councils lay the work of theologians, who gave precision to the words which the councils
employed. It was the supreme achievement of St Athanasius of
Alexandria to draw out the full implications of the key word in
the Nicene Creed: *homoousios*, one in essence or substance,
consubstantial. Complementary to his work was that of the
three Cappadocian Fathers, Saints Gregory of Nazianzus,
known in the Orthodox Church as Gregory the Theologian
(?329–?90), Basil the Great (?330–79), and his younger brother
Gregory of Nyssa (died 394). While Athanasius emphasized
the unity of God – Father and Son are one in essence (*ousia*) –
the Cappadocians stressed God's threeness: Father, Son, and
Holy Spirit are three persons (*hypostasis*). Preserving a delicate
balance between the threeness and the oneness in God, they
gave full meaning to the classic summary of Trinitarian doctrine, *three persons in one essence*. Never before or since has the
Church possessed four theologians of such stature within a
single generation.

After 381 Arianism quickly ceased to be a living issue, except
in certain parts of western Europe. The controversial aspect of
the council's work lay in its third Canon, which was resented
alike by Rome and by Alexandria. Old Rome wondered where
the claims of New Rome would end: might not Constantinople
before long claim first place? Rome chose therefore to ignore
the offending Canon, and not until the Lateran Council (1215)
did the Pope formally recognize Constantinople's claim to
second place. (Constantinople was at that time in the hands of
the Crusaders and under the rule of a Latin Patriarch.) But the
Canon was equally a challenge to Alexandria, which hitherto
had occupied the first place in the east. The next seventy years

witnessed a sharp conflict between Constantinople and Alexandria, in which for a time the victory went to the latter. The first major Alexandrian success was at the Synod of the Oak, when Theophilus of Alexandria secured the deposition and exile of the Bishop of Constantinople, St John Chrysostom, 'John of the Golden Mouth' (?334–407). A fluent and eloquent preacher – his sermons must often have lasted for an hour or more – John expressed in popular form the theological ideas put forward by Athanasius and the Cappadocians. A man of strict and austere life, he was inspired by a deep compassion for the poor and by a burning zeal for social righteousness. Of all the Fathers he is perhaps the best loved in the Orthodox Church, and the one whose works are most widely read.

Alexandria's second major success was won by the nephew and successor of Theophilus, St Cyril of Alexandria (died 444), who brought about the fall of another Bishop of Constantinople, Nestorius, at the third General Council, held in Ephesus (431). But at Ephesus there was more at stake than the rivalry of two great sees. Doctrinal issues, quiescent since 381, once more emerged, centring now not on the Trinity but on the Person of Christ. Cyril and Nestorius agreed that Christ was fully God, one of the Trinity, but they diverged in their descriptions of His humanity and in their method of explaining the union of the divine and the human in a single person. They represented different traditions or schools of theology. Nestorius, brought up in the school of Antioch, upheld the integrity of Christ's humanity, but distinguished so emphatically between the humanity and the Godhead that he seemed in danger of ending, not with one person, but with two persons coexisting in the same body. Cyril, the protagonist of the opposite tradition of Alexandria, started from the unity of Christ's person rather than the diversity of His humanity and Godhead, but spoke about Christ's humanity less vividly than the Antiochenes. Either approach, if pressed too far, could lead to heresy, but the Church had need of both in order to form a balanced picture of the whole Christ. It was a tragedy for Christendom that the two schools, instead of balancing one another, entered into conflict.

Nestorius precipitated the controversy by declining to call the Virgin Mary 'Mother of God' (*Theotokos*). This title was already accepted in popular devotion, but it seemed to Nestorius to imply a confusion of Christ's humanity and His Godhead. Mary, he argued – and here his Antiochene 'separatism' is evident – is only to be called 'Mother of Man' or at the most 'Mother of Christ', since she is mother only of Christ's humanity, not of His divinity. Cyril, supported by the council, answered with the text 'The Word was made flesh' (John i, 14): Mary is God's mother, for 'she bore the Word of God made flesh'.[1] What Mary bore was not a man loosely united to God, but a single and undivided person, who is God and man at once. The name *Theotokos* safeguards the unity of Christ's person: to deny her this title is to separate the Incarnate Christ into two, breaking down the bridge between God and humanity and erecting within Christ's person a middle wall of partition. Thus we can see that not only titles of devotion were involved at Ephesus, but the very message of salvation. The same primacy that the word *homoousios* occupies in the doctrine of the Trinity, the word *Theotokos* holds in the doctrine of the Incarnation.

Alexandria won another victory at a second council held in Ephesus in 449, but this gathering – so it was felt by a large part of the Christian world – pushed the Alexandrian position too far. Dioscorus of Alexandria, Cyril's successor, insisted that there is in Christ only one nature (*physis*); the Saviour is *from* two natures, but after His Incarnation there is only 'one incarnate nature of God the Word'. This is the position commonly termed 'Monophysite'. It is true that Cyril himself had used such language, but Dioscorus omitted the balancing statements that Cyril had made in 433 as a concession to the Antiochenes. To many it seemed that Dioscorus was denying the integrity of Christ's humanity, although this is almost certainly an unjust interpretation of his standpoint.

Only two years later, in 451, the Emperor Marcian summoned to Chalcedon a fresh gathering of bishops, which the

---

1. See the first of Cyril's *Twelve Anathemas*.

Church of Byzantium and the west regarded as the fourth General Council. The pendulum now swung back in an Antiochene direction. The council, rejecting the Monophysite position of Dioscorus, proclaimed that, while Christ is a single, undivided person, He is not only *from* two natures but *in* two natures. The bishops acclaimed the *Tome* of St Leo the Great, Pope of Rome (died 461), in which the distinction between the two natures is clearly stated, although the unity of Christ's person is also emphasized. In their proclamation of faith they stated their belief in 'one and the same Son, perfect in Godhead and perfect in humanity, truly God and truly human ... acknowledged *in two natures* unconfusedly, unchangeably, indivisibly, inseparably; the difference between the natures is in no way removed because of the union, but rather the peculiar property of each nature is preserved, and both combine in one person and in one *hypostasis*'. The Definition of Chalcedon, we may note, is aimed not only at the Monophysites ('in two natures, unconfusedly, unchangeably'), but also at the followers of Nestorius ('one and the same Son ... indivisibly, inseparably').

But Chalcedon was more than a defeat for Alexandrian theology: it was a defeat for Alexandrian claims to rule supreme in the east. Canon XXVIII of Chalcedon confirmed Canon III of Constantinople, assigning to New Rome the place next in honour after Old Rome. Leo repudiated this Canon, but the east has ever since recognized its validity. The council also freed Jerusalem from the jurisdiction of Caesarea and gave it the fifth place among the great sees. The system later known among Orthodox as the Pentarchy was now complete, whereby five great sees in the Church were held in particular honour, and a settled order of precedence was established among them: in order of rank, Rome, Constantinople, Alexandria, Antioch, Jerusalem. All five claimed Apostolic foundation. The first four were the most important cities in the Roman Empire; the fifth was added because it was the place where Christ had suffered on the Cross and risen from the dead. The bishop in each of these cities received the title *Patriarch*. The five Patriarchates between them divided into spheres of jurisdiction the whole of the known world, apart from Cyprus, which was granted independence by the Council of Ephesus and has remained self-governing ever since.

When speaking of the Orthodox conception of the Pentarchy there are two possible misunderstandings which must be avoided. First, the system of Patriarchs and Metropolitans is a matter of *ecclesiastical organization*. But if we look at the Church from the viewpoint not of ecclesiastical order but of *divine right*, then we must say that all bishops are essentially equal, however humble or exalted the city over which each presides. All bishops share equally in the apostolic succession, all have the same sacramental powers, all are divinely appointed teachers of the faith. If a dispute about doctrine arises, it is not enough for the Patriarchs to express their opinion: *every* diocesan bishop has the right to attend a general council, to speak, and to cast his vote. The system of the Pentarchy does not impair the essential equality of all bishops, nor does it deprive each local community of the importance which Ignatius assigned to it.

In the second place, Orthodox believe that among the five Patriarchs a special place belongs to the Pope. The Orthodox Church does not accept the doctrine of Papal authority set forth in the decrees of the Vatican Council of 1870, and taught today in the Roman Catholic Church; but at the same time Orthodoxy does not deny to the Holy and Apostolic See of Rome a *primacy of honour*, together with the right (under certain conditions) to hear appeals from all parts of Christendom. Note that we have used the word 'primacy', not 'supremacy'. Orthodox regard the Pope as the bishop 'who presides in love', to adapt a phrase of St Ignatius: Rome's mistake – so Orthodox believe – has been to turn this primacy or 'presidency of love' into a supremacy of external power and jurisdiction.

This primacy which Rome enjoys takes its origin from three factors. First, Rome was the city where St Peter and St Paul were martyred, and where Peter was bishop. The Orthodox Church acknowledges Peter as the first among the Apostles: it does not forget the celebrated 'Petrine texts' in the Gospels (Matthew xvi, 18–19; Luke xxii, 32; John xxi, 15–17) –

although Orthodox theologians do not understand these texts in quite the same way as modern Roman Catholic commentators. And while many Orthodox theologians would say that not only the Bishop of Rome but all bishops are successors of Peter, yet most of them at the same time admit that the Bishop of Rome is Peter's successor in a special sense. Secondly, the see of Rome also owed its primacy to the position occupied by the city of Rome in the Empire: she was the capital, the chief city of the ancient world, and such in some measure she continued to be even after the foundation of Constantinople. Thirdly, although there were occasions when Popes fell into heresy, on the whole during the first eight centuries of the Church's history the Roman see was noted for the purity of its faith: other Patriarchates wavered during the great doctrinal disputes, but Rome for the most part stood firm. When hard pressed in the struggle against heretics, people felt that they could turn with confidence to the Pope. Not only the Bishop of Rome, but *every* bishop, is appointed by God to be a teacher of the faith; yet because the see of Rome had in practice taught the faith with an outstanding loyalty to the truth, it was above all to Rome that everyone appealed for guidance in the early centuries of the Church.

But as with Patriarchs, so with the Pope: the primacy assigned to Rome does not overthrow the essential equality of all bishops. The Pope is the first bishop in the Church – but he is the *first among equals*.

Ephesus and Chalcedon were a rock of Orthodoxy, but they were also a grave rock of offence. The Arians had been gradually reconciled and formed no lasting schism. But to this day there exist Christians belonging to the Church of the East (frequently, although misleadingly, called 'Nestorians') who cannot accept the decisions of Ephesus, and who consider it incorrect to call the Virgin Mary *Theotokos*; and to this day there also exist Non-Chalcedonians who follow the Monophysite teaching of Dioscorus, and who reject the Chalcedonian Definition and the *Tome* of Leo. The Church of the East lay almost entirely outside the Byzantine Empire, and little more is heard of it in Byzantine history. But large numbers of

Non-Chalcedonians, particularly in Egypt and Syria, were subjects of the Emperor, and repeated though unsuccessful efforts were made to bring them back into communion with the Byzantine Church. As so often, theological differences were made more bitter by cultural and national tension. Egypt and Syria, both predominantly non-Greek in language and background, resented the power of Greek Constantinople, alike in religious and in political matters. Thus ecclesiastical schism was reinforced by political separatism. Had it not been for these non-theological factors, the two sides might perhaps have reached a theological understanding after Chalcedon. Many modern scholars are inclined to think that the difference between 'Non-Chalcedonians' and 'Chalcedonians' was basically one of terminology, not of theology. The two parties understood the word 'nature' (*physis*) in different ways, but both were concerned to affirm the same basic truth: that Christ the Saviour is fully divine and fully human, and yet He is one and not two.

The Definition of Chalcedon was supplemented by two later councils, both held at Constantinople. The fifth Ecumenical Council (553) reinterpreted the decrees of Chalcedon from an Alexandrian point of view, and sought to explain, in more constructive terms than Chalcedon had used, how the two natures of Christ unite to form a single person. The sixth Ecumenical Council (680–81) condemned the heresy of the Monothelites, who argued that, although Christ has two natures, yet since He is a single person, He has only one will. The Council replied that, if He has two natures, then He must also have two wills. The Monothelites, it was felt, impaired the fullness of Christ's humanity, since human nature without a human will would be incomplete, a mere abstraction. Since Christ is true man as well as true God, He must have a human as well as a divine will.

During the fifty years before the meeting of the sixth Council, Byzantium was faced with a sudden and alarming development: the rise of Islam. The most striking fact about Muslim expansion was its speed. When the Prophet died in 632, his authority scarcely extended beyond the Hejaz. But within fifteen years his Arab followers had taken Syria, Palestine, and

Egypt; within fifty they were at the walls of Constantinople and almost captured the city; within a hundred they had swept across North Africa, advanced through Spain, and forced western Europe to fight for its life at the Battle of Poitiers. The Arab invasions have been called 'a centrifugal explosion, driving in every direction small bodies of mounted raiders in quest of food, plunder, and conquest. The old empires were in no state to resist them.'[1] Christendom survived, but only with difficulty. The Byzantines lost their eastern possessions, and the three Patriarchates of Alexandria, Antioch, and Jerusalem passed under infidel control; within the Christian Empire of the East, the Patriarchate of Constantinople was now without rival. Henceforward Byzantium was never free for very long from Muslim attacks, and although it held out for eight centuries more, yet in the end it succumbed.

THE HOLY ICONS

Disputes concerning the Person of Christ did not cease with the council of 681, but were extended in a different form into the eighth and ninth centuries. The struggle centred on the Holy Icons, the pictures of Christ, the Mother of God, and the saints, which were kept and venerated both in churches and in private homes. The Iconoclasts or icon-smashers, suspicious of any religious art which represented human beings or God, demanded the destruction of icons; the opposite party, the Iconodules or venerators of icons, vigorously defended the place of icons in the life of the Church. The struggle was not merely a conflict between two conceptions of Christian art. Deeper issues were involved: the character of Christ's human nature, the Christian attitude towards matter, the true meaning of Christian redemption.

The Iconoclasts may have been influenced from the outside by Jewish and Muslim ideas, and it is significant that, three years before the first outbreak of Iconoclasm in the Byzantine

1. H. St L. B. Moss, in Baynes and Moss, *Byzantium: an Introduction* (Oxford 1948), pp. 11–12.

Empire, the Muslim Caliph Yezid ordered the removal of all icons within his dominions. But Iconoclasm was not simply imported from outside; within Christianity itself there had always existed a 'puritan' outlook, which condemned icons because it saw in all images a latent idolatry. When the Isaurian Emperors attacked icons, they found plenty of support inside the Church.

The Iconoclast controversy, which lasted some 120 years, falls into two phases. The first period opened in 726 when Leo III began his attack on icons, and ended in 780 when the Empress Irene suspended the persecution. The Iconodule position was upheld by the seventh and last Ecumenical Council (787), which met, as the first had done, at Nicaea. Icons, the council proclaimed, are to be kept in churches and honoured with the same relative veneration as is shown to other material symbols, such as the 'precious and life-giving Cross' and the Book of Gospels. A new attack on icons, started by Leo V the Armenian in 815, continued until 843 when the icons were again reinstated, this time permanently, by another Empress, Theodora. The final victory of the Holy Images in 843 is known as 'the Triumph of Orthodoxy', and is commemorated in a special service celebrated on 'Orthodoxy Sunday', the first Sunday in Lent. The chief champion of the icons in the first period was St John of Damascus (?675–749), in the second St Theodore of Stoudios (759–826). John was able to work the more freely because he dwelt in Muslim territory, out of reach of the Byzantine government. It was not the last time that Islam acted unintentionally as the protector of Orthodoxy.

One of the distinctive features of Orthodoxy is the place which it assigns to icons. An Orthodox church today is filled with them: dividing the sanctuary from the body of the building there is a solid screen, the iconostasis, entirely covered with icons, while other icons are placed in special shrines around the church; and perhaps the walls are covered with icons in fresco or mosaic. An Orthodox prostrates himself before these icons, he kisses them and burns candles in front of them; they are censed by the priest and carried in procession. What do these gestures and actions mean? What do icons signify, and why did John of Damascus and others regard them as important?

We shall consider first the charge of idolatry, which the Iconoclasts brought against the Iconodules; then the positive value of icons as a means of instruction; and finally their doctrinal importance.

(1) *The question of idolatry*. When an Orthodox kisses an icon or prostrates himself before it, he is not guilty of idolatry. The icon is not an idol but a symbol; the veneration shown to images is directed, not towards stone, wood and paint, but towards the person depicted. This had been pointed out some time before the Iconoclast controversy by Leontius of Neapolis (died about 650):

> We do not make obeisance to the nature of wood, but we revere and do obeisance to Him who was crucified on the Cross ... When the two beams of the Cross are joined together I adore the figure because of Christ who was crucified on the Cross, but if the beams are separated, I throw them away and burn them.[1]

Because icons are only symbols, Orthodox do not *worship* them, but *reverence* or *venerate* them. John of Damascus carefully distinguished between the relative honour of veneration shown to material symbols, and the worship due to God alone.

(2) *Icons as part of the Church's teaching*. Icons, said Leontius, are 'opened books to remind us of God';[2] they are one of the means which the Church employs in order to teach the faith. He who lacks learning or leisure to study works of theology has only to enter a church to see unfolded before him on the walls all the mysteries of the Christian religion. If a pagan asks you to show him your faith, said the Iconodules, take him into church and place him before the icons. In this way icons form a part of Holy Tradition.

(3) *The doctrinal significance of icons*. Here we come to the real heart of the Iconoclast dispute. Granted that icons are not idols; granted that they are useful for instruction; but are

1. Migne, *Patrologia Graeca* (*P.G.*), xciv, 1384D.
2. *P.G.* xciv, 1276A.

they not only permissible but necessary? Is it *essential* to have icons? The Iconodules held that it is, because icons safeguard a full and proper doctrine of the Incarnation. Iconoclasts and Iconodules agreed that God cannot be represented in His eternal nature: 'no one has seen God at any time' (John i, 18). But, the Iconodules continued, the Incarnation has made a representational religious art possible: God can be depicted because He became human and took flesh. Material images, argued John of Damascus, can be made of Him who took a material body:

Of old God the incorporeal and uncircumscribed was not depicted at all. But now that God has appeared in the flesh and lived among humans, I make an image of the God who can be seen. I do not worship matter but I worship the Creator of matter, who for my sake became material and deigned to dwell in matter, who through matter effected my salvation. I will not cease from worshipping the matter through which my salvation has been effected.[1]

The Iconoclasts, by repudiating all representations of God, failed to take full account of the Incarnation. They fell, as so many puritans have done, into a kind of dualism. Regarding matter as a defilement, they wanted a religion freed from all contact with what is material; for they thought that what is spiritual must be non-material. But this is to betray the Incarnation, by allowing no place to Christ's humanity, to His body; it is to forget that our body as well as our soul must be saved and transfigured. The Iconoclast controversy is thus closely linked to the earlier disputes about Christ's person. It was not merely a controversy about religious art, but about the Incarnation, about human salvation, about the salvation of the entire material cosmos.

God took a material body, thereby proving that matter can be redeemed: 'The Word made flesh has deified the flesh,' said John of Damascus.[2] God has 'deified' matter, making it 'spirit-bearing'; and if flesh has become a vehicle of the Spirit, then so – though in a different way – can wood and paint. The

1. *On Icons*, i, 16 (*P.G.* xciv, 1245A).
2. *On Icons*, i, 21 (*P.G.* xciv, 1253B).

Orthodox doctrine of icons is bound up with the Orthodox belief that the whole of God's creation, material as well as spiritual, is to be redeemed and glorified. In the words of Nicolas Zernov (1898–1980) – what he says of Russians is true of all Orthodox:

[Icons] were for the Russians not merely paintings. They were dynamic manifestations of man's spiritual power to redeem creation through beauty and art. The colours and lines of the [icons] were not meant to imitate nature; the artists aimed at demonstrating that men, animals, and plants, and the whole cosmos, could be rescued from their present state of degradation and restored to their proper 'Image'. The [icons] were pledges of the coming victory of a redeemed creation over the fallen one ... The artistic perfection of an icon was not only a reflection of the celestial glory – it was a concrete example of matter restored to its original harmony and beauty, and serving as a vehicle of the Spirit. The icons were part of the transfigured cosmos.[1]

As John of Damascus put it:

The icon is a song of triumph, and a revelation, and an enduring monument to the victory of the saints and the disgrace of the demons.[2]

The conclusion of the Iconoclast dispute, the meeting of the seventh Ecumenical Council, the Triumph of Orthodoxy in 843 – these mark the end of the second period in Orthodox history, the period of the seven councils. These seven councils are of immense importance to Orthodoxy. For members of the Orthodox Church, their interest is not merely historical but contemporary; they are the concern not only of scholars and clergy, but of all the faithful. 'Even illiterate peasants,' said Dean Stanley, 'to whom, in the corresponding class of life in Spain and Italy, the names of Constance and Trent would probably be quite unknown, are well aware that their Church reposes on the basis of the seven councils, and retain a hope that they may yet live to see an eighth general council, in which the evils of the time will be set straight.'[3] Orthodox

1. *The Russians and their Church* (London 1945), pp. 107–8.
2. *On Icons,* 11, 11 (*P.G.* xciv, 1296B).
3. *Lectures on the History of the Eastern Church* (Everyman Edition), p. 99.

often call themselves 'the Church of the Seven Councils'. By this they do not mean that the Orthodox Church has ceased to think creatively since 787. But they see in the period of the councils the great age of theology; and, next to the Bible, it is the seven councils which the Orthodox Church takes as its standard and guide in seeking solutions to the new problems which arise in every generation.

SAINTS, MONKS, AND EMPERORS

Not without reason has Byzantium been called 'the image of the heavenly Jerusalem'. Religion entered into every aspect of Byzantine life. Byzantine holidays were religious festivals; the races which took place in the Circus began with the singing of hymns; and trade contracts invoked the Trinity and were marked with the sign of the Cross. Today, in an untheological age, it is all but impossible to realize how burning an interest was felt in religious questions by every part of society, by laity as well as clergy, by the poor and uneducated as well as the Court and the scholars. Gregory of Nyssa describes the unending theological arguments in Constantinople at the time of the second general council:

The whole city is full of it, the squares, the market places, the cross-roads, the alleyways; old-clothes men, money changers, food sellers: they are all busy arguing. If you ask someone to give you change, he philosophizes about the Begotten and the Unbegotten; if you inquire about the price of a loaf, you are told by way of reply that the Father is greater and the Son inferior; if you ask 'Is my bath ready?' the attendant answers that the Son was made out of nothing.[1]

This curious complaint indicates the atmosphere in which the councils met. So violent were the passions aroused that sessions were not always restrained or dignified. 'Synods and councils I salute from a distance,' Gregory of Nazianzus dryly remarked, 'for I know how troublesome they are.' 'Never again will I sit in those gatherings of cranes and

1. *On the Deity of the Son* (*P.G.* xlvi, 557B).

geese.'[1] The Fathers at times supported their cause by question-able means: Cyril of Alexandria, for example, in his struggle against Nestorius, bribed the Court heavily and terrorized the city of Ephesus with a private army of monks. Yet if Cyril was intemperate in his methods, it was because of his consuming desire that the right cause should triumph; and if Christians were at times acrimonious, it was because they cared about the Christian faith. Perhaps disorder is better than apathy. Ortho-doxy recognizes that the councils were attended by imperfect humans, but it believes that these imperfect humans were guided by the Holy Spirit.

The Byzantine bishop was not only a distant figure who attended councils; he was also in many cases a true father to his people, a friend and protector to whom people confidently turned when in trouble. The concern for the poor and op-pressed which John Chrysostom displayed is found in many others. St John the Almsgiver, Patriarch of Alexandria (died 619), for example, devoted all the wealth of his see to helping those whom he called 'my brothers and sisters, the poor'. When his own resources failed, he appealed to others: 'He used to say,' a contemporary recorded, 'that if, without ill-will, some-one were to strip the rich right down to their shirts in order to give to the poor, he would do no wrong.'[2] 'Those whom you call poor and beggars,' John said, 'these I proclaim my masters and helpers. For they, and they alone, can really help us and bestow upon us the kingdom of heaven.'[3] The Church in the Byzantine Empire did not overlook its social obligations, and one of its principal functions was charitable work.

Monasticism played a decisive part in the religious life of Byzantium, as it has done in that of all Orthodox countries. It has been rightly said that 'the best way to penetrate Orthodox spirituality is to enter it through monasticism'.[4] 'There is a great richness of forms of the spiritual life to be found within

1. *Letter* 124; *Poems about Himself*, xvii, 91.
2. Leontius of Neapolis, *A Supplement to the Life of John the Almsgiver*, 21.
3. Leontius, *Supplement*, 2.
4. P. Evdokimov, *L'Orthodoxie* (Paris 1959), p. 20.

the bounds of Orthodoxy, but monasticism remains the most classic of all.'[1] The monastic life first emerged as a definite institution in Egypt and Syria during the fourth century, and from there it spread rapidly across Christendom. It is no coincidence that monasticism should have developed immediately after Constantine's conversion, at the very time when the persecutions ceased and Christianity became fashionable. The monks with their austerities were martyrs in an age when martyrdom of blood no longer existed; they formed the counterbalance to an established Christendom. People in Byzantine society were in danger of forgetting that Byzantium was an image and symbol, not the reality; they ran the risk of identifying the kingdom of God with an earthly kingdom. The monks by their withdrawal from society into the desert fulfilled a prophetic and eschatological ministry in the life of the Church. They reminded Christians that the kingdom of God is not of this world.

Monasticism has taken three chief forms, all of which had appeared in Egypt by the year 350, and all of which are still to be found in the Orthodox Church today. There are first the *hermits*, ascetics leading the solitary life in huts or caves, and even in tombs, among the branches of trees, or on the tops of pillars. The great model of the eremitic life is the father of monasticism himself, St Antony of Egypt (251–356). Secondly there is the *community life*, where monks dwell together under a common rule and in a regularly constituted monastery. Here the great pioneer was St Pachomius of Egypt (286–346), author of a rule later used by St Benedict in the west. Basil the Great, whose ascetic writings have exercised a formative influence on eastern monasticism, was a strong advocate of the community life, although he was probably influenced more by Syria than by the Pachomian houses that he visited. Giving a social emphasis to monasticism, he urged that religious houses should care for the sick and poor, maintaining hospitals and orphanages, and working directly for the benefit of society at large. But in general eastern monasticism has been far less concerned than

1. V. Lossky, *The Mystical Theology of the Eastern Church*, p. 17.

western with active work; in Orthodoxy a monk's primary task is the life of prayer, and it is through this that he serves others. It is not so much what a monk *does* that matters, as what he *is*. Finally there is a form of the monastic life intermediate between the first two, the *semi-eremitic life*, a 'middle way' where instead of a single highly organized community there is a loosely knit group of small settlements, each settlement containing perhaps between two and six members living together under the guidance of an elder. The great centres of the semi-eremitic life in Egypt were Nitria and Scetis, which by the end of the fourth century had produced many outstanding monks – Ammon the founder of Nitria, Macarius of Egypt and Macarius of Alexandria, Evagrius of Pontus, and Arsenius the Great. (This semi-eremitic system is found not only in the east but in the far west, in Celtic Christianity.) From its very beginnings the monastic life was seen, in both east and west, as a vocation for women as well as men, and throughout the Byzantine world there were numerous communities of nuns.

Because of its monasteries, fourth-century Egypt was regarded as a second Holy Land, and travellers to Jerusalem felt their pilgrimage to be incomplete unless it included the ascetic houses of the Nile. In the fifth and sixth centuries leadership in the monastic movement shifted to Palestine, with St Euthymius the Great (died 473) and his disciple St Sabas (died 532). The monastery founded by St Sabas in the Jordan valley can claim an unbroken history to the present day; it was to this community that John of Damascus belonged. Almost as old is another important house with an unbroken history to the present, the monastery of St Catherine at Mount Sinai, founded by the Emperor Justinian (reigned 527–65). With Palestine and Sinai in Arab hands, monastic pre-eminence in the Byzantine Empire passed in the ninth century to the monastery of Stoudios in Constantinople. St Theodore, who became Abbot here in 799, reactivated the community and revised its rule, attracting vast numbers of monks.

Since the tenth century the chief centre of Orthodox monasticism has been Athos, a rocky peninsula in North Greece jutting out into the Aegean and culminating at its tip in a peak 6,670 feet high. Known as 'the Holy Mountain', Athos contains twenty 'ruling' monasteries and a large number of smaller houses, as well as hermits' cells; the whole peninsula is given up entirely to monastic settlements, and in the days of its greatest expansion it is said to have contained nearly forty thousand monks. The Great Lavra, the oldest of the twenty ruling monasteries, has by itself produced 26 Patriarchs and more than 144 bishops: this gives some idea of the importance of Athos in Orthodox history.

There are no 'Orders' in Orthodox monasticism. In the west a monk belongs to the Carthusian, the Cistercian, or some other Order; in the east he is simply a member of the one great fellowship which includes all monks and nuns, although of course he is attached to a particular monastic house. Western writers sometimes refer to Orthodox monks as 'Basilian monks' or 'monks of the Basilian Order', but this is not correct. St Basil is an important figure in Orthodox monasticism, but he founded no Order, and although two of his works are known as the *Longer Rules* and the *Shorter Rules*, these are in no sense comparable to the *Rule* of St Benedict.

A characteristic figure in Orthodox monasticism is the 'elder' or 'old man' (Greek *gerōn*; Russian *starets*, plural *startsy*). The elder is a monk of spiritual discernment and wisdom, whom others – either monks or people in the world – adopt as their guide and spiritual director. He is sometimes a priest, but often a lay monk; he receives no special ordination or appointment to the work of eldership, but is guided to it by the direct inspiration of the Spirit. A woman as well as a man may be called to this ministry, for Orthodoxy has its 'spiritual mothers' as well as its 'spiritual fathers'. The elder sees in a concrete and practical way what the will of God is in relation to each person who comes to consult him: this is the elder's special gift or *charisma*. The earliest and most celebrated of the monastic *startsy* was St Antony himself. The first part of his life, from eighteen to fifty-five, he spent in withdrawal and solitude; then, though still living in the desert, he abandoned this life of strict enclosure, and began to receive visitors. A group of disciples gathered round him, and besides these disciples there was a far larger circle of people who came, often from a long distance, to ask his advice; so great was the stream of visitors that, as Antony's biographer Athanasius put it, he became a physician to all Egypt. Antony has had many successors, and in most of them the same outward pattern of events is found – *a withdrawal in order to return.* A monk must first withdraw, and in silence must learn the truth about himself and God. Then, after this long and rigorous preparation in solitude, having gained the gifts of discernment which are required of an elder, he can open the door of his cell and admit the world from which formerly he fled.

At the heart of the Christian polity of Byzantium was the Emperor, who was no ordinary ruler, but God's representative on earth. If Byzantium was an icon of the heavenly Jerusalem, then the earthly monarchy of the Emperor was an image or icon of the monarchy of God in heaven; in church people prostrated themselves before the icon of Christ, and in the palace before God's living icon – the Emperor. The labyrinthine palace, the Court with its elaborate ceremonial, the throne room where mechanical lions roared and musical birds sang: these things were designed to make clear the Emperor's status as vicegerent of God. 'By such means,' wrote the Emperor Constantine VII Porphyrogenitus, 'we figure forth the harmonious movement of God the Creator around this universe, while the imperial power is preserved in proportion and order.'[1] The Emperor had a special place in the Church's worship: he could not of course celebrate the Eucharist, but he received communion within the sanctuary 'as priests do' – taking the consecrated bread in his hands and drinking from the chalice, instead of being given the sacrament in a spoon – and he also preached sermons and on certain feasts censed the altar. The vestments which Orthodox bishops now wear are the vestments once worn by the Emperor.

The life of Byzantium formed a unified whole, and there was no rigid line of separation between the religious and the secular, between Church and State: the two were seen as parts

1. *Book of Ceremonies*, Prologue.

of a single organism. Hence it was inevitable that the Emperor played an active part in the affairs of the Church. Yet at the same time it is not just to accuse Byzantium of Caesaro-Papism, of subordinating the Church to the State. Although Church and State formed a single organism, yet within this one organism there were two distinct elements, the priesthood (*sacerdotium*) and the imperial power (*imperium*); and while working in close co-operation, each of these elements had its own proper sphere in which it was autonomous. Between the two there was a 'symphony' or 'harmony', but neither element exercised absolute control over the other.

This is the doctrine expounded in the great code of Byzantine law drawn up under Justinian (see the sixth *Novel*) and repeated in many other Byzantine texts. Take for example the words of Emperor John Tzimisces: 'I recognize two authorities, priesthood and empire; the Creator of the world entrusted to the first the care of souls and to the second the control of men's bodies. Let neither authority be attacked, that the world may enjoy prosperity.'[1] Thus it was the Emperor's task to summon councils and to carry their decrees into effect, but it lay beyond his powers to dictate the content of those decrees: it was for the bishops gathered in council to decide what the true faith was. Bishops were appointed by God to teach the faith, whereas the Emperor was the protector of Orthodoxy, but not its exponent. Such was the theory, and such in great part was the practice also. Admittedly there were many occasions on which the Emperor interfered unwarrantably in ecclesiastical matters; but when a serious question of principle arose, the authorities of the Church quickly showed that they had a will of their own. Iconoclasm, for example, was vigorously championed by a whole series of Emperors, yet for all that it was successfully rejected by the Church. In Byzantine history Church and State were closely interdependent, but neither was subordinate to the other.

There are many today, not only outside but within the

1. Quoted in N. H. Baynes, *Byzantine Studies* (London 1955), p. 52.

Orthodox Church, who sharply criticize the Byzantine Empire and the idea of a Christian society for which it stands. Yet were the Byzantines entirely wrong? They believed that Christ, who lived on earth as a man, has redeemed every aspect of human existence, and they held that it was therefore possible to baptize not human individuals only but the whole spirit and organization of society. So they strove to create a polity entirely Christian in its principles of government and in its daily life. Byzantium in fact was nothing less than an attempt to accept and to apply the full implications of the Incarnation. Certainly the attempt had its dangers: in particular the Byzantines often fell into the error of identifying the earthly kingdom of Byzantium with the Kingdom of God, the Greek people – or rather, the 'Roman' people, to use the term by which they themselves described their own identity – with God's people. Certainly Byzantium fell far short of the high ideal which it set itself, and its failure was often lamentable and disastrous. The tales of Byzantium duplicity, violence and cruelty are too well known to call for repetition here. They are true – but they are only a part of the truth. For behind all the shortcomings of Byzantium can always be discerned the great vision by which the Byzantines were inspired: to establish here on earth a living image of God's government in heaven.

CHAPTER 3

Byzantium, II:
The Great Schism

> We are unchanged; we are still the same as we were in the
> eighth century ... Oh that you could only consent to be
> again what you were once, when we were both united in faith
> and communion!
>
> *Alexis Khomiakov*

THE ESTRANGEMENT OF EASTERN AND
WESTERN CHRISTENDOM

One summer afternoon in the year 1054, as a service was about
to begin in the Church of the Holy Wisdom[1] at Constantinople,
Cardinal Humbert and two other legates of the Pope entered
the building and made their way up to the sanctuary. They
had not come to pray. They placed a Bull of Excommunication
upon the altar and marched out once more. As he passed
through the western door, the Cardinal shook the dust from
his feet with the words: 'Let God look and judge.' A deacon
ran out after him in great distress and begged him to take back
the Bull. Humbert refused; and it was dropped in the street.

It is this incident which has conventionally been taken to
mark the beginning of the great schism between the Orthodox
east and the Latin west. But the schism, as historians now
generally recognize, is not really an event whose beginning can
be exactly dated. It was something that came about gradually,
as the result of a long and complicated process, starting well
before the eleventh century and not completed until some time
after.

In this long and complicated process, many different influences were at work. The schism was conditioned by cultural,

1. In Greek, 'Hagia Sophia'; often called 'St Sophia' or 'Sancta Sophia' by
English writers.

political, and economic factors; yet its fundamental cause was not secular but theological. In the last resort it was over matters of doctrine that east and west quarrelled – two matters in particular: the Papal claims and the *Filioque*. But before we look more closely at these two major differences, and before we consider the actual course of the schism, something must be said about the wider background. Long before there was an open and formal schism between east and west, the two sides had become *strangers* to one another; and in attempting to understand how and why the communion of Christendom was broken, we must start with this fact of increasing estrangement.

When Paul and the other Apostles travelled around the Mediterranean world, they moved within a closely knit political and cultural unity: the Roman Empire. This Empire embraced many different national groups, often with languages and dialects of their own. But all these groups were governed by the same Emperor; there was a broad Greco-Roman civilization in which educated people throughout the Empire shared; either Greek or Latin was understood almost everywhere in the Empire, and many could speak both languages. These facts greatly assisted the early Church in its missionary work.

But in the centuries that followed, the unity of the Mediterranean world gradually disappeared. The political unity was the first to go. From the end of the third century the Empire, while still theoretically one, was usually divided into two parts, an eastern and a western, each under its own Emperor. Constantine furthered this process of separation by founding a second imperial capital in the east, alongside Old Rome in Italy. Then came the barbarian invasions at the start of the fifth century: apart from Italy, much of which remained within the Empire for some time longer, the west was carved up among barbarian chiefs. The Byzantines never forgot the ideals of Rome under Augustus and Trajan, and still regarded their Empire as in theory universal; but Justinian was the last Emperor who seriously attempted to bridge the gulf between theory and fact, and his conquests in the west were soon abandoned. The political unity of the Greek east and the Latin west was destroyed by the barbarian invasions, and never permanently restored.

During the late sixth and the seventh centuries, east and west were further isolated from each other by the Avar and Slav invasions of the Balkan peninsula; Illyricum, which used to serve as a bridge, became in this way a barrier between Byzantium and the Latin world. The severance was carried a stage further by the rise of Islam: the Mediterranean, which the Romans once called *mare nostrum*, 'our sea', now passed largely into Arab control. Cultural and economic contacts between the eastern and western Mediterranean never entirely ceased, but they became far more difficult.

The Iconoclast controversy contributed still further to the division between Byzantium and the west. The Popes were firm supporters of the Iconodule standpoint, and so for many decades they found themselves out of communion with the Iconoclast Emperor and Patriarch at Constantinople. Cut off from Byzantium and in need of help, in 754 Pope Stephen turned northwards and visited the Frankish ruler, Pepin. This marked the first step in a decisive change of orientation so far as the Papacy was concerned. Hitherto Rome had continued in many ways to be part of the Byzantine world, but now it passed increasingly under Frankish influence, although the effects of this reorientation did not become fully apparent until the middle of the eleventh century.

Pope Stephen's visit to Pepin was followed half a century later by a much more dramatic event. On Christmas Day in the year 800 Pope Leo III crowned Charles the Great, King of the Franks, as Emperor. Charlemagne sought recognition from the ruler at Byzantium, but without success; for the Byzantines, still adhering to the principle of imperial unity, regarded Charlemagne as an intruder and the Papal coronation as an act of schism within the Empire. The creation of a Holy Roman Empire in the west, instead of drawing Europe closer together, only served to alienate east and west more than before.

The cultural unity lingered on, but in a greatly attenuated form. In both east and west, people of learning still lived within the classical tradition which the Church had taken over and made its own; but as time went on they began to interpret this tradition in increasingly divergent ways. Matters were made more difficult by problems of language. The days when educated people were bilingual were over. By the year 450 there were very few in western Europe who could read Greek, and after 600, although Byzantium still called itself the *Roman* Empire, it was rare for a Byzantine to speak Latin, the language of the Romans. Photius, the greatest scholar in ninth-century Constantinople, could not read Latin; and in 864 a 'Roman' Emperor at Byzantium, Michael III, even called the language in which Virgil once wrote 'a barbarian and Scythic tongue'. If Greeks wished to read Latin works or vice versa, they could do so only in translation, and usually they did not trouble to do even that: Psellus, an eminent Greek savant of the eleventh century, had so sketchy a knowledge of Latin literature that he confused Caesar with Cicero. Because they no longer drew upon the same sources nor read the same books, Greek east and Latin west drifted more and more apart.

It was an ominous but significant precedent that the cultural renaissance in Charlemagne's Court should have been marked at its outset by a strong anti-Greek prejudice. In fourth-century Europe there had been one Christian civilization, in thirteenth-century Europe there were two. Perhaps it is in the reign of Charlemagne that the schism of civilizations first becomes clearly apparent. The Byzantines for their part remained enclosed in their own world of ideas, and did little to meet the west half way. Alike in the ninth and in later centuries they usually failed to take western learning as seriously as it deserved. They dismissed all Franks as barbarians and nothing more.

These political and cultural factors could not but affect the life of the Church, and make it harder to maintain religious unity. Cultural and political estrangement can lead only too easily to ecclesiastical disputes, as may be seen from the case of Charlemagne. Refused recognition in the political sphere by the Byzantine Emperor, he was quick to retaliate with a charge of heresy against the Byzantine Church: he denounced the Greeks for not using the *Filioque* in the Creed (of this we shall say more in a moment) and he declined to accept the decisions of the seventh Ecumenical Council. It is true that Charlemagne only knew of these decisions through a faulty translation which seriously distorted their true meaning; but he seems in any case to have been semi-Iconoclast in his views.

The different political situations in east and west made the Church assume different outward forms, so that people came gradually to think of Church order in conflicting ways. From the start there had been a certain difference of emphasis here between east and west. In the east there were many Churches whose foundation went back to the Apostles; there was a strong sense of the equality of all bishops, of the collegial and conciliar nature of the Church. The east acknowledged the Pope as the first bishop in the Church, but saw him as the first among equals. In the west, on the other hand, there was only one great see claiming Apostolic foundation – Rome – so that Rome came to be regarded as *the* Apostolic see. The west, while it accepted the decisions of the Ecumenical Councils, did not play a very active part in the Councils themselves; the Church was seen less as a college and more as a monarchy – the monarchy of the Pope.

This initial divergence in outlook was made more acute by political developments. As was only natural, the barbarian invasions and the consequent breakdown of the Empire in the west served greatly to strengthen the autocratic structure of the western Church. In the east there was a strong secular head, the Emperor, to uphold the civilized order and to enforce law. In the west, after the advent of the barbarians, there was only a plurality of warring chiefs, all more or less usurpers. For the most part it was the Papacy alone which could act as a centre of unity, as an element of continuity and stability in the spiritual and political life of western Europe. By force of circumstances, the Pope assumed a part which the Greek Patriarchs were not called to play, issuing commands not only to his ecclesiastical subordinates but to secular rulers as well. The western Church gradually became centralized to a degree unknown anywhere in the four Patriarchates of the east (except possibly in Egypt). Monarchy in the west; in the east collegiality.

Nor was this the only effect which the barbarian invasions had upon the life of the Church. In Byzantium there were many educated laymen who took an active interest in theology. The 'lay theologian' has always been an accepted figure in Orthodoxy: some of the most learned Byzantine Patriarchs – Photius, for example – were laymen before their appointment to the Patriarchate. But in the west the only effective education which survived through the Dark Ages was provided by the Church for its clergy. Theology became the preserve of the priests, since most of the laity could not even read, much less comprehend the technicalities of theological discussion. Orthodoxy, while assigning to the episcopate a special teaching office, has never known this sharp division between clergy and laity which arose in the western Middle Ages.

Relations between eastern and western Christendom were also made more difficult by the lack of a common language. Because the two sides could no longer communicate easily with one another, and each could no longer read what the other wrote, misunderstandings arose much more easily. The shared 'universe of discourse' was progressively lost.

East and west were becoming strangers to one another, and this was something from which both were likely to suffer. In the early Church there had been unity in the faith, but a diversity of theological schools. From the start Greeks and Latins had each approached the Christian Mystery in their own way. At the risk of some oversimplification, it can be said that the Latin approach was more practical, the Greek more speculative; Latin thought was influenced by juridical ideas, by the concepts of Roman law, while the Greeks understood theology in the context of worship and in the light of the Holy Liturgy. When thinking about the Trinity, Latins started with the unity of the Godhead, Greeks with the threeness of the persons; when reflecting on the Crucifixion, Latins thought primarily of Christ the Victim, Greeks of Christ the Victor; Latins talked more of redemption, Greeks of deification; and so on. Like the schools of Antioch and Alexandria within the east, these two distinctive approaches were not in themselves contradictory; each served to supplement the other, and each had its place in the fullness of Catholic tradition. But now that the two sides were becoming strangers to one another – with no political and little cultural unity, with no common language – there was a danger that each side would follow its own approach in isolation and push it to extremes, forgetting the value in the other point of view.

We have spoken of the different doctrinal approaches in east and west; but there were two points of doctrine where the two sides no longer supplemented one another, but entered into direct conflict – the Papal claims and the *Filioque*. The factors which we have mentioned in previous paragraphs were sufficient in themselves to place a serious strain upon the unity of Christendom. Yet for all that, unity might still have been maintained, had there not been these two further points of difficulty. To them we must now turn. It was not until the middle of the ninth century that the full extent of the disagreement first came properly into the open, but the two differences themselves date back considerably earlier.

We have already had occasion to mention the Papacy when speaking of the different political situations in east and west; and we have seen how the centralized and monarchical structure of the western Church was reinforced by the barbarian invasions. Now so long as the Pope claimed an absolute power only in the west, Byzantium raised no objections. The Byzantines did not mind if the western Church was centralized, so long as the Papacy did not interfere in the east. The Pope, however, believed his immediate power of jurisdiction to extend to the east as well as to the west; and as soon as he tried to enforce this claim within the eastern Patriarchates, trouble was bound to arise. The Greeks assigned to the Pope a primacy of honour, but not the universal supremacy which he regarded as his due. The Pope viewed infallibility as his own prerogative; the Greeks held that in matters of the faith the final decision rested not with the Pope alone, but with a Council representing *all* the bishops of the Church. Here we have two different conceptions of the visible organization of the Church.

The Orthodox attitude to the Papacy is admirably expressed by a twelfth-century writer, Nicetas, Archbishop of Nicomedia:

My dearest brother, we do not deny to the Roman Church the primacy amongst the five sister Patriarchates; and we recognize her right to the most honourable seat at an Ecumenical Council. But she has separated herself from us by her own deeds, when through pride she assumed a monarchy which does not belong to her office . . . How shall we accept decrees from her that have been issued without consulting us and even without our knowledge? If the Roman Pontiff, seated on the lofty throne of his glory, wishes to thunder at us and, so to speak, hurl his mandates at us from on high, and if he wishes to judge us and even to rule us and our Churches, not by taking counsel with us but at his own arbitrary pleasure, what kind of brotherhood, or even what kind of parenthood can this be? We should be the slaves, not the sons, of such a Church, and the Roman See would not be the pious mother of sons but a hard and imperious mistress of slaves.[1]

That was how an Orthodox felt in the twelfth century, when the whole question had come out into the open. In earlier centuries the Greek attitude to the Papacy was basically the same, although not yet sharpened by controversy. Up to 850, Rome and the east avoided an open conflict over the Papal claims, but the divergence of views was not the less serious for being partially concealed.

The second great difficulty was the *Filioque*. The dispute involved the words about the Holy Spirit in the Nicene-Constantinopolitan Creed. Originally the Creed ran: 'I believe . . . in the Holy Spirit, the Lord, the Giver of Life, *who proceeds from the Father*, who with the Father and the Son together is worshipped and together glorified.' This, the original form, is recited unchanged by the east to this day. But the west inserted an extra phrase 'and from the Son' (in Latin, *Filioque*), so that the Creed now reads 'who proceeds from the Father *and the Son*'. It is not certain when and where this addition was first made, but it seems to have originated in Spain, as a safeguard against Arianism. At any rate the Spanish Church interpolated the *Filioque* at the third Council of Toledo (589), if not before. From Spain the addition spread to France and thence to Germany, where it was welcomed by Charlemagne and adopted at

1. Quoted in S. Runciman, *The Eastern Schism*, p. 116.

the semi-Iconoclast Council of Frankfort (794). It was writers at Charlemagne's court who first made the *Filioque* into an issue of controversy, accusing the Greeks of heresy because they recited the Creed in its original form. But Rome, with typical conservatism, continued to use the Creed without the *Filioque* until the start of the eleventh century. In 808 Pope Leo III wrote in a letter to Charlemagne that, although he himself believed the *Filioque* to be doctrinally sound, yet he considered it a mistake to tamper with the wording of the Creed. Leo deliberately had the Creed, without the *Filioque*, inscribed on silver plaques and set up in St Peter's. For the time being Rome acted as a mediator between the Franks and Byzantium.

It was not until 850 that the Greeks paid much attention to the *Filioque*, but once they did so, their reaction was sharply critical. The Orthodox objected (and still object) to this addition to the Creed, for two reasons. First, the Creed is the common possession of the whole Church, and if any change is to be made in it, this can only be done by an Ecumenical Council. The west, in altering the Creed without consulting the east, is guilty (as Khomiakov put it) of moral fratricide, of a sin against the unity of the Church. In the second place, most Orthodox believe the *Filioque* to be theologically untrue. They hold that the Spirit proceeds from the Father alone, and consider it a heresy to say that He proceeds from the Son as well. There are, however, some Orthodox who consider that the *Filioque* is not in itself heretical, and is indeed admissible as a theological opinion – not a dogma – provided that it is properly explained. But even those who take this more moderate view still regard it as an unauthorized addition.

Besides these two major issues, the Papacy and the *Filioque*, there were certain lesser matters of Church worship and discipline which caused trouble between east and west: the Greeks allowed married clergy, the Latins insisted on priestly celibacy; the two sides had different rules of fasting; the Greeks used leavened bread in the Eucharist, the Latins unleavened bread or 'azymes'.

*

Around 850 east and west were still in full communion with one another and still formed one Church. Cultural and political divisions had combined to bring about an increasing estrangement, but there was no open schism. The two sides had different conceptions of Papal authority and recited the Creed in different forms, but these questions had not yet been brought fully into the open.

But in 1190 Theodore Balsamon, Patriarch of Antioch and a great authority on Canon Law, looked at matters very differently:

> For many years [he does not say how many] the western Church has been divided in spiritual communion from the other four Patriarchates and has become alien to the Orthodox ... So no Latin should be given communion unless he first declares that he will abstain from the doctrines and customs that separate him from us, and that he will be subject to the Canons of the Church, in union with the Orthodox.[1]

In Balsamon's eyes, communion had been broken; there was a definite schism between east and west. The two no longer formed one visible Church.

In this transition from estrangement to schism, four incidents are of particular importance: the quarrel between Photius and Pope Nicolas I (usually known as the 'Photian schism': the east would prefer to call it the 'schism of Nicolas'); the incident of the Diptychs in 1009; the attempt at reconciliation in 1053–4 and its disastrous sequel; and the Crusades.

FROM ESTRANGEMENT TO SCHISM: 858–1204

In 858, fifteen years after the triumph of icons under Theodora, a new Patriarch of Constantinople was appointed – Photius, known to the Orthodox Church as St Photius the Great. He has been termed 'the most distinguished thinker, the most outstanding politician, and the most skilful diplomat ever to hold office as Patriarch of Constantinople'.[2] Soon after his

---

1. Quoted in Runciman, *The Eastern Schism*, p. 139.
2. G. Ostrogorsky, *History of the Byzantine State*, p. 199.

accession he became involved in a dispute with Pope Nicolas I (858–67). The previous Patriarch, St Ignatius, had been exiled by the Emperor and while in exile had resigned under pressure. The supporters of Ignatius, declining to regard this resignation as valid, considered Photius a usurper. When Photius sent a letter to the Pope announcing his accession, Nicolas decided that before recognizing Photius he would look further into the quarrel between the new Patriarch and the Ignatian party. Accordingly in 861 he sent legates to Constantinople.

Photius had no desire to start a dispute with the Papacy. He treated the legates with great deference, inviting them to preside at a council in Constantinople, which was to settle the issue between Ignatius and himself. The legates agreed, and together with the rest of the council they decided that Photius was the legitimate Patriarch. But when his legates returned to Rome, Nicolas declared that they had exceeded their powers, and he disowned their decision. He then proceeded to retry the case himself at Rome: a council held under his presidency in 863 recognized Ignatius as Patriarch, and proclaimed Photius to be deposed from all priestly dignity. The Byzantines took no notice of this condemnation, and sent no answer to the Pope's letters. Thus an open breach existed between the Churches of Rome and Constantinople.

The dispute clearly involved the Papal claims. Nicolas was a great reforming Pope, with an exalted idea of the prerogatives of his see, and he had already done much to establish an absolute power over all bishops in the west. But he believed this absolute power to extend to the east also: as he put it in a letter of 865, the Pope is endowed with authority 'over all the earth, that is, over *every* Church'. This was precisely what the Byzantines were not prepared to grant. Confronted with the dispute between Photius and Ignatius, Nicolas thought that he saw a golden opportunity to enforce his claim to universal jurisdiction: he would make both parties submit to his arbitration. But he realized that Photius had submitted *voluntarily* to the inquiry by the Papal legates, and that his action could not be taken as a recognition of Papal supremacy. This (among other reasons) was why Nicolas had cancelled his legates' decisions. The Byzantines for their part were willing to allow appeals to Rome, but only under the specific conditions laid down in Canon III of the Council of Sardica (343). This Canon states that a bishop, if under sentence of condemnation, can appeal to Rome, and the Pope, if he sees cause, can order a retrial; this retrial, however, is not to be conducted by the Pope himself at Rome, but by the bishops of the provinces adjacent to that of the condemned bishop. Nicolas, so the Byzantines felt, in reversing the decisions of his legates and demanding a retrial at Rome itself, was going far beyond the terms of this Canon. They regarded his behaviour as an unwarrantable and uncanonical interference in the affairs of another Patriarchate.

Soon not only the Papal claims but the *Filioque* became involved in the dispute. Byzantium and the west (chiefly the Germans) were both launching great missionary ventures among the Slavs.[1] The two lines of missionary advance, from the east and from the west, soon converged; and when Greek and German missionaries found themselves at work in the same land, it was difficult to avoid a conflict, since the two missions were run on widely different principles. The clash naturally brought to the fore the question of the *Filioque*, used by the Germans in the Creed, but not used by the Greeks. The chief point of trouble was Bulgaria, a country which Rome and Constantinople alike were anxious to add to their sphere of jurisdiction. The Khan Boris was at first inclined to ask the German missionaries for baptism: threatened, however, with a Byzantine invasion, he changed his policy and around 865 accepted baptism from Greek clergy. But Boris wanted the Church in Bulgaria to be independent, and when Constantinople refused to grant autonomy, he turned to the west in hope of better terms. Given a free hand in Bulgaria, the Latin missionaries promptly launched a violent attack on the Greeks, singling out the points where Byzantine practice differed from their own: married clergy, rules of fasting, and above all the *Filioque*. At Rome itself the *Filioque* was still not in use, but Nicolas gave full support to the Germans when they insisted

1. See pp. 73–6.

upon its insertion in Bulgaria. The Papacy, which in 808 had mediated between the Franks and the Greeks, was now neutral no longer.

Photius was naturally alarmed by the extension of German influence in the Balkans, on the very borders of the Byzantine Empire; but he was much more alarmed by the question of the *Filioque*, now brought forcibly to his attention. In 867 he took action. He wrote an Encyclical Letter to the other Patriarchs of the east, denouncing the *Filioque* at length and charging those who used it with heresy. Photius has often been blamed for writing this letter: even the great Roman Catholic historian Francis Dvornik, who is in general highly sympathetic to Photius, calls his action on this occasion a 'futile attack', and says 'the lapse was inconsiderate, hasty, and big with fatal consequences'.[1] But if Photius really considered the *Filioque* heretical, what else could he do except speak his mind? It must also be remembered that it was not Photius who first made the *Filioque* a matter of controversy, but Charlemagne and his scholars seventy years before: the west was the original aggressor, not the east. Photius followed up his letter by summoning a council to Constantinople, which declared Pope Nicolas excommunicate, terming him 'a heretic who ravages the vineyard of the Lord'.

At this critical point in the dispute, the whole situation suddenly changed. In this same year (867) Photius was deposed from the Patriarchate by the Emperor. Ignatius became Patriarch once more, and communion with Rome was restored. In 869–70 another council was held at Constantinople, known as the 'Anti-Photian Council', which condemned and anathematized Photius, reversing the decisions of 867. This council, later reckoned in the west as the eighth Ecumenical Council, opened with the unimpressive total of 12 bishops, although numbers at subsequent sessions rose to 103.

But there were further changes to come. The 869–70 council requested the Emperor to resolve the status of the Bulgarian Church, and not surprisingly he decided that it should be assigned to the Patriarchate of Constantinople. Realizing that

1. F. Dvornik, *The Photian Schism*, p. 433.

Rome would allow him less independence than Byzantium, Boris accepted this decision. From 870, then, the German missionaries were expelled and the *Filioque* was heard no more in the confines of Bulgaria. Nor was this all. At Constantinople, Ignatius and Photius were reconciled to one another, and when Ignatius died in 877, Photius once more succeeded him as Patriarch. In 879 yet another council was held in Constantinople, attended by 383 bishops – a notable contrast with the meagre total at the anti-Photian gathering ten years previously. The council of 869 was anathematized and all condemnations of Photius were withdrawn; these decisions were accepted without protest at Rome. So Photius ended victorious, recognized by Rome and ecclesiastically master of Bulgaria. Until recently it was thought that there was a second 'Photian schism', but Dr Dvornik has proved with devastating conclusiveness that this second schism is a myth: in Photius' later period of office (877–86) communion between Constantinople and the Papacy remained unbroken. The Pope at this time, John VIII (872–82), was no friend to the Franks and did not press the question of the *Filioque*, nor did he attempt to enforce the Papal claims in the east. Perhaps he recognized how seriously the policy of Nicolas had endangered the unity of Christendom.

Thus the schism was outwardly healed, but no real solution had been reached concerning the two great points of difference which the dispute between Nicolas and Photius had forced into the open. Matters had been patched up, and that was all.

Photius, always honoured in the east as a saint, a leader of the Church, and a theologian, has in the past been regarded by the west with less enthusiasm, as the author of a schism and little else. His good qualities are now more widely appreciated. 'If I am right in my conclusions,' so Dr Dvornik ends his monumental study, 'we shall be free once more to recognize in Photius a great Churchman, a learned humanist, and a genuine Christian, generous enough to forgive his enemies, and to take the first step towards reconciliation.'[1]

1. *The Photian Schism*, p. 432.

At the beginning of the eleventh century there was fresh trouble over the *Filioque*. The Papacy at last adopted the addition: at the coronation of Emperor Henry II at Rome in 1014, the Creed was sung in its interpolated form. Five years earlier, in 1009, the newly-elected Pope Sergius IV sent a letter to Constantinople which may have contained the *Filioque*, although this is not certain. Whatever the reason, the Patriarch of Constantinople, also called Sergius, did not include the new Pope's name in the Diptychs: these are lists, kept by each Patriarch, which contain the names of the other Patriarchs, living and departed, whom he recognizes as orthodox. The Diptychs are a visible sign of the unity of the Church, and deliberately to omit a person's name from them is tantamount to a declaration that one is not in communion with him. After 1009 the Pope's name did not appear again in the Diptychs of Constantinople; technically, therefore, the Churches of Rome and Constantinople were out of communion from that date. But it would be unwise to press this technicality too far. Diptychs were frequently incomplete, and so do not form an infallible guide to Church relations. The Constantinopolitan lists before 1009 often lacked the Pope's name, simply because new Popes at their accession failed to notify the east. The omission in 1009 aroused no comment at Rome, and even at Constantinople people quickly forgot why and when the Pope's name had first been dropped from the Diptychs.

As the eleventh century proceeded, new factors brought relations between the Papacy and the eastern Patriarchates to a further crisis. The previous century had been a period of grave instability and confusion for the see of Rome, a century which Cardinal Baronius justly termed an age of iron and lead in the history of the Papacy. But under German influence Rome now reformed itself, and through the rule of men such as Hildebrand (Pope Gregory VII) it gained a position of power in the west such as it had never before achieved. The reformed Papacy naturally revived the claims to universal jurisdiction which Nicolas had made. The Byzantines on their side had grown accustomed to dealing with a Papacy that was for the most part weak and disorganized, and so they found it difficult to adapt themselves to the new situation. Matters were made worse by political factors, such as the military aggression of the Normans in Byzantine Italy, and the commercial encroachments of the Italian maritime cities in the eastern Mediterranean during the eleventh and twelfth centuries.

In 1054 there was a severe quarrel. The Normans had been forcing the Greeks in Byzantine Italy to conform to Latin usages; the Patriarch of Constantinople, Michael Cerularius, in return demanded that the Latin churches at Constantinople should adopt Greek practices, and in 1052, when they refused, he closed them. This was perhaps harsh, but as Patriarch he was fully entitled to act in this manner. Among the practices to which Michael and his supporters particularly objected was the Latin use of 'azymes' or unleavened bread in the Eucharist, an issue which had not figured in the dispute of the ninth century. In 1053, however, Cerularius took up a more conciliatory attitude and wrote to Pope Leo IX, offering to restore the Pope's name to the Diptychs. In response to this offer, and to settle the disputed questions of Greek and Latin usages, Leo in 1054 sent three legates to Constantinople, the chief of them being Humbert, Bishop of Silva Candida. The choice of Cardinal Humbert was unfortunate, for both he and Cerularius were men of stiff and intransigent temper, whose mutual encounter was not likely to promote good will among Christians. The legates, when they called on Cerularius, did not create a favourable impression. Thrusting a letter from the Pope at him, they retired without giving the usual salutations; the letter itself, although signed by Leo, had in fact been drafted by Humbert, and was distinctly unfriendly in tone. After this the Patriarch refused to have further dealings with the legates. Eventually Humbert lost patience, and laid a Bull of Excommunication against Cerularius on the altar of the Church of the Holy Wisdom: among other ill-founded charges in this document, Humbert accused the Greeks of *omitting* the *Filioque* from the Creed! Humbert promptly left Constantinople without offering any further explanation of his act, and on returning to Italy he represented the whole incident as a great victory for the see of Rome. Cerularius and his synod retaliated by anathematizing Humbert (but not the Roman Church as such). The attempt at reconciliation left matters worse than before.

But even after 1054 friendly relations between east and west continued. The two parts of Christendom were not yet conscious of a great gulf of separation between them, and people on both sides still hoped that the misunderstandings could be cleared up without too much difficulty. The dispute remained something of which ordinary Christians in east and west were largely unaware. It was the Crusades which made the schism definitive: they introduced a new spirit of hatred and bitterness, and they brought the whole issue down to the popular level.

From the military point of view, however, the Crusades began with great éclat. Antioch was captured from the Turks in 1098, Jerusalem in 1099: the first Crusade was a brilliant, if bloody,[1] success. At both Antioch and Jerusalem the Crusaders proceeded to set up Latin Patriarchs. At Jerusalem this was reasonable, since the see was vacant at the time; and although in the years that followed there existed a succession of Greek Patriarchs of Jerusalem, living exiled in Cyprus, yet within Palestine itself the whole population, Greek as well as Latin, at first accepted the Latin Patriarch as their head. A Russian pilgrim at Jerusalem in 1106–7, Abbot Daniel of Tchernigov, found Greeks and Latins worshipping together in harmony at the Holy Places, though he noted with satisfaction that at the ceremony of the Holy Fire the Greek lamps were lit miraculously while the Latin had to be lit from the Greek. But at Antioch the Crusaders found a Greek Patriarch actually in residence: shortly afterwards, it is true, he withdrew to Constantinople, but the local Greek population was unwilling to recognize the Latin Patriarch whom the Crusaders set up in his place. Thus from 1100 there existed in effect a local schism at Antioch. After 1187, when Saladin captured Jerusalem, the

1. 'In the Temple and the porch of Solomon,' wrote Raymond of Argiles, 'men rode in blood up to their knees and bridle reins ... The city was filled with corpses and blood.'(Quoted in A. C. Krey, *The First Crusade* [Princeton 1921], p. 261.)

situation in the Holy Land deteriorated: two rivals, resident within Palestine itself, now divided the Christian population between them – a Latin Patriarch at Acre, a Greek at Jerusalem. These local schisms at Antioch and Jerusalem were a sinister development. Rome was very far away, and if Rome and Constantinople quarrelled, what practical difference did it make to the average Christian in Syria or Palestine? But when two rival bishops claimed the same throne and two hostile congregations existed in the same city, the division became an immediate reality in which simple believers were directly implicated. It was the Crusades that turned the dispute into something that involved whole Christian congregations, and not just church leaders; the Crusaders brought the schism down to the local level.

But worse was to follow in 1204, with the taking of Constantinople during the Fourth Crusade. The Crusaders were originally bound for Egypt, but were persuaded by Alexius, son of Isaac Angelus, the dispossessed Emperor of Byzantium, to turn aside to Constantinople in order to restore him and his father to the throne. This western intervention in Byzantine politics did not go happily, and eventually the Crusaders, disgusted by what they regarded as Greek duplicity, lost patience and sacked the city. Eastern Christendom has never forgotten those three appalling days of pillage. 'Even the Saracens are merciful and kind,' protested Nicetas Choniates, 'compared with these men who bear the Cross of Christ on their shoulders.' In the words of Sir Steven Runciman, 'The Crusaders brought not peace but a sword; and the sword was to sever Christendom.'[1] The long-standing doctrinal disagreements were now reinforced on the Greek side by an intense national hatred, by a feeling of resentment and indignation against western aggression and sacrilege. After 1204 there can be no doubt that Christian east and Christian west were divided into two.

Orthodoxy and Rome each believes itself to have been right and its opponent wrong upon the points of doctrine that arose between them; and so Rome and Orthodoxy since the schism

1. *The Eastern Schism*, p. 101.

have each claimed to be the true Church. Yet each, while believing in the rightness of its own cause, must look back at the past with sorrow and repentance. Both sides must in honesty acknowledge that they could and should have done more to prevent the schism. Both sides were guilty of mistakes on the human level. Orthodox, for example, must blame themselves for the pride and contempt with which during the Byzantine period they regarded the west; they must blame themselves for incidents such as the riot of 1182, when many Latin residents at Constantinople were massacred by the Byzantine populace. (None the less there is no action on the Byzantine side which can be compared to the sack of 1204.) And each side, while claiming to be the one true Church, must admit that on the human level it has been grievously impoverished by the separation. The Greek east and the Latin west needed and still need one another. For both parties the great schism has proved a great tragedy.

TWO ATTEMPTS AT REUNION;
THE HESYCHAST CONTROVERSY

In 1204 the Crusaders set up a short-lived Latin kingdom at Constantinople, which came to an end in 1261 when the Greeks recovered their capital. Byzantium survived for two centuries more, and these years proved a time of great cultural, artistic, and religious revival. But politically and economically the restored Byzantine Empire was in a precarious state, and found itself more and more helpless in the face of the Turkish armies which pressed upon it from the east.

Two important attempts were made to secure reunion between the Christian east and west, the first in the thirteenth and the second in the fifteenth century. The moving spirit behind the first attempt was Michael VIII (reigned 1259–82), the Emperor who recovered Constantinople. While doubtless sincerely desiring Christian unity on religious grounds, his motive was also political: threatened by attacks from Charles of Anjou, sovereign of Sicily, he desperately needed the support and protection of the Papacy, which could best be secured

61

through a union of the Churches. A reunion council was held at Lyons in 1274. The Orthodox delegates who attended agreed to recognize the Papal claims and to recite the Creed with the *Filioque*. But the union proved no more than an agreement on paper, since it was fiercely rejected by the overwhelming majority of clergy and laity in the Byzantine Church, as well as by Bulgaria and the other Orthodox countries. The general reaction to the Council of Lyons was summed up in words attributed to the Emperor's sister: 'Better that my brother's Empire should perish, than the purity of the Orthodox faith.' The union of Lyons was formally repudiated by Michael's successor, and Michael himself, for his 'apostasy', was deprived of Christian burial.

Meanwhile east and west continued to grow further apart in their theology and in their whole manner of understanding the Christian life. Byzantium continued to live in a Patristic atmosphere, using the ideas and language of the Greek Fathers of the fourth century. But in western Europe the tradition of the Fathers was replaced by Scholasticism – that great synthesis of philosophy and theology worked out in the twelfth and thirteenth centuries. Western theologians now came to employ new categories of thought, a new theological method, and a new terminology which the east did not understand. To an ever-increasing extent the two sides were losing a common 'universe of discourse'.

Byzantium on its side also contributed to this process: here too there were theological developments in which the west had neither part nor share, although there was nothing so radical as the scholastic revolution. These theological developments were connected chiefly with the *Hesychast Controversy*, a dispute which arose at Byzantium in the middle of the fourteenth century, and which involved the doctrine of God's nature and the methods of prayer used in the Orthodox Church.

To understand the Hesychast Controversy, we must turn back for the moment to the earlier history of eastern mystical theology. The main features of this mystical theology were worked out by St Clement of Alexandria (died 215) and by Origen of Alexandria (died 253/4), whose ideas were developed in the fourth century by the Cappadocians, especially St Gregory of Nyssa, and by their disciple Evagrius of Pontus (died 399), a monk in the Egyptian desert. This mystical tradition is marked, particularly in the case of Clement and Gregory, by a strong use of the apophatic approach, whereby God is described in negative rather than positive terms. Since God cannot be properly comprehended by the human mind, all language that is applied to Him is inevitably inexact. It is therefore less misleading to use negative language about God rather than positive — to refuse to say what God is, and to state simply what He is not. As Gregory of Nyssa put it: 'The true knowledge and vision of God consist in this — in seeing that He is invisible, because what we seek lies beyond all knowledge, being wholly separated by the darkness of incomprehensibility.'[1]

Negative theology reaches its classic expression in the so-called 'Dionysian' writings. For many centuries these books were thought to be the work of St Dionysius the Areopagite, Paul's convert at Athens (Acts xvii, 34); but they are in fact by an unknown author, who probably lived in Syria towards the end of the fifth century and who may have belonged to circles sympathetic to the Non-Chalcedonians. St Maximus the Confessor (died 662) composed commentaries on the Dionysian writings, and so ensured for them a permanent place in Orthodox theology. Dionysius has also had a great influence on the west: it has been reckoned that he is quoted 1,760 times by Thomas Aquinas in the *Summa*, while a fourteenth-century English chronicler records that the *Mystical Theology* of Dionysius 'ran through England like the wild deer'. The apophatic language of Dionysius was repeated by many others. 'God is infinite and incomprehensible,' wrote John of Damascus, 'and all that is comprehensible about Him is His infinity and incomprehensibility . . . God does not belong to the class of existing things: not that He has no existence, but that He is above all existing things, nay even above existence itself.'[2]

This emphasis on divine unknowability might seem at first

1. *The Life of Moses*, ii, 163 (377A).
2. *On the Orthodox Faith*, i, 4 (*P.G.* xciv, 800B).

sight to exclude any direct experience of God. But in fact many of those who used the apophatic approach saw it, not just as a philosophical device for indicating God's utter transcendence, but also, and much more fundamentally, as a means for attaining union with Him through prayer. The negations, as well as serving to qualify positive statements about God, acted as a springboard or trampoline whereby the mystical theologian sought to leap up with all the fullness of his or her being into the living mystery of God. This is the case, for example, with Gregory of Nyssa, Dionysius and Maximus, all of whom made heavy use of the apophatic approach; for them the 'way of negation' was at the same time the 'way of union'. But how, it may be asked, can we attain a meeting face to face with the One who is utterly transcendent? How can God be both knowable and unknowable at once?

This was one of the questions that confronted the fourteenth-century Hesychasts. (The name is derived from the Greek word *hesychia*, meaning inner stillness. The Hesychast is one who devotes himself to the prayer of silence – to prayer that is stripped, so far as possible, of all images, words and discursive thinking.) Connected with this first question was another: what is the place of the body in prayer? Evagrius, like Origen, sometimes borrowed too heavily from Platonism: he wrote of prayer in intellectual terms, as an activity of the mind rather than of the whole person, and he seemed to allow no positive role to the human body in the process of redemption and deification. But the balance between mind and body is redressed in another ascetic writing, the Macarian Homilies. (These were traditionally attributed to St Macarius of Egypt (?300–90), but it is now thought that they were written in Syria or perhaps Asia Minor during the 380s.) The Macarian Homilies uphold a more Biblical idea of the human person – not a soul imprisoned in a body (as in Greek thought), but a single and united whole, soul and body together. Where Evagrius speaks of the *mind* or *intellect* (in Greek *nous*), Macarius uses the Hebraic idea of the *heart*. The change of emphasis is significant, for the heart includes the *whole* person – not only intellect, but will, emotions, and even body.

Using 'heart' in this Macarian sense, Orthodox often talk about 'prayer of the heart'. What does the phrase mean? When someone begins to pray, at first using the lips, the person must make a conscious intellectual effort in order to realize the meaning of what is said. But if that person perseveres, praying continually with recollection, intellect and heart become united: finding 'the place of the heart', the spirit acquires the power of 'dwelling in the heart', and so the prayer becomes 'prayer of the heart'. It becomes something not merely said by the lips, not merely thought by the mind, but offered spontaneously by the whole of one's being – lips, intellect, emotions, will, and body. The prayer fills the entire consciousness, and no longer has to be forced out, but says itself. Such prayer of the heart cannot be attained simply through our own efforts, but is a gift conferred by the grace of God.

When Orthodox writers use the term 'prayer of the heart', they usually have in mind one particular prayer, the Jesus Prayer. Among Greek spiritual writers, first Diadochus of Photice (mid fifth century) and later St John Climacus of Mount Sinai (?579–?649) recommended, as a specially valuable form of prayer, the constant repetition or remembrance of the name 'Jesus'. In course of time the Invocation of the Name became crystallized into a short sentence, known as the Jesus Prayer: *Lord Jesus Christ, Son of God, have mercy on me.*[1] By the thirteenth century (if not before), the recitation of the Jesus Prayer had become linked to certain physical exercises, designed to assist concentration. Breathing was carefully regulated in time with the Prayer, and a particular bodily posture was recommended: head bowed, chin resting on the chest, eyes fixed on the place of the heart.[2] This is often called 'the Hesychast method of prayer', but it should not be thought that for the Hesychasts these exercises constituted the essence of prayer. They were regarded, not as an end in themselves, but

1. In modern Orthodox practice the Prayer sometimes ends, '. . . have mercy on me *a sinner*'. (Compare the Publican's Prayer, Luke xviii, 13.)

2. There are interesting parallels between the Hesychast 'method' and Hindu *Yoga* or Muslim *Dhikr*; but the points of similarity must not be pressed too far.

as a help to concentration – as an accessory useful to some, but not obligatory upon all. The Hesychasts knew that there can be no mechanical means of acquiring God's grace, and no techniques leading automatically to the mystical state.

For the Hesychasts of Byzantium, the culmination of mystical experience was the vision of Divine and Uncreated Light. The works of St Symeon the New Theologian (949–1022), the greatest of the Byzantine mystics, are full of this 'Light mysticism'. When he writes of his own experiences, he speaks again and again of the Divine Light: 'fire truly divine,' he calls it, 'fire uncreated and invisible, without beginning and immaterial'. The Hesychasts believed that this light which they experienced was identical with the Uncreated Light which the three disciples saw surrounding Jesus at His Transfiguration on Mount Tabor. But how was this vision of Divine Light to be reconciled with the apophatic doctrine of God the transcendent and unapproachable?

All these questions concerning the transcendence of God, the role of the body in prayer, and the Divine Light came to a head in the middle of the fourteenth century. The Hesychasts were attacked by a learned Greek from Italy, Barlaam the Calabrian, who stated the doctrine of God's 'otherness' and unknowability in an extreme form. It is sometimes suggested that Barlaam was influenced here by the Nominalist philosophy that was current in the west at this date; but more probably he derived his teaching from Greek sources. Starting from a one-sided exegesis of Dionysius, he argued that God can only be known *indirectly*; Hesychasm (so he maintained) was wrong to speak of an immediate experience of God, for any such experience is impossible in this present life. Seizing on the bodily exercises which the Hesychasts employed, Barlaam accused them of holding a grossly materialistic conception of prayer. He was also scandalized by their claim to attain a vision of the Divine and Uncreated Light: here again he charged them with falling into a gross materialism. How can someone see God's essence with his bodily eyes? The light which the Hesychasts beheld, in his view, was not the eternal light of the Divinity, but a temporary and created light.

The defence of the Hesychasts was taken up by St Gregory Palamas (1296–1359), Archbishop of Thessalonica. He upheld a doctrine of the human person which allowed for the use of bodily exercises in prayer, and he argued, against Barlaam, that the Hesychasts did indeed experience the Divine and Un-created Light of Tabor. To explain how this was possible, Gregory developed the distinction between the essence and the energies of God. It was Gregory's achievement to set Hesy-chasm on a firm dogmatic basis by integrating it into Orthodox theology as a whole. His teaching was confirmed by two coun-cils held at Constantinople in 1341 and 1351, which, although local and not Ecumenical, yet possess a doctrinal authority in Orthodox theology scarcely inferior to the seven general coun-cils themselves. But western Christendom has never officially recognized these two councils, although many western Chris-tians personally accept the theology of Palamas.

Gregory began by reaffirming the Biblical doctrine of the human person and of the Incarnation. The human being is a single, united whole; not only the human mind but the *whole* person was created in the image of God. Our body is not an enemy, but partner and collaborator with our soul. Christ, by taking a human body at the Incarnation, has 'made the *flesh* an inexhaustible source of sanctification'.[1] Here Gregory took up and developed the ideas implicit in earlier writings, such as the Macarian Homilies; the same emphasis on the human body, as we have seen, lies behind the Orthodox doctrine of icons. Gregory went on to apply this doctrine of the person to the Hesychast methods of prayer: the Hesychasts, so he argued, in placing such emphasis on the part of the body in prayer, are not guilty of a gross materialism but are simply remaining faithful to the Biblical doctrine of personhood as a unity. Christ took human flesh and saved the whole person; therefore it is the *whole* person – body and soul together – that prays to God.

From this Gregory turned to the main problem: how to combine the two affirmations, that we humans know God and that God is by nature unknowable. Gregory answered: we

1. *Homily* 16 (*P.G.* cli, 193B).

know the *energies* of God, but not His *essence*. This distinction between God's essence (*ousia*) and His energies goes back to the Cappadocian Fathers. 'We know our God from His energies,' wrote St Basil, 'but we do not claim that we can draw near to His essence. For His energies come down to us, but His essence remains unapproachable.'[1] Gregory accepted this distinction. He affirmed, as emphatically as any exponent of negative theology, that God is in essence absolutely unknowable. 'God is not a nature,' he wrote, 'for He is above all nature; He is not a being, for He is above all beings ... No single thing of all that is created has or ever will have even the slightest communion with the supreme nature or nearness to it.'[2] But however remote from us in His essence, yet in His energies God has revealed Himself to us. These energies are not something that exists apart from God, not a gift which God confers upon humans; they are God Himself in His action and revelation to the world. God exists complete and entire in each of His divine energies. The world, as Gerard Manley Hopkins said, is charged with the grandeur of God; all creation is a gigantic Burning Bush, permeated but not consumed by the ineffable and wondrous fire of God's energies.[3]

It is through these energies that God enters into a direct and immediate relationship with humankind. In relation to us humans, the divine energy is in fact nothing else than the *grace of God*; grace is not just a 'gift' of God, not just an object which God bestows on humans, but a direct manifestation of the living God Himself, a personal encounter between creature and Creator. 'Grace signifies all the abundance of the divine nature, in so far as it is communicated to men.'[4] When we say that the saints have been transformed or 'deified' by the grace of God, what we mean is that they have a direct experience of God Himself. They *know* God – that is to say, God in His energies, not in His essence.

God is Light, and therefore the experience of God's energies

1. *Letter* 234, 1.
2. *P.G.* cl, 1176c.
3. Compare Maximus, *Ambigua, P.G.* xci, 1148D.
4. V. Lossky, *The Mystical Theology of the Eastern Church*, p. 162.

takes the form of Light. The vision which the Hesychasts receive is (so Palamas argued) not a vision of some created radiance but of the Light of the Godhead Itself – the same Light of the Godhead which surrounded Christ on Mount Tabor. This Light is not a sensible or material light, but it can be seen with physical eyes (as by the disciples at the Transfiguration), since when a person is deified, his bodily faculties as well as his soul are transformed. The Hesychasts' vision of Light is therefore a true vision of God in His divine energies; and they are quite correct in identifying it with the Uncreated Light of Tabor.

Palamas, therefore, preserved God's transcendence and avoided the pantheism to which an unguarded mysticism easily leads; yet he allowed for God's immanence, for His continual presence in the world. God remains 'the Wholly Other', and yet through His energies (which are God Himself) He enters into an immediate relationship with the world. God is a living God, the God of history, the God of the Bible, who became Incarnate in Christ. Barlaam, in excluding all direct knowledge of God and in asserting that the Divine Light is something created, set too wide a gulf between God and humanity. Gregory's fundamental concern in opposing Barlaam was therefore the same as that of Athanasius and the general councils: to safeguard our direct approach to God, to uphold our full deification and entire redemption. That same doctrine of salvation which underlay the disputes about the Trinity, the Person of Christ, and the Holy Icons, lies also at the heart of the Hesychast controversy.

'Into the closed world of Byzantium,' wrote Dom Gregory Dix, 'no really fresh impulse ever came after the sixth century . . . Sleep began . . . in the ninth century, perhaps even earlier, in the sixth.'[1] The Byzantine controversies of the fourteenth century amply demonstrate the falsity of such an assertion. Certainly Gregory Palamas was no revolutionary innovator, but firmly rooted in the tradition of the past; yet he was a creative theologian of the first rank, and his work shows that

1. *The Shape of the Liturgy* (London 1945), p. 548.

Orthodox theology did not cease to be active after the eighth century and the seventh Ecumenical Council.

Among the contemporaries of Gregory Palamas was the lay theologian St Nicolas Cabasilas, who was sympathetic to the Hesychasts, although not closely involved in the controversy. Cabasilas is the author of a *Commentary on the Divine Liturgy*, which has become the classic Orthodox work on this subject; he also wrote a treatise on the sacraments entitled *The Life in Christ*. The writings of Cabasilas are marked by two things in particular: a vivid sense of the person of Christ the Saviour, who, as he puts it, 'is closer to us than our own soul';[1] and a constant emphasis upon the sacraments. For him the mystical life is essentially a life in Christ and a life in the sacraments. There is a danger that mysticism may become speculative and individualist – divorced from the historical revelation in Christ and from the corporate life of the Church with its sacraments; but the mysticism of Cabasilas is always Christocentric, sacramental, ecclesial. His work shows how closely mysticism and the sacramental life were linked together in Byzantine theology. Palamas and his circle did not regard mystical prayer as a means of bypassing the normal institutional life of the Church.

A second reunion council was held at Florence in 1438–9. The Emperor John VIII (reigned 1425–48) attended in person, together with the Patriarch of Constantinople and a large delegation from the Byzantine Church, as well as representatives from the other Orthodox Churches. There were prolonged discussions, and a genuine attempt was made by both sides to reach a true agreement on the great points of dispute. At the same time it was difficult for the Greeks to discuss theology dispassionately, for they knew that the political situation had now become desperate: the only hope of defeating the Turks lay in help from the west. Eventually a formula of union was drawn up, covering the *Filioque*, Purgatory, 'azymes', and the Papal claims; and this was signed by all the Orthodox present

1. *P.G.* cl, 712A.

at the council except one – Mark, Archbishop of Ephesus, later canonized by the Orthodox Church. The Florentine Union was based on a twofold principle: unanimity in matters of doctrine; respect for the legitimate rites and traditions peculiar to each Church. Thus in matters of doctrine, the Orthodox accepted the Papal claims (although here the wording of the formula of union was in some respects vague and ambiguous); they accepted the doctrine of the Double Procession of the Holy Spirit, although they were not required to insert the *Filioque* into the text of the Creed at the Divine Liturgy; they accepted the Roman teaching on Purgatory (as a point of dispute between east and west, this only came into the open in the thirteenth century). But so far as 'azymes' were concerned, no uniformity was demanded: Greeks were allowed to use leavened bread, while Latins were to continue to employ unleavened.

But the Union of Florence, though celebrated throughout western Europe – bells were rung in all the parish churches of England – proved no more of a reality in the east than its predecessor at Lyons. John VIII and his successor Constantine XI, the last Emperor of Byzantium and the eightieth in succession since Constantine the Great, both remained loyal to the union; but they were powerless to enforce it on their subjects, and did not even dare to proclaim it publicly at Constantinople until 1452. Many of those who signed at Florence revoked their signatures when they reached home. The decrees of the council were never accepted by more than a minute fraction of the Byzantine clergy and people. The Grand Duke Lucas Notaras, echoing the words of the Emperor's sister after Lyons, remarked, 'I would rather see the Muslim turban in the midst of the city than the Latin mitre.'

John and Constantine had hoped that the Union of Florence would secure them military help from the west, but small indeed was the help which they actually received. On 7 April 1453 the Turks began to attack Constantinople by land and sea. Outnumbered by more than twenty to one, the Byzantines maintained a brilliant but hopeless defence for seven long weeks. In the early hours of 29 May the last Christian service

was held in the great Church of the Holy Wisdom. It was a
united service of Orthodox and Roman Catholics, for at this
moment of crisis the supporters and opponents of the Florentine Union forgot their differences. The Emperor went out
after receiving communion, and died fighting on the walls.
Later the same day the city fell to the Turks, and the most
glorious church in Christendom became a mosque.

It was the end of the Byzantine Empire. But it was not the
end of the Patriarchate of Constantinople, far less the end of
Orthodoxy.

CHAPTER 4

The Conversion of the Slavs

> The religion of grace spread over the earth and finally reached
> the Russian people ... The gracious God who cared for all
> other countries now no longer neglects us. It is His desire to
> save us and lead us to reason.
>
> *Hilarion, Metropolitan of Russia (1051–?1054)*

CYRIL AND METHODIUS

For Constantinople the middle of the ninth century was a
period of intensive missionary activity. The Byzantine Church,
freed at last from the long struggle against the Iconoclasts,
turned its energies to the conversion of the pagan Slavs who
lay beyond the frontiers of the Empire, to the north and the
north-west – Moravians, Bulgarians, Serbs and Russians. Photius was the first Patriarch of Constantinople to initiate missionary work on a large scale among these Slavs. He selected for
the task two brothers, Greeks from Thessalonica, Constantine
(826–69) and Methodius (?815–85). In the Orthodox Church
Constantine is usually called by the name Cyril which he took
on becoming a monk. Known in earlier life as 'Constantine the
Philosopher', he was the ablest among the pupils of Photius,
and was familiar with a wide range of languages, including
Hebrew, Arabic, and even the Samaritan dialect. But the special qualification which he and his brother enjoyed was their
knowledge of Slavonic: in childhood they had learnt the dialect
of the Slavs around Thessalonica, and they could speak it
fluently.

The first missionary journey of Cyril and Methodius was a
short visit around 860 to the Khazars, who lived north of the
Caucasus region. This expedition had no permanent results,
and some years later the Khazars adopted Judaism. The
brothers' real work began in 863 when they set out for Moravia

(roughly equivalent to the modern Czechoslovakia). They went in answer to an appeal from the Prince of the land, Rostislav, who asked that Christian missionaries be sent, capable of preaching to the people in their own tongue and of taking services in Slavonic. Slavonic services required a Slavonic Bible and Slavonic service books. Before they set out for Moravia the brothers had already set to work on this enormous task of translation. They had first to invent a suitable Slavonic alphabet. In their translation the brothers used the form of Slavonic familiar to them from childhood, the Macedonian dialect spoken by the Slavs around Thessalonica. In this way the dialect of the Macedonian Slavs became *Church Slavonic*, which remains to the present day the liturgical language of the Russian and certain other Slavonic Orthodox Churches.

One cannot overestimate the significance, for the future of Orthodoxy, of the Slavonic translations which Cyril and Methodius carried with them as they left Byzantium for the unknown north. Few events have been so important in the missionary history of the Church. From the start the Slav Christians enjoyed a precious privilege, such as none of the peoples of western Europe shared at this time: they heard the Gospel and the services of the Church in a tongue which they could understand. Unlike the Church of Rome in the west with its insistence on Latin, the Orthodox Church has never been rigid in the matter of languages; its normal policy is to hold services in the language of the people.

In Moravia, as in Bulgaria, the Greek mission soon clashed with German missionaries at work in the same area. The two missions not only depended on different Patriarchates, but worked on different principles. Cyril and Methodius used Slavonic in their services, the Germans Latin; Cyril and Methodius recited the Creed in its original form, the Germans inserted the *Filioque*. To free his mission from German interference, Cyril decided to place it under the immediate protection of the Pope. Cyril's action in appealing to Rome shows that he did not take the quarrel between Photius and Nicolas too seriously; for him east and west were still united as one Church, and it was not a matter of primary importance whether he depended on Constantinople or Rome, so long as he could continue to use Slavonic in Church services. The brothers travelled to Rome in person in 868 and were entirely successful in the appeal. Hadrian II, Nicolas I's successor at Rome, received them favourably and gave full support to the Greek mission, confirming the use of Slavonic as the liturgical language of Moravia. He approved the brothers' translations, and laid copies of their Slavonic service books on the altars of the principal churches in the city.

Cyril died at Rome (869), but Methodius returned to Moravia. Sad to say, the Germans ignored the Pope's decision and obstructed Methodius in every possible way, even putting him in prison for more than a year. When Methodius died in 885, the Germans expelled his followers from the country, selling a number of them into slavery. Traces of the Slavonic mission lingered on in Moravia for two centuries more, but were eventually eradicated; and Christianity in its western form, with Latin culture and the Latin language (and of course the *Filioque*), became universal. The attempt to found a Slavonic national Church in Moravia came to nothing. The work of Cyril and Methodius, so it seemed, had ended in failure.

Yet in fact this was not so. Other countries, where the brothers had not themselves preached, benefited from their work, most notably Bulgaria, Serbia and Russia. Boris, Khan of Bulgaria, as we have seen, wavered for a time between east and west, but finally accepted the jurisdiction of Constantinople. The Byzantine missionaries in Bulgaria, however, lacking the vision of Cyril and Methodius, at first used Greek in Church services, a language as unintelligible as Latin to the ordinary Bulgar. But after their expulsion from Moravia, the disciples of Methodius turned naturally to Bulgaria, and here introduced the principles employed in the Moravian mission. Greek was replaced by Slavonic, and the Christian culture of Byzantium was presented to the Bulgars in a Slavonic form which they could assimilate. The Bulgarian Church grew rapidly. Around 926, during the reign of Tsar Symeon the Great (reigned 893–927), an independent Bulgarian Patriarchate was created, and this was recognized by the Patriarchate of Constantinople in 927. The dream of Boris – an autocephalous Church of his own – became a reality within half a century of his death. Bulgaria was the first national Church of the Slavs.

Byzantine missionaries went likewise to Serbia, which accepted Christianity in the second half of the ninth century, around 867–74. Serbia also lay on the dividing line between eastern and western Christendom, but after a period of uncertainty it followed the example of Bulgaria, not of Moravia, and came under Constantinople. Here too the Slavonic service books were introduced and a Slavonic–Byzantine culture grew up. The Serbian Church gained a partial independence under St Sava (1176–1235), the greatest of Serbian national saints, who in 1219 was consecrated at Nicaea as Archbishop of Serbia. In 1346 a Serbian Patriarchate was created, which was recognized by the Church of Constantinople in 1375.

The conversion of Russia was also due indirectly to the work of Cyril and Methodius; but of this we shall speak further in the next section. With Bulgars, Serbs, and Russians as their 'spiritual children', the two Greeks from Thessalonica abundantly deserve their title 'Apostles of the Slavs'.

Another Orthodox nation in the Balkans, Romania, has a more complex history. The Romanians, though influenced by their Slav neighbours, are primarily Latin in language and ethnic character. Dacia, corresponding to part of modern Romania, was a Roman province during 106–271; but the Christian communities founded there in this period seem to have disappeared after the Romans withdrew. Part of the Romanian people was apparently converted to Christianity by the Bulgarians in the late ninth or early tenth century, but the full conversion of the two Romanian principalities of Wallachia and Moldavia did not occur until the fourteenth century. Those who think of Orthodoxy as being exclusively 'eastern', as Greek and Slav in character, should not overlook the fact that the Church of Romania, the second largest Orthodox Church today, is predominantly Latin in its national identity.

Byzantium conferred two gifts upon the Slavs: a fully articulated system of Christian doctrine and a fully developed

Christian civilization. When the conversion of the Slavs began in the ninth century, the great period of doctrinal controversies, the age of the seven councils, was at an end; the main outlines of the faith – the doctrines of the Trinity and the Incarnation – had already been worked out, and were delivered to the Slavs in their definitive form. Perhaps this is why the Slavonic Churches have produced few original theologians, while the religious disputes which have arisen in Slavonic lands have usually not been dogmatic in character. But this faith in the Trinity and the Incarnation did not exist in a vacuum; with it went a whole Christian culture and civilization, and this too the Greek missionaries brought with them from Byzantium. The Slavs were Christianized and civilized at the same time.

The Greeks communicated this faith and civilization not in an alien but in a Slavonic garb (here the translations of Cyril and Methodius were of capital importance); what the Slavs borrowed from Byzantium they were able to make their own. Byzantine culture and the Orthodox faith, if at first limited mainly to the ruling classes, became in time an integral part of the daily life of the Slavonic peoples as a whole. The link between Church and people was made even firmer by the system of creating independent national Churches.

Certainly this close identification of Orthodoxy with the life of the people, and in particular the system of national Churches, has had unfortunate consequences. Because Church and nation were so closely associated, the Orthodox Slavs have often confused the two and have made the Church serve the ends of national politics. They have sometimes tended to think of their faith as primarily Serb, Russian, or Bulgar, and to forget that it is primarily Orthodox and Catholic; and this has also been a temptation for the Greeks in modern times. Nationalism has been the bane of Orthodoxy for the last ten centuries. Yet the integration of Church and people has in the end proved immensely beneficial. Christianity among the Slavs became in very truth the religion of the *whole* people, a *popular* religion in the best sense.

77

THE BAPTISM OF RUSSIA:
THE KIEVAN PERIOD (988–1237)

Photius also made plans to convert the Slavs of Russia. Around 864 he sent a bishop to Russia, but this first Christian foundation was exterminated by Oleg, who assumed power at Kiev (the chief Russian city at this time) in 878. Russia, however, continued to undergo a steady Christian infiltration from Byzantium, Bulgaria, and Scandinavia, and there was certainly a church at Kiev in 945. The Russian Princess Olga became a Christian in 955, but her son Svyatoslav refused to follow her example, saying that his retinue would laugh at him if he received Christian baptism. Around 988, however, Olga's grandson Vladimir (reigned 980–1015) was converted to Christianity and married Anna, the sister of the Byzantine Emperor. Orthodoxy became the State religion of Russia, and such it remained until 1917. Vladimir set to in earnest to Christianize his realm: priests, relics, sacred vessels, and icons were imported; mass baptisms were held in the rivers; Church courts were set up, and ecclesiastical tithes instituted. The great idol of the god Perun, with its silver head and gold moustaches, was rolled ignominiously down from the hill-top above Kiev. 'Angel's trumpet and Gospel's thunder sounded through all the towns. The air was sanctified by the incense that ascended towards God. Monasteries stood on the mountains. Men and women, small and great, all people filled the holy churches.'[1] So the Metropolitan Hilarion described the event sixty years afterwards, doubtless idealizing a little; for Kievan Russia was not at once completely converted to Christianity, and the Church was at first restricted mainly to the cities, while much of the countryside remained pagan until the fourteenth and fifteenth centuries.

Vladimir placed the same emphasis upon the social implications of Christianity as John the Almsgiver had done. Whenever he feasted with his Court, he distributed food to the poor and sick; nowhere else in medieval Europe were there such

1. Quoted in G. P. Fedotov, *The Russian Religious Mind*, vol. 1, p. 410.

highly organized 'social services' as in tenth-century Kiev. Other rulers in Kievan Russia followed Vladimir's example. Prince Vladimir Monomachos (reigned 1113–25) wrote in his *Testament* to his sons, 'Above all things forget not the poor, and support them to the extent of your means. Give to the orphan, protect the widow, and permit the mighty to destroy no man.'[1] Vladimir was also deeply conscious of the Christian law of mercy, and when he introduced the Byzantine law code at Kiev, he insisted on mitigating its more savage and brutal features. There was no death penalty in Kievan Russia, no mutilation, no torture; corporal punishment was very little used.[2]

The same gentleness can be seen in the story of Vladimir's two sons, Boris and Gleb. On Vladimir's death in 1015, their elder brother Svyatopolk attempted to seize their principalities. Taking literally the commands of the Gospel, they offered no resistance, although they could easily have done so; and each in turn was murdered by Svyatopolk's emissaries. If any blood were to be shed, Boris and Gleb preferred that it should be their own. Although they were not martyrs for the faith, but victims in a political quarrel, they were both canonized, being given the special title of 'Passion Bearers': it was felt that by their innocent and voluntary suffering they had shared in the Passion of Christ. Russians have always laid great emphasis on the place of suffering in the Christian life.

In Kievan Russia, as in Byzantium and the medieval west, monasteries played an important part. The most influential of them all was the *Petchersky Lavra*, the Monastery of the Caves at Kiev. Founded as a semi-eremitic brotherhood by St Antony, a Russian who had lived on Mount Athos, it was reorganized by his successor St Theodosius (died 1074), who introduced there the full community life, as followed at the monastery of Stoudios in Constantinople. Like Vladimir, Theodosius was conscious of the social consequences of Christianity, and applied them in a radical fashion, identifying himself

1. Quoted in G. Vernadsky, *Kievan Russia* (New Haven 1948), p. 195.
2. In Byzantium the death penalty existed, but was hardly ever applied; the punishment of mutilation, however, was employed with distressing frequency.

closely with the poor, much as St Francis of Assisi did in the west. Boris and Gleb followed Christ in his sacrificial death; Theodosius followed Christ in his life of poverty and voluntary 'self-emptying' (*kenosis*). Of noble birth, he chose in childhood to wear coarse and patched garments and to work in the fields with the slaves. 'Our Lord Jesus Christ,' he said, 'became poor and humbled Himself, offering Himself as an example, so that we should humble ourselves in His name. He suffered insults, was spat upon, and beaten, for our salvation; how just it is, then, that we should suffer in order to gain Christ.'[1] Even when Abbot he wore the meanest kind of clothing and rejected all outward signs of authority. Yet at the same time he was the honoured friend and adviser of nobles and princes. The same ideal of kenotic humility is seen in others, for example Bishop Luke of Vladimir (died 1185) who, in the words of the *Vladimir Chronicle*, 'bore upon himself the humiliation of Christ, not having a city here but seeking a future one'. It is an ideal found often in Russian folklore, and in writers such as Tolstoy and Dostoyevsky.

Vladimir, Boris and Gleb, and Theodosius were all intensely concerned with the practical implications of the Gospel: Vladimir in his concern for social justice and his desire to treat criminals with mercy; Boris and Gleb in their resolution to follow Christ in His voluntary suffering and death; Theodosius in his self-identification with the humble. These four saints embody some of the most attractive features in Kievan Christianity.

The Russian Church during the Kievan period was subject to Constantinople, and until 1237 the Metropolitans of Russia were usually Greek. In memory of the days when the Metropolitan came from Byzantium, the Russian Church continues to sing in Greek the solemn greeting to a bishop, *eis polla eti, despota* ('unto many years, O master'). But of the rest of the bishops, about half were native Russians in the Kievan period; one was even a converted Jew, and another a Syrian.

---

1. Nestor, 'Life of Saint Theodosius', in G. P. Fedotov, *A Treasury of Russian Spirituality*, p. 27.

Kiev enjoyed close relations not only with Byzantium but with western Europe, and certain features in the organization of the early Russian Church, such as ecclesiastical tithes, were not Byzantine but western. Many western saints who do not appear in the Byzantine calendar were venerated at Kiev; a prayer to the Holy Trinity composed in Russia during the eleventh century lists English saints such as Alban and Botolph, and a French saint, Martin of Tours. Some writers have even argued that until 1054 Russian Christianity was as much Latin as Greek, but this is a great exaggeration. Russia was closer to the west in the Kiev period than at any other time until the reign of Peter the Great, but she owed immeasurably more to Byzantine than to Latin culture. Napoleon was correct histori-cally when he called Emperor Alexander I of Russia 'a Greek of the Lower Empire'.

It has been said that it was Russia's greatest misfortune that she was allowed too little time to assimilate the full spiritual inheritance of Byzantium. In 1237 Kievan Russia was brought to a sudden and violent end by the Mongol invasions; Kiev was sacked, and the whole Russian land was overrun, except the far north around Novgorod. A visitor to the Mongol Court in 1246 recorded that he saw in Russian territory neither town nor village, but only ruins and countless human skulls. But if Kiev was destroyed, the Christianity of Kiev remained a living memory:

Kievan Russia, like the golden days of childhood, was never dimmed in the memory of the Russian nation. In the pure fountain of her literary works anyone who wills can quench his religious thirst; in her venerable authors he can find his guide through the complexities of the modern world. Kievan Christianity has the same value for the Russian religious mind as Pushkin for the Russian artistic sense: that of a standard, a golden measure, a royal way.[1]

1. Fedotov, *The Russian Religious Mind*, vol. 1, p. 412.

THE RUSSIAN CHURCH UNDER THE MONGOLS
(1237-1448)

The suzerainty of the Mongol Tartars over Russia lasted from 1237 until 1480. But after the great battle of Kulikovo (1380), when the Russians dared at last to face their oppressors in an open fight and actually defeated them, Mongol overlordship was considerably weakened; by 1450 it had become largely nominal. More than anything else, it was the Church which kept alive Russian national consciousness in the thirteenth and fourteenth centuries, as the Church was later to preserve a sense of unity among the Greeks under Turkish rule. The Russia which emerged from the Mongol period was a Russia greatly changed in outward appearance. Kiev never recovered from the sack of 1237, and its position of leadership was taken in the fourteenth century by the Principality of Moscow. It was the Grand Dukes of Moscow who inspired the resistance to the Mongols and who led Russia at Kulikovo. The rise of Moscow was closely bound up with the Church. When the town was still small and comparatively unimportant, Peter, Metropolitan of Russia from 1308 to 1326, decided to settle there. This led eventually to the division of the Russian Church between two metropolitans, one at Moscow and the other at Kiev, but this arrangement did not become fixed and permanent until the middle of the fifteenth century.

Three figures in the history of the Russian Church during the Mongol period call for particular mention, all of them saints: Alexander Nevsky, Stephen of Perm, and Sergius of Radonezh.

Alexander Nevsky (died 1263), one of the great warrior saints of Russia, has been compared with his western contemporary, St Louis, King of France. He was Prince of Novgorod, the one major principality in Russia to escape unharmed in 1237. But soon after the coming of the Tartars, Alexander found himself threatened by other enemies from the west: Swedes, Germans, and Lithuanians. It was impossible to fight on two fronts at once. Alexander decided to submit to Tartar overlordship and to pay tribute; but against his western opponents he put up a vigorous resistance, inflicting two decisive defeats upon them – over the Swedes in 1240 and over the Teutonic Knights in 1242. His reason for treating with the Tartars rather than the west was primarily religious: the Tartars took tribute but refrained from interfering in the life of the Church, whereas the Teutonic Knights had as their avowed aim the reduction of the Russian 'schismatics' to the jurisdiction of the Pope. This was the very period when a Latin Patriarch reigned in Constantinople, and the German Crusaders in the north aimed to break Orthodox Novgorod, just as their fellow Crusaders in the south had broken Orthodox Constantinople in 1204. But Alexander, despite the Mongol menace, refused any religious compromise. 'Our doctrines are those preached by the Apostles,' he is reported to have replied to messengers from the Pope. '. . . The tradition of the Holy Fathers of the seven councils we scrupulously keep. As for your words, we do not listen to them and we do not want your doctrine.'[1] Two centuries later the Greeks after the Council of Florence made the same choice: political submission to the infidel rather than what they felt would be spiritual capitulation to the Church of Rome.

Stephen of Perm brings us to another aspect of Church life under the Mongols: missionary work. From its early days the Russian Church was a missionary Church, and the Russians were quick to send evangelists among their pagan conquerors. In 1261 a certain Mitrophan went as missionary bishop to Sarai, the Tartar capital on the Volga. Others preached, not among the Mongols, but among the primitive pagan tribes in the north-east and far north of the Russian continent. True to the example of Cyril and Methodius, these missionaries translated the Bible and Church services into the languages and dialects of the people to whom they ministered.

St Stephen, Bishop of Perm (?1340–96), worked among the Zyrian tribes. He spent thirteen years of preparation in a monastery, studying not only the native dialects but also Greek, to be the better fitted for the work of translation. While the followers

1. From the thirteenth-century life of Alexander Nevsky; quoted in Fedotov, *The Russian Religious Mind*, vol. 1, p. 383.

of Cyril and Methodius had employed an adapted Greek alphabet in their Slavonic translations, Stephen made use of the native runes. He was an icon painter, and sought to show forth God as the God not of truth only, but of beauty. Like many other of the early Russian missionaries, he did not follow in the wake of military and political conquest, but was ahead of it.

Sergius of Radonezh (?1314–92), the greatest national saint of Russia, is closely connected with the recovery of the land in the fourteenth century. The outward pattern of his life recalls that of St Antony of Egypt. In early manhood Sergius withdrew into the forests (the northern equivalent of the Egyptian desert) and here he founded a hermitage dedicated to the Holy Trinity. After several years of solitude, his place of retreat became known, disciples gathered round him, and he grew into a spiritual guide, an 'elder' or *starets*. Finally (and here the parallel with Antony ends) he turned his group of disciples into a regular monastery, which became within his own lifetime the greatest religious house in the land. What the Monastery of the Caves was to Kievan Russia, the Monastery of the Holy Trinity was to Muscovy.

Sergius displayed the same *kenosis* and deliberate self-humiliation as Theodosius, living (despite his noble birth) as a peasant, dressing in the poorest of clothing. 'His garb was of coarse peasant felt, old and worn, unwashed, saturated with sweat, and heavily patched.'[1] At the height of his fame, when Abbot of a great community, he still worked in the kitchen garden. Often when he was pointed out to visitors, they could not believe that it was really the celebrated Sergius. 'I came to see a prophet,' exclaimed one man in disgust, 'and you show me a beggar.'[2] Like Theodosius, Sergius played an active part in politics. A close friend of the Grand Dukes of Moscow, he encouraged the city in its expansion, and it is significant that before the Battle of Kulikovo the leader of the Russian forces, Prince Dimitry Donskoy, went specially to Sergius to secure his blessing.

1. St Epiphanius, 'The Life of Saint Sergius', in Fedotov, *A Treasury of Russian Spirituality*, pp. 69–70.
2. Epiphanius, in Fedotov, op. cit., p. 70.

But while there exist many parallels in the lives of Theodosius and Sergius, two important points of difference must be noted. First, whereas the Monastery of the Caves, like most monasteries in Kievan Russia, lay on the outskirts of a city, the Monastery of the Holy Trinity was founded in the wilderness at a distance from the civilized world. Sergius was in his way an explorer and a colonist, pushing forward the boundaries of civilization and subjecting the forest to cultivation. Nor is he the only example of a colonist monk at this time. Others went like him into the forests to become hermits but, in their case as in his, what started as a hermitage soon grew into a regular monastery, with a civilian town outside the walls. Then the whole process would start all over again: a fresh generation of monks in search of the solitary life would make their way into the yet more distant forest, disciples would follow, new communities would form, fresh land would be cleared for agriculture. This steady advance of colonist monks is one of the most striking features of fourteenth- and fifteenth-century Russia. From Radonezh and other centres a vast network of religious houses spread swiftly across the whole of north Russia as far as the White Sea and the Arctic Circle. Fifty communities were founded by disciples of Sergius in his own lifetime, forty more by his followers in the next generation. These explorer monks were not only colonists but missionaries, for as they penetrated farther north, they preached Christianity to the wild pagan tribes in the forests around them.

In the second place, while there is in the religious experience of Theodosius nothing that can be termed specifically mystical, in Sergius a new dimension of the spiritual life becomes evident. Sergius was a contemporary of Gregory Palamas, and it is not impossible that he knew something of the Hesychast movement in Byzantium. At any rate some of the visions granted to Sergius in prayer, which his biographer Epiphanius recorded, can only be interpreted in a mystical sense.

Sergius has been called a 'Builder of Russia', and such he was in three senses: politically, for he encouraged the rise of Moscow and the resistance against the Tartars; geographically, for it was he more than any other who inspired the great advance of monks into the forests; and spiritually, for through his experience of mystical prayer he deepened the inner life of the Russian Church. Better, perhaps, than any other Russian saint, he succeeded in balancing the social and mystical aspects of monasticism. Under his influence and that of his followers, the two centuries from 1350 to 1550 proved a golden age in Russian spirituality.

These two centuries were also a golden age in Russian religious art. During these years Russian painters carried to perfection the iconographic traditions which they had taken over from Byzantium. Icon painting flourished above all among the spiritual children of St Sergius. It is no coincidence that the finest of all Orthodox icons from the artistic point of view – the Holy Trinity, by St Andrew Rublev (?1370–?1430) – should have been painted in honour of St Sergius and placed in his monastery at Radonezh.

Sixty-one years after the death of Sergius, the Byzantine Empire fell to the Turks. The new Russia which took shape after Kulikovo, and which the saint himself had done so much to build, was now called to take Byzantium's place as protector of the Orthodox world. It proved both worthy and unworthy of this vocation.

CHAPTER 5

The Church under Islam

> The stable perseverance in these our days of the Greek
> Church ... notwithstanding the Oppression and Contempt
> put upon it by the *Turk*, and the Allurements and Pleasures
> of this World, is a Confirmation no less convincing than the
> Miracles and Power which attended its first beginnings. For
> indeed it is admirable to see and consider with what
> Constancy, Resolution, and Simplicity, ignorant and poor
> men keep their faith.
>
> *Sir Paul Rycaut*, The Present State of the
> Greek and Armenian Churches (*1679*)

IMPERIUM IN IMPERIO

'It doth go hugely against the grain to see the crescent exalted
everywhere, where the Cross stood so long triumphant': so
wrote Edward Browne in 1677, soon after arriving as Chaplain
to the English Embassy in Constantinople. To the Greeks in
1453 it must also have gone hugely against the grain. For more
than a thousand years people had taken the Christian Empire
of Byzantium for granted as a permanent element in God's
providential dispensation to the world. Now the 'God-
protected city' had fallen, and the Greeks were under the rule of
the infidel.

It was not an easy transition: but it was made less hard by
the Turks themselves, who treated their Christian subjects
with remarkable generosity. The Muslims in the fifteenth century were far more tolerant towards Christianity than western
Christians were towards one another during the Reformation
and the seventeenth century. Islam regards the Bible as a
holy book and Jesus Christ as a prophet; in Muslim eyes,
therefore, the Christian religion is at some points erroneous
but not entirely false, and Christians, being 'People of the

87

Book', should not be treated as if on a level with mere pagans. According to Muslim teaching, Christians are to undergo no persecution, but may continue without interference in the observance of their faith, so long as they submit quietly to the power of Islam.

Such were the principles which guided the conqueror of Constantinople, Sultan Mohammed II. Before the fall of the city, Greeks called him 'the precursor of Antichrist and the second Sennacherib', but they found that in practice his rule was very different in character. Learning that the office of Patriarch was vacant, Mohammed summoned the monk Gennadius and installed him on the Patriarchal throne. Gennadius (?1405–?72), known as George Scholarios before he became a monk, was a voluminous writer and the leading Greek theologian of his time. He was a determined opponent of the Church of Rome, and his appointment as Patriarch meant the final abandonment of the Union of Florence. Doubtless for political reasons, the Sultan deliberately chose a man of anti-Latin convictions: with Gennadius as Patriarch, there would be less likelihood of the Greeks seeking secret aid from Roman Catholic powers.

The Sultan himself instituted the Patriarch, ceremonially investing him with his pastoral staff, exactly as the autocrats of Byzantium had formerly done. The action was symbolic: Mohammed the Conqueror, champion of Islam, became also the protector of Orthodoxy, taking over the role once exercised by the Christian Emperor. Thus Christians were assured a definite place in the Turkish order of society; but, as they were soon to discover, it was a place of guaranteed inferiority. Christianity under Islam was a second-class religion, and its adherents second-class citizens. They paid heavy taxes, wore a distinctive dress, were not allowed to serve in the army, and were forbidden to marry Muslim women. The Church was allowed to undertake no missionary work, and it was a crime to convert a Muslim to the Christian faith. From the material point of view there was every inducement for a Christian to apostatize to Islam. Direct persecution often serves to strengthen a Church; but the Greeks in the Ottoman Empire were usually denied the

more heroic ways of witnessing to their faith, and were subjected instead to the demoralizing effects of an unrelenting
social pressure.

Nor was this all. After the fall of Constantinople the
Church was not allowed to revert to the situation before the
conversion of Constantine; paradoxically enough, the things
of Caesar now became more closely associated with the things
of God than they had ever been before. For the Muslims
drew no distinction between religion and politics: from their
point of view, if Christianity was to be recognized as an independent religious faith, it was necessary for Christians to be
organized as an independent political unit, an Empire within
the Empire. The Orthodox Church therefore became a civil
as well as a religious institution: it was turned into the *Rum
Millet*, the 'Roman nation'. The ecclesiastical structure was
taken over *in toto* as an instrument of secular administration.
The bishops became government officials, the Patriarch was
not only the spiritual head of the Greek Orthodox Church,
but the civil head of the Greek nation – the *ethnarch* or
millet-bashi. This situation continued in Turkey until 1923,
and in Cyprus until the death of Archbishop Makarios III
(1977).

The *millet* system performed one invaluable service: it made
possible the survival of the Greek nation as a distinctive unit
through four centuries of alien rule. But on the life of the
Church it had two melancholy effects. It led first to a sad
confusion between Orthodoxy and nationalism. With their civil
and political life organized completely around the Church, it
became all but impossible for the Greeks to distinguish between
Church and nation. The Orthodox faith, being universal, is
limited to no single people, culture, or language; but to the
Greeks of the Turkish Empire 'Hellenism' and Orthodoxy
became inextricably intertwined, far more so than they had
ever been in the Byzantine Empire. The effects of this confusion continue to the present day.

In the second place, the Church's higher administration
became caught up in a degrading system of corruption and
simony. Involved as they were in wordly affairs and matters

political, the bishops fell a prey to ambition and financial greed. Each new Patriarch required a *berat* from the Sultan before he could assume office, and for this document he was obliged to pay heavily. The Patriarch recovered his expenses from the episcopate, by exacting a fee from each bishop before instituting him in his diocese; the bishops in turn taxed the parish clergy, and the clergy taxed their flocks. What was once said of the Papacy was certainly true of the Ecumenical Patriarchate under the Turks: everything was for sale.

When there were several candidates for the Patriarchal throne, the Turks virtually sold it to the highest bidder; and they were quick to see that it was in their financial interests to change the Patriarch as frequently as possible, so as to multiply occasions for selling the *berat*. Patriarchs were removed and reinstated with kaleidoscopic rapidity. 'Out of 159 Patriarchs who have held office between the fifteenth and the twentieth century, the Turks have on 105 occasions driven Patriarchs from their throne; there have been 27 abdications, often involuntary; 6 Patriarchs have suffered violent deaths by hanging, poisoning, or drowning; and only 21 have died natural deaths while in office.'[1] The same man sometimes held office on four or five different occasions, and there were usually several ex-Patriarchs watching restively in exile for a chance to return to the throne. The extreme insecurity of the Patriarch naturally gave rise to continual intrigues among the Metropolitans of the Holy Synod who hoped to succeed him, and the leaders of the Church were usually separated into bitterly hostile parties. 'Every good Christian,' wrote an English resident in the seventeenth-century Levant, 'ought with sadness to consider, and with compassion to behold this once glorious Church to tear and rend out her own bowels, and give them for food to vultures and ravens, and to the wild and fierce Creatures of the World.'[2]

1. B. J. Kidd, *The Churches of Eastern Christendom* (London 1927), p. 304.

2. Sir Paul Rycaut, *The Present State of the Greek and Armenian Churches* (London 1679), p. 107.

But if the Patriarchate of Constantinople suffered an inward decay, outwardly its power expanded as never before. The Turks looked on the Patriarch of Constantinople as the head of all Orthodox Christians in their dominions. The other Patriarchates also within the Ottoman Empire – Alexandria, Antioch, Jerusalem – remained theoretically independent but were in practice subordinate. The Churches of Bulgaria and Serbia – likewise within Turkish dominions – gradually lost all independence, and by the mid eighteenth century had passed directly under the Ecumenical Patriarch's control. But in the nineteenth century, as Turkish power declined, the frontiers of the Patriarchate contracted. The nations which gained freedom from the Turks found it impracticable to remain subject ecclesiastically to a Patriarch resident in the Turkish capital and closely involved in the Turkish political system. The Patriarch resisted as long as he could, but in each case he bowed eventually to the inevitable. A series of national Churches were carved out of the Patriarchate: the Church of Greece (organized in 1833, recognized by the Patriarch of Constantinople in 1850); the Church of Romania (organized in 1864, recognized in 1885); the Church of Bulgaria (re-established in 1871, not recognized by Constantinople until 1945); the Church of Serbia (restored and recognized in 1879). The diminution of the Patriarchate has continued in the present century, chiefly as a result of war, and its membership in the Balkans is now but a tiny fraction of what it once was in the palmy days of Ottoman suzerainty.

The Turkish occupation had two opposite effects upon the intellectual life of the Church: it was the cause on the one hand of an immense conservatism and on the other of a certain westernization. Orthodoxy under the Turks felt itself on the defensive. The great aim was *survival* – to keep things going in hope of better days to come. The Greeks clung with miraculous tenacity to the Christian civilization which they had taken over from Byzantium, but they had little opportunity to develop this civilization creatively. Understandably enough, they were usually content to repeat accepted formulae, to entrench themselves in the positions which they had inherited from the past. Greek thought underwent an ossification and a hardening which one cannot but regret; yet conservatism had its advantages. In a dark and difficult period the Greeks did in fact maintain the Orthodox tradition substantially unimpaired. The Orthodox under Islam took as their guide Paul's words to Timothy, 'Guard the deposit: keep safe what has been entrusted to you' (1 Timothy vi, 20). Could they in the end have chosen a better motto?

Yet alongside this traditionalism there is another and contrary current in Orthodox theology of the seventeenth and eighteenth centuries: the current of western infiltration. It was difficult for the Orthodox under Ottoman rule to maintain a good standard of scholarship. Greeks who wished for a higher education were obliged to travel to the non-Orthodox world, to Italy and Germany, to Paris, and even as far as Oxford. Among the distinguished Greek theologians of the Turkish period, a few were self-taught, but the overwhelming majority had been trained in the west under Roman Catholic or Protestant masters.

Inevitably this had an effect upon the way in which they interpreted Orthodox theology. Certainly Greek students in the west read the Fathers, but they only became acquainted with such of the Fathers as were held in esteem by their non-Orthodox professors. Thus Gregory Palamas was still read, for his spiritual teaching, by the monks of Athos; but to most learned Greek theologians of the Turkish period he was utterly unknown. In the works of Eustratios Argenti (died ?1758), the ablest Greek theologian of his time, there is not a single citation from Palamas; and his case is typical. It is symbolic of the state of Greek Orthodox learning in the last four centuries that one of the chief works of Palamas, *The Triads in Defence of the Holy Hesychasts*, should have remained in great part unpublished until 1959.

There was a real danger that Greeks who studied in the west, even though they remained fully loyal in intention to their own Church, would lose their Orthodox mentality and become cut off from Orthodoxy as a living tradition. It was difficult for them not to look at theology through western spectacles; whether consciously or not, they used terminology and forms of argument foreign to their own Church. Orthodox theology underwent what the Russian theologian Fr Georges Florovsky (1893–1979) has appropriately termed a *pseudomorphosis*. Religious thinkers of the Turkish period can be divided for the most part into two broad groups, the 'Latinizers' and the 'Protestantizers'. Yet the extent of this westernization must not be exaggerated. Greeks used the outward forms which they had learnt in the west, but in the substance of their thought the great majority remained fundamentally Orthodox. The tradition was at times distorted by being forced into alien moulds – distorted, but not wholly destroyed.

Keeping in mind this twofold background of conservatism and westernization, let us consider the challenge presented to the Orthodox world by Reformation and Counter-Reformation.

REFORMATION AND COUNTER-REFORMATION: THEIR DOUBLE IMPACT

The forces of Reform stopped short when they reached the borders of Russia and the Turkish Empire, so that the Orthodox Church has not undergone either a Reformation or a Counter-Reformation. Yet it would be a mistake to conclude that these two movements have had no influence whatever upon Orthodoxy. There were many means of contact: Orthodox, as we have seen, went to study in the west; Jesuits and Franciscans, sent out to the eastern Mediterranean, undertook missionary work among Orthodox; the Jesuits were also at work in Ukraine; the foreign embassies at Constantinople, both of Roman Catholic and of Protestant powers, played a religious as well as a political role. During the seventeenth century these contacts led to significant developments in Orthodox theology.

The first important exchange of views between Orthodox and Protestants began in 1573, when a delegation of Lutheran scholars from Tübingen, led by Jakob Andreae and

Martin Crusius, visited Constantinople and gave the Patri-arch, Jeremias II, a copy of the Augsburg Confession trans-lated into Greek. Doubtless they hoped to initiate some sort of Reformation among the Greeks; as Crusius somewhat naïvely wrote: 'If they wish to take thought for the eternal salvation of their souls, they must join us and embrace our teaching, or else perish eternally!' Jeremias, however, in his three *Answers* to the Tübingen theologians (dated 1576, 1579, 1581), adhered strictly to the traditional Orthodox position and showed no inclination to Protestantism. To his first two letters the Lutherans sent replies, but in his third letter the Patriarch brought the correspondence to a close, feeling that matters had reached a deadlock: 'Go your own way, and do not write any more on doctrinal matters; and if you do write, then write only for friendship's sake.' The whole incident shows the interest felt by the Reformers in the Orthodox Church. The Patriarch's *Answers* are important as the first clear and authoritative *critique* of the doctrines of the Refor-mation from an Orthodox point of view. The chief matters discussed by Jeremias were free will and grace, Scripture and Tradition, the sacraments, prayers for the dead, and the invo-cation of the saints.

During the Tübingen interlude, Lutherans and Orthodox both showed great courtesy to one another. A very different spirit marked the first major contact between Orthodoxy and the Counter-Reformation. This occurred outside the limits of the Turkish Empire, in Ukraine. After the destruction of Kievan power by the Tartars, a large area in the south-west of Russia, including the city of Kiev itself, became absorbed by Lithuania and Poland; this south-western part of Russia is commonly known as 'Little Russia' or Ukraine. The crowns of Poland and Lithuania were united under a single ruler from 1386; thus while the monarch of the joint realm, together with the majority of the population, was Roman Catholic, an appreci-able minority of his subjects was Russian and Orthodox. These Orthodox in Ukraine were in an uncomfortable predicament. The Patriarch of Constantinople, to whose jurisdiction they belonged, could exercise no very effective control in Poland;

their bishops were appointed not by the Church but by the Roman Catholic king of Poland and were sometimes courtiers lacking in spiritual qualities.

Towards the end of the sixteenth century a Romeward movement developed among the eastern Christians of Ukraine. In 1596 at the Council of Brest-Litovsk six out of the eight bishops present, including the Metropolitan of Kiev, Michael Ragoza, decided in favour of union with Rome, although the two remaining bishops, along with a significant number of the monastic and parish delegates, chose to remain Orthodox. So a sharp division occurred: on the one side, the continuing Orthodox; on the other, the 'Greek Catholics', 'Catholics of the Eastern rite' or 'Uniates', as they have been variously styled. The Greek Catholics accepted the principles proclaimed at the Council of Florence: they acknowledged the supremacy of the Pope, but were allowed to keep their traditional practices, such as married clergy, and they continued as before to use the Byzantine Liturgy, although in course of time western elements crept into it. Outwardly, therefore, there was very little to distinguish Catholics of the Eastern rite from Orthodox. How far, one wonders, did the uneducated peasantry appreciate what the dispute was really about?

The continuing Orthodox in Polish Ukraine suffered severe repression from the Roman Catholic authorities, and there is no doubt that the Union of Brest has embittered relations between Orthodoxy and Rome from 1596 until the present day. Persecution, however, had in many ways an invigorating effect. The laity rallied to the defence of Orthodoxy and, in many places where the higher clergy had defected to Rome, the Orthodox tradition was upheld by powerful lay associations, known as the Brotherhoods (*Bratstva*). To answer Jesuit propaganda they maintained printing presses and issued books in defence of Orthodoxy; to counteract the influence of the Jesuit schools they organized Orthodox schools of their own. By 1650 the level of learning in Ukraine was higher than anywhere else in the Orthodox world; scholars from Kiev, travelling to Moscow at this time, did much to raise intellectual standards in Great Russia. In this revival of learning a particularly brilliant part was played by Peter of Moghila, Metropolitan of Kiev from 1633 to 1647. To him we must shortly return.

One of the representatives of the Patriarchate of Constantinople at Brest in 1596 was a young Greek priest called Cyril Lukaris (1572–1638). Whether as a result of his experiences in Ukraine or because of friendships that he subsequently made in Constantinople, he showed in later life a strong hostility towards the Church of Rome. On becoming Ecumenical Patriarch, he devoted his full energies to combating Roman Catholic influence in the Turkish Empire. It was unfortunate, though perhaps inevitable, that in his struggle against 'the Papic Church' (as the Greeks termed it) he should have become deeply involved in politics. He turned naturally for help to the Protestant embassies at Constantinople, while his Jesuit opponents for their part used the diplomatic representatives of the Roman Catholic powers. Besides invoking the political assistance of Protestant diplomats, Cyril also fell under Protestant influence in matters of theology, and his *Confession*,[1] first published at Geneva in 1629, is distinctively Calvinist in much of its teaching.

Cyril's reign as Patriarch is one long series of stormy intrigues, and forms a lurid example of the troubled state of the Ecumenical Patriarchate under the Ottomans. Six times deposed from office and six times reinstated, he was finally strangled by Turkish janissaries and his body cast into the Bosphorus. In the last resort there is something deeply tragic about his career, since he was possibly the most brilliant man to have held office as Patriarch since the days of St Photius. Had he but lived under happier conditions, freed from political intrigue, his exceptional gifts might have been put to better use.

Cyril's Calvinism was sharply and speedily repudiated by his fellow Orthodox, his *Confession* being condemned by no less than six local councils between 1638 and 1691. In direct

1. By 'Confession' in this context is meant a statement of faith, a solemn declaration of religious belief.

reaction to Cyril two other Orthodox hierarchs, Peter of Moghila and Dositheus of Jerusalem, produced Confessions of their own. Peter's *Orthodox Confession*, written in 1640, was based directly on Roman Catholic manuals. It was approved by the Council of Jassy in Romania (1642), but only after it had been revised by a Greek, Meletius Syrigos, who in particular altered the passages about the consecration in the Eucharist (which Peter attributed solely to the Words of Institution) and about Purgatory. Even in its revised form the Confession of Moghila is still the most Latin document ever to be adopted by an official council of the Orthodox Church. Dositheus, Patriarch of Jerusalem from 1669 to 1707, likewise drew heavily upon Latin sources. His *Confession*, ratified in 1672 by the Council of Jerusalem (also known as the Council of Bethlehem), answers Cyril's *Confession* point by point with concision and clarity. The chief matters over which Cyril and Dositheus diverge are four: the question of free will, grace, and predestination; the doctrine of the Church; the number and nature of the sacraments; and the veneration of icons. In his statement upon the Eucharist, Dositheus adopted not only the Latin term *transubstantiation* but the Scholastic distinction between *substance* and *accidents*;[1] and in defending prayers for the dead he came very close to the Roman doctrine of Purgatory, without actually using the word Purgatory itself. On the whole, however, the *Confession* of Dositheus is less Latin than that of Moghila, and must certainly be regarded as a document of primary importance in the history of seventeenth-century Orthodox theology. Faced by the Calvinism of Lukaris, Dositheus used the weapons which lay nearest to hand – Latin weapons (under the circumstances it was perhaps the only thing that he could do); but the faith which he defended with these Latin weapons was not Roman, but Orthodox.

Outside Ukraine, relations between Orthodox and Roman Catholics were often friendly in the seventeenth century. In many places in the eastern Mediterranean, particularly

1. See p. 284, note 1.

in the Greek islands under Venetian rule, Greeks and Latins shared in one another's worship: we even read of Roman Catholic processions of the Blessed Sacrament, which the Orthodox clergy attended in force, wearing full vestments, with candles and banners. Greek bishops invited the Latin missionaries to preach to their flocks or to hear confessions. But after 1700 these friendly contacts grew less frequent, and by 1750 they had largely ceased. In 1724 a large part of the Orthodox Patriarchate of Antioch submitted to Rome; after this the Orthodox authorities, fearing that the same thing might happen elsewhere in the Turkish Empire, were far stricter in their dealings with Roman Catholics. The climax in anti-Roman feeling came in 1755, when the Patriarchs of Constantinople, Alexandria, and Jerusalem declared Latin baptism to be entirely invalid and demanded that all converts to Orthodoxy be baptized anew. 'The baptisms of heretics are to be rejected and abhorred,' the decree stated; they are 'waters which cannot profit . . . nor give any sanctification to such as receive them, nor avail at all to the washing away of sins'. This measure remained in force in the Greek world until the end of the nineteenth century, but it did not extend to the Church of Russia; the Russians generally baptized Roman Catholic converts between 1441 and 1667, but since 1667 they have not normally done so.

The Orthodox of the seventeenth century came into contact not only with Roman Catholics, Lutherans and Calvinists but also with the Church of England. Cyril Lukaris corresponded with Archbishop Abbot of Canterbury, and a future Patriarch of Alexandria, Metrophanes Kritopoulos, studied at Oxford from 1617 to 1624. Kritopoulos is the author of a *Confession*, slightly Protestant in tone, but widely used in the Orthodox Church. Around 1694 there was even a plan to establish a 'Greek College' at Gloucester Hall, Oxford (now Worcester College), and about ten Greek students were actually sent to Oxford; but the plan failed for lack of money, and the Greeks found the food and lodging so poor that many of them ran away. From 1716 to 1725 a most interesting correspondence was maintained between the Orthodox and the Non-Jurors (a group of Anglicans who separated from the main body of the

Church of England in 1688, rather than swear allegiance to the usurper William of Orange). The Non-Jurors approached both the four Eastern Patriarchs and the Church of Russia, in the hope of establishing communion with the Orthodox. But the Non-Jurors could not accept the Orthodox teaching concerning the presence of Christ in the Eucharist; they were also troubled by the veneration shown by Orthodoxy to the Mother of God, the saints, and the Holy Icons. Eventually the correspondence was suspended without any agreement being reached.

Looking back on the work of Moghila and Dositheus, on the councils of Jassy and Jerusalem, and on the correspondence with the Non-Jurors, one is struck by the limitations of Greek theology in this period: one does not find the Orthodox tradition in its *fullness*. Nevertheless the councils of the seventeenth century made a permanent and constructive contribution to Orthodoxy. The Reformation controversies raised problems which neither the Ecumenical Councils nor the Church of the later Byzantine Empire was called to face: in the seventeenth century the Orthodox were forced to think more carefully about the sacraments, and about the nature and authority of the Church. It was important for Orthodoxy to express its mind on these topics, and to define its position in relation to the new teachings which had arisen in the west; this was the task which the seventeenth-century councils achieved. These councils were local, but the substance of their decisions has been accepted by the Orthodox Church as a whole. The seventeenth-century councils, like the Hesychast councils three hundred years before, show that creative theological work did not come to an end in the Orthodox Church after the period of the Ecumenical Councils. There are important doctrines not defined by the general councils, which every Orthodox is bound to accept as an integral part of his faith.

Throughout the Turkish period the traditions of Hesychasm remained alive, particularly on Mount Athos. Here during the second half of the eighteenth century there arose an important movement of spiritual renewal, whose effects can still be felt today. Its members, known as the Kollyvades, were alarmed at the way in which all too many of their fellow Greeks were falling under the influence of the western Enlightenment. The Kollyvades were convinced that a regeneration of the Greek nation would come, not through embracing the secular ideas fashionable in the west, but only through a return to the true roots of Orthodox Christianity – through a rediscovery of Patristic theology and Orthodox liturgical life. In particular they advocated frequent communion – if possible, daily – although at this time most Orthodox communicated only three or four times a year. For this the Kollyvades were fiercely attacked on the Holy Mountain and elsewhere, but a council held at Constantinople in 1819 endorsed their standpoint and affirmed that in principle the faithful, if properly prepared, may receive the sacrament at every celebration of the Eucharist.

One of the most notable fruits of this spiritual renewal was the appearance of the *Philokalia*, a vast anthology of ascetic and mystical texts dating from the fourth to the fifteenth century. Published in Venice in 1782, this is a weighty tome of some 1,207 folio pages. The editors, both leading members of the Kollyvades movement, were St Macarius (Notaras), Metropolitan of Corinth (1731–1805), and St Nicodemus of the Holy Mountain ('The Hagiorite', 1748–1809), who was justly termed 'an encyclopaedia of the Athonite learning of his time'. The *Philokalia*, which was intended by its editors for laypeople living in the world as well as for monks, is devoted especially to the theory and practice of inner prayer, and in particular the Jesus Prayer. Initially its impact in the Greek world was limited, and more than a century passed before it was reissued. But the Slavonic translation published in Moscow in 1793 contributed decisively to the renaissance of Russian spirituality in the nineteenth century, while more recently, from the 1950s onwards, much more attention has been given to the *Philokalia* by the Greeks. Translations have also begun to appear in western languages, and these have appealed to a surprisingly wide public. Indeed the *Philokalia* has acted as a spiritual 'time bomb', for the true 'age of the *Philokalia*' has been not the late eighteenth but the late twentieth century.

Nicodemus helped in the editing of numerous other texts,

most notably the writings of Symeon the New Theologian, and he prepared an edition of Gregory Palamas, although this was never published. Somewhat surprisingly, in view of the strong anti-Catholic feeling in the Greek world at this time, he also drew on Roman Catholic devotional literature, adapting for a Greek Orthodox readership works by Lorenzo Scupoli and by Ignatius Loyola, the founder of the Jesuits.

Another monk of Mount Athos in the eighteenth century, St Kosmas the Aetolian (1714–79), contributed to the revival of the Greek people not through books but through missionary preaching. His ministry resembles that of John Wesley. At a time when the religious and cultural life of the Greeks under Turkish rule had sunk in many places to a very low ebb, he undertook a series of apostolic journeys throughout mainland Greece and the islands, addressing huge crowds. He saw the Greek Orthodox faith and the Greek language as integrally linked, and wherever he went he founded Greek schools. Eventually he was executed by the Ottoman authorities. He is one of the many 'New Martyrs' who suffered for their faith in the Turkish period.

It has been rightly said that if there is much to pity in the state of Orthodoxy during the Turkish period, there is also much to admire. Despite innumerable discouragements, the Orthodox Church under Ottoman rule never lost heart. There were of course many cases of apostasy to Islam, but in Europe at any rate they were not as frequent as might have been expected. The corruption in the higher administration of the Church, depressing though it was, had very little effect on the daily life of the ordinary Christian, who was still able to worship Sunday by Sunday in his parish church. More than anything else it was the Holy Liturgy which kept Orthodoxy alive in those dark days.

CHAPTER 6

Moscow and St Petersburg

The sense of God's presence – of the supernatural – seems to me to penetrate Russian life more completely than that of any of the western nations.

H. P. Liddon, Canon of St Paul's,
after a visit to Russia in 1867

MOSCOW THE THIRD ROME

After the taking of Constantinople in 1453, there was only one nation capable of assuming leadership in eastern Christendom. The greater part of Bulgaria, Serbia, and Romania had already been conquered by the Turks, while the rest was absorbed before long. The Metropolia of Kiev had passed under the Roman Catholic rulers of Poland and Lithuania. Muscovy alone remained. To the Muscovites it seemed no coincidence that at the very moment when the Byzantine Empire came to an end, they themselves were at last throwing off the few remaining vestiges of Tartar suzerainty: God, it seemed, was granting them their freedom because He had chosen them to be the successors of Byzantium.

At the same time as the land of Muscovy, the Muscovite Church gained its independence, more by chance than from any deliberate design. Hitherto the Patriarch of Constantinople had appointed the head of the Russian Church, the Metropolitan. At the Council of Florence the Metropolitan was a Greek, Isidore. A leading supporter of the union with Rome, Isidore returned to Moscow in 1441 and proclaimed the decrees of Florence, but he met with no support from the Muscovites: he was imprisoned by the Grand Duke, but after a time was allowed to escape, and went back to Italy. The chief see was thus left vacant; but the Russians could not ask the Patriarch for a new Metropolitan, because until 1453 the official Church at Constantinople continued to accept the Florentine Union.

Reluctant to take action on their own, the Russians delayed for several years. Eventually in 1448 a council of Russian bishops in Moscow proceeded to elect a Metropolitan without further reference to Constantinople. After 1453, when the Florentine Union was abandoned at Constantinople, communion between the Patriarchate and Russia was restored, but Russia continued to appoint its own chief hierarch. Henceforward the Church of Moscow was autocephalous. The Metropolia of Kiev, however, continued to be within the jurisdiction of Constantinople until 1686, when it passed under Moscow, although this happened without any proper blessing from the Ecumenical Patriarch.

The idea of Moscow as successor of Byzantium was assisted by a marriage. In 1472 Ivan III 'the Great' (reigned 1462–1505) married Sophia, niece of the last Byzantine Emperor. Although Sophia had brothers and was not the legal heir to the throne, the marriage served to establish a dynastic link with Byzantium. The Grand Duke of Moscow began to assume the Byzantine titles of 'autocrat' and 'Tsar' (an adaption of the Roman 'Caesar') and to use the double-headed eagle of Byzantium as his State emblem. People came to think of Moscow as 'the third Rome'. The first Rome (so they argued) had fallen to the barbarians and then lapsed into heresy; the second Rome, Constantinople, had in turn fallen into heresy at the Council of Florence, and as a punishment had been taken by the Turks. Moscow therefore had succeeded Constantinople as the third and last Rome, the centre of Orthodox Christendom. The monk Philotheus of Pskov set forth this line of argument in a famous letter written in 1510 to Tsar Basil III:

I wish to add a few words on the present Orthodox Empire of our ruler: he is on earth the sole Emperor [Tsar] of the Christians, the leader of the Apostolic Church which stands no longer in Rome or in Constantinople, but in the blessed city of Moscow. She alone shines in the whole world brighter than the sun ... All Christian Empires are fallen and in their stead stands alone the Empire of our ruler in accordance with the Prophetical books. Two Romes have fallen, but the third stands and a fourth there will not be.[1]

1. Quoted in Baynes and Moss, *Byzantium: an Introduction*, p. 385.

This idea of Moscow the third Rome had a certain appropriateness when applied to the Tsar: the Emperor of Byzantium had once acted as champion and protector of Orthodoxy, and now the autocrat of Russia was called to perform the same task. Its application in the religious sphere, however, has been more limited, for the head of the Russian Church has never superseded the Patriarch of Constantinople, but has always ranked no higher than fifth among the Orthodox leaders, after the Patriarch of Jerusalem.

Now that the dream for which St Sergius worked – the liberation of Russia from the Tartars – had become a reality, a sad division occurred among his spiritual descendants. Sergius had united the social with the mystical side of monasticism, but under his successors these two aspects became separated. The separation first came into the open at a Church council in 1503. As this council drew to its close, St Nilus of Sora (Nil Sorsky, ?1433–1508), a monk from a remote hermitage in the forests beyond the Volga, rose to speak, and launched an attack on the ownership of land by monasteries (about a third of the land in Russia belonged to monasteries at this time). St Joseph, Abbot of Volokalamsk (1439–1515), replied in defence of monastic landholding. The majority of the council supported Joseph; but there were others in the Russian Church who agreed with Nilus – chiefly hermits living like him beyond the Volga. Joseph's party were known as the Possessors, Nilus and the 'Transvolga hermits' as the Non-Possessors. During the next twenty years there was considerable tension between the two groups. Finally in 1525–6 the Non-Possessors attacked Tsar Basil III for unjustly divorcing his wife (the Orthodox Church grants divorce, but only for certain reasons); the Tsar then imprisoned the leading Non-Possessors and closed the Transvolga hermitages. The tradition of St Nilus was driven underground, and although it never entirely disappeared, its influence in the Russian Church was very much restricted. For the time being the outlook of the Possessors reigned supreme.

Behind the question of monastic property lay two different conceptions of the monastic life, and ultimately two different views of the relation of the Church to the world. The Possessors emphasized the social obligations of monasticism: it is part of the work of monks to care for the sick and poor, to show hospitality and to teach; to do these things efficiently, monasteries need money and therefore they must own land. Monks (so they argued) do not use their wealth on themselves, but hold it in trust for the benefit of others. There was a saying among the followers of Joseph, 'The riches of the Church are the riches of the poor'.

The Non-Possessors argued on the other hand that almsgiving is the duty of the laity, while a monk's primary task is to help others by praying for them and by setting an example. To do these things properly a monk must be detached from the world, and only those who are vowed to complete poverty can achieve true detachment. Monks who are landowners cannot avoid being tangled up in secular anxieties, and because they become absorbed in worldly concerns, they act and think in a worldly way. In the words of the monk Vassian (Prince Patrikiev), a disciple of Nilus:

Where in the traditions of the Gospels, Apostles, and Fathers are monks ordered to acquire populous villages and enslave peasants to the brotherhood? . . . We look into the hands of the rich, fawn slavishly, flatter them to get out of them some little village . . . We wrong and rob and sell Christians, our brothers. We torture them with scourges like wild beasts.[1]

Vassian's protest against torture and scourges brings us to a second matter over which the two sides disagreed, the treatment of heretics. Joseph upheld the view all but universal in Christendom at this time: if heretics are recalcitrant, the Church must call in the civil arm and resort to prison, torture, and if necessary fire. But Nilus condemned all forms of coercion and violence against heretics. One has only to recall how Protestants and Roman Catholics treated one another in western Europe during the Reformation, to realize how exceptional Nilus was in his tolerance and respect for human freedom.

1. Quoted in B. Pares, *A History of Russia* (3rd edn., London ?1936), p. 93.

The question of heretics in turn involved the wider problem of relations between Church and State. Nilus regarded heresy as a spiritual matter, to be settled by the Church without the State's intervention; Joseph invoked the help of the secular authorities. In general Nilus drew a clearer line than Joseph between the things of Caesar and the things of God. The Possessors were great supporters of the ideal of Moscow the third Rome; believing in a close alliance between Church and State, they took an active part in politics, as Sergius had done, but perhaps they were less careful than Sergius to guard the Church from becoming the servant of the State. The Non-Possessors for their part had a sharper awareness of the prophetic and other-worldly witness of monasticism. The Josephites were in danger of identifying the Kingdom of God with a kingdom of this world; Nilus saw that the Church on earth must always be a Church in pilgrimage. While Joseph and his party were great patriots and nationalists, the Non-Possessors thought more of the universality and Catholicity of the Church.

Nor did the divergences between the two sides end here: they also had different ideas of Christian piety and prayer. Joseph emphasized the place of rules and discipline, Nilus the inner and personal relation between God and the soul. Joseph stressed the place of beauty in worship, Nilus feared that beauty might become an idol: the monk (so Nilus maintained) is dedicated not only to an outward poverty, but to an absolute self-stripping, and he must be careful lest a devotion to beautiful icons or Church music comes between him and God. (In this suspicion of beauty, Nilus displays a Puritanism – almost an Iconoclasm – most unusual in Russian spirituality.) Joseph realized the importance of corporate worship and of liturgical prayer:

A man can pray in his own room, but he will never pray there as he prays in church ... where the singing of many voices rises united towards god, where all have but one thought and one voice in the unity of love ... On high the seraphim proclaim the *Trisagion*, here below the human multitude raises the same hymn. Heaven and earth keep festival together, one in thanksgiving, one in happiness, one in joy.[1]

Nilus on the other hand was chiefly interested not in liturgical but in mystical prayer: before he settled at Sora he had lived as a monk on Mount Athos, and he knew the Byzantine Hesychast tradition at first hand.

The Russian Church rightly saw good things in the teaching of both Joseph and Nilus, and has canonized them both. Each inherited a part of the tradition of St Sergius, but no more than a part: Russia needed both the Josephite and the Transvolgian forms of monasticism, for each supplemented the other. It was sad indeed that the two sides entered into conflict, and that the tradition of Nilus was largely suppressed: without the Non-Possessors, the spiritual life of the Russian Church became one-sided and unbalanced. The close integration which the Josephites upheld between Church and State, their Russian nationalism, their devotion to the outward forms of worship – these things were to lead to trouble in the next century.

One of the most interesting participants in the dispute of Possessors and Non-Possessors was St Maximus the Greek (?1470–1556), a 'bridge figure' whose long life embraces the three worlds of Renaissance Italy, Mount Athos, and Muscovy. Greek by birth, he spent the years of early manhood in Florence and Venice, as a friend of Humanist scholars such as Pico della Mirandola; he also fell under the influence of Savonarola, and for two years was a Dominican. Returning to Greece in 1504, he became a monk on Athos; in 1517 he was invited to Russia by the Tsar, to translate Greek works into Slavonic and to correct the Russian service books, which were disfigured by numerous errors. Like Nilus, he was devoted to the Hesychast ideals, and on arriving in Russia he threw in his lot with the Non-Possessors. He suffered with the rest, and was imprisoned for twenty-six years, from 1525 to 1551. He was attacked with

1. Quoted by J. Meyendorff, 'Une controverse sur le rôle social de l'Église. La querelle des biens ecclésiastiques au XVIe siècle en Russie', in the periodical *Irénikon*, vol. XXIX (1956), p. 29.

particular bitterness for the changes which he proposed in the
service books, and the work of revision was broken off and left
unfinished. His great gifts of learning, from which the Russians
could have benefited so much, were largely wasted in imprisonment. He was as strict as Nilus in his demand for self-stripping
and spiritual poverty. 'If you truly love Christ crucified,' he
wrote, '. . . be a stranger, unknown, without country, without
name, silent before your relatives, your acquaintances, and
your friends; distribute all that you have to the poor, sacrifice
all your old habits and all your own will.'[1]

Although the victory of the Possessors meant a close alliance
between Church and State, the Church did not forfeit all independence. When Ivan the Terrible's power was at its height,
the Metropolitan of Moscow, St Philip (died 1569), dared to
protest openly against the Tsar's bloodshed and injustice, and
rebuked him to his face during the public celebration of the
Liturgy. Ivan put him in prison and later had him strangled.
Another who sharply criticized Ivan was St Basil the Blessed,
the 'Fool in Christ' (died 1552). Folly for the sake of Christ is
a form of sanctity found in Byzantium, but particularly prominent in medieval Russia: the 'Fool' carries the ideal of self-
stripping and humiliation to its furthest extent, by renouncing
all intellectual gifts, all forms of earthly wisdom, and by voluntarily taking upon himself the Cross of madness. These Fools
often performed a valuable social role: simply because they
were fools, they could criticize those in power with a frankness
which no one else dared to employ. So it was with Basil, the
'living conscience' of the Tsar. Ivan listened to the shrewd
censure of the Fool, and so far from punishing him, treated
him with marked honour.

In 1589, with the consent of the Patriarch of Constantinople,
the head of the Russian Church was raised from the rank of
Metropolitan to that of Patriarch, receiving the fifth place,
after Jerusalem. As things turned out, the Moscow Patriarchate
was to last for little more than a century.

1. Quoted by E. Denissoff, *Maxime le Grec et l'Occident* (Paris 1943),
pp. 275–6.

THE SCHISM OF THE OLD BELIEVERS

The seventeenth century in Russia opened with a period of confusion and disaster, known as the Time of Troubles, when the land was divided against itself and fell a victim to outside enemies. But after 1613 Russia made a sudden recovery, and the next forty years were a time of reconstruction and reform in many branches of the nation's life. In this work of reconstruction the Church played a large part. The reforming movement in the Church was led at first by the Abbot Dionysius of the Trinity–St Sergius Monastery and by Philaret, Patriarch of Moscow from 1619 to 1633 (he was the father of the Tsar); after 1633 the leadership passed to a group of married parish clergy, and in particular to the Archpriests John Neronov and Avvakum Petrovitch. The work of correcting service books, begun in the previous century by Maximus the Greek, was now cautiously resumed; a Patriarchal Press was set up at Moscow, and more accurate Church books were issued, although the authorities did not venture to make too many drastic alterations. On the parish level, the reformers did all they could to raise moral standards alike among the clergy and the laity. They fought against drunkenness; they insisted that the fasts be observed; they demanded that the Liturgy and other services in the parish churches should be sung with reverence and without omissions; they encouraged frequent preaching.

The reforming group represented much of what was best in the tradition of St Joseph of Volokalamsk. Like Joseph they believed in authority and discipline, and saw the Christian life in terms of ascetic rules and liturgical prayer. They expected not only monks but parish priests and laity – husband, wife, children – to keep the fasts and to spend long periods at prayer each day, either in church or before the icons in their own homes. Their programme made few concessions to human weakness, and was too ambitious ever to be completely realized. Nevertheless Muscovy around 1650 went far to justify the title 'Holy Russia'. Orthodox from the Turkish Empire who visited Moscow were amazed (and often filled with dismay) by the austerity of the fasts, by the length and magnificence of the services. The whole nation appeared to live as 'one vast religious house'.[1] Archdeacon Paul of Aleppo, an Arab Orthodox from the Patriarchate of Antioch, who stayed in Russia from 1654 to 1656, found that banquets at Court were accompanied not by music but by readings from the Lives of the Saints, as at meals in a monastery. Services lasting seven hours or more were attended by the Tsar and the whole Court: 'Now what shall we say of these duties, severe enough to turn children's hair grey, so strictly observed by the Emperor, Patriarch, grandees, princesses and ladies, standing upright on their legs from morning to evening? Who would believe that they should thus go beyond the devout anchorites of the desert?'[2] The children were not excluded from these rigorous observances: 'What surprised us most was to see the boys and little children . . . standing bareheaded and motionless, without betraying the smallest gesture of impatience.'[3] Paul found Russian strictness not entirely to his taste. He complains that they permit no 'mirth, laughter and jokes', no drunkenness, no 'opium eating' and no smoking, 'For the special crime of drinking tobacco they even put men to death.'[4] It is an impressive picture which Paul and other visitors to Russia present, but there is perhaps too much emphasis on externals. One Greek remarked on his return home that Muscovite religion seemed to consist largely in bell-ringing.

In 1652–3 there began a fatal quarrel between the reforming group and the new Patriarch, Nikon (1605–81). A peasant by origin, Nikon was probably the most brilliant and gifted man ever to become head of the Russian Church; but he suffered from an overbearing and authoritarian temper. Nikon was a strong admirer of things Greek: 'I am a Russian and the son of a Russian,' he used to say, 'but my faith and my religion are Greek.'[5] He demanded that Russian practices should be made

1. N. Zernov, *Moscow the Third Rome* (London 1937), p. 51.

2. 'The Travels of Macarius', in W. Palmer, *The Patriarch and the Tsar*, vol. 2 (London 1873), p. 107.

3. *The Travels of Macarius*, ed. Lady Laura Ridding (London 1936), p. 68.

4. ibid., p. 21.

5. ibid., p. 37.

to conform at every point to the standard of the four ancient Patriarchates, and that the Russian service books should be altered whenever they differed from the Greek. In particular he insisted that the sign of the Cross, still made by the Russians in the older manner with two fingers, should henceforward be made with three fingers, as the Greeks were now doing.

This policy was resented by many who were heirs to the Josephite tradition. They regarded Moscow as the third Rome, and Russia as the stronghold and norm of Orthodoxy. They respected the memory of the Mother Church of Byzantium, from which Russia had received the faith, but they did not feel the same reverence for contemporary Greeks. They remembered how the Greek hierarchs had betrayed the faith at Florence, and they may well have known something of the corruption within the Patriarchate of Constantinople under Turkish rule. All this made them unwilling slavishly to copy modern Greek usages, and in particular they saw no reason why the Russians should now be required to make the sign of the Cross in the Greek way, when their Russian practice was in fact the more ancient. The question of the sign of the Cross may seem trivial, but it has to be remembered how great an importance Orthodox in general, and Russians in particular, have always attached to ritual actions, to the symbolic gestures whereby the inner belief of the Christian is expressed. In the eyes of many, a change in the symbol constituted a change in the faith. This divergence over the sign of the Cross served to crystallize in a specific way the whole issue of Muscovite versus Greek Orthodoxy.

Had Nikon proceeded gently and tactfully, all might yet have been well, but unfortunately he was not a tactful man. He pressed on with his reforming programme, despite the opposition from Neronov and Avvakum, along with many others among parish clergy, the monks and lay people. The opponents of the Nikonian reforms were severely persecuted, suffering exile, imprisonment and in some cases death. Although Neronov finally submitted, Avvakum (1620–82) refused to give way, and after ten years of exile and twenty-two years of imprisonment – twelve of them spent in an underground hut – he was finally burnt at the stake. His supporters saw him as a martyr for the faith. He has left a full account of all his sufferings in his vivid and extraordinary autobiography, which forms one of the classics of Russian religious literature.

The dispute between Nikon and the opponents of reform led eventually to a lasting schism. Those who like Avvakum rejected the Nikonian service books came to be known as *Raskolniki* ('sectarians') or *Old Believers*, although it would be more accurate to term them 'Old Ritualists'. Thus there arose in seventeenth-century Russia a movement of Dissent; but if we compare it with English Dissent of the same period, we notice two great differences. First, the Old Believers – the Russian Dissenters – differed from the official Church solely in ritual, not in doctrine; and secondly, while English Dissent was radical – a protest against the official Church for not carrying reform far enough – Russian Dissent was the protest of conservatives against an official Church which in their eyes had carried reform too far. The schism of the Old Believers has continued to the present day. Before 1917 their numbers were officially assessed at two million, but the true figure may well have been over five times as great. They are divided into two main groups, the *Popovtsy*, who have retained the priesthood and who since 1846 have also possessed their own succession of bishops; and the *Bezpopovtsy*, who have no priests.

There is much to admire in the Old Believers, who embody many of the finest elements in the tradition of medieval Russian piety. But they do not embrace all the richness of that tradition, for they represent only one aspect of it – the viewpoint of the Possessors. The defects of the Old Believers are the Josephite defects writ large: too narrow a nationalism, too great an emphasis on the externals of worship. Nikon too, despite his Hellenism, is in the end a Josephite: he demanded an absolute uniformity in the externals of worship, and like the Possessors he freely invoked the help of the civil arm in order to suppress all religious opponents. More than anything else, it was his readiness to resort to persecution which made the schism definitive. Had the development of Church life in Russia between 1550 and 1650 been less one-sided, perhaps a lasting separation would have been avoided. If people had thought more (as Nilus did) of tolerance and freedom instead of using persecution, then a reconciliation might have been effected; and if they had attended more to mystical prayer, they might have argued less bitterly about ritual. Behind the division of the seventeenth century lie the disputes of the sixteenth.

As well as establishing Greek practices in Russia, Nikon pursued a second aim: to make the Church supreme over the State. In the past the theory governing relations between Church and State had been the same in Russia as in Byzantium – a dyarchy or symphony of two co-ordinated powers, *sacerdotium* and *imperium*, each supreme in its own sphere. In practice the Church had enjoyed a wide measure of independence and influence in the Kievan and Mongol periods. But under the Moscow Tsardom, although the theory of two co-ordinated powers remained the same, in practice the civil power came to control the Church more and more; the Josephite policy naturally encouraged this tendency. Nikon attempted to reverse the situation. Not only did he demand that the Patriarch's authority be absolute in religious matters, but he also claimed the right to intervene in civil affairs, and assumed the title 'Great Lord', hitherto reserved to the Tsar alone. Tsar Alexis had a deep respect for Nikon, and at first submitted to his control. 'The Patriarch's authority is so great,' wrote Olearius, visiting Moscow in 1654, 'that he in a manner divides the sovereignty with the Grand Duke.'[1]

But after a time Alexis began to resent Nikon's interference in secular affairs. In 1658 Nikon, perhaps in hopes of restoring his influence, decided upon a curious step: he withdrew into semi-retirement, but did not resign the office of Patriarch. For eight years the Russian Church remained without an effective head, until at the Tsar's request a great council was held at Moscow in 1666–7 over which the Patriarchs of Alexandria and Antioch presided. The council decided in favour of Nikon's *reforms*, but against his *person*: Nikon's changes in the service books and above all his ruling on the sign of the Cross were

---

1. Palmer, *The Patriarch and the Tsar*, vol. 2, p. 407.

confirmed, but Nikon himself was deposed and exiled, a new Patriarch being appointed in his place. The council was therefore a triumph for Nikon's policy of imposing Greek practices on the Russian Church, but a defeat for his attempt to set the Patriarch above the Tsar. The council reasserted the Byzantine theory of a harmony of two interdependent powers.

But the decisions of the Moscow Council upon the relations of Church and State did not remain long in force. The pendulum which Nikon had pushed too far in one direction soon swung back in the other with redoubled violence. Peter the Great (reigned 1682–1725) altogether suppressed the office of Patriarch, whose powers Nikon had so ambitiously striven to aggrandize.

THE SYNODICAL PERIOD (1700–1917)

Peter was determined that there should be no more Nikons. In 1700, when Patriarch Adrian died, Peter took no steps towards the appointment of a successor; and in 1721 he proceeded to issue the celebrated *Spiritual Regulation*, which declared the Patriarchate to be abolished, and he set up in its place a commission, the Spiritual College or Holy Synod. This was composed of twelve members, three of whom were bishops, and the rest drawn from the heads of monasteries or from the married clergy.

The constitution of the Synod was not based on Orthodox Canon Law, but copied from the Protestant ecclesiastical synods in Germany. Its members were not chosen by the Church but nominated by the Emperor; and the Emperor who nominated could also dismiss them at will. Whereas a Patriarch, holding office for life, could perhaps defy the Tsar, a member of the Holy Synod was allowed no scope for heroism: he was simply retired. The Emperor was not called 'Head of the Church', but he was given the title 'Supreme Judge of the Spiritual College'. Meetings of the Synod were not attended by the Emperor himself, but by a government official, the Chief Procurator. The Procurator, although he sat at a separate table and took no part in the discussions, in practice wielded considerable power over Church affairs and was in effect if not in name a 'Minister for Religion'.

The *Spiritual Regulation* sees the Church not as a divine institution but as a department of State. Based largely on secular presuppositions, it makes little allowance for what were termed in the English Reformation 'the Crown rights of the Redeemer'. This is true not only of its provisions for the higher administration of the Church, but of many of its other rulings. A priest who learns, while hearing confessions, of any scheme which the government might consider seditious, is ordered to violate the secrecy of the sacrament and to supply the police with names and full details. Monasticism is bluntly termed 'the origin of innumerable disorders and disturbances' and placed under many restrictions. New monasteries are not to be founded without special permission; monks are forbidden to live as hermits; no woman under the age of fifty is allowed to take vows as a nun.

There was a deliberate purpose behind these restrictions on the monasteries, the chief centres of social work in Russia up to this time. The abolition of the Patriarchate was part of a wider process: Peter sought not only to deprive the Church of leadership, but to eliminate it from participation in social work. Peter's successors circumscribed the work of the monasteries still more drastically. Elizabeth (reigned 1741–62) confiscated most of the monastic estates, and Catherine II (reigned 1762–96) suppressed more than half the monasteries, while on such houses as remained open she imposed a strict limitation on the number of monks. The closing of the monasteries was little short of a disaster in the more distant provinces of Russia, where they formed virtually the only cultural and charitable centres. But although the social work of the Church was grievously restricted, it never completely ceased.

Peter's religious reforms aroused considerable opposition in Russia, but it was ruthlessly silenced. Outside Russia the redoubtable Dositheus made a vigorous protest; but the Orthodox Churches under Turkish rule were in no position to intervene effectively, and in 1723 the four ancient Patriarchates

accepted the abolition of the Patriarchate of Moscow and
recognized the constitution of the Holy Synod.

The system of Church government which Peter the Great
established continued in force until 1917. The Synodical period
in the history of Russian Orthodoxy is usually represented
as a time of decline, with the Church in complete subservience
to the State. Certainly a superficial glance at the eighteenth
century would serve to confirm this verdict. It was an age of
ill-advised westernization in Church art, Church music and
theology. Those who rebelled against the dry scholasticism of
the theological academies turned, not to the teachings of Byzantium and ancient Russia, but to religious or pseudo-religious
movements in the contemporary west: Protestant mysticism,
German pietism, Freemasonry[1] and the like. Prominent
among the higher clergy were Court prelates such as Ambrose
(Zertiss-Kamensky), Archbishop of Moscow and Kaluga, who
at his death in 1771 left (among many other possessions) 252
shirts of fine linen and nine eye-glasses framed in gold.

But this is only one side of the picture in the eighteenth
century. The Holy Synod, however objectionable its theoretical
constitution, in practice governed efficiently. Reflective
Churchmen were well aware of the defects in Peter's reforms,
and submitted to them without necessarily agreeing with them.
Theology was westernized, but standards of scholarship were
high. Behind the façade of westernization, the true life of Orthodox Russia continued without interruption. Ambrose Zertiss-
Kamensky represented one type of Russian bishop, but there
were other bishops of a very different character, true monks
and pastors, such as St Tikhon of Zadonsk (1724–83), Bishop
of Voronezh. A great preacher and a fluent writer, Tikhon is
particularly interesting as an example of one who, like most of
his contemporaries, borrowed heavily from the west, but who
remained at the same time firmly rooted in the classic tradition
of Orthodox spirituality. He drew upon German and Anglican

1. Orthodox are strictly forbidden, on pain of excommunication, to become
Freemasons.

books of devotion; his detailed meditations upon the physical sufferings of Jesus are more typical of Roman Catholicism than of Orthodoxy; in his own life of prayer he underwent an experience similar to the Dark Night of the Soul, as described by western mystics such as St John of the Cross. But Tikhon was also close in outlook to Theodosius and Sergius, to Nilus and the Non-Possessors. Like so many Russian saints, both lay and monastic, he took a special delight in helping the poor, and he was happiest when talking with simple people – peasants, beggars and even criminals.

The second part of the Synodical period, the nineteenth century, so far from being a period of decline, was a time of great revival in the Russian Church. People turned away from religious and pseudo-religious movements in the contemporary west, and fell back once more upon the true spiritual forces of Orthodoxy. Hand in hand with this revival in the spiritual life went a new enthusiasm for missionary work, while in theology, as in spirituality, Orthodoxy freed itself from a slavish imitation of the west.

It was from Mount Athos that this religious renewal took its origin, through the work and witness of St Paissy Velichkovsky (1722–94). Ukrainian by birth, during his studies at the theological academy of Kiev he was repelled by the secular tone of the teaching, and he fled to Mount Athos, where he became a monk. In 1763 he went to Romania and became Abbot of the monastery of Niamets, which he made a great spiritual centre, gathering round him more than 500 brethren. Under his guidance, the community devoted itself specially to the work of translating Greek Fathers into Slavonic. At Athos Paissy had learnt at first hand about the Hesychast tradition, and he was in close sympathy with his contemporary Nicodemus. He made a Slavonic translation of the *Philokalia*, which was published at Moscow in 1793. Paissy laid great emphasis upon the practice of continual prayer – above all the Jesus Prayer – and on the need for obedience to an elder or *starets*. He was deeply influenced by Nilus and the Non-Possessors, but he did not overlook the good elements in the Josephite form of monasticism: he allowed more place than Nilus had done to liturgical prayer and to social work, and in this way he attempted, like Sergius, to combine the mystical with the corporate and social aspect of the monastic life.

Paissy himself never returned to Russia, but many of his disciples travelled thither from Romania and under their inspiration a monastic revival spread across the land. Existing houses were reinvigorated, and many new foundations were made: in 1810 there were 452 monasteries in Russia, whereas in 1914 there were 1,025. This monastic movement, while outward-looking and concerned to serve the world, also restored to the centre of the Church's life the tradition of the Non-Possessors, largely suppressed since the sixteenth century. It was marked in particular by a high development of the practice of spiritual direction. Although the 'elder' has been a characteristic figure in many periods of Orthodox history, nineteenth-century Russia is *par excellence* the age of the *starets*.

The first and greatest of the *startsy* of the nineteenth century was St Seraphim of Sarov (1759–1833), who of all the saints of Russia is perhaps the most immediately attractive to non-Orthodox Christians. Entering the monastery of Sarov at the age of nineteen, Seraphim first spent sixteen years in the ordinary life of the community. Then he withdrew to spend the next twenty years in seclusion, living at first in a hut in the forest, then (when his feet swelled up and he could no longer walk with ease) enclosed in a cell in the monastery. This was his training for the office of eldership. Finally in 1815 he opened the doors of his cell. From dawn until evening he received all who came to him for help, healing the sick, giving advice, often supplying the answer before his visitor had time to ask any questions. Sometimes scores or hundreds would come to see him in a single day. The outward pattern of Seraphim's life recalls that of Antony of Egypt fifteen centuries before: there is the same withdrawal in order to return. Seraphim is rightly regarded as a characteristically Russian saint, but he is also a striking example of how much the best of Russian Orthodoxy has in common with Byzantium and the universal Orthodox tradition throughout the ages.

Seraphim was extraordinarily severe to himself (at one point in his life he spent a thousand successive nights in continual prayer, standing motionless throughout the long hours of darkness on a rock), but he was gentle to others, without ever being sentimental or indulgent. Asceticism did not make him gloomy, and if ever a saint's life was illuminated by joy, it was Seraphim's. The vision of the Divine Light of Tabor took in his case a visible form, outwardly transforming his body. One of Seraphim's 'spiritual children', Nicolas Motovilov, described what happened one winter day as the two of them were talking together in the forest. Seraphim had spoken of the need to acquire the Holy Spirit, and Motovilov asked how someone could be sure of 'being in the Spirit of God':

Then Father Seraphim took me very firmly by the shoulders and said: 'My son, we are both at this moment in the Spirit of God. Why don't you look at me?'

'I cannot look, Father,' I replied, 'because your eyes are flashing like lightning. Your face has become brighter than the sun, and it hurts my eyes to look at you.'

'Don't be afraid,' he said. 'At this very moment you yourself have become as bright as I am. You yourself are now in the fullness of the Spirit of God; otherwise you would not be able to see me as you do.'

Then bending his head towards me, he whispered softly in my ear: 'Thank the Lord God for His infinite goodness towards us . . . But why, my son, do you not look me in the eyes? Just look, and don't be afraid; the Lord is with us.'

After these words I glanced at his face, and there came over me an even greater reverent awe. Imagine in the centre of the sun, in the dazzling light of its midday rays, the face of a man talking to you. You see the movement of his lips and the changing expression of his eyes, you hear his voice, you feel someone holding your shoulders; yet you do not see his hands, you do not even see yourself or his body, but only a blinding light spreading far around for several yards and lighting up with its brilliance the snow-blanket which covers the forest glade and the snow-flakes which continue to fall unceasingly . . .

'What do you feel?' Father Seraphim asked me.

'An immeasurable well-being,' I said.

'But what sort of well-being? How exactly do you feel well?'

'I feel such a calm,' I answered, 'such peace in my soul that no words can express it.'

'This,' said Father Seraphim, 'is the peace of which the Lord said to His disciples: My peace I give to you; not as the world gives do I give to you [John xiv, 27], the peace which passes all understanding [Philippians iv, 7] . . . What else do you feel?'

'Infinite joy in all my heart.'

And Father Seraphim continued: 'When the Spirit of God comes down to someone and overshadows him with the fullness of His presence, then that person's soul overflows with unspeakable joy, for the Holy Spirit fills with joy whatever He touches . . .'[1]

So the conversation continues. The whole passage is of extraordinary importance for understanding the Orthodox doctrine of deification and union with God. It shows how the Orthodox idea of sanctification includes the body: it is not Seraphim's (or Motovilov's) soul only, but the whole body which is transfigured by the grace of God. We may note that neither Seraphim nor Motovilov is in a state of ecstasy; both can talk in a coherent way and are still conscious of the outside world, but both are filled with the Holy Spirit and surrounded by the light of the age to come.

Seraphim had no teacher in the art of direction and he left no successor. After his death the work was taken up by another community, the hermitage of Optino. From 1829 until 1923, when the monastery was closed by the Bolsheviks, a succession of *startsy* ministered here, their influence extending like that of Seraphim over the whole of Russia. The best known of the Optino elders are Leonid (1768–1841), Macarius (1788–1860), and Ambrose (1812–91). While these elders all belonged to the school of Paissy and were all devoted to the Jesus Prayer, each of them had a strongly marked character of his own: Leonid, for example, was simple, vivid, and direct, appealing specially to peasants and merchants, while Macarius was highly educated, a Patristic scholar, a man in close contact with the intellectual movements of the day. Optino influenced a number of writers, including Gogol, Khomiakov, Dostoyevsky, Soloviev, and Tolstoy.[2] The remarkable figure of the elder Zossima

1. Fedotov, *A Treasury of Russian Spirituality*, pp. 273–5.
2. The story of Tolstoy's relations with the Orthodox Church is extremely

in Dostoyevsky's novel *The Brothers Karamazov* was based partly on St Macarius or St Ambrose of Optino, although Dostoyevsky says that he was inspired primarily by the life of St Tikhon of Zadonsk.

'There is one thing more important than all possible books and ideas,' wrote the Slavophil Ivan Kireyevsky, 'to find an Orthodox *starets*, before whom you can lay each of your thoughts, and from whom you can hear not your own opinion, but the judgement of the Holy Fathers. God be praised, such *startsy* have not yet disappeared in Russia.'[1]

Through the *startsy*, the monastic revival influenced the life of many lay people. The spiritual atmosphere of the time is vividly expressed in an anonymous book, *The Way of a Pilgrim*, which describes the experiences of a Russian peasant who tramped from place to place practising the Jesus Prayer. This is a most attractive little work, striking in its simplicity, although somewhat one-sided in its emphasis upon the invocation of the Holy Name to the exclusion of almost everything else. One of the book's aims is to show that the Jesus Prayer is not limited to monks but can be used by everyone, in every form of life. As he travelled, the Pilgrim carried with him a copy of the *Philokalia*, presumably the Slavonic translation by Paissy. St Theophan the Recluse (1815–94) during the years 1876–90 issued a greatly expanded translation of the *Philokalia* in five volumes, this time not in Slavonic but in Russian.

Hitherto we have spoken chiefly of the movement centring on the monasteries. But among the great figures of the Russian Church in the nineteenth century there was also a member of the married parish clergy, St John of Kronstadt (1829–1908). Throughout his ministry he worked in the same place, Kronstadt, a naval base and suburb of St Petersburg. He was totally devoted to his parochial work – visiting the poor and the sick,

---

sad. In later life he publicly attacked the Church with great violence, and the Holy Synod after some hesitation excommunicated him (February 1901). As he lay dying in the stationmaster's house at Astapovo, one of the Optino elders travelled to see him, but was refused admittance by Tolstoy's family.

1. Quoted by Metropolitan Seraphim (of Berlin and Western Europe), *L'Église orthodoxe* (Paris 1952), p. 219.

organizing charitable services, teaching religion to the children of his parish, preaching continually, and above all praying with and for his flock. He had an intense awareness of the power of prayer, and as he celebrated the Liturgy he was entirely carried away: 'He could not keep the prescribed measure of liturgical intonation: he called out to God; he shouted; he wept in the face of the visions of Golgotha and the Resurrection which presented themselves to him with such shattering immediacy.'[1] The same sense of immediacy can be felt on every page of the spiritual autobiography which he wrote, *My Life in Christ*. Like St Seraphim, he possessed the gifts of healing, of insight, and of spiritual direction.

St John insisted on frequent communion, although in Russia at this date it was unusual for the laity to communicate more than three or four times a year. Because he had no time to hear individually the confessions of all who came for communion, he established a form of public confession, with everybody shouting their sins aloud simultaneously. He turned the iconostasis into a low screen, so that altar and celebrant might be visible throughout the service. In his emphasis on frequent communion and his reversion to the more ancient form of chancel screen, he anticipated liturgical developments in contemporary Orthodoxy.

In nineteenth-century Russia there was a striking revival of missionary work. Since the days of Mitrophan of Sarai and Stephen of Perm, Russians had been active missionaries, and as Muscovite power advanced eastward, a great field was opened up for evangelism among the native tribes and among the Muslim Mongols. But although the Church never ceased to send out preachers to the heathen, in the seventeenth and eighteenth centuries missionary efforts had somewhat languished, particularly after the closing of monasteries by Catherine. But in the nineteenth century the missionary challenge was taken up with fresh energy and enthusiasm: the Academy of Kazan, opened in 1842, was especially concerned with missionary studies; native clergy were trained; the

---

1. Fedotov, *A Treasury of Russian Spirituality*, p. 348.

scriptures and the Liturgy were translated into a wide variety of languages. In the Kazan area alone the Liturgy was celebrated in twenty-two different languages or dialects. It is significant that one of the first leaders in the missionary revival, Archimandrite Macarius (Glukharev, 1792–1847), was a student of Hesychasm and knew the disciples of Paissy Velichkovsky: the missionary revival had its roots in the revival of the spiritual life. The greatest of the nineteenth-century missionaries was St Innocent (John Veniaminov, 1797–1879), Bishop in Alaska, honoured by millions of American Orthodox today as their chief 'Apostle'.

In the field of theology, nineteenth-century Russia broke away from its excessive dependence upon the west. This was due chiefly to the work of Alexis Khomiakov (1804–60), leader of the Slavophil circle and perhaps the first original theologian in the history of the Russian Church. A country landowner and a retired cavalry captain, Khomiakov belonged to the tradition of lay theologians which has always existed in Orthodoxy. Khomiakov argued that all western Christianity, whether Roman or Protestant, shares the same assumptions and betrays the same fundamental point of view, while Orthodoxy is something entirely distinct. Since this is so (Khomiakov continued), it is not enough for Orthodox to borrow their theology from the west, as they had been doing since the seventeenth century; instead of using Protestant arguments against Rome, and Roman arguments against the Protestants, they must return to their own authentic sources, and rediscover the true Orthodox tradition, which in its basic presuppositions is neither Roman nor Reformed, but unique. As his friend G. Samarin put it, before Khomiakov 'our Orthodox school of theology was not in a position to define either Latinism or Protestantism, because in departing from its own Orthodox standpoint, it had itself become divided into two, and each of these halves had taken up a position *opposed* indeed to its opponent, Latin or Protestant, but not *above* him. It was Khomiakov who first looked upon Latinism and Protestantism from the point of view *of the Church*, and therefore from a *higher* standpoint: and this is the reason why he was also able to define them.'[1] Khomiakov was particularly concerned with the doctrine of the Church, its unity and authority; and here he made a lasting contribution to Orthodox theology.

Khomiakov during his lifetime exercised little or no influence on the theology taught in the academies and seminaries, but here too there was an increasing independence from the west. By 1900 Russian academic theology was at its height, and there were a number of theologians, historians and liturgists, thoroughly trained in western academic disciplines, yet not allowing western influences to distort their Orthodoxy. In the years following 1900 there was also an important intellectual revival outside the theological schools. Since the time of Peter the Great, unbelief had been common among Russian 'intellectuals', but now a number of thinkers, by various routes, found their way back to the Church. Some were former Marxists, such as Sergius Bulgakov (1871–1944) (later ordained priest) and Nicolas Berdyaev (1874–1948), both of whom subsequently played a prominent part in the life of the Russian emigration in Paris.

When one reflects on the lives of Tikhon and Seraphim, on the Optino *startsy* and John of Kronstadt, on the missionary and theological work in nineteenth-century Russia, it can be seen how unfair it is to regard the Synodical period simply as a time of decline. One of the greatest of Russian Church historians, Professor Kartashev (1875–1960), has rightly said:

The subjugation was ennobled from within by Christian humility . . . The Russian Church was suffering under the burden of the régime, but she overcame it from within. She grew, she spread and flourished in many different ways. Thus the period of the Holy Synod could be called the most brilliant and glorious period in the history of the Russian Church.[2]

On 15 August 1917, six months after the abdication of Emperor Nicolas II, when the Provisional Government was in

1. Quoted in Birkbeck, *Russia and the English Church*, p. xlv.
2. Article in the periodical *The Christian East*, vol. xvi (1936), pp. 114 and 115.

power, an All-Russian Church Council was convened at Moscow, which did not finally disperse until September of the following year. More than half the delegates were laymen – the bishops and clergy present numbered 250, the laity 314 – but (as Canon Law demanded) the final decision on specifically religious questions was reserved to the bishops alone. The council carried through a far-reaching programme of reform, its chief act being to abolish the Synodical form of government established by Peter the Great, and to restore the Patriarchate. The election of the Patriarch took place on 5 November 1917, when St Tikhon, Metropolitan of Moscow (1866–1925), was chosen.

Outside events gave a note of urgency to the Council's deliberations. At the earlier sessions members could hear the sound of Bolshevik artillery shelling the Kremlin, and two days before the election of the new Patriarch, Lenin and his associates gained full mastery of Moscow. The Church was allowed no time to consolidate the work of reform. Before the Council came to a close in the summer of 1918, its members learnt with horror of the brutal murder of St Vladimir, Metropolitan of Kiev, by the Bolsheviks. Persecution had already begun.

CHAPTER 7

The Twentieth Century, I: Greeks and Arabs

The Church is the living image of eternity in time.
Fr Georges Florovsky

The Orthodox Church of today exists in five different situations. There are, first, the Orthodox who live in the area of the eastern Mediterranean, as a minority in a society that is predominantly Muslim. This is basically the situation of the four ancient Patriarchates of Constantinople, Alexandria, Antioch and Jerusalem (this last exists under Muslim rule in Jordan, but not of course in Israel). Secondly, there are two Orthodox Churches, Cyprus and Greece, in which a Church–State alliance of the Byzantine type still persists, although in an attenuated form. In the third place, there are the Orthodox Churches in eastern Europe, which until recently were living under Communist rule and facing persecution of a more or less severe character. This is by far the largest of the five groups, comprising as it does the Churches of Russia, Serbia, Romania, Bulgaria, Georgia, Poland, Albania and Czechoslovakia, and amounting to over 85 per cent of the total membership of the Orthodox Church today. Fourthly, there are the Orthodox communities of the diaspora, living in the western world, and formed mainly of immigrants and exiles and their descendants, but including also some western converts. Fifthly and finally, there are some small missionary movements within Orthodoxy, with communities in East Africa, Japan, China, Korea and elsewhere. Altogether, these five groups amount to about 110–140 million persons, of whom perhaps 50–80 million are in some measure actively practising their faith.

The present chapter will be devoted to the first two of these five groups – to the Greeks and Arabs living in a Muslim

environment, and to the Greeks belonging to what are fundamentally still 'State Churches'. The next chapter will look at
the Orthodox in what used to be termed the 'second world',
behind the now vanished 'Iron Curtain'. A third chapter is
devoted to the Orthodox 'dispersion' and to present-day missionary work within Orthodoxy.

(1) The *Patriarchate of Constantinople*, which in the tenth
century contained 624 dioceses, is today enormously reduced
in size. At present within the Patriarch's jurisdiction are:

  (i)   Turkey;
  (ii) Crete and the Dodecanese;
 (iii) All Greeks of the dispersion, together with certain
       Russian, Ukrainian, Polish and Albanian groups in
       emigration (on these see Chapter 9);
 (iv) Mount Athos;
  (v) Finland.

This amounts in all to about six million persons, more than
half of whom are Greeks dwelling in North America.

At the start of this century, Turkey contained a population of nearly two million Greek Orthodox, including a
flourishing community of 250,000 in Constantinople (Istanbul). But, following the disastrous defeat of the Greek army
in Asia Minor in 1922, large numbers of these Greeks were
massacred, especially in Smyrna. Worse was to follow. Under
the terms of the Treaty of Lausanne (July 1923), there was
an 'exchange of populations' whereby all the Orthodox were
expelled to Greece; many thousands died *en route* during
deportation. Only the Greek population in Istanbul and its
immediate environs was allowed to remain. Even here they
existed under restrictions: apart from the Patriarch himself,
Orthodox clergy were forbidden to appear in the streets in
clerical dress (but the same rule applied also to Muslim
clergy).

The position of the Greeks in Istanbul worsened in the
1950s, because of Turkish resentment over the movement in
Cyprus for union with Greece (*Enosis*). In a savage anti-Greek

(and anti-Christian) riot on 6 September 1955, sixty out of the eighty Orthodox churches in the city were sacked or gutted and incalculable damage was done to Christian property, with widespread raping and some loss of life. For several hours the Turkish authorities did little to intervene, allowing the rioters a virtually free hand. In the years that followed, many Greeks fled from Istanbul in fear, while others were forcibly deported, and by the early 1990s the Greek community had dwindled to a mere three or four thousand, mostly elderly and poor. The Patriarchate's printing press was shut down by the Turkish authorities in the early 1960s, and all its publications suspended; the celebrated theological school on the island of Halki, near Istanbul, was forced to close in 1971. There were even rumours that the Patriarchate itself would be expelled from Turkish soil, but in fact this did not happen. In the 1980s, however, there was a slight improvement in the situation. The Turks gave permission for the main building of the Patriarchate, accidentally burnt down in 1941, to be fully reconstructed, and it was reopened in 1987. Also the Patriarch and bishops, whose movements for some twenty years had been severely circumscribed by the Turks, were allowed once more to travel freely abroad.

Since the closure of Halki, the Patriarchate has had to depend on theological schools in Crete, Patmos, Athos, North America and Australia. It maintains two active foundations in Greece: the Patriarchal Institute for Patristic Studies at Vlatadon Monastery, Thessalonica, opened in 1968, which publishes the scholarly journal *Kleronomia,* and the Orthodox Academy at Gonia, Crete, also established in 1968, which is especially concerned with social and ecological studies. Under the Patriarchate there is likewise the Orthodox Centre at Chambésy (near Geneva, Switzerland), which has particular responsibility for promoting inter-Orthodox relations.

The most celebrated occupant of the Ecumenical throne since the Second World War has been Patriarch Athenagoras (in office 1948–72). A bold visionary, he devoted himself particularly to two tasks: the strengthening of links between the different Orthodox Churches, especially through the Rhodes conferences,[1] and the promotion of world-wide Christian unity. His initiatives in this second sphere, and especially his attempts at *rapprochement* with Rome, were sharply attacked by more conservative Orthodox in Greece and elsewhere. His successor, Patriarch Dimitrios (in office 1972–91), a man of peace and prayer, did much to restore confidence, but pursued basically the same policy in his work for Christian unity. Patriarch Bartholomew (elected 1991), a specialist in canon law who has studied in Rome, maintains close links with western Christendom.

Mount Athos, the main centre of Orthodox monasticism over the past millennium, is not only Greek but international. Of the twenty ruling monasteries, at the present day seventeen are Greek, one Russian, one Serbian, and one Bulgarian; in Byzantine times one of the twenty was Georgian, and there was also a Latin house, with monks from Amalfi in Italy. Besides the ruling monasteries there are several other large houses, and innumerable smaller settlements known as *sketes* or *kellia*; there are also hermits, a number of whom live above alarming precipices at the southern tip of the peninsula, in huts or caves often accessible only by decaying ladders. Thus the three forms of monastic life, dating back to fourth-century Egypt – the community life, the semi-eremitic life, and the hermits – continue side by side on the Holy Mountain today. It is a remarkable illustration of the continuity of Orthodoxy.

The period from 1914 to the mid 1960s was a time of decline for the Holy Mountain. There was a spectacular decrease in numbers. At the start of the century there were about 7,500 monks, of whom nearly half were Russians; the Russian monastery of St Panteleimon (Roussikon) had by itself nearly 2,000 members. Fr Amphilochios, spiritual father at Patmos, used to recount to me the impression made on him as a Greek by the Russian singing when he visited St Panteleimon around 1912: it was the nearest he had ever known to 'heaven on earth'. But after the First World War no more novices could come from Russia, while recruits from the Russian emigration amounted to a mere trickle, and by the 1960s there were less than sixty

---

1. See below, p. 187.

monks at Roussikon. After 1945 the supply of novices from
Romania, Bulgaria and Serbia was also drastically reduced.
At the same time very few young Greeks made their way to
Athos. By the late 1950s there was a regular decrease of about
forty to fifty monks annually, and in 1971 the total monastic
population had sunk to only 1,145. Almost all of these were old
men: in human terms it seemed doubtful whether the Holy
Mountain had any future. Only a minute proportion of the
monks was well educated, and Athos had largely ceased to
exercise an effective spiritual influence in Greece or in world-
wide Orthodoxy.

It would be a mistake, however, to judge Athos or any other
monastic centre by numbers or learning alone, for the true
criterion is not size or scholarship but the quality of the spiritual life. Even in this period of outward decadence, high standards were maintained in some houses, notably at the Monastery
of Dionysiou under Fr Gabriel (1886–1983), abbot for nearly
fifty years. One of the monks here, Fr Theoklitos (still active),
wrote a remarkable study of the monastic life entitled *Between
Heaven and Earth* (in Greek: Athens 1956), which showed
clearly the continuing vitality of Athonite spirituality. In a
hidden and unostentatious way, the Mountain went on nurtur-
ing saints, ascetics and men of prayer formed in the classic
traditions of Orthodoxy. One such was St Silouan (1866–1938;
proclaimed a saint in 1988), at the Russian monastery of St
Panteleimon: of peasant background, a simple and humble
man, his life was outwardly uneventful, but he left behind him
some deeply moving meditations, poetic in style and profound
in their theological vision, which have been edited by his disciple Archimandrite Sophrony (1896–1993) and published in
many languages. Another such monk was Fr Joseph (died
1959), a Greek who lived in the semi-eremitic settlement of
New Skete, gathering round him a group of disciples dedicated
to the practice of *noera prosevchi* ('mental' or 'inner' prayer,
signifying in particular the Jesus Prayer). So long as Athos
continued to produce men such as St Silouan and Fr Joseph, it
was by no means failing in its task.

Suddenly and unexpectedly, after this half-century of

external decline, there began in the late 1960s a new chapter of Athonite history. Signs of fresh life became evident – at first faint and hesitant, but by the 1980s clear and unmistakable. In the first place there was an influx of new monks. After sinking to a low point in 1971 with only 1,145 monks, numbers slowly picked up, and by 1990 there were about 1,500 monks resident on the Mountain. In itself this may not seem a very striking improvement. More significant, however, has been the shift in the age-pattern: in 1971 the great majority were over sixty years old; by 1990 the majority were under forty. The change in many monasteries was nothing short of dramatic: houses which in 1971 were silently decaying, occupied by perhaps a dozen ageing inhabitants, only half of them able to attend services, after no more than ten or fifteen years were full of young and active members, with scarcely a grey beard in sight.

Much more important than the quantity of the new arrivals has been their quality. Many of them are not only highly educated but spiritually gifted. Some have talents as writers, others as spiritual fathers and confessors. There is a renewed sense of prayer on the Mountain: the liturgical services, often performed in the recent past in a perfunctory manner, are now marked by attentiveness and joy, and the monks receive communion far more frequently. The singing is vastly improved. Through this new generation of monks, Athos has acquired once more an articulate voice, heard with respect outside its own boundaries, and it is acting again as a beacon and power-house for Orthodoxy as a whole.

What are the reasons for this striking transformation? It is not easy to say. One factor, however, is undoubtedly the presence in many communities of an abbot possessing the gift of 'eldership'. What draws recruits to a particular monastery is most commonly the presence of a spiritual father able to provide personal guidance. Among the abbots especially valued as *gerontes* or elders are Fr Vasileios of Iviron (formerly of Stavronikita), author of the widely-read study *Hymn of Entry*; Fr Aimilianos of Simonos Petras; Fr George of Grigoriou; and Fr Ephraim, until recently abbot of Philotheou, a disciple of Fr Joseph of New Skete.

Problems still remain. The non-Greek houses continue to be depleted in numbers, and the Greek civil authorities – contravening the spirit and sometimes also the letter of the legal constitution of Athos – make it exceedingly difficult for recruits to come from Romania and the Slav countries. There have been several serious fires, some inside the monasteries, some in the surrounding forest. The stillness of Athos is being eroded by an ever-expanding network of roads, by a growing number of vehicles, and by a steadily increasing flood of visitors (mainly Greeks rather than foreigners). Among some monks there exists a narrow and fanatical spirit, which makes them hostile to any *rapprochement* with non-Orthodox Christians and over-zealous in stigmatizing their fellow-Orthodox as traitors to Holy Tradition. Yet, despite every difficulty, this is a time of hope for Athos. In the words of a Russian *starets* on the Mountain, Fr Nikon of Karoulia (1875–1963), 'Here every stone breathes prayers.' This remains as true today as in the past.

Outside Athos, but still within the jurisdiction of Constantinople, there is the celebrated monastery of St John the Theologian (the Evangelist) on the island of Patmos, founded by St Christodoulos in 1088. One of the outstanding monks here in the present century was Fr Amphilochios (1888–1970), already widely revered as a saint. His most striking characteristic, which I myself can vividly recall, was his gentleness and ardent compassion; as one of his spiritual children remarked, 'He spoke the language of love.' He attached deep value to the Jesus Prayer, and he was also an ecologist, long before this had become fashionable. 'Whoever does not love trees, does not love Christ,' he used to say; and, if imposing a penance on the farmers who came to him for confession, he would tell them to plant two or three trees. The women's community that he founded on Patmos, the Monastery of the Annunciation, now numbers more than fifty, and has daughter houses on the islands of Rhodes and Kalymnos.

The Orthodox *Church of Finland* owes its origin to monks from the Russian monastery of Valamo on Lake Ladoga, who preached among the pagan Finnish tribes in Karelia during the

Middle Ages. The Finnish Orthodox were dependent on the Russian Church until the Revolution, but since 1923 they have been under the spiritual care of the Patriarchate of Constantinople, although the Russian Church did not accept this situation until 1957. The vast majority of Finns are Lutheran, and the 56,000 Orthodox comprise less than 1.5 per cent of the population. The traditions of Valamo monastery are continued today by the monastery of New Valamo at Heinävesi in central Finland; nearby is a women's community at Lintula. There is a seminary at Joensu. Although in the parishes there are many whose membership is largely nominal, there is an active youth movement, much involved in inter-Orthodox and ecumenical contacts. The present head of the Church of Finland, Archbishop John (elected 1987), was originally a Lutheran: he is the first western convert to become the head of a local Orthodox Church. With its roots deep in Russian history yet its face turned towards the west, Finnish Orthodoxy is able to play a special role as a bridge and mediator between the 'traditional' Orthodox lands and the newly-established Orthodox diaspora.

(2) The *Patriarchate of Alexandria* has been a small Church ever since 451, when the overwhelming majority of Christians in Egypt rejected the Council of Chalcedon. Territorially it includes the whole of the continent of Africa. Early in this century there was a flourishing Greek community in Cairo and Alexandria, but it is now much diminished through emigration. Most of the Alexandrian flock today live either in Uganda and Kenya, where a native African Orthodox movement has sprung up,[1] or else in South Africa. The recent head of the Alexandrian Patriarchate, Pope Parthenios III (died 1996),[2] was intellectually one of the more adventurous of Orthodox Church leaders, and even expressed himself in favour of the ordination of women priests.

1. See below, pp. 189–90.
2. In Orthodoxy the title 'Pope' is not limited to the Bishop of Rome, but is also borne by the Patriarch of Alexandria. Among his other honorary titles are 'Shepherd of Shepherds', 'Thirteenth Apostle', and 'Judge of the Universe'.

(3) The *Patriarchate of Antioch* has in its care the Orthodox of Syria and Lebanon. Its numbers have been reduced through emigration, due to the long-extended agony of the war in Lebanon, but it has a lively diaspora, especially in North America. The Patriarch lives, not in the ancient Antioch (now within the borders of Turkey), but in Damascus. During 1724–1898 the Patriarch and many of the higher clergy were Greek, but today they are entirely Arab. Early in this century the Patriarchate bore all the marks of a 'sleeping' Church, but since then there has been an awakening, due especially to the Orthodox Youth Movement (Mouvement de la Jeunesse Orthodoxe), founded in 1942. Numbering today around 7,000 members, with leadership predominantly from the laity, the MJO has always assigned priority to Christian education. It issues a periodical, *An-Nour*, and has published over 120 books. It is also firmly committed to social and medical work and to the fight against poverty; its initiatives here were particularly valuable in Lebanon during the war years. Under the aegis of the MJO there has been a revival of the monastic life, for both men and women. Several of its members now hold high rank within the hierarchy, including the present Patriarch Ignatius IV (elected 1979) and Metropolitan George (Khodre) of Mount Lebanon. In 1970 the Patriarchate established the St John of Damascus Academy of Theology at Balamand (near Tripoli, Lebanon).

(4) The *Patriarchate of Jerusalem* has always occupied a special position in the Church: never large in numbers, its primary task has been to guard the Holy Places. Its territory covers Israel and Jordan. As at Antioch, Arabs form the majority of the people; they number today about 60,000 but are on the decrease, as elsewhere in the Near East, through emigration. Before the war of 1948 there were only 5,000 Greeks within the Patriarchate and at present there are far fewer (? not more than 500). But the Patriarch of Jerusalem is still a Greek, and the Brotherhood of the Holy Sepulchre, which looks after the Holy Places, is completely in Greek control. This situation has caused considerable tension over the last seventy years. Unfortunately the present Patriarch

Diodoros (elected 1981) has met with little success in his efforts to solve the internal problems of the Patriarchate.

Before the Bolshevik Revolution, a notable feature in the life of Orthodox Palestine was the annual influx of Russian pilgrims, of whom there were often more than ten thousand staying in the Holy City at the same time. For the most part they were elderly peasants, to whom this pilgrimage was the most notable event in their lives: after a walk of perhaps several thousand miles across Russia, they took ship at the Crimea and endured a voyage of what to us today must seem unbelievable discomfort, arriving at Jerusalem if possible in time for Easter.[1] The Russian Spiritual Mission in Palestine, as well as looking after the Russian pilgrims, did most valuable pastoral work among the Arab Orthodox and maintained a large number of schools. This Russian Mission has naturally been sadly reduced in size since 1917, but has not entirely disappeared, and there are still three Russian convents in Jerusalem; two of them receive Arab girls as novices. With the recent changes in Russia, Russian pilgrims have begun to reappear in the Holy City, while the number of Greek pilgrims increased noticeably in the 1980s.

The *Church of Sinai*, headed at present by Archbishop Damianos (elected 1973), is sometimes reckoned as autocephalous, but is more correctly classified as autonomous, since its leader is consecrated by the Patriarch of Jerusalem. It consists basically of just a single monastery, St Catherine's, at the foot of the Mountain of Moses in the Sinai peninsula (Egypt). The monks, who are Greeks and number about twenty, have pastoral care of the Christian Bedouin families living in the region, and also of a small monastery for women nearby. St Catherine's has an outstanding library and a unique collection of icons, some dating back to pre-Iconclast times; these escaped destruction because of Sinai's remote situation outside the Byzantine Empire. Sad to say, the future of the monastery is threatened

1. See the striking eye-witness account of Stephen Graham, *With the Russian Pilgrims to Jerusalem* (London 1913). The author, who was fluent in Russian, himself travelled as one of the pilgrims.

by the plans of the Egyptian government to develop the area as a tourist park.

(5) The *Church of Cyprus*, autocephalous since the Council of Ephesus (431), suffered heavy losses from the Turkish invasion in 1974, but still remains wealthy and well organized. There are about 450 parishes, with 550 priests, and also 16 monasteries, with over 50 monks and 120 nuns. (There are also about 150 Cypriot monks on Mount Athos; three of the twenty monasteries have Cypriot abbots.) There is a theological school at Nicosia. The Ottoman system, whereby the head of the Church was regarded also as 'ethnarch' or civil leader of the Greek Christian population, was continued by the British when they took over the island in 1878. This explains the double role, both ecclesiastical and civil, which was played by Archbishop Makarios III (in office 1950–77), and which was so widely misunderstood by the British public during the Greek Cypriot struggle for independence in the 1950s. Those who regarded Makarios as a churchman who was meddling gratuitously in politics failed to appreciate that he was heir to a long historical tradition. His successor, however, Archbishop Chrysostom (elected 1977), acts solely as a religious leader.

(6) The *Church of Greece*, despite the many inroads of secularism and indifference since the Second World War, continues to occupy a central place in the life of the country as a whole. In the 1951 census only 121 persons, out of a total population of more than 7,500,000, stated that they were atheists. Today the number of declared atheists would doubtless be larger, but not dramatically so; for most Greeks, whether or not they are active in practising their faith, still regard Orthodox Christianity as an integral part of their Greek identity. Recent estimates suggest that some 97 per cent of the population have been baptized as Christians, and of these around 96.5 per cent belong to the Orthodox Church. Within the small minority of non-Orthodox Christians, the largest body are the Roman Catholics with some 45,000 members, of whom around 2,500 are Catholics of the Eastern rite. There are also about 120,000 Muslims in Greece.

The link in Greece between Church and State, which in the past was extremely close, is today being steadily weakened. Orthodox religious education now plays a smaller part in the State school syllabus. In the 1980s the government introduced civil marriage and legalized abortion; the second of these measures in particular was fiercely opposed by the Church, but to no effect. On its side the Church has gained a greater internal autonomy, and the politicians interfere less in the appointment of bishops. But few if any in Greece envisage a complete separation between State and Church. The theological seminaries for the training of future priests continue to be supported financially by the government and to form part of the State educational system, and the State still pays the salaries of the clergy.

Greek dioceses of today, as in the primitive Church, are small: there are 80 for a population of about 9 million (contrast Russia before 1917, with 67 dioceses for 100 million faithful). The largest Greek diocese contains no more than 247 parishes, while more than half have less than 100 parishes. In ideal and sometimes in reality, the Greek bishop is not merely a distant administrator, but an accessible figure with whom his flock can have personal contact, and in whom the poor and simple freely confide, calling daily in large numbers for practical as well as spiritual advice. So far as outward organization is concerned, over the past decades there has been a steady expansion in the Church of Greece.[1]

	1971	1981	1992
Parishes	7,426	7,477	7,742
Clergy	7,176	8,335	8,670
Monks	776	822	927
Nuns	1,499	1,971	2,305

Along with this network of parishes and monasteries, the Church of Greece also supports a vast number of philanthropic foundations – orphanages, old people's homes, psychiatric clinics, organized groups for hospital and prison visiting. Those

1. These statistics are taken from the annual *Calendar of the Church of Greece* for the years 1971, 1981 and 1992. The figures given for 1992 may need some adjustment, since the details in the *Calendar* are incomplete.

who imagine that Orthodoxy is narrowly 'other-worldly' and uninterested in social work should pay a visit to the Church of Greece.

But while the outward organization has been expanding, there can be no doubt that church attendance in Greece over the past thirty years has declined. When a poll was carried out by the newspaper *Ta Nea* in Athens on 21 September 1963, the replies to the question 'How often do you go to church?' were as follows:

	Per Cent
Every Sunday	31
Two or three times a month	32
Once a month	15
On Great Feasts	14
When I have time	3

In a similar poll held during the spring of 1980, also in the Athens area, the answers were:

	Per Cent
Every Sunday	9
Fairly often	20
Only for Great Feasts or special occasions such as weddings	60
Never	11

Even if people do not always tell the truth in polls of this kind, it is manifest that church-going is on the decrease. Allowance should of course be made for the fact that, in Greece as elsewhere, church attendance is on the whole lower in the centre of large cities than it is in small towns or rural areas.

At an average Sunday congregation there are more women than men, and more old than young; but Greece is certainly not unique in this respect. Many students in higher education, and young people generally, were alienated from the Church because of the apparent collaboration of the hierarchy with the military dictatorship during 1967–74, at the time when Archbishop Ieronymos was head of the Greek Church. In fact the extent of this collaboration has usually been exaggerated, and it was in any case the Colonels who exploited the Church, rather than vice-versa. But it remains true that the Church's reputation was gravely compromised in the eyes of the younger generation. In the early 1990s, however, there have been signs of a modest but significant return of young people to the Church.

In the past the parish priests of Greece received little or no formal training, and from 1833 onwards one of the Church's major concerns has been to raise the educational level of the clergy. In the Turkish period, and indeed up to the Second World War, the priest was firmly rooted within the local community which he served. Usually he was a native of the place in which he exercised his ministry and he would expect to remain in the same parish throughout his life. Only in rare cases had he been to a seminary; he was no better educated than the laity around him and, like most of them, he was married. After ordination he would continue with his previous work, whatever that might have been – carpentry, for instance, or shoemaking, or most commonly farming. Usually he did not preach sermons: that was done, if at all, by the bishop or by visiting monks, or perhaps by lay preachers appointed by the bishop. In most cases the parish priest did not hear confessions; for this his flock would probably go to a nearby monastery or rely on visiting monk-priests (but the sacrament of Confession was in any case much neglected in the Turcocratia).

This firm association between pastor and flock had undoubted advantages in the stable agricultural society of the past. Greek Orthodoxy was fortunate to avoid the cultural gap between priest and people that has generally existed, for example, in the Church of England since the Reformation. But in the present century, with the rise of educational standards in Greek society as a whole, there is an obvious need for parish clergy who can teach, preach and give spiritual guidance. Otherwise, in the contemporary world, especially in the cities, the parish priest risks being marginalized: he is no longer, as he once was, a natural leader within the community.

The contemporary Church of Greece has in fact developed an elaborate programme of theological education. There are two faculties of theology, in the universities of Athens and Thessalonica (but by no means all the theological students here intend to be ordained), and there are in addition twenty-eight theological schools of various levels. Scarcely anyone is ordained today unless he has studied some theology either at university or at seminary. The number of theology graduates among the clergy is at last showing a significant increase. In 1919, out of 4,433 clergy serving in the Church of Greece, less than one per cent – no more than forty-three, not counting the bishops – had a university degree in theology. In 1975 the number of theology graduates was still only 589, about 8 per cent of the total clergy. But by 1981 there were 1,406 graduates in theology, and in 1992 there were 2,019. That is still less than a quarter of the clergy as a whole, but it represents a marked improvement. Not that degrees and diplomas necessarily make a good priest!

What is the present state of theology in Greece? During the past ninety years the university professors in theology have produced a formidable *corpus* of scholarly writing. Two works are particularly representative of this tradition of 'scientific' theology: the *Dogmatics* of Christos Androutsos (1869–1935), first published in 1907,[1] and its successor, the three-volume *Dogmatics* of Panagiotis Trembelas (1886–1977), published in 1959–61.[2] Similar in approach, although briefer, is the *Synopsis* of Ioannis Karmiris (1904–91).[3] Weighty and systematic though these books are, they are also in some ways disappointing. Western readers, familiar with the theologians of the Russian emigration such as Lossky, Florovsky and Evdokimov will not find in their Greek contemporaries the same sense of excitement and creative exploration. The theology of Androutsos, Trembelas and Karmiris is very much a theology of the university lecture room, academic and scholastic rather than liturgical

1. This is extensively (and rather boringly) summarized in Frank Gavin, *Some Aspects of Contemporary Greek Orthodox Thought* (Milwaukee 1923).

2. Available in French: *Dogmatique de l'Église Orthodoxe Catholique*, tr. Pierre Dumont (3 vols., Bruges 1966–68).

3. *A Synopsis of the Dogmatic Theology of the Orthodox Catholic Church*, tr. George Dimopoulos (Scranton 1973).

and mystical. Moreover, although the content of these works is strictly Orthodox, the method and the categories employed are very often borrowed from the west. Trembelas, for all his passionate commitment to Orthodox tradition, is none the less a 'westernizer', in the sense that he belongs to that long series of Orthodox theologians who, like Moghila and Dositheus in the seventeenth century, have been shaped by western intellectual patterns. The Fathers are frequently quoted by Trembelas, but they are fitted into a framework that is on the whole not Patristic.

These shortcomings have led a younger generation of Greek theologians to adopt a very different theological approach. They are less systematic than their predecessors, less magisterial and self-confident. They are much more critical of western intellectual categories. They make use of the mystical theologians such as Isaac the Syrian and Symeon the New Theologian, whom their predecessors altogether neglected; they lay emphasis on the apophatic approach, and give full scope to the essence–energies distinction elaborated by Gregory Palamas. The boldest and most controversial of these younger theologians is Christos Yannaras, who adopts a strongly 'personalist' approach, partly indebted to the existentialism of Heidegger, but drawing also, and much more fundamentally, on the dogmatic and ascetic writings of the Fathers. Important contributions have also been made by Panagiotis Nellas (1936–86), whose early death has been a sad loss, by John Zizioulas, Metropolitan of Pergamon, and by Fr John Romanides. They do not by any means agree invariably with Yannaras, or indeed with each other; but they all alike share a desire to develop a style of theology that will be, as they see it, both more faithful to the 'mind' of the Fathers and more responsive to the anguish and thirst of the present-day world.

In Greek religious art there has been a similar reaction against westernization. The debased Italianate style, universal at the beginning of the present century, has largely been abandoned in favour of the older Byzantine tradition. A number of churches in Athens and elsewhere have recently been decorated with a full scheme of icons and frescoes, executed in strict conformity with the traditional rules. The leader of this artistic renewal, Photios Kontoglou (1896–1965), was noted for his uncompromising advocacy of Byzantine art. Typical of his outlook is his comment on the art of the Italian renaissance: 'Those who see in a secular way say that it progressed, but those who see in a religious way say that it declined.'[1]

A decisive role was played in Greek Church life, during the first half of this century, by 'home missionary' movements devoted to evangelistic and social work. The most dynamic of these, *Zoe* ('Life'), also known as 'The Brotherhood of Theologians', was started by Fr Eusebius Matthopoulos in 1907, although its roots extend back to similar movements during the late nineteenth century. It has a semi-monastic structure: all its full members, whether laymen or priests (bishops are excluded), are celibate, although they take no permanent vows. From its foundation *Zoe* has advocated frequent communion, wider use of the sacrament of Confession, regular preaching, catechism classes for children, organized youth groups, and Bible study circles. All of this is surely admirable; indeed, the main points in the programme of *Zoe* have now been taken over and applied by the Greek Church as a whole. But while *Zoe* has done much that is highly positive, its secrecy and its authoritarian spirit – here it resembles the Roman Catholic movement *Opus Dei* – have made it many enemies. The influence of *Zoe* was at its height during 1920–60, but has diminished since then. In the early 1960s a split occurred among its members, and a rival organization *Sotir* was set up. In the 1970s *Zoe* was accused of links with the Colonels – in large measure unjustly – and this did further damage to its standing. The moralistic, puritanical tone which tends to mark its publications has little appeal for the younger generation of Greeks today.

Modern Greece has its kenotic saints, similar in their loving compassion to St Seraphim of Sarov and St Silouan of Athos. The most widely revered is St Nektarios (1846–1920), for a

1. C. Cavarnos, *Byzantine Sacred Art: Selected Writings of the Contemporary Greek Icon Painter Fotis Kontoglous* (New York 1957), p. 21.

time Metropolitan of Pentapolis in Egypt until he was driven from there by false accusations – in his humility he refused to make any answer to his slanderers. His later years were spent in great poverty as chaplain to the nuns at the monastery of the Holy Trinity which he had founded on the island of Aegina. Another such kenotic figure – a parish priest like St John of Kronstadt – was St Nicolas Planas (1851–1932), greatly loved for his simplicity of heart and closeness to the poor. He had a special enthusiasm for all-night vigil services; the chanters were often the two writers Alexander Papadiamantis (1851–1911) and Alexander Moraitidis (1850–1929).

What of the monastic life? The revival on Mount Athos has yet to spread on a significant scale to the men's monasteries elsewhere in Greece. Most houses are depleted in numbers, although there are some notable exceptions such as the monastery of the Paraclete at Oropos (Attica). The women's communities, on the other hand, present a striking contrast. There has been an impressive increase since 1920, with new foundations springing up everywhere. Amounting to only a few hundreds at the start of the century, the nuns in Greece are today numbered in thousands. Among the larger houses are the monasteries of St Patapios at Loutraki (outside Corinth), of the Dormition at Panorama (near Thessalonica), of Our Lady of Help in Chios, and of Kechrovouni in Tinos (the island famous for its pilgrimage shrine to the Mother of God). Particularly impressive is the Monastery of the Annunciation at Ormylia (Chalcidice, Northern Greece), which has over a hundred nuns and novices; the community here, which depends on the Athonite monastery of Simonos Petras, has embarked recently on a special project for organic farming. The Old Calendarists[1] in Greece also have several large monasteries for women.

Changes are happening in Greek society today with bewildering rapidity. To those who first visited Greece forty years ago, it seems now a new and unfamiliar world. Is the Church responding to these fresh challenges with sufficient resilience?

---

1. See below, pp. 301–3.

It has not been easy for Archbishop Seraphim (elected 1974) to provide the imaginative leadership that is essential at such a time of crisis and opportunity. But in Athens, Thessalonica and other cities, the high calibre of many of the younger married clergy is unmistakable. Wherever there is a parish priest of energy and intelligence, the response from the laity, and not least from the youth, is usually most encouraging. Greek Orthodoxy has been passing through some difficult times, but there is still vigour and new life in the old tree.

CHAPTER 8

The Twentieth Century, II: Orthodoxy and the Militant Atheists

> 'Those who desire to see Me shall pass through tribulation and despair.'
>
> *Epistle of Barnabas vii, 11*

'THE ASSAULT UPON HEAVEN'

From October 1917, when the Bolsheviks seized power, until around 1988, the year when Russian Christianity celebrated its millennium, the Orthodox Church in the Soviet Union existed in a state of siege. The intensity of persecution varied at different points in those seventy years, but the basic attitude of the Communist authorities remained the same: religious belief, in all its manifestations, was an error to be repressed and extirpated. In Stalin's words, 'The Party cannot be neutral towards religion. It conducts an anti-religious struggle against all and any religious prejudices.'[1] To appreciate the full force of his words, it has to be remembered that the Party, under Soviet Communism, to all intents and purposes meant the State.

In this way, from 1917 onwards, Orthodox and other Christians found themselves in a situation for which there was no exact precedent in earlier Christian history. The Roman Empire, although persecuting Christians from time to time, was in no sense an atheist state, committed to the suppression of religion as such. The Ottoman Turks, while non-Christians, were still worshippers of the one God and, as we have seen, allowed the Church a large measure of toleration. But Soviet Communism was committed by its fundamental principles to an aggressive and militant atheism. It could not rest satisfied merely with a neutral separation between Church and State,

---

1. *Works*, vol. 10 (Moscow 1953), p. 132.

but sought by every means, direct and indirect, to overthrow all organized Church life and to eliminate all religious belief.

The Bolsheviks, newly come to power, were quick to carry their programme into effect. Legislation in 1918 excluded the Church from all participation in the educational system, and confiscated all Church property. The Church ceased to possess any rights; quite simply, it was not a legal entity. The terms of the Soviet constitution grew progressively more severe. The constitution of 1918 allowed 'freedom of religious and anti-religious propaganda' (Article 13), but in the 'Law on Religious Associations' enacted in 1929 this was changed to 'freedom of religious *belief* and of anti-religious *propaganda*'. The distinction here is important: Christians were allowed – at any rate in theory – freedom of belief, but they were not allowed any freedom of propaganda. The Church was seen merely as a cultic association. It was in principle permitted to celebrate religious services, and in practice – more particularly from 1943 onwards – there were a certain number of church buildings open for worship. Also, after 1943, the Church was allowed to maintain a few institutions for training priests, and to undertake a limited publishing programme. But it was allowed to do virtually nothing beyond this.

The bishops and clergy, in other words, could not engage in charitable or social work. Sick visiting was severely restricted; pastoral work in prisons, hospitals or psychiatric wards was impossible. Parish priests could not organize any kind of youth group or any study circle. They could not hold catechism classes or Sunday schools for children. The only instruction that they could give to their flock was through sermons during church services. (Often they took full advantage of this: I can recall attending celebrations of the Liturgy in the 1970s at which four or five different sermons were preached; the congregation listened with rapt attention, and thanked the preacher at the end with a great cry of gratitude – an experience I do not usually have when preaching in the west!) The clergy could not form a parish library, since the only books which they were permitted to keep in church were service books for use in worship. They had no pamphlets to distribute to their people, no informative literature, however basic; even copies of the Bible were a great rarity, exchanged on the black market at exorbitant prices. Worst of all, every member of the clergy, from the bishop to the humblest parish priest, required permission from the State to exercise his ministry, and was subject to close and relentless supervision from the secret police. Every word that the priest spoke in his sermons was carefully noted. Throughout the day, watchful and unfriendly eyes would observe who came to him in church for baptisms and weddings, for confession or for private talks.

The totalitarian Communist State employed to the full all forms of anti-religious propaganda, while denying the Church any right of reply. There was, first of all, the atheist instruction that was given systematically in every school. Teachers received such injunctions as these:

A Soviet teacher must be guided by the principle of the Party spirit of science; he is obliged not only to be an unbeliever himself, but also to be an active propagandist of godlessness among others, to be the bearer of the ideas of militant proletarian atheism. Skilfully and calmly, tactfully and persistently, the Soviet teacher must expose and overcome religious prejudices in the course of his activity in school and out of school, day in and day out.[1]

Outside school, a vast anti-religious campaign was carried on by the League of Militant Atheists; this was replaced in 1942 by the slightly less aggressive All-Union Society for the Dissemination of Scientific and Political Knowledge. Atheism was actively propagated among the new generation through the Young Communist League. Museums of Religion and Atheism were opened, often in former churches such as Kazan Cathedral in St Petersburg. In the 1920s, anti-religious processions of a crude and offensive character were held in the streets, especially at Easter and Christmas. Here is a description by an eye-witness:

There were no protests from the silent streets – the years of terror

1. F. N. Oleschuk (formerly Secretary of the League of Militant Atheists), in *Uchitelskaya Gazeta*, 26 November 1949.

had done their work – but nearly everyone tried to turn off the road when they met this shocking procession. I, personally, as a witness of the Moscow carnival, may certify that there was not a drop of popular pleasure in it. The parade moved along empty streets and its attempts at creating laughter or provocation met with dull silence on the part of the occasional witnesses.[1]

Not only were churches closed on a massive scale in the 1920s and 1930s, but huge numbers of bishops and clergy, monks, nuns and laity were sent to prison and to concentration camps. How many were executed or died from ill-treatment we simply cannot calculate. Nikita Struve provides a list of martyr-bishops running to 130 names, and even this he terms 'provisional and incomplete'.[2] The sum total of priest-martyrs must extend to tens of thousands. Of course religious believers were by no means the only group to suffer in Stalin's reign of terror, but they suffered more than most. Nothing on a remotely comparable scale had happened in the persecutions under the Roman Empire. The words of Archpriest Avvakum, spoken in the seventeenth century, were certainly fulfilled under Communism three hundred years later: 'Satan has obtained our radiant Russia from God, that she may become red with the blood of martyrs.'[3]

What effect did Communist propaganda and persecution have upon the Church? In many places there was an amazing quickening of the spiritual life. Cleansed of worldly elements, freed from the burden of insincere members who had merely conformed outwardly for social reasons, purified as by fire, the true Orthodox believers gathered themselves together and resisted with heroism and humility. A Russian of the emigration wrote, 'In every place where the faith has been put to the test, there have been abundant outpourings of grace, the most astonishing miracles – icons renewing themselves before the eyes of astonished spectators; the cupolas of churches shining with a

1. G. P. Fedotov, *The Russian Church since the Revolution* (London 1928), p. 47.

2. Nikita Struve, *Christians in Contemporary Russia*, pp. 393–8.

3. From Avvakum's *Life*; see Fedotov, *A Treasury of Russian Spirituality*, p. 167.

light not of this world . . . Nevertheless, all this was scarcely noticed. The glorious aspect of what had taken place in Russia remained almost without interest for the generality of mankind . . . The crucified and buried Christ will always be judged thus by those who are blind to the light of His resurrection.'[1] It is not surprising that enormous numbers should have deserted the Church in the hour of persecution, for this has always happened, and will doubtless happen again. Far more surprising is the fact that so many remained faithful.

'RENDER TO CAESAR THE THINGS THAT ARE CAESAR'S': WHERE TO DRAW THE LINE?

In a time of religious persecution the underlying principles involved are usually clear-cut, but the practical course of action which each believer ought to follow is often not clear-cut at all. How far could bishops, priests and laity go in co-operating with a regime that was openly dedicated to the overthrow of religion? Russian Orthodox Christians in the years 1917–88 have answered this crucial question in many conflicting ways. Persons in the west, who have never lived under persecution, need to be highly circumspect in passing any moral judgement on the actions of those within Russia. But we can at least note certain variations in attitude.

Church–State relations in the Soviet Union may be divided into five main periods:

(1) *1917–25*: Patriarch Tikhon struggles to preserve the liberty of the Church.

(2) *1925–43*: Metropolitan Sergius seeks a *modus vivendi*.

(3) *1943–59*: Stalin allows a revival of Church life in the post-war years.

(4) *1959–64*: Khrushchev renews the persecution.

(5) *1964–88*: a dissident movement emerges and is crushed.

1. Lossky, *The Mystical Theology of the Eastern Church*, pp. 245–6. The miraculous 'renewal of icons', to which Lossky refers, has occurred in a number of places under Communist rule. Icons and frescoes, darkened and disfigured with age, have suddenly and without any human intervention resumed fresh and bright colours.

(1) *1917–25*. At the outset the Patriarch of Moscow, St Tikhon, adopted a firm and uncompromising attitude towards the Bolsheviks. On 1 February 1918 he anathematized and excommunicated those whom he termed 'the enemies of Christ, open or disguised', 'the godless rulers of the darkness of our time'. This anathema was confirmed by the All-Russian Council in session at Moscow at the time, and it has never subsequently been revoked. Later in 1918 the Patriarch publicly denounced the murder of Emperor Nicolas II as a heinous crime, adding, 'Whoever does not condemn it will be guilty of his blood.' When the Communists were preparing to celebrate the first anniversary of the October Revolution, he called on them to desist from 'the persecution and destruction of the innocent'. No one else at that moment had the courage openly to raise their voice on behalf of justice and human rights. At the same time, however, Tikhon avoided taking sides on any strictly political question, and refused to send his blessing to General Denikin, the White Army leader in the Crimea.

The Communists were naturally dissatisfied with Tikhon's stance and made determined efforts to break down his resistance. From May 1922 to June 1923 he was kept in prison, and, while there, he was persuaded to hand over the control of the Church to a group of married clergy, which unknown to him was acting in co-operation with the Communist authorities. This group, which came to be known as the 'Renewed' or 'Living Church', initiated a sweeping programme of ecclesiastical reform, including the introduction of married bishops.[1] Even though many of the reforms were not objectionable in themselves, the movement was compromised from the start by its collaboration with the atheist authorities. Tikhon, as soon as he realized its true character, broke off relations with it. Despite initial successes, it soon lost support among the faithful, and as a result the Communists ceased to be interested in it. After 1926 the Living Church and its offshoots no longer possessed any great importance, and during the Second World

1. In the Orthodox Church bishops have to be monks (see p. 291).

War they disappeared altogether. The first attempt by the Bolsheviks to take over the Church had proved a fiasco.

What pressures St Tikhon underwent in custody we do not know, but on emerging from prison he spoke in a more conciliatory tone than he had done in 1917–18. This is evident in his 'Confession', issued shortly before his release in 1923, and in his 'Will', signed on the day of his death (there is some dispute over the authenticity of this last). Yet he still strove to adopt a neutral, non-political position, such as would safeguard the inner freedom of the Church. As he put it in 1923:

> The Russian Orthodox Church is non-political, and henceforward does not want to be either a Red or a White Church; it should and will be the One Catholic Apostolic Church, and all attempts coming from any side to embroil the Church in the political struggle should be rejected and condemned.

St Tikhon died suddenly, under mysterious circumstances. Certainly a confessor for the faith, very possibly he was also a martyr.

(2) *1925–43*. Tikhon realized that when he died it would not be possible for a council to assemble freely, as in 1917, and to elect a new Patriarch. He therefore designated his own successor, appointing three *locum tenentes* or 'guardians' of the Patriarchal throne: Metropolitans Cyril, Agathangel and Peter. The first two were already in prison at the time of Tikhon's death, so that in April 1925 Peter, Metropolitan of Krutitsy, became Patriarchal *locum tenens*. In December 1925 Peter was arrested and exiled to Siberia, where he remained until his death in 1936. After Peter's arrest, Sergius (Stragorodsky) (1867–1944), Metropolitan of Nizhni-Novgorod, took over the leadership in his stead, with the unusual title 'Deputy to the *locum tenens*'. Sergius had joined the Living Church in 1922, but in 1924 had made his submission to Tikhon, who restored him to his former position.

At first Sergius sought to continue the policy adopted by Tikhon in the last years of his Patriarchate. In a declaration issued on 10 June 1926, while emphasizing that the Church respected the laws of the Soviet Union, he said that bishops could not be expected to enter into any special undertaking to prove their loyalty. He continued, 'We cannot accept the duty of watching over the political tendencies of our co-religionists.' This was in effect a request for a true separation between Church and State: Sergius wanted to keep the Church out of politics, and therefore declined to make it an agent of Soviet policy. In this same declaration he also spoke openly of the incompatibility and the 'contradictions' existing between Christianity and Communism. 'Far from promising reconciliation with the irreconcilable and from pretending to adapt our faith to Communism, we will remain from the religious point of view what we are, that is, members of the traditional Church.'

But in 1927 – a crucial year for Church–State relations in Russia – Sergius changed his position. He spent from December 1926 to March 1927 in prison; as in Tikhon's case, we do not know to what pressures he was subjected during internment. After his release, he issued a new declaration on 29 July 1927, significantly different from that of the previous year. He said nothing this time about the 'contradictions' between Christianity and Communism; he no longer pleaded for a separation between Church and State, but associated the two as closely as possible:

We wish to be Orthodox and at the same time to recognize the Soviet Union as our civil fatherland, whose joys and successes are our joys and successes, and whose failures are our failures. Every blow directed against the Union . . . we regard as a blow directed against us.

In 1926 Sergius had declined to watch over the political tendencies of his co-religionists; but he now demanded from the clergy abroad 'a written promise of their complete loyalty to the Soviet government'.[1]

This 1927 declaration caused great distress to many Orthodox both within and outside Russia. It seemed that Sergius had compromised the Church in a way that Tikhon had never

1. For the full text of the 1926 and 1927 declarations by Sergius, see Matthew Spinka, *The Church in Soviet Russia* (New York 1956), pp. 157–65.

done. In identifying the Church so closely with a government dedicated wholeheartedly to the overthrow of all religion, he appeared to be attempting the very thing which in 1926 he had refused to do – to reconcile the irreconcilable. The victory of atheism would certainly be a joy and success for the Soviet State; would it also be a joy and success for the Church? The dissolution of the League of Militant Atheists would be a blow to the Communist government, but scarcely a blow to the Church. How could the Russian clergy abroad be expected to put their signature to a written promise of complete loyalty to the Soviet government, when many of them had now become citizens of another country? It is hardly surprising that Metropolitan Antony, head of the Karlovtsy Synod (representing the Russian bishops in exile),[1] should have replied to Sergius by quoting 2 Corinthians vi, 14–15: 'Can light consort with darkness? Can Christ agree with Belial, or a believer with an unbeliever?' He continued, 'The Church cannot bless anti-Christian, much less atheistical politics.' It was the 1927 declaration of Sergius which led to a final breach between the Karlovtsy Synod and the Church authorities in Moscow. Ever since then, the Synod in Exile has condemned what it labels 'Sergianism', that is to say, the capitulation of the Church to the atheist government. Metropolitan Evlogy of Paris, the Exarch for western Europe, sought at first to conform to Sergius' requests, but from 1930 he too found it impossible to maintain direct links with the Church in Moscow.

The policy of Sergius also provoked widespread opposition within Russia. Many recalled that he had been a supporter of the Living Church, and they felt he was now pursuing the same collaborationist policy under a slightly different form. The Communists had failed in their first attempt to take over the Church through the reforming movement; now it seemed that, with Sergius' help, they were succeeding in their second attempt. Had Sergius summoned a council of all his fellow bishops in 1927 – of course, the conditions of the time made this impossible – it is very doubtful whether a majority would

1. See below, p. 176.

have supported him. It was rumoured that even the Patriarchal *locum tenens*, Metropolitan Peter, was opposed to the 1927 declaration, but it is impossible to be sure of this. Certainly Metropolitan Joseph of Petrograd, together with a number of senior hierarchs, disapproved so strongly of Sergius' policy that they broke off all communion with him.

Although Joseph and his main supporters were quickly removed from the scene and died in internment, the movement which they had started continued to exist underground. A 'Catacomb Church' was formed, with bishops and priests working in secret, without any links with the official Church under Sergius. Bishop Maximus (Shishilenko) of Serpukhov played an important part in the establishment of this secret Church; he had been Patriarch Tikhon's private physician, and claimed that it was Tikhon's wish that the Church should go underground if Communist pressure became intolerable. The Catacomb Church – it might be more correct to say 'the Catacomb Christians', for it is not clear how far there was a single unified organization – survived into the 1980s, although probably with only a limited number of members. Sometimes it was called the 'True Orthodox Church'.

There were other Russian Orthodox, however, who supported the policy of Metropolitan Sergius. They felt that he was sincerely seeking to protect the Church. They defended his actions as a 'necessary sin'; to save his flock from destruction, he had humbly taken upon himself the 'martyrdom' of lying. It was indeed the case that he was required to tell many lies. In an interview with foreign journalists in 1930, for example, he went so far as to claim that there had never been any persecution of religion in the Soviet Union. To many inside Russia and abroad, this seemed to be a cruel denial of the sufferings of the new Russian martyrs for Christ's sake. Members of the Russian Orthodox Church remain to this day deeply divided in their estimate of Sergius' conduct.

The concessions which Sergius made in 1927 at first brought the Church little apparent advantage. The closure of churches and the liquidation of the clergy continued unabated in the 1930s. At the outbreak of the Second World War in 1939, the outward structure of the Church had been all but annihilated. Only about four bishops were still allowed to function, and there were probably no more than a few hundred churches open in the whole of Russia; all the theological schools and all the monasteries had long since been closed. It was a dark moment for the Russian Church, but a startling change was soon to come. The entire situation was transformed by a new development – the war.

(3) *1943–59*. On 21 June 1941 Germany invaded Russia; and on that very same day, without waiting for matters to develop, Metropolitan Sergius issued a pastoral letter calling on Orthodox Christians to spring to the defence of their threatened country. From that point onwards the Moscow Patriarchate gave unwavering support to the war effort; as the Church leaders saw it, they were fighting not for Communism but for their fatherland. Meanwhile the Germans, in the parts of Russia which they occupied, permitted the restoration of religious life. The revival was immediate, spontaneous and intense. Churches were reopened everywhere in Ukraine and Byelorussia; a particularly dynamic renewal occurred in the diocese of Pskov, under the leadership of its young Metropolitan Sergius (Voskresensky) (1899–1944).[1] It was abundantly clear that twenty years of persecution had not destroyed the faith of the people.

Desperately hard pressed in the struggle against the Germans, Stalin thought it prudent to make some concessions to the Christians under his rule. It was clear that believers still formed a significant portion of the population, and Stalin needed the help of every single Russian if he were to win the war. In gratitude for the support of Sergius and his clergy – and doubtless conscious also that he could hardly afford to be less generous than the Germans – he relaxed the pressure on the Church. At first the concessions were small, but on 4 September 1943 Stalin summoned Sergius and two other metropolitans

1. See Struve, *Christians in Contemporary Russia*, pp. 68–73. Sergius Voskresensky is not to be confused with the Patriarchal *locum tenens* Sergius Stragorodsky.

into his presence, and gave permission for the election of a new Patriarch. Three days later a modest council of nineteen bishops elected Sergius. Already an old man, he died in the following year, and in February 1945 Metropolitan Alexis of Leningrad (1877–1970), a staunch supporter of Sergius since 1927, was elected Patriarch in his place.

Permission to restore the Patriarchate was no more than the first step. In the immediate post-war years Stalin also permitted a major reconstruction of the Church. According to statistics issued by the Moscow Patriarchate, by 1947 the number of open churches had risen to over 20,000; there were some sixty-seven functioning monasteries, two theological academies and eight seminaries. Here was a situation utterly different from the late 1930s. It might be thought that the post-war resurrection of Church life was a posthumous vindication of Sergius' policy since 1927. But this would be a false conclusion. What saved the Church was not the leadership of Sergius, but an historical accident – the war – and also, more fundamentally, the faithful endurance of the believing Russian people.

There were, however, limits to Stalin's toleration. The Church was not allowed to do anything except conduct Church services and train future priests. It still could undertake no social activities, no youth work, no religious education of children. The Soviet government continued to treat religion as an enemy to be combated through all forms of propaganda, while the Church was not allowed to answer back. The secret police interfered in every aspect of the Church's inner life. Moreover, in return for restricted toleration, the Church leaders were expected to be 'loyal' to the government. This meant not only that they had to refrain from any criticism of the Soviet authorities, but they were also required to support Communist policies actively at home and more particularly abroad. None of the legislation against religion was repealed, and it was open to the authorities to resume active persecution at any time, whenever they should judge it expedient.

(4) *1959–64.* Up to his death in 1953, Stalin maintained the post-war status quo. The last eight years of his rule (1945–53)

were the most favourable period for the Russian Church during the whole of the Communist era. But in 1959 Khrushchev launched a major offensive against the Church, displaying a harshness that was all the more striking because of the liberalization that he allowed in other directions. Bishops, priests, monks and nuns were tried and imprisoned on fabricated 'criminal charges'; the clergy everywhere underwent a good deal of harassment and some physical violence. Churches were closed on a massive scale, and the total number was reduced to around 7,000, representing a loss of two-thirds. The seminaries were reduced from eight to three, and the number of functioning monasteries fell from sixty-seven to twenty-one. Particularly severe restrictions were placed upon Church work with the young: priests were often forbidden to give communion to children, and parents arriving for the Liturgy with their young families were turned back at the church door by plain-clothes police. The dimensions of this persecution passed largely unnoticed in the west, in particular because the Church authorities in Russia made no open protests. When speaking in the west in such forums as the World Council of Churches or the Prague Peace Conference, they pretended that all was 'normal' in Church–State relations. The anti-religious campaign ceased abruptly with Khrushchev's removal from power, but the Church was not allowed to make good the losses which it had suffered.

(5) *1964–88.* So far as official Church–State relations were concerned, this was a period of outward calm. The State continued to supervise the Church closely, through the KGB and in other ways; the leadership of the Moscow Patriarchate continued to work as best it could within the narrow limits permitted by the Communist authorities. Had this leadership been more dynamic and vociferous – as many prominent Baptists were in Russia at this time – might not the Church in fact have obtained far greater concessions from the State? Need the Church hierarchy have been so consistently submissive?

These were questions that began to be asked more and more during the late 1960s and 1970s, not only by western observers but by Orthodox Christians within the Soviet Union. And it is precisely this that constitutes the most striking new development in the fifth period of Church–State relations under Communism. Even if the leadership kept silent, others did not. A dissident movement emerged within the Orthodox Church in Russia, which openly protested against State interference in the Church's internal life. The protestors received no encouragement whatever from the Patriarch and the Holy Synod – quite the contrary – but none the less their numbers grew steadily.

The first prominent figure among the Orthodox dissidents was Anatoly Krasnov-Levitin, who from 1958 onwards produced a stream of *samizdat*[1] articles, describing the religious persecution and the sufferings of believers. Similar accounts were compiled by the layman Boris Talantov, who died in a labour camp. But the most influential single document to come from the religious dissident movement was the Open Letter addressed in November 1965 to Patriarch Alexis by two Moscow priests, Fr Nicolas Eshliman and Fr Gleb Yakunin. They mentioned in detail the repressive measures taken against the Church by the Communist authorities and the lack of resistance, even the apparent co-operation, of the Church authorities. They appealed to the Patriarch to act: 'The suffering Church turns to you with hope. You have been invested with the staff of primatial authority. You have the power as Patriarch to put an end to this lawlessness with one word! Do this!'[2]

Sadly, yet perhaps predictably, the Patriarch's only response was to suspend the two priests from their ministry. But the letter acted as a catalyst, inspiring many other believers to express their long-pent-up feelings. At last the Church seemed to be breaking free from the oppressive web of evasion and half-truths that was smothering it. One of those inspired

1. Writings not published officially, but circulated more or less secretly in typescript or manuscript.

2. Ellis, *The Russian Orthodox Church: A Contemporary History*, p. 292. The two priests wrote a second letter to Podgorny, Chairman of the Presidium of the Supreme Soviet.

by the example of Fr Gleb and Fr Nicolas was the novelist Alexander Solzhenitsyn, who in 1972 wrote a forceful 'Lenten Letter' addressed to Patriarch Pimen (1910–90), the successor of Alexis, in which he emphasized the tragic irony of the Church's present predicament:

By what reasoning is it possible to convince oneself that the planned *destruction* of the spirit and body of the Church under the guidance of the atheists is the best way of *preserving* it? Rescuing it *for whom*? Certainly not for Christ. Preserving it *by what means*? By falsehood? But after the falsehood by whose hands are the holy sacraments to be celebrated?

His own solution to the Church's problems lay in the one word 'sacrifice': 'Though deprived of all material strength the Church is always victorious in sacrifice.'[1]

In 1976 the Christian Committee for the Defence of Believers' Rights was founded, which aimed to help Orthodox and non-Orthodox believers alike. The committee was set up in close co-operation with the Helsinki Monitoring Group, which dealt with the infringement of human rights in general. Recognizing that freedom is indivisible, the Christian dissidents sought to work constructively with the broader dissident movement. Important protests against religious oppression were also made by the Christian Seminar, an informal study group for young Russian Orthodox intellectuals founded in 1974 by Alexander Ogorodnikov, and headed after Ogorodnikov's arrest in 1978 by Lev Regelson. The Russian feminist movement which began in Leningrad in 1979 included a number of Orthodox believers such as Tatiana Goricheva.

From 1976 onwards the Communist authorities reacted to the dissident movement with increasing severity, and by 1980 most of the leading Orthodox members had been silenced. Some were sent to labour camps and exile, others were discredited by the KGB in various ways. The general prospect was discouraging. More than a decade of public dissent had brought about, so it seemed, no change in the basic relationship between the Church and the atheist State. The Church had not secured

1. Ellis, p. 304.

freedom from Communist interference, and there seemed little likelihood that it would do so in the immediate future. So far as both the government and the leadership of the Moscow Patriarchate were concerned, it was 'business as usual'.

And then, contrary to all human expectation, there was an abrupt and fundamental change. The Communist regime, seemingly all-powerful over the past seven decades, collapsed like a house of cards.

A TROUBLED RENAISSANCE

On 11 March 1985 Mikhail Gorbachev became General Secretary of the Communist Party of the Soviet Union. Seven years later, at the beginning of 1992, Gorbachev was no longer in power and the Soviet Union had ceased to exist. But as a result of the policies of *glasnost* ('openness') and *perestroika* ('restructuring') which he had initiated, the Russian Church found itself suddenly liberated from all the repressive measures that had crippled its life since 1917. Without recovering the position of privilege that it had enjoyed under the Tsarist regime, the Church was at last basically free. Yet the qualification 'basically' needs still to be added, for there continued to be cases of obstruction by government officials at the local level, and even of intimidation from the KGB. After all, especially in the middle and lower strata of the administration, most of those who worked for Communism were still in office. Leopards do not change their spots overnight.

The most significant change has been at the level of legislation. During 1990–91, in almost all parts of what was once the Soviet Union, new regulations came into force, cancelling the 'Law on Religious Associations' originally enacted in 1929. There is now, for the first time, a true and genuine separation between Church and State. The State no longer promotes atheism. The Orthodox Church – along with other religious bodies – is recognized as a legal entity, with the right to own property. Some restrictions still remain, however, as regards the opening of churches, since permission is needed from the civil authorities. But the Church is now at liberty to engage in social and philanthropic work, and services can be held in hospitals and prisons. Missionary activities are permitted. Youth groups and Bible study circles are allowed. The Church can publish religious literature and teach religion to children; indeed, religious instruction may even be given in State institutions.

Legislation, however, is valueless if it remains a dead letter and is not carried into practical effect. In fact, from 1988 onwards the Church had already been allowed to do most of the things that were now permitted by law. During 1989–92 Russian Orthodoxy was able to make an important start in rebuilding its outward structures. The accompanying chart (see p. 162) indicates the vicissitudes of the Church during the past seven decades: almost total annihilation by the eve of the Second World War; revival in the immediate post-war years; heavy losses (chiefly because of the persecution during 1959–64); and then from 1988 rapid reconstruction (although there are still far fewer churches and priests than in 1947). Churches have been opened, during 1989–92, at the rate of about thirty a week; the State has given back many historic monasteries; educational institutions for future clergy have expanded.

Yet it would be grossly misleading to suggest that all is now well. The political and economic situation in the former Soviet Union during recent years has been highly unstable, and the future remains uncertain. The problems facing the Church are formidable. The State is handing back church buildings and monasteries in a condition of shocking dilapidation, and the cost of repairs is stretching the Church's finances to the utmost. The central administration of the Patriarchate, from all accounts, is virtually bankrupt; local congregations are providing donations on a sacrificial scale, but they can do all too little with Russia in the grip of an economic crisis. The constant creation of new parishes is placing the existing clergy under immense strain; even before 1988 they were severely overworked, and there are now far too few to go round. The Church needs at least 7,000 more priests in the immediate future. There are regular complaints that the curriculum in the theological schools is narrow and outdated, and fails to prepare the clergy for the

Institutions of the Russian Orthodox Church

	1914	1939	1947	1988	1996
Churches	54,174	some 100s	?20,000	about 7,000	over 17,000
Priests and deacons	51,105	some 100s	?30,000	about 7,000	about 13,000
Monasteries (for both men and women)	1,025	none	67	21	337
Monks and nuns	94,629	?	?10,000	1,190	?
Theological academies	4	none	2	2	3
Seminaries	57	none	8	3 } forbidden by law	about 50
Pre-theological schools	185	forbidden by law	forbidden by law		
Students	?	none	?	2,000	?
Parochial schools	37,528	forbidden by law	forbidden by law	forbidden by law	no statistics available; rapidly proliferating
Homes for the aged	1,113				
Hospitals	291				
Parish libraries	34,497				

radically new pastoral situation that awaits them. The supply of religious literature, despite help from the west, falls pitiably short of the needs. For seventy years the Church has been excluded from all social and charitable work, and although everywhere there are open doors – State hospitals and old people's homes are for the most part only too eager to welcome voluntary help from believers – the Church authorities simply have no practical expertise in this field. Equally they have no experience whatever in organized youth work or in the religious teaching of children. They are having to start from nothing.

Nor is this all. Less tangible but equally grave problems confront the Church as it comes to terms with what is now a pluralist society. Russian Orthodoxy under Communism was in a paradoxical way still to some extent a 'State Church', protected by the authorities as well as persecuted. Now this is no longer so. Roman Catholics and Protestants are free to carry out missionary work in Russia. The Orthodox resent this as an intrusion, but they are powerless to stop it. All kinds of other religious or pseudo-religious movements – Hare Krishna, occultism, even explicitly satanic cults – are likewise offering their own particular version of the spiritual way to a bewildered Russian public that is eagerly seeking the meaning of life, but has little idea where to turn. In the post-Communist era Russian Orthodoxy is having to face competition from all sides.

There are other reasons for disquiet. The organization of the KGB still survives more or less intact, and many elements in it are hostile to religion. It is widely believed that the brutal murder of Fr Alexander Men (1935–90), a priest of energy and independent views, was instigated by the secret police. There are also sinister elements within the Church itself. The strongly nationalist Orthodox organization *Pamyat* ('Remembrance'), in which some priests are active, is more or less openly anti-Semitic. Despite firm condemnation from leading bishops, anti-Semitism continues to enjoy a good deal of popular support. Unfortunately, this is true of other Orthodox Churches as well as the Russian.

How far is the present hierarchy able to cope with all these difficulties? Its moral authority is somewhat tarnished. With the opening up of the KGB files in 1992, many of the laity have been scandalized to discover the extent of the collaboration under Communism between certain bishops and the secret police. There is also a feeling among laypeople that the bishops, formed in the Soviet period when all their pastoral activities were strictly supervised, are all too often over-passive in the new situation, and lack the intelligence and imagination to seize the opportunities now before them. But this is certainly not true of such leading hierarchs as Metropolitan Kyrill of Smolensk and Archbishop Chrysostom of Irkutsk. Opinions differ over the past collaboration or otherwise between the present Patriarch Alexis II (elected in 1990) and the Communist authorities, but on the whole he is thought to have shown firmness and independence in his dealings as a diocesan bishop with the Soviet State. Under his leadership the episcopate in 1992 proceeded for the first time to canonize some of the new martyrs who suffered under Communism. For Russian Orthodoxy this is a step of great spiritual significance. Three saints in particular were proclaimed: the sister-in-law of Emperor Nicolas II, the Grand Duchess Elizabeth, who became a nun after the assassination of her husband by terrorists in 1905 and was herself killed by the Bolsheviks in 1918; Metropolitan Vladimir of Kiev, assassinated in 1918; and Metropolitan Benjamin of Petrograd, shot after a show trial in 1922.

A particularly thorny problem troubling Russian Orthodoxy is the revival of Eastern-rite Catholicism. In 1946 the Greek Catholic Church of Ukraine, set up in 1596 through the Union of Brest-Litovsk[1] and numbering about 3,500,000, was reincorporated into the Russian Orthodox Church and ceased to exist. While there were doubtless some Ukrainian Catholics whose return to Orthodoxy was voluntary, there can be little doubt that the vast majority wished to continue as they were, in union with the Papacy. Not one of the Ukrainian bishops was in favour of the return; all alike were arrested, and most died in prison or exile. Because of direct coercion and police terrorism, many clergy and laity chose to conform outwardly

1. See above, p. 95.

to the Orthodox Church, while still remaining Catholic in their inward convictions; others preferred to go underground. The hierarchs of the Moscow Patriarchate, in conniving at the persecution of their fellow Christians by Stalin and the atheist authorities, were placed in an unenviably equivocal situation. Surely, as a matter of basic principle, no Christian should ever support acts of violence against the conscience of other Christians. The fate of the Greek Catholics after the Second World War is perhaps the darkest chapter in the story of the Moscow Patriarchate's collusion with Communism.

Yet, though driven underground, eastern Catholicism was not exterminated. One of the fruits of Gorbachev's *glasnost* was that at the end of 1989 the Greek Catholic Church of Ukraine was once more legalized. By 1987 it was already becoming abundantly clear that the Greek Catholics would re-emerge from the catacombs and seek to recover the churches, now in Orthodox hands, that had once belonged to them. If only the Moscow Patriarchate had taken the initiative in proposing a peaceful and negotiated solution, it would have won immense moral authority, and much subsequent bitterness could have been avoided. Regrettably there was no such initiative. In 1987, and again in 1988, the head of the Ukrainian Catholic Church, Cardinal Myroslav Lubachivsky, approached the Moscow Patriarchate both verbally and in writing, proposing that the two sides, Orthodox and Catholic, should make a public and formal gesture of mutual forgiveness; but no response came from the Moscow Patriarchate. It is easy to understand how wounding the Greek Catholics found this silence. Now the moment of opportunity has passed. From 1989 onwards there have been sharp local disputes, often marked by violence, over the possession of church buildings. With passions thoroughly aroused on both sides, reconciliation is going to prove slow.

Alongside the problem of relations between Orthodox and Greek Catholics in Ukraine, and closely connected with it, there is the question of Ukrainian nationalism. Ukraine has now become an independent state, and so most Ukrainian Orthodox want their Church to be independent as well. A Ukrainian Autocephalous Church was in fact founded after the revolution.

At an assembly in Kiev in 1921, the delegates – unable to find any Orthodox hierarch who would join the autocephalist movement – decided to create a Ukrainian episcopate by themselves, without any consecrating bishop. The resulting 'self-consecrated' Ukrainian hierarchy, as it was termed, has never been recognized by the rest of the Orthodox Church; for a time, however, the Ukrainian Autocephalous Church flourished, with 26 bishops, 2,500 priests and 2,000 parishes, but in the 1930s it was liquidated by Stalin. It was revived in the Second World War under German occupation, this time with bishops possessing the apostolic succession, but was suppressed once more by Stalin when the war ended. In 1989 the Ukrainian Autocephalous Church was once more revived, with the support of a retired bishop of the Moscow Patriarch, John (Bodnarchuk).

By the mid-1990s the ecclesiastical situation in Ukraine had become highly confused. The Greek Catholics have around 2,700 parishes; the Ukrainian Autocephalous Orthodox Church, by now split into two groups (neither of them recognized by any other Orthodox Church), have about 1,500 parishes; the main body of Orthodox – forming an autonomous local Church under the jurisdiction of the Moscow Patriarchate – has some 5,500 parishes. On the Orthodox side, the only long-term solution would seem to be a fully independent Ukrainian Autocephalous Church; this would need the recognition of the Moscow Patriarchate and also that of the Ecumenical Patriarchate, to whose jurisdiction Ukraine belonged before 1686. But this is going to make a major difference to the situation of the Moscow Patriarchate, since in the post-war period no less than two-thirds of all the open churches in the entire Soviet Union were located in Ukraine, while perhaps as many as 70 per cent of the students in the seminaries were Ukrainian. For Orthodox everywhere in the former Soviet Union, this is a time of great hope – and also great anxiety.

EASTERN EUROPE: A VARIED PICTURE

Hope and anxiety: the same words apply to the present situation of the other seven Orthodox Churches previously under

Communist rule. Apart from the Church of Georgia, their experience of Communism has been briefer than that of Russian Orthodoxy – forty rather than seventy years. The Communist regimes established after the Second World War followed the same general principles as the Soviet Union had done. The Church was excluded from social and charitable work. In most cases, it was also forbidden to undertaken educational activities, except for the training of priests. The Church authorities were expected to support the government; semi-political 'confederations of priests' were formed under Communist patronage, and priests had usually to take an oath of loyalty to the Communist authorities. But the number of arrests and the extent to which churches were closed varied from country to country.

Conditions were worst of all for the *Church of Albania*, which had been granted autocephaly in 1937 by the Patriarchate of Constantinople. In 1967 the government of Hoxha announced that Albania was now the first truly atheist state in the world: every place of worship had been closed and every visible expression of religious faith eliminated. Repression fell with equal severity on Orthodox, Roman Catholics and Muslims. The last primate of the Albanian Orthodox Church, Archbishop Damian, died in prison in 1973. In 1991, when religion began to emerge from underground, no Orthodox bishops at all had survived, and less than twenty Orthodox priests were still alive, half of them too infirm to officiate. Churches are now being reopened, new clergy ordained, and a small theological school has been started. In 1992 Bishop Anastasios (Yannoulatos), a Greek who has worked as a missionary in East Africa, was appointed head of the Albanian Church; he has declared his willingness to resign as soon as a suitable Albanian candidate can be found.

At the other extreme, the Orthodox Church under Communist rule which has best preserved its outward structure is the *Church of Romania*. When the Communists took over in 1948, there was little closure of churches. The Romanian Patriarchate retained its theological academies and was able to go on publishing periodicals and other books on a large scale. This favourable situation was due partly to the friendly links that Patriarch Justinian (in office 1948–77) maintained with the new rulers.

At times he identified himself to a surprising degree with Marxist ideology, but he was also a devoted pastor, respected and loved by his Orthodox flock. Throughout the Communist period the number of clergy in Romania continued to rise, and many new churches were opened. Under Justinian's inspiration, there was also a striking monastic renewal, based on the best traditions of Hesychasm, with an emphasis on the Jesus Prayer. The spirit of St Paissy Velichkovsky is very much alive in Romania today, and there are some outstanding 'elders' such as Fr Cleopas of Sihastria. In 1946 an edition of the *Philokalia* began to appear, prepared by the greatest Romanian theologian of the twentieth century, Fr Dumitru Staniloae (1903–93). Far more than a mere translation from the Greek, this contains introductions and notes drawing on western critical research, but displaying also a fine appreciation of Orthodox spirituality. The Romanian *Philokalia* reached its eleventh volume in 1990. The Romanian Church, however, has also had to face persecution, especially in 1958 when many priests, monks and nuns were imprisoned, including Fr Staniloae. In his later years Ceausescu closed and destroyed numerous churches.

There was a heavy price to pay for the relative toleration that Romanian Orthodoxy enjoyed. Church life was closely supervised in all its aspects by the secret police, and this meant that, by the time Ceausescu fell in December 1989, the Church's moral authority had been gravely impaired because of its co-operation with the hated regime. Patriarch Teoctist (elected 1986) thought it right to resign from office in January 1990, but he was reinstated by the Holy Synod in the following April. The future leadership of the Romanian Church, however, will certainly depend on the younger bishops appointed since the end of Communism, such as Metropolitan Daniel (Cibotea) of Moldavia.

Until 1948 Romania contained a large group of Greek Catholics, numbering about 1,500,000; but in that year, like their brothers and sisters in the Ukraine, they were forced to reunite with the Orthodox Church. Since 1990 they have re-emerged and sought to recover their church property, and as in Ukraine there has been much tension and bitterness.

The *Church of Serbia* enjoyed under Communism less out-ward prosperity than the Romanian Church, but it maintained a much greater inner independence. The services are less well attended than in Romania, and in some areas there is a shortage of priests; but the number of students training for ordination is now considerably more than it was in the 1930s. There is a lack of monks but, as in Greece, a revival of monasticism for women. The Communists sought to weaken the Serbian Church by subdivision, and encouraged the foundation of a schismatic *Church of Macedonia* in 1967. This regards itself as autocephalous, but has not been recognized by any other Ortho-dox Church.

In the twentieth-century Serbian Church there have been countless martyrs. Some of these suffered at the hands of the Communists, but far more were killed during the Second World War by the infamous Fascist State of Croatia, under the Ustashi leader Ante Pavelich, who claimed the blessing of the Roman Catholic Church. In Croatia and the rest of Yugoslavia during the war years, out of the twenty-one Orthodox bishops, five were murdered, two died of beatings, two died in intern-ment, five others were imprisoned or expelled from their dio-ceses; a quarter of the Orthodox priests were killed, and about one-half imprisoned. In Croatia half the Serbian population perished, and many Orthodox were forcibly 'converted' to Roman Catholicism at gunpoint. Memories of this were still vivid in the minds of the Serbs when an independent Croatia was once more set up in 1991 and began at once to take repres-sive measures against the Serbian Orthodox churches and clergy on its territory. But, to its credit, the Serbian hierarchy, led by the revered Patriarch Pavle (elected 1990), has con-demned the atrocities committed by the invading Serbian armies and the Serbian irregulars in Croatia and Bosnia. The Serbian Church, so the Patriarch insisted on the day of Pente-cost 1992, 'has never taught its people to seize the possessions of others and to kill in order to obtain them, but only to defend its own sanctuaries'.

In the four other Orthodox Churches formerly under Com-munist rule, relations with the State have been very similar to those prevailing in Russia. Since the Communists came to power in 1944, the *Church of Bulgaria* has closely followed the policies of the Moscow Patriarchate. To judge from evidence in the early 1980s, church attendance in Bulgaria was a good deal worse than in Romania or Serbia. The monasteries were much depleted, although there were some women's communities with young nuns. With the re-establishment of freedom, a group of six Bulgarian bishops had the courage in July 1990 to issue a public act of repentance, seeking forgiveness for their failures and acts of compromise under the Communist regime; but the head of the Bulgarian Church, Patriarch Maksim (elected 1971), was not one of the six. With the demise of Communism, let us hope that forces of renewal will now emerge within Bulgarian Orthodoxy.

Another Church that was until recently closely dependent on Moscow is the ancient *Church of Georgia*. Founded in the early fourth century through the missionary witness of a woman, St Nina 'the equal of the Apostles', it was for a time under the jurisdiction of the Patriarchate of Antioch; but it gained internal autonomy by the eighth century, and complete autocephaly around 1053. Incorporated into the Russian Church in 1811, it reasserted its independence in 1917. Its autocephaly was formally recognized by Moscow in 1943, and by Constantinople in 1990. Out of 2,455 churches functioning in Georgia in 1917, less than 100 were active in the 1980s; but with the coming of *glasnost* there has been a modest renewal. In 1992, besides the Catholicos-Patriarch Ilia II (elected 1977), there were fourteen diocesan bishops.

The *Orthodox Church of Poland* was granted autocephaly by the Ecumenical Patriarchate in 1924. In the inter-war period it numbered about four million, but with the alteration of frontiers in 1939 most of its members found themselves within the Soviet Union. In the 1930s it suffered much harassment from the Latin Catholic government of Pilsudski, and many churches were closed. Following the Communist takeover in 1948, the head of the Polish Orthodox Church, Metropolitan Dionysius, was deposed and put under house arrest, and the Orthodox Poles were forced to seek a new grant of autocephaly from the Moscow Patriarchate, under whose control they largely remained until the 1980s. At the moment there are about 250 parishes, with 325 priests. From all accounts Orthodox Church life is expanding, and there is an active youth movement.

The *Orthodox Church of the Czech Republic and Slovakia* has been closely linked with the Moscow Patriarchate since 1946. It was granted autocephaly by Moscow in 1951, but this has not yet been recognized by Constantinople. In the inter-war period, the leading Czech Orthodox was Bishop Gorazd, originally a Roman Catholic priest, who was consecrated as an Orthodox bishop in 1921, and killed by the Germans in 1942; he was proclaimed a saint in 1987. The numbers of Czechoslovak Orthodox were greatly increased in 1950, when the Greek Catholics in Slovakia, amounting to around 200,000, were forcibly reunited with Orthodoxy. But most of these new members were lost again when the Greek Catholic Church was re-established during the 'Prague spring' of 1968. Following the fall of Communism, the government handed back to the Catholics most of the church buildings that were being used by the Orthodox. Czech and Slovak Orthodoxy is now struggling hard to build new places of worship.

For most Orthodox Christians in the twentieth century, Communism has been *the* enemy. But it is wise to remember that our enemy lies not only outside us but within. As Solzhenitsyn discovered in the prison camp, we should not simply project evil upon others, but we need to search our own hearts:

Gradually it was disclosed to me that the line separating good and evil passes not through states, nor between classes, nor between political parties either – but right through every human heart – and through all human hearts. This line shifts. Inside us, it oscillates with the years. And even within hearts overwhelmed by evil, one small bridgehead of good is retained. And even in the best of all hearts, there remains . . . an unuprooted small corner of evil.[1]

1. *The Gulag Archipelago*, vol. 2 (London 1975), part iv, p. 597.

CHAPTER 9

The Twentieth Century, III: Diaspora and Mission

> Every foreign country is our motherland, and every mother-
> land is foreign.
>
> *Epistle to Diognetus* v,5

DIVERSITY IN UNITY

In the past Orthodoxy has appeared, from the cultural and
geographical point of view, almost exclusively as an 'eastern'
Church. Today this is no longer so. Outside the boundaries of
the traditional Orthodox countries there now exists a large
Orthodox 'dispersion', its chief centre in North America, but
with branches in every part of the world. In numbers and
influence Greeks and Russians predominate, but the diaspora
is by no means limited to them alone: Serbs, Romanians, Arabs,
Bulgarians, Albanians and others all have a place.

The origins of this Orthodox diaspora extend some way
back. The first Greek church in London was opened as long
ago as 1677, in the then fashionable district of Soho. It had a
brief but troubled career, and was closed in 1682. Henry Comp-
ton, the Anglican Bishop of London, forbade the Greeks to
have a single icon in the church and demanded that their
clergy omit all prayers to the saints, disown the Council of
Jerusalem (1672), and repudiate the doctrine of Transubstantiation. When the Patriarch of Constantinople protested against
these conditions to the English Ambassador, Sir John Finch,
the latter retorted that it was 'illegal for any public church in
England to express Romish beliefs, and that it was just as bad
to have them professed in Greek as in Latin'![1] The next Orthodox place of worship founded in London, the Russian embassy

---

1. See E. Carpenter, *The Protestant Bishop* (London 1956), pp. 357–64.

chapel – opened around 1721 – enjoyed diplomatic immunity, and so it was no concern of the Anglican Bishop of London what went on inside it. During the eighteenth century this chapel was used by Greeks and by English converts as well as by Russians. In 1838 the Greeks were able to open a church of their own in London, without any irksome restrictions from the Anglican authorities.

There was an Orthodox presence in the North American continent from the middle of the eighteenth century. The Russian explorers Bering and Chirikov sighted the coast of Alaska on 15 July 1741, and five days later, on the feast of the Prophet Elijah, the first Orthodox Liturgy in America was celebrated in Sitka Bay on board the ship *St Peter*. A few years later, in 1768, a large group of Greeks arrived in Florida to establish the colony of New Smyrna, but the venture proved a disastrous failure.[1]

Yet, if the fact of an Orthodox diaspora is not itself new, it is only in the twentieth century that the diaspora has attained such dimensions as to make the presence of Orthodoxy a significant factor in the religious life of non-Orthodox countries. Even today, as a result of national and jurisdictional divisions, the influence of the diaspora is not nearly so great as it ought to be.

The most important single event in the story of the dispersion has been the Bolshevik Revolution, which drove into exile more than a million Russians, including the cultural and intellectual élite of the nation. Before 1914 the majority of the Orthodox immigrants, whether Greek or Slav, were poor and little educated – peasants and manual labourers looking for land or work. But the great wave of exiles after the Russian Revolution contained many people qualified to make contact with the west on a scholarly level, who could present Orthodoxy to the non-Orthodox world in a way that most earlier immigrants manifestly could not. The output of the post-1917 Russian emigration, particularly in its first years, was astonishing: in the two decades between the world wars, so it has been

---

1. See E. P. Panagopoulos, *New Smyrna: An Eighteenth Century Greek Odyssey* (Gainesville 1966).

calculated, its members published 10,000 books and 200 journals, not counting literary and scientific reviews. Today the second and third generations of Greeks in the west, especially in the USA, are also coming to play a prominent part in the political, academic and professional life of their adopted countries.

On the religious side, the Orthodox emigration has come to be organized on strongly national lines. In the nineteenth and the early twentieth century, the first initiative usually came not from above but from below – from the laity rather than the hierarchy. A group of immigrants would join together and invite a priest from their old country, and so a parish would be formed. Often it was only much later that any bishop became directly involved in this arrangement. For the first generation, the local parish church was their chief link with the mother country; it was the place where they could hear their native language spoken, the ark and guardian of their national customs. Thus, for fully understandable reasons, Orthodoxy in the west possessed from the start a markedly ethnic character.

Now nationhood is certainly a gift from God. Alexander Solzhenitsyn was right to say, in his 1970 Nobel Prize speech, 'Nations are the wealth of mankind, its collective personalities; the very least of them wears its own special colours and bears within itself a special facet of divine intention.'[1] Unfortunately, however, in the religious life of the diaspora, national loyalties, in themselves legitimate, have been allowed to prevail at the expense of Orthodox Catholicity, and this has led to a grievous fragmentation of ecclesial structures. Instead of a single diocese in each place, under one bishop, almost everywhere in the west there has grown up a multiplicity of parallel jurisdictions, with several Orthodox bishops side by side in every major city. Whatever the historical causes of this, it is certainly contrary to the Orthodox understanding of the Church; the Ecumenical Patriarch Dimitrios, visiting the USA in 1990, was right to speak of the ethnic divisions in American Orthodoxy as 'truly a

1. Leopold Labedz, *Solzhenitsyn: A Documentary Record* (2nd ed., Harmondsworth 1974), p. 314.

scandal'. Today many of us would like to see, in each western country, a single local Church embracing all the Orthodox in a unified organization; individual parishes could retain their ethnic character, if they so desired, but all would acknowledge the same local hierarch, and all the hierarchs in each country would sit together in a single synod. Regrettably this is as yet no more than a distant hope. Ethnic divisions are proving hard to transcend.

In addition to these ethnic divisions, there have also been internal splits within many of the national groups; and spiritually these have had a far more harmful effect on the life of Orthodoxy in the west than the ethnic divisions have done. Since 1922, apart from certain local tensions, the Greek emigration has been ecclesiastically more or less united under the Ecumenical Patriarchate. But the Orthodox peoples who fled from Communism became divided in almost every instance into warring factions, with one group maintaining its links with the Mother Church and another group setting up an independent 'Church in Exile'. Despite the collapse of Communism in the late 1980s, most of these schisms remain still unhealed.

The story of the Russian diaspora is particularly complex and tragic. There are four main jurisdictions:

(1) *The Moscow Patriarchate*, comprising those parishes in the emigration which have chosen to maintain direct links with the Church authorities inside Russia (?30,000–40,000 members, in all parts of the west).

(2) *The Russian Orthodox Church Outside Russia* (ROCOR); also known as 'The Russian Orthodox Church in Exile', 'The Russian Orthodox Church Abroad', 'The Synodal Church', 'The Karlovtsy Synod' (perhaps 150,000 members). Present head: Metropolitan Vitaly (elected 1986).

(3) *The Russian Orthodox Archdiocese in Western Europe*, under the Ecumenical Patriarchate; also known as the 'Paris Jurisdiction' (perhaps 50,000 members). Present head: Archbishop Sergius (elected 1993).

(4) *The Russian Orthodox Greek Catholic Church of America*,

also known as 'The Metropolia'. In 1970 this became 'The Orthodox Church in America' (OCA, total membership: 1,000,000). Present head: Metropolitan Theodosius (elected 1977).

How did these divisions arise? On 20 November 1920 the Patriarch of Moscow, St Tikhon, issued a decree authorizing bishops of the Russian Church to set up independent organizations of their own on a temporary basis, should it become impossible to maintain normal relations with the Patriarchate. After the collapse of the White Armies, the Russian bishops in exile decided to carry into effect the terms of this decree, even though it is questionable whether Tikhon intended it to apply outside the borders of Russia. A first meeting was held in Constantinople in 1920; and then in 1921, with the support of Patriarch Dimitrije of Serbia, a further council was convened at Sremski-Karlovci (Karlovtsy) in Yugoslavia. A temporary administration for the Russian Orthodox in exile was set up, under a synod of bishops that was to meet annually at Karlovtsy. The first head of the Karlovtsy Synod (ROCOR) was Antony (Khrapovitsky) (1863–1936), formerly Metropolitan of Kiev, one of the most daring and original theologians in the Russian hierarchy at this time. Among other decisions, the Karlovtsy council of 1921 passed a motion – against the wishes of many participants – calling for the restoration of the Romanov dynasty in Russia.

The vehemently anti-Communist attitude of the Karlovtsy bishops placed Patriarch Tikhon in a delicate situation. In 1922 he ordered the Synod to be dissolved, but the bishops reconstituted it in what was virtually the same form. The Karlovtsy bishops totally rejected the 1927 declaration by Metropolitan Sergius, the Patriarchal *locum tenens*, while on his side Sergius stated in 1928 that all the acts of the Karlovtsy Synod were null and void. After the Second World War the Synod moved its headquarters to Munich, and since 1949 its centre has been in New York. In 1990 ROCOR extended its work to the former Soviet Union, consecrating two bishops there and establishing parishes in Moscow, St Petersburg and elsewhere;

the branch of ROCOR within Russia is known as the 'Free Russian Orthodox Church'. Naturally this step has led to further tension between ROCOR and the Moscow Patriarchate.

From the early 1960s, ROCOR has become increasingly isolated, although still maintaining links with the Serbian Church. This state of separation has been largely by ROCOR's own choice: its leaders feel strongly that the other Orthodox Churches have compromised the true faith through their participation in the Ecumenical Movement. Whatever the reasons, the isolation of ROCOR is certainly much to be regretted. It has preserved with loving faithfulness the ascetic, monastic and liturgical traditions of Orthodox Russia, and this traditional spirituality is something of which western Orthodoxy stands greatly in need.

Initially, all the Russian bishops in exile tried to work with the Karlovtsy Synod, but from 1926 onwards divisions occurred which led to the establishment of the third and fourth among the four groups mentioned above. The Paris jurisdiction owed its origin to the Russian bishop in Paris, Metropolitan Evlogy (1864–1946), whom Patriarch Tikhon had appointed as his Exarch in western Europe. Evlogy broke with the Karlovtsy Synod in 1926–7; then in 1930 he was disowned by the Patriarchal *locum tenens*, Sergius, because he had taken part in a service of prayer in Westminster Abbey, London, on behalf of persecuted Christians in the Soviet Union. In 1931 Evlogy appealed to the Ecumenical Patriarch Photius II, who received him and his parishes under the jurisdiction of Constantinople. Evlogy returned to the jurisdiction of Moscow in 1945, shortly before his death, but the great majority of his flock chose to remain under Constantinople. Despite difficulties during 1965–71, the Russian Archdiocese in Paris has continued until now within the jurisdiction of the Ecumenical throne.

Finally there is the fourth group, the North American Metropolia. After the revolution, the Russians in America stood in a slightly different position from the Russian *émigrés* elsewhere, since here alone among the countries outside Russia there were regularly constituted Russian dioceses before 1917, with resident bishops. Metropolitan Platon of New York

(1866–1934), like Evlogy, separated from the Karlovtsy Synod after 1926; he had already severed contact in 1924 with the Moscow Patriarchate, so that from 1926 onwards the Russians in the USA formed *de facto* an autonomous group. During 1935–46 the Metropolia maintained links with the Karlovtsy Synod, but at the Synod of Cleveland in 1946 a majority of the delegates voted to return to the jurisdiction of the Moscow Patriarchate on condition that Moscow allowed them to retain their 'complete autonomy as it exists at present'. At that time the Patriarchate was unable to consent to this. In 1970, however, the Church of Russia granted the Metropolia not just autonomy but autocephaly. This 'Autocephalous Orthodox Church in America' (OCA) has been formally recognized by the Churches of Bulgaria, Georgia, Poland and Czechoslovakia, but not as yet by Constantinople or any other Orthodox Church. The Ecumenical Patriarchate takes the view that it alone, acting in consultation with the other Orthodox Churches, has the right to establish an autocephalous Church in America. But, despite this unresolved dispute, the OCA continues in full communion with the rest of the Orthodox Churches.

WESTERN ORTHODOXY

Without attempting to be exhaustive, let us briefly survey the Orthodox scene in western Europe, North America and (more briefly) Australia. In western Europe, the chief intellectual and spiritual centre is Paris. Here the celebrated Theological Institute of St Sergius (under the Paris jurisdiction of Russians), founded in 1925, has acted as an important point of encounter between Orthodox and non-Orthodox. Particularly during the inter-war period, the Institute numbered among its professors an extraordinarily brilliant group of scholars. Those formerly on the staff of St Sergius include Archpriest Sergius Bulgakov (1871–1944), the first rector; Bishop Cassian (1892–1965), his successor; Anton Kartashev (1875–1960); George P. Fedotov (1886–1951); and Paul Evdokimov (1901–70). Among its professors at present are Constantin Andronikoff, Fr Boris Bobrinskoy, and the French Orthodox writer Olivier Clément.

DIASPORA AND MISSION

Three members of St Sergius, Fathers Georges Florovsky, Alexander Schmemann (1921–83) and John Meyendorff (1926–92), moved to America, where they played a decisive role in the development of American Orthodoxy. A list of books and articles published by teachers at the Institute between 1925 and 1947 runs to ninety-two pages, and includes seventy full-scale books – a remarkable achievement, rivalled by the staffs of few theological academies (however large) in any Church. St Sergius is also noted for its choir, which has done much to revive the use of the ancient ecclesiastical chants of Russia. Almost entirely Russian between the two wars, the Institute now attracts students of many other nationalities, and the teaching is given mainly in French. There are at present more than fifty full-time students, and about 400 others who are following correspondence courses.

The Moscow Patriarchate has also made a distinguished contribution to Orthodox life in western Europe. Among its theologians have been Vladimir Lossky (1903–58), Archbishop Basil (Krivocheine) of Brussels (1900–85), and Archbishop Alexis (van der Mensbrugghe) (1899–1980) (originally a Roman Catholic). Nicholas Lossky, the son of Vladimir, is an expert on the seventeenth-century theologian Lancelot Andrewes, in whose thinking he has discerned striking Orthodox affinities.[1] Leonid Ouspensky (1902–87) was widely influential both as an iconographer and as a writer on the theology of the icon, while the monk-iconographer Gregory Kroug (1909–69) has shown through his work how a loyalty to iconographic tradition can be combined with a wide measure of artistic creativity.[2] In Great Britain the head of the Moscow Patriarchal diocese, Metropolitan Anthony (Bloom) of Sourozh, is much respected as a teacher on prayer. His diocese has taken the lead in Britain in using the English language at services, and at its annual diocesan conference there is an unusually close collaboration between clergy and laity.

1. See his book *Lancelot Andrewes the Preacher (1555–1626): The Origins of the Mystical Theology of the Church of England* (Oxford 1991).
2. See Andrew Tregubov, *The Light of Christ: Iconography of Gregory Kroug* (New York 1990).

179

Western Orthodoxy has so far produced few composers of religious music, but there is at least one notable exception, the British convert John Tavener. Well known initially for his secular music, he now confines himself exclusively to religious themes, experimenting creatively with the traditional eight tones of Byzantine hymnography and with ancient Russian chant, which he transposes into an idiom that is timeless yet contemporary. Summing up his approach to his work, he has observed, 'I would say that the *dictum* for all sacred Christian art must be as St Paul expressed it in another context: "It is not I who live, but Christ in me".'

Orthodoxy in Great Britain is particularly blessed by the presence of a growing monastic community, with both monks and nuns, at Tolleshunt Knights, Essex (Ecumenical Patriarchate), founded by Archimandrite Sophrony, disciple of St Silouan of Athos. Here a central place is given to the Jesus Prayer. The monastery is widely visited by pilgrims, especially Greek Cypriots, who comprise the great majority of Orthodox in Britain. In France there are two well-established monasteries for women, at Provement, Normandy (ROCOR), and at Bussy-en-Othe, Yonne (Ecumenical Patriarchate). Archimandrite Placide (Deseille) (a former Roman Catholic) has founded two communities, one for women and one for men, at St Laurent-en-Royans; these depend on the Athonite house of Simonos Petras.

A highly distinctive Orthodox figure in western Europe was the Frenchman Archimandrite Lev (Gillet) (1893–1980), the 'Monk of the Eastern Church', to use the name under which most of his books were published. At first a Catholic priest of the Eastern rite, he was received into Orthodoxy in 1928, and in later life served in London as chaplain to the Fellowship of St Alban and St Sergius.[1] He has expressed, better than most, the paradox of the Orthodox Church in the twentieth century:

O strange Orthodox Church, so poor and so weak, at the same time so traditional and yet so free, so archaic and yet so alive, so ritualistic and yet so personally mystical, Church where the pearl of great price

1. See p. 318.

of the Gospel is preciously preserved, sometimes beneath a layer of dust – Church that has so often proved incapable of action, yet which knows, as does no other, how to sing the joy of Easter.[1]

In North America (the USA and Canada) there are more than three million Orthodox, with over forty bishops and around 2,250 parishes subdivided into at least fifteen different jurisdictions. The Russians, as we have seen, were the first Orthodox arrivals on the American continent. In 1794 an ecclesiastical mission was established in Alaska – part of the Russian Empire until 1867 – by a group of monks from the Russian monastery of Valamo on Lake Ladoga. One of its members, St Herman (died 1836), the hermit of Spruce Island, came to be especially loved by the native people. Missionary work in Alaska was placed for the first time on a firm basis by St Innocent (Veniaminov), who worked in Alaska from 1824 until 1853, first as priest and then as bishop. He took a close and sympathetic interest in the native customs and beliefs, and his writings in this field remain a primary source for modern ethnography. Following the tradition of St Cyril and St Methodius, he was quick to translate the Gospels and the Liturgy into Aleutian. He sought to build up a native priesthood, opening a seminary at Sitka in 1845. A man of great physical strength, an indefatigable traveller, he undertook year-long missionary journeys of extreme hardship to the more remote islands, often travelling through heavy seas in a frail native boat, 'with not a single plank to save you from death – just skins', as he put it.

Meanwhile, as the nineteenth century proceeded, large numbers of Orthodox immigrants – Greek, Slav, Romanian, Arab – began to settle on the eastern seaboard of America and to move gradually westwards. In 1891 and the years following, many Eastern-rite Catholics, led by St Alexis Tóth (1854–1909), joined the Russian Orthodox archdiocese, chiefly because the Roman Catholic hierarchy refused to allow them to retain married priests. Under St Tikhon, the future Patriarch of Moscow, who was in North America for nine years (1898–1907), the

1. Quoted in Elisabeth Behr-Sigel, *Lev Gillet, 'Un Moine de l'Eglise d'Orient'* (Paris 1993), p. 173.

Russian archdiocese began to assume an increasingly multi-national character, and in 1904 a Syrian, Raphael (Hawaweeny), was consecrated as one of his assistant bishops, to minister to the Arab Orthodox. Tikhon encouraged the use of English in services and promoted the publication of English translations, in particular the well-known *Service Book* prepared by I. F. Hapgood.

Up to the end of the First World War, the Russian arch-diocese was the only organized Orthodox presence in North America, and most Orthodox parishes, whatever their ethnic character, looked to the Russian archbishop and his suffragans for pastoral care. Although this arrangement was never formally accepted by the Ecumenical Patriarchate and the Church of Greece, canonical and organizational unity existed *de facto*. But after the 1917 revolution a time of grave confusion ensued. The Russians became divided into conflicting groups, although the majority remained within the Metropolia.[1] A separate Greek Orthodox archdiocese was set up in 1922, and in due course the other national groups followed suit by establishing dioceses of their own. So there arose the present multiplicity of 'jurisdictions', a situation as bewildering to the American Ortho-dox themselves as it is to outside observers.

The largest Orthodox group in North America today is the Greek Archdiocese, with around 475 parishes. Crippled by internal schisms in the 1920s, it was reorganized and unified by Athenagoras, Archbishop during 1931–48 and later Ecumenical Patriarch. Archbishop Iakovos, head of the Archdiocese during 1959–96, has done more than any other single person to make Orthodoxy known and respected by the American public at large. Next in size after the Greek Archdiocese is the OCA, the former Russian Metropolia, now multi-national in character, with English as the main liturgical language and with many convert clergy. The third largest body is the Antiochian Archdiocese (within the Patriarchate of Antioch), under the dynamic leadership of Metropolitan Philip. In 1986 he received into Orthodoxy a group of former Protestants, the 'Evangelical Orthodox Church', headed by Peter Gillquist.

1. See above, pp. 177–8.

In Canada, the most numerous Orthodox community is that of the Ukrainians: canonically isolated for many years, in 1991 they were received into the Ecumenical Patriarchate.

The Orthodox in America have ten theological schools, of which the best known are St Vladimir's, at Crestwood, outside New York (OCA), and Holy Cross, at Brookline, Boston (Greek Archdiocese). The first of these issues *St Vladimir's Theological Quarterly*, while the second produces *The Greek Orthodox Theological Review*. Orthodox theologians at work in North America today include Archbishop Peter (l'Huillier) (OCA), Fr Thomas Hopko, Fr John Breck and John Erickson (St Vladimir's), Fr Joseph Allen (Antiochian Archdiocese), Bishop Maximos of Pittsburg (Greek Archdiocese) and Fr Stanley Harakas (Holy Cross). Orthodox monasticism has found North America on the whole a stony terrain: if St Theodore of Stoudios was right to say, 'Monastics are the sinews and foundations of the Church',[1] the American Orthodox scene leaves room for some disquiet. Monastic life is strongest in ROCOR, where the leading monastery is Holy Trinity, Jordanville, NY (with a seminary attached). The OCA has a long-established monastery, St Tikhon's, South Canaan, PA (also with a seminary). In the Greek Archdiocese during the early 1990s over ten small communities – mainly for women – were established by Fr Ephraim, formerly Abbot of Philotheou (Athos).

The Orthodox emigration in Australia is of more recent date than the North American diaspora, and most Australian Orthodox parishes have been founded since the Second World War. The Greek Archdiocese is the largest body, with over 121 parishes and a recently opened theological college in Sydney. There are also many Russian parishes (belonging mainly to ROCOR) and a significant Arab presence (under the Patriarchate of Antioch).

Two basic problems confront the Orthodox diaspora. There is, first of all, the transition from a first generation of Orthodox immigrants to a second generation of Orthodox born and

1. *Little Catecheses* 114: ed. J. Cozza-Luzi, *Nova Patrum Bibliotheca* 9 (Rome 1888), p. 266.

brought up in the west. The first generation of immigrants, even if not always active in practising their faith, will in most cases retain until death the sense that they are Orthodox Christians. But what of the second generation? Will they remain faithful to their Orthodox inheritance, or will they grow indifferent and become assimilated to the secular western society around them? In North America, where a high proportion of the immigrants arrived before the First World War, most Orthodox groups have already passed through this crucial cultural transition from the first generation to the second; the losses have been immense, yet Orthodoxy has survived. But in western Europe and Australia the bulk of the immigrants arrived only after the Second World War, and the transition is by no means complete.

In effecting the transition, it is vitally important that all Orthodox groups should draw their future clergy from young Orthodox born and trained in the west, rather than importing priests 'ready-made' from the mother country. It is still more important that the local language – English, French, German and so on – should be widely used in liturgical worship. Otherwise the young people will drift away, alienated by a Church that seems more concerned with maintaining the culture and language of the 'old country' than with preaching the Christian faith. Unfortunately the Orthodox authorities in the west, anxious to preserve their national heritage, have usually been slow to introduce the local vernacular into their Church services. In North America, English has now come to be widely employed, alike in the OCA, in the Antiochian Archdiocese, and in many Greek parishes. But in Britain most of the Greek parishes use as yet virtually no English at all.

The second obvious problem facing the diaspora is its fragmentation into separate jurisdictions. However understandable this may be from the historical point of view, it is doing grievous harm both to the pastoral work of the Orthodox Church among its own members in the west, and also to the witness of western Orthodoxy before the outside world. With increasing frustration, both laity and clergy are asking: When shall we be *visibly* one? How can we testify more effectively to the *universality* of Orthodoxy? A small beginning has been made through the establishment of episcopal committees in most western countries (although not yet in Great Britain). In the American continent, for example, the Standing Conference of Canonical Orthodox Bishops in the Americas (SCOBA) was founded in 1960, but so far it has failed to contribute as positively to Orthodox unity as was originally hoped. At the local level, throughout the USA there are active Orthodox Christian Fellowships, involving both clergy and laity, which seek to build up friendship and co-operation across jurisdictional boundaries. Similar work is being done in France by the Fraternité Orthodoxe, and in Britain by the Orthodox Fellowship of St John the Baptist. The potential contribution of such grassroots organizations is very great; for Orthodox unity in the west, when eventually realized, will probably come not so much from above, through the decisions of pan-Orthodox conferences, as from below, through the mutual love and the holy impatience of the people of God.

There is one further aspect of western Orthodoxy which calls for special mention: the existence, albeit limited and tentative, of an Orthodoxy of the Western rite (equivalent to Eastern-rite Catholicism, but in reverse). In the first millennium of Christian history, before the schism between west and east, the west used its own Liturgies, different from the Byzantine rite, yet fully Orthodox. People often talk about 'the Orthodox Liturgy', when what in fact they mean is the *Byzantine* Liturgy. But we should not speak as if that alone were Orthodox, for the ancient Roman, Gallican, Celtic and Mozarabic Liturgies, dating back to the pre-schism era, also have their place in the fullness of Orthodoxy. Western-rite Orthodox parishes exist both in the USA, within the Antiochian Archdiocese (with a membership of about 10,000), and in France, where there is a very active group known as the Catholic-Orthodox Church of France. The origins of this last extend back to 1937, when a former Roman Catholic priest, Louis-Charles Winnaert (1880–1937), who had received episcopal consecration in the Liberal Catholic Church, was received at Paris with his followers into the Moscow

Patriarchate.[1] By special decision of the Patriarchal *locum tenens*, Metropolitan Sergius, they were allowed to continue using the Western rite. Winnaert's successor, Fr Evgraph Kovalevsky (1905–70) – consecrated in 1964 as Bishop Jean de St-Denys – devised a Liturgy based on the ancient Gallican rite, but incorporating Byzantine elements. Under its present leader, Bishop Germain, this French movement has ceased to be in communion with other Orthodox Churches, and its future is problematic. Since 1995 there have been some Western-rite parishes in Britain, under the Patriarchate of Antioch.

A small minority in an alien environment, the Orthodox of the diaspora have often found it a hard struggle simply to survive. But some of them, at any rate, realize that besides mere survival they have a greater challenge to meet. If they really believe Orthodoxy to be the true Catholic faith, then they should not cut themselves off from the non-Orthodox majority around them, but as a duty and privilege they should share their Orthodoxy with others. It is surely not by chance that God has allowed Orthodox to be scattered throughout the west in the twentieth century. This dispersal, so far from being fortuitous and tragic, constitutes on the contrary our *kairos*, our moment of opportunity. But if we are to respond as we should to this *kairos*, we Orthodox need both to understand and to listen: to understand more profoundly our own Orthodox inheritance, and to listen more humbly to what is being said by our western contemporaries, both religious and secular.

It is not only in the diaspora that Orthodoxy suffers from a lack of reciprocal contacts. For a long time all the different Patriarchates and autocephalous Churches, often through no fault of their own, have been far too isolated from one another. At times the only formal contact has been the regular exchange of letters between the heads of the Churches. Today this isolation still continues, but there is a growing desire for much closer co-operation. Orthodox participation in the World

1. When Winnaert was received, it was specified that he should officiate only as a priest; the validity of his episcopal consecration by the Liberal Catholics was deemed doubtful.

Council of Churches has played its part here: at the great gatherings of the World Council of Churches, the Orthodox delegates have often found themselves ill-prepared to speak with a united voice. Why, they have asked, does it require the World Council to bring us Orthodox together? Why do we ourselves never meet to discuss our common problems? The urgent need for pan-Orthodox co-operation has been felt particularly by youth movements, and here valuable work has been done by Syndesmos, the international youth organization founded in 1953.

In the attempts at co-operation a leading part is naturally played by the senior hierarch of the Orthodox Church, the Ecumenical Patriarch. After the First World War the Patriarchate of Constantinople contemplated gathering a 'Great Council' of the whole Orthodox Church; and, as a first step towards this, plans were made for a 'Pro-Synod' which was to prepare the agenda for the council. A preliminary Inter-Orthodox Committee met on Mount Athos in 1930, but the Pro-Synod itself never materialized, largely owing to obstruction by the Turkish government. Around 1950 the Ecumenical Patriarch Athenagoras revived the idea, and after repeated postponements a 'Pan-Orthodox Conference' eventually met at Rhodes in September 1961. There were further Rhodes conferences in 1963 and 1964, and since then inter-Orthodox conferences and committees have been meeting regularly in Geneva. The chief items on the agenda of the 'Great and Holy Council', when and if it eventually meets, will probably be the problems of Orthodox disunity in the diaspora, the relations of Orthodoxy with other Christian Churches (ecumenism), and the application of Orthodox moral teaching in the modern world.

MISSIONS

Orthodoxy has often been criticized for failing to be a missionary Church, and there is truth in the charge. Yet if we reflect on the conversion of the Slavs by Cyril and Methodius and their disciples, it has to be acknowledged that Byzantium can claim missionary achievements in no way inferior to those of

Celtic or Roman Christianity during the same period. The Greeks and Arabs under Turkish rule were, of course, precluded from doing any missionary work, but the Russian Church in the nineteenth century maintained a wide range of missions among the many non-Christian nationalities within the Russian Empire.[1] The whole of this missionary programme was suppressed under Communism, but it is now being resumed on a limited scale.

Russian missions before 1917 extended also outside Russia, not only to Alaska (of which we have already spoken), but also to China, Japan and Korea. One of the concerns of the Russian missionaries, wherever they went, was to establish a native clergy as soon as possible. The origins of the Chinese mission extend back to the late seventeenth century, although systematic work did not develop until the late nineteenth century. About 400 Chinese Orthodox suffered martyrdom in the Boxer Rebellion (1901). In 1957, when the Chinese Orthodox Church became autonomous, there were two Chinese bishops, with perhaps 20,000 faithful, but repression by the 'Red Guards' in 1966 drove Chinese Orthodoxy almost entirely underground. Today the Liturgy is celebrated in several places by elderly Chinese priests, but there are no surviving bishops and few remaining faithful.

The Japanese Orthodox Church was founded by St Nicolas (Kassatkin) (1836–1912), one of the greatest missionaries of modern times in any Christian community. Sent to Hakodate in 1861 as chaplain to the Russian consulate, he decided from the start to devote himself to preaching the Christian faith among the Japanese, even though at that time missionary work was strictly forbidden by the Japanese laws. He baptized his first converts in 1868, and the first Japanese clergy were ordained in 1875. When he died in 1912, there were 266 congregations, with a membership of 33,017, served by thirty-five Japanese priests and twenty-two deacons. Losses were suffered in the inter-war period, but today there are about 25,000 faith-

1. See pp. 122–3.

ful, with one bishop and about forty priests. The present head, Metropolitan Theodosius (elected 1972), was originally a Buddhist; in common with all his clergy he is Japanese. The Church of Japan is autonomous, under the spiritual care of its mother Church, the Church of Russia.

The Korean mission, founded by Russian clergy in 1898, almost came to an end in the 1950s, but it has revived in the last fifteen years under the leadership of a Greek priest, Archimandrite Sotirios (Trambas), consecrated bishop in 1993. There are now over five parishes, a seminary and a monastery. In the 1980s, under the auspices of the Ecumenical Patriarchate, missionary work was also started in Indonesia, the Philippines, Hong Kong and South Bengal (India).

Besides these Orthodox missions in Asia, there is also an exceedingly lively African Orthodox Church in Kenya, Uganda and Tanzania. Indigenous from the start, African Orthodoxy did not arise through the preaching of missionaries from the traditional Orthodox lands, but was a spontaneous movement among Africans themselves. The founders of the African Orthodox movement were two native Ugandans, Rauben Sebanja Mukasa Spartas (born 1899, bishop 1972, died 1982) and his friend Obadiah Kabanda Basajjakitalo. Originally brought up as Anglicans, they were converted to Orthodoxy in the 1920s, not as a result of personal contact with other Orthodox, but through their own reading and study. At first the canonical position of Ugandan Orthodoxy was in some doubt, as originally Rauben and Obadiah established contact with an organization emanating from the USA, the 'African Orthodox Church', which, though using the title 'Orthodox', has in fact no connection with the true and historical Orthodox communion. In 1932 they were both ordained by a certain Archbishop Alexander of this Church, but towards the end of that same year they became aware of the questionable status of the 'African Orthodox Church', whereupon they severed all relations with it and approached the Patriarchate of Alexandria. But only in 1946, when Rauben visited Alexandria in person, did the Patriarch formally recognize the African Orthodox community in Uganda, and definitely take it under his care.

Rauben and Obadiah preached their new-found faith with great enthusiasm to their fellow Africans, and the movement expanded rapidly. One reason was that the Orthodox mission, while condemning polygamy, was in practice less strict than the European missions in its treatment of those who had already contracted polygamous marriages. Political factors were also involved: before Kenya gained its independence in 1959, the Kenyan Orthodox were closely linked with African liberation movements such as Mau Mau. One of the obvious attractions of Orthodox Christianity in African eyes was its freedom from colonial links.[1] Following independence, much of the support for the Orthodox mission fell away. But more recently African Orthodoxy has become better organized and has begun once more to grow. Some observers reckon the number of Orthodox in Kenya at between 70,000 and 250,000, and in Uganda at 30,000; but Greek Orthodox sources often quote a much lower figure of around 40,000 native Orthodox in the whole of East Africa. At present there is an African bishop in Kampala (Uganda), Theodore Nankyamas, a graduate of Athens University. In 1992 there were nineteen native clergy in Uganda, sixty-one in Kenya, and seven in Tanzania. The Orthodox theological school at Nairobi, founded in 1982, has about fifty students.

The spontaneous growth of African Orthodoxy has had a significant effect on the Greek Orthodox both in Greece itself and in North America, making them much more directly aware of the missionary dimension of the Church. The visits of Rauben Spartas to Greece in 1959 and of Theodore Nankyamas to the USA in 1965 proved widely influential, with many parishes – and, more especially, youth groups – pledging themselves to prayer and financial help. It could be argued that the African Orthodox have in this way given to Greek Orthodoxy more than they have received.

Every Christian body is today confronted by grave problems, but the Orthodox have perhaps greater difficulties to face than

1. On the background here, see F. B. Welbourn, *East African Rebels* (London 1961).

most. In contemporary Orthodoxy it is not always easy 'to recognize victory beneath the outward appearance of failure, to discern the power of God fulfilling itself in weakness, the true Church within the historic reality'.[1] But if there are obvious weaknesses, there are also many signs of life. Whatever the compromises of Church leaders under Communist rule, Orthodoxy also produced countless martyrs and confessors. In the highly unstable situation following the demise of Communism, there are reasons not only for unease but for great hope. The decline of Orthodox monasticism has been dramatically reversed on the Holy Mountain, and Athos will perhaps prove the source of a wider monastic resurrection. The spiritual treasures of Orthodoxy – for example, the *Philokalia* and the Jesus Prayer – so far from being forgotten, are used and appreciated more and more. Orthodox theologians are few in number, but some of them, often under the stimulus of western contacts, are rediscovering forgotten yet vital elements in their theological inheritance. A short-sighted nationalism is hindering the Church in its work, but there are sporadic attempts at co-operation. Missions are still on a very small scale, but Orthodoxy is showing a growing awareness of their importance. We Orthodox, if we are realistic and honest, can scarcely feel complacent or triumphalist about the present state of our Church. Yet, despite its many problems and manifest human shortcomings, Orthodoxy can at the same time look to the future with confidence and sober optimism.

1. V. Lossky, *The Mystical Theology of the Eastern Church*, p. 246.

Part Two
FAITH AND WORSHIP

CHAPTER 10

Holy Tradition:
The Source of the Orthodox Faith

Guard the deposit. *I Timothy vi, 20*

Tradition is the life of the Holy Spirit in the Church.
Vladimir Lossky

THE INNER MEANING OF TRADITION

Orthodox history is marked outwardly by a series of sudden breaks: the capture of Alexandria, Antioch, and Jerusalem by Arab Muslims; the burning of Kiev by the Mongols; the two sacks of Constantinople; the October Revolution in Russia. Yet these events, while they have transformed the external appearance of the Orthodox world, have never broken the inward continuity of the Orthodox Church. The thing that first strikes a stranger on encountering Orthodoxy is usually its air of antiquity, its apparent changelessness. Orthodox still baptize by threefold immersion, as in the primitive Church; they still bring babies and small children to receive Holy Communion; in the Liturgy the deacon still cries out: 'The doors! The doors!' – recalling the early days when the church's entrance was jealously guarded, and none but members of the Christian family could attend the family worship; the Creed is still recited without any additions.

These are but a few outward examples of something which pervades every aspect of Orthodox life. When Orthodox are asked at contemporary inter-Church gatherings to sum up what they see as the distinctive characteristic of their Church,[1] they often point precisely to its changelessness, its determination to

1. See, for example, Panagiotis Bratsiotis and Georges Florovsky, in *Orthodoxy: A Faith and Order Dialogue* (Geneva 1960).

remain loyal to the past, its sense of *living continuity* with the Church of ancient times. At the start of the eighteenth century, in words that recall the language of the Ecumenical Councils, the Eastern Patriarchs said exactly the same to the Non-Jurors:

We preserve the Doctrine of the Lord uncorrupted, and firmly adhere to the Faith He delivered to us, and keep it free from blemish and diminution, as a Royal Treasure, and a monument of great price, *neither adding any thing, nor taking any thing from it.*[1]

This idea of living continuity is summed up for the Orthodox in the one word *Tradition*. 'We do not change the everlasting boundaries which our fathers have set,' wrote John of Damascus, 'but *we keep the Tradition, just as we received it.*'[2]

Orthodox are always talking about Tradition. What do they mean by the word? A tradition is commonly understood to signify an opinion, belief or custom handed down from ancestors to posterity. Christian Tradition, in that case, is the faith and practice which Jesus Christ imparted to the Apostles, and which since the Apostles' time has been handed down from generation to generation in the Church.[3] But to an Orthodox Christian, Tradition means something more concrete and specific than this. It means the books of the Bible; it means the Creed; it means the decrees of the Ecumenical Councils and the writings of the Fathers; it means the Canons, the Service Books, the Holy Icons – in fact, the whole system of doctrine, Church government, worship, spirituality and art which Orthodoxy has articulated over the ages. Orthodox Christians of today see themselves as heirs and guardians to a rich inheritance received from the past, and they believe that it is their duty to transmit this inheritance unimpaired to the future.

Note that the Bible forms a part of Tradition. Sometimes Tradition is defined as the oral teaching of Christ, not recorded in writing by His immediate disciples. Not only non-Orthodox

1. Letter of 1718, in G. Williams, *The Orthodox Church of the East in the Eighteenth Century*, p. 17.
2. *On Icons*, 11, 12 (*P.G.* xciv, 1297B).
3. Compare Paul in 1 Corinthians xv, 3.

but many Orthodox writers have adopted this way of speaking, treating Scripture and Tradition as two different things, two distinct sources of the Christian faith. But in reality there is only one source, since Scripture exists *within* Tradition. To separate and contrast the two is to impoverish the idea of both alike.

Orthodox, while reverencing this inheritance from the past, are also well aware that not everything received from the past is of equal value. Among the various elements of Tradition, a unique pre-eminence belongs to the Bible, to the Creed, to the doctrinal definitions of the Ecumenical Councils: these things the Orthodox accept as something absolute and unchanging, something which cannot be cancelled or revised. The other parts of Tradition do not have quite the same authority. The decrees of Jassy or Jerusalem do not stand on the same level as the Nicene Creed, nor do the writings of an Athanasius, or a Symeon the New Theologian, occupy the same position as the Gospel of St John.

Not everything received from the past is of equal value, nor is everything received from the past necessarily true. As one of the bishops remarked at the Council of Carthage in 257: 'The Lord said, I am truth. He did not say, I am custom.'[1] There is a difference between 'Tradition' and 'traditions': many traditions which the past has handed down are human and accidental – pious opinions (or worse), but not a true part of the one Tradition, the fundamental Christian message.

It is absolutely essential to question the past. In Byzantine and post-Byzantine times, Orthodox have often been far too uncritical in their attitude to the past, and the result has been stagnation. Today this uncritical attitude can no longer be maintained. Higher standards of scholarship, increasing contacts with western Christians, the inroads of secularism and atheism, have forced Orthodox in this present century to look more closely at their inheritance and to distinguish more carefully between Tradition and traditions. The task of discrimination is never easy. It is necessary to avoid alike the error of the Old Believers and the error of the 'Living Church': the one

1. *The Opinions of the Bishops on the Baptizing of Heretics*, 30.

party fell into an extreme conservatism which suffered no change whatever in traditions, the other into spiritual compromises which undermined Tradition. Yet despite certain manifest handicaps, the Orthodox of today are perhaps in a better position to discriminate aright than their predecessors have been for many centuries; and often it is precisely their contact with the west which is helping them to see more and more clearly what is indispensable in their own inheritance.

True Orthodox fidelity to the past must always be a *creative* fidelity; for true Orthodoxy can never rest satisfied with a barren 'theology of repetition', which, parrot-like, repeats accepted formulae without striving to understand what lies behind them. Loyalty to Tradition, properly understood, is not something mechanical, a passive and automatic process of transmitting the accepted wisdom of an era in the distant past. An Orthodox thinker must see Tradition *from within*, he must enter into its inner spirit, he must re-experience the meaning of Tradition in a manner that is exploratory, courageous, and full of imaginative creativity. In order to live within Tradition, it is not enough simply to give intellectual assent to a system of doctrine; for Tradition is far more than a set of abstract propositions – it is a life, a personal encounter with Christ in the Holy Spirit. Tradition is not only kept by the Church – it lives in the Church, it is the life of the Holy Spirit in the Church. The Orthodox conception of Tradition is not static but dynamic, not a dead acceptance of the past but a living discovery of the Holy Spirit in the present. Tradition, while inwardly changeless (for God does not change), is constantly assuming new forms, which supplement the old without superseding them. Orthodox often speak as if the period of doctrinal formulation were wholly at an end, yet this is not the case. Perhaps in our own day new Ecumenical Councils will meet, and Tradition will be enriched by fresh statements of the faith.

This idea of Tradition as a living thing has been well expressed by Georges Florovsky:

Tradition is the witness of the Spirit; the Spirit's unceasing revelation and preaching of good tidings ... To accept and understand

Tradition we must live within the Church, we must be conscious of the grace-giving presence of the Lord in it; we must feel the breath of the Holy Ghost in it ... Tradition is not only a protective, conservative principle; it is, primarily, the principle of growth and regeneration ... Tradition is the constant abiding of the Spirit and not only the memory of words.[1]

Tradition is the witness of the Spirit: in the words of Christ, 'When the Spirit of truth has come, He will guide you into all truth' (John xvi, 13). It is this divine promise that forms the basis of the Orthodox devotion to Tradition.

THE OUTWARD FORMS

Let us take in turn the different outward forms in which Tradition is expressed:

(1)   *The Bible*

(a)   *The Bible and the Church.* The Christian Church is a Scriptural Church: Orthodoxy believes this just as firmly, if not more firmly, than Protestantism. The Bible is the supreme expression of God's revelation to the human race, and Christians must always be 'People of the Book'. But if Christians are People of the Book, the Bible is the Book of the People; it must not be regarded as something set up *over* the Church, but as something that lives and is understood *within* the Church (that is why one should not separate Scripture and Tradition). It is from the Church that the Bible ultimately derives its authority, for it was the Church which originally decided which books form a part of Holy Scripture; and it is the Church alone which can interpret Holy Scripture with authority. There are many sayings in the Bible which by themselves are far from clear, and individual readers, however sincere, are in danger of error if they trust their own personal interpretation. 'Do you

1. 'The Catholicity of the Church', in *Bible, Church, Tradition*, pp. 46–7. Compare also his essay, 'Saint Gregory Palamas and the Tradition of the Fathers', in the same volume, pp. 105–20; and V. Lossky, 'Tradition and Traditions', in Ouspensky and Lossky, *The Meaning of Icons*, pp. 13–24. To all three of these essays I am heavily indebted.

understand what you are reading?' Philip asked the Ethiopian eunuch; and the eunuch replied, 'How can I, unless someone guides me?' (Acts viii, 30–1). Orthodox, when they read the Scripture, accept the guidance of the Church. When received into the Orthodox Church, a convert promises, 'I will accept and understand Holy Scripture in accordance with the interpretation which was and is held by the Holy Orthodox Catholic Church of the East, our Mother.'

(b) *The Text of the Bible: Biblical Criticism.* The Orthodox Church has the same New Testament as the rest of Christendom. As its authoritative text for the Old Testament, it uses the ancient Greek translation known as the Septuagint. When this differs from the original Hebrew (which happens quite often), Orthodox believe that the changes in the Septuagint were made under the inspiration of the Holy Spirit, and are to be accepted as part of God's continuing revelation. The best-known instance is Isaiah vii, 14 – where the Hebrew says 'A *young woman* shall conceive and bear a son', which the Septuagint translates 'A *virgin* shall conceive', etc. The New Testament follows the Septuagint text (Matthew i, 23).

The Hebrew version of the Old Testament contains thirty-nine books. The Septuagint contains in addition ten further books, not present in the Hebrew, which are known in the Orthodox Church as the 'Deutero-Canonical Books'.[1] These were declared by the Councils of Jassy (1642) and Jerusalem (1672) to be 'genuine parts of Scripture'; most Orthodox scholars at the present day, however, following the opinion of Athanasius and Jerome, consider that the Deutero-Canonical Books, although part of the Bible, stand on a lower footing than the rest of the Old Testament.

1. In the west the Deutero-Canonical Books are commonly termed 'The Apocrypha'. The works in question are 1 (*alias* 3) Esdras; Tobit; Judith; 1, 2 and 3 Maccabees; The Wisdom of Solomon; Ecclesiasticus (*alias* Sirach); Baruch; the Letter of Jeremias. Some Orthodox editions of the Bible also contain 4 Maccabees. These works can all be found in English translation in *The New Oxford Annotated Bible with the Apocrypha, Expanded Edition: Revised Standard Version*, ed. Herbert G. May and Bruce M. Metzger (New York 1977).

Christianity, if true, has nothing to fear from honest inquiry. Orthodoxy, while regarding the Church as the authoritative interpreter of Scripture, does not forbid the critical and historical study of the Bible, although hitherto Orthodox scholars have not been prominent in this field.

(c) *The Bible in worship.* It is sometimes thought that Orthodox attach less importance than western Christians to the Bible. Yet in fact Holy Scripture is read constantly at Orthodox services: during the course of Matins and Vespers the entire Psalter is recited each week, and in Lent twice a week;[1] Old Testament readings occur at Vespers on the eves of many feasts, and at the Sixth Hour and Vespers on weekdays in Lent (but it is a pity that there is no Old Testament reading at the Liturgy); the reading of the Gospel forms the climax of Matins on Sundays and feasts; at the Liturgy a special Epistle and Gospel are assigned for each day of the year, so that the whole New Testament (except the Revelation of St John) is read at the Eucharist. The *Nunc Dimittis* is used at Vespers; Old Testament canticles, with the *Magnificat* and *Benedictus*, are sung at Matins; the Lord's Prayer is read at every service. Besides these specific extracts from Scripture, the whole text of each service is shot through with Biblical language, and it has been calculated that the Liturgy contains 98 quotations from the Old Testament and 114 from the New.[2]

Orthodoxy regards the Bible as a verbal icon of Christ, the seventh Ecumenical Council laying down that the Holy Icons and the Book of the Gospels should be venerated in the same way. In every church the Gospel Book has a place of honour on the altar; it is carried in procession at the Liturgy and at Matins on Sundays and feasts; the faithful kiss it and prostrate themselves before it. Such is the respect shown in the Orthodox Church for the Word of God.

1. Such is the rule laid down by the service books. In practice, in many parish churches Matins and Vespers are not recited daily, but only at weekends and on feasts; and even then, unfortunately, the portions appointed from the Psalter are often abbreviated or (worse still) omitted entirely.

2. P. Evdokimov, *L'Orthodoxie*, p. 241, note 96.

(2)   *The Seven Ecumenical Councils: The Creed*

The doctrinal definitions of an Ecumenical Council are infallible. Thus in the eyes of the Orthodox Church, the statements of faith put out by the seven councils possess, along with the Bible, an abiding and irrevocable authority.

The most important of all the Ecumenical statements of faith is the *Nicene-Constantinopolitan Creed*, which is read or sung at every celebration of the Eucharist, and also daily at the Midnight Office and at Compline. The other two Creeds used by the west, the *Apostles' Creed* and the *'Athanasian Creed'*, do not possess the same authority as the Nicene, because they have not been proclaimed by an Ecumenical Council. Orthodox honour the Apostles' Creed as an ancient statement of faith, and accept all its teaching; but it is simply a local western Baptismal Creed, never used in the services of the Eastern Patriarchates. The 'Athanasian Creed' likewise is not used in Orthodox worship, but it is sometimes printed (without the *Filioque*) in the *Horologion* (Book of Hours).

(3)   *Later Councils*

The formulation of Orthodox doctrine, as we have seen, did not cease with the seventh Ecumenical Council. Since 787 there have been two chief ways whereby the Church has expressed its mind: (1) definitions by local councils (that is, councils attended by members of one or more Patriarchates or autocephalous Churches, but not claiming to represent the Orthodox Catholic Church as a whole) and (2) letters or statements of faith put out by individual bishops. While the doctrinal decisions of general councils are infallible, those of a local council or an individual bishop are always liable to error; but if such decisions are accepted by the rest of the Church, then they come to acquire Ecumenical authority (i.e. a universal authority similar to that possessed by the doctrinal statements of an Ecumenical Council). The doctrinal decisions of an Ecumenical Council cannot be revised or corrected, but must be accepted in their entirety; but the Church has often been selective in its treatment of the acts of local councils: in the case of the seventeenth-century councils, for example, their statements of faith have in part been received by the whole Orthodox Church, but in part set aside or corrected.

The following are the chief Orthodox doctrinal statements since 787:

(i) The Encyclical Letter of St Photius (867).

(ii) The First Letter of Michael Cerularius to Peter of Antioch (1054).

(iii) The decisions of the Councils of Constantinople in 1341 and 1351 on the Hesychast Controversy.

(iv) The Encyclical Letter of St Mark of Ephesus (1440–1).

(v) The Confession of Faith by Gennadius, Patriarch of Constantinople (1455–6).

(vi) The Replies of Jeremias II to the Lutherans (1573–81).

(vii) The Confession of Faith by Metrophanes Kritopoulos (1625).

(viii) The Orthodox Confession by Peter of Moghila, in its revised form (ratified by the Council of Jassy, 1642).

(ix) The Confession of Dositheus (ratified by the Council of Jerusalem, 1672).

(x) The Answers of the Orthodox Patriarchs to the Non-Jurors (1718, 1723).

(xi) The Reply of the Orthodox Patriarchs to Pope Pius IX (1848).

(xii) The Reply of the Synod of Constantinople to Pope Leo XIII (1895).

(xiii) The Encyclical Letters by the Patriarchate of Constantinople on Christian unity and on the 'Ecumenical Movement' (1920, 1952).

These documents – particularly items v–ix – are sometimes called the 'Symbolical Books' of the Orthodox Church, but many Orthodox scholars today regard this title as misleading and do not use it.

(4) *The Fathers*

The definitions of the councils must be studied in the wider context of the Fathers. But as with local councils, so with the Fathers, the judgement of the Church is selective: individual writers have at times fallen into error and at times contradict one another. Patristic wheat needs to be distinguished from Patristic chaff. The Orthodox must not simply know and quote the Fathers; they must enter more deeply into the inner spirit of the Fathers and acquire a 'Patristic mind', and must treat the Fathers not merely as relics from the past, but as living witnesses and contemporaries.

The Orthodox Church has never attempted to define exactly who the Fathers are, still less to classify them in order of importance. But it has a particular reverence for the writers of the fourth century, and especially for those whom it terms 'the Three Great Hierarchs': Basil the Great, Gregory of Nazianzus (known in Orthodoxy as Gregory the Theologian), and John Chrysostom. In the eyes of Orthodoxy, the 'Age of the Fathers' did not come to an end in the fifth century, for many later writers are also 'Fathers' – Maximus, John of Damascus, Theodore of Stoudios, Symeon the New Theologian, Gregory Palamas, Mark of Ephesus. Indeed, it is dangerous to look on 'the Fathers' as a closed cycle of writings belonging wholly to the past, for might not our own age produce a new Basil or Athanasius? To say that there can be no more Fathers is to suggest that the Holy Spirit has deserted the Church.

(5) *The Liturgy*

The Orthodox Church is not as much given to making formal dogmatic definitions as is the Roman Catholic Church. But it would be false to conclude that because some belief has never been specifically proclaimed as a dogma by Orthodoxy, it is therefore not a part of Orthodox Tradition, but merely a matter of private opinion. Certain doctrines, never formally defined, are yet held by the Church with an unmistakable inner conviction, an unruffled unanimity, which is just as binding as an explicit formulation. 'Some things we have from written teaching,' said St Basil, 'others we have received from the Apostolic Tradition handed down to us in a mystery; and both these things have the same force for piety.'[1]

This inner Tradition 'handed down to us in a mystery' is preserved above all in the Church's worship. *Lex orandi lex credendi*: our faith is expressed in our prayer. Orthodoxy has made few explicit definitions about the Eucharist and the other Sacraments, about the next world, the Mother of God, the saints, and the faithful departed: our belief on these points is contained mainly in the prayers and hymns used at services. Nor is it merely the *words* of the services which are a part of Tradition; the various *gestures* and *actions* – immersion in the waters of Baptism, the different anointings with oil, the sign of the Cross, and so on – all have a special meaning, and all express in symbolical or dramatic form the truths of the faith.

(6) *Canon Law*

Besides doctrinal definitions, the Ecumenical Councils drew up *Canons*, dealing with Church organization and discipline; other Canons were made by local councils and by individual bishops. Theodore Balsamon, Zonaras, and other Byzantine writers compiled collections of Canons, with explanations and commentaries. The standard modern Greek commentary, the *Pedalion* ('Rudder'), published in 1800, is the work of that indefatigable saint, Nicodemus of the Holy Mountain.

The Canon Law of the Orthodox Church has been very little studied in the west, and as a result western writers sometimes fall into the mistake of regarding Orthodoxy as an organization with virtually no outward regulations. On the contrary, the life of Orthodoxy has many rules, often of great strictness and rigour. It must be confessed, however, that at the present day many of the Canons are difficult or impossible to apply, and have fallen widely into disuse. When and if a new general council of the Church is assembled, one of its chief tasks may well be the revision and clarification of Canon Law.

The doctrinal definitions of the councils possess an absolute

---

1. *On the Holy Spirit*, xxvii (66).

and unalterable validity which Canons as such cannot claim; for doctrinal definitions deal with eternal truths, Canons with the earthly life of the Church, where conditions are constantly changing and individual situations are infinitely various. Yet between the Canons and the dogmas of the Church there exists an essential connexion: Canon Law is simply the attempt to apply dogma to practical situations in the daily life of each Christian. Thus in a relative sense the Canons form a part of Holy Tradition.

(7) *Icons*

The Tradition of the Church is expressed not only through words, not only through the actions and gestures used in worship, but also through art – through the line and colour of the Holy Icons. An icon is not simply a religious picture designed to arouse appropriate emotions in the beholder; it is one of the ways whereby God is revealed to us. Through icons the Orthodox Christian receives a vision of the spiritual world. Because the icon is a part of Tradition, icon painters are not free to adapt or innovate as they please; for their work must reflect, not their own aesthetic sentiments, but the mind of the Church. Artistic inspiration is not excluded, but it is exercised within certain prescribed rules. It is important that icon painters should be good artists, but it is even more important that they should be sincere Christians, living within the spirit of Tradition, preparing themselves for their work by means of Confession and Holy Communion.

Such are the primary elements which from an outward point of view make up the Tradition of the Orthodox Church – Scripture, Councils, Fathers, Liturgy, Canons, Icons. These things are not to be separated and contrasted, for it is the same Holy Spirit which speaks through them all, and together they make up a single whole, each part being understood in the light of the rest.

It has sometimes been said that the underlying cause for the break-up of western Christendom in the sixteenth century was the separation between theology and mysticism, between liturgy and personal devotion, which existed in the later Middle Ages. Orthodoxy for its part has always tried to avoid any such division. All true Orthodox theology is mystical; just as mysticism divorced from theology becomes subjective and heretical, so theology, when it is not mystical, degenerates into an arid scholasticism, 'academic' in the bad sense of the word.

Theology, mysticism, spirituality, moral rules, worship, art: these things must not be kept in separate compartments. Doctrine cannot be understood unless it is prayed: a theologian, said Evagrius, is one who knows how to pray, and he who prays in spirit and in truth is by that very act a theologian.[1] And doctrine, if it is to be prayed, must also be lived: theology without action, as St Maximus put it, is the theology of demons.[2] The Creed belongs only to those who live it. Faith and love, theology and life, are inseparable. In the Byzantine Liturgy, the Creed is introduced with the words, 'Let us love one another, that with one mind we may confess Father, Son, and Holy Spirit, Trinity one in essence and undivided.' This exactly expresses the Orthodox attitude to Tradition. If we do not love one another, we cannot love God; and if we do not love God, we cannot make a true confession of faith and cannot enter into the inner spirit of Tradition, for there is no other way of knowing God than to love Him.

1. *On Prayer*, 60 (*P.G.* lxxix, 1180B).
2. *Letter* 20 (*P.G.* xci, 601C).

CHAPTER 11

God and Humankind

> In His unbounded love, God became what we are that He
> might makes us what He is.
>
> *St Irenaeus (died 202)*

GOD IN TRINITY

Our social programme, said the Russian thinker Feodorov, is
the dogma of the Trinity. Orthodoxy believes most passion-
ately that the doctrine of the Holy Trinity is not a piece of
'high theology' reserved for the professional scholar, but
something that has a living, *practical* importance for every
Christian. The human person, so the Bible teaches, is made
in the image of God, and to Christians God means the Trinity: thus it is only in the light of the dogma of the Trinity
that we can understand who we are and what God intends
us to be. Our private lives, our personal relations, and all
our plans of forming a Christian society depend upon a right
theology of the Trinity. 'Between the Trinity and Hell there
lies no other choice.'[1] As an Anglican writer put it, 'In this
doctrine is summed up the new way of thinking about God,
in the power of which the fishermen went out to convert the
Greco-Roman world. It marks a saving revolution in human
thought.'[2]

The basic elements in the Orthodox doctrine of God have
already been indicated in the first part of this book, so that
here they will only be summarized briefly:

(1) *God is absolutely transcendent.* 'No single thing of all that
is created has or ever will have even the slightest communion

1. V. Lossky, *The Mystical Theology of the Eastern Church*, p. 66.
2. D. J. Chitty, 'The Doctrine of the Holy Trinity told to the Children', in
Sobornost 4:5 (1961), p. 241.

with the supreme nature or nearness to it.'[1] This absolute transcendence Orthodoxy safeguards by its emphatic use of the 'way of negation', of 'apophatic' theology. Positive or 'cataphatic' theology – the 'way of affirmation' – must always be balanced and corrected by the employment of negative language. Our positive statements about God – that He is good, wise, just and so on – are true as far as they go, yet they cannot adequately describe the inner nature of the deity. These positive statements, said John of Damascus, reveal 'not the nature, but the things around nature'. '*That* there is a God is clear; but *what* He is by essence and nature, this is altogether beyond our comprehension and knowledge.'[2]

(2) *God, although absolutely transcendent, is not cut off from the world which He has made.* God is above and outside His creation, yet He also exists within it. As a much used Orthodox prayer puts it, God is 'everywhere present and filling all things'. Orthodoxy therefore distinguishes between God's essence and His energies, thus safeguarding both divine transcendence and divine immanence: God's essence remains unapproachable, but His energies come down to us. God's energies, *which are God Himself*, permeate all His creation, and we experience them in the form of deifying grace and divine light. Truly our God is a God who hides Himself, yet He is also a God who acts – the God of History, intervening directly in concrete situations.

(3) *God is personal, that is to say, Trinitarian.* This God who acts is not only a God of energies, but a personal God. When humans participate in the divine energies, they are not overwhelmed by some vague and nameless power, but they are brought face to face with a person. Nor is this all: God is not simply a single person confined within His own being, but a Trinity of three persons, Father, Son, and Holy Spirit, each of whom 'dwells' in the other two by virtue of a perpetual movement of love. God is not only a unity but a union.

1. Gregory Palamas, *P.G.* cl, 1176c (quoted on p. 68).
2. *On the Orthodox Faith*, 1, 4 (*P.G.* xciv, 800B, 797B).

(4) *Our God is an Incarnate God.* God has come down to humankind, not only through His energies, but in His own person. The Second Person of the Trinity, 'true God from true God', was made human: 'The word became flesh and dwelt among us' (John i, 14). A closer union than this between God and His creation there could not be. God Himself became one of His creatures.[1]

Those brought up in other traditions have sometimes found it difficult to accept the Orthodox emphasis on apophatic theology and the distinction between essence and energies; but apart from these two matters, Orthodox agree in their doctrine of God with the overwhelming majority of all who call themselves Christians. Non-Chalcedonians and Lutherans, members of the Church of the East and Roman Catholics, Calvinists, Anglicans, and Orthodox: all alike worship One God in Three Persons and confess Christ as Incarnate Son of God.[2]

Yet there is one point in the doctrine of God the Trinity over which east and west seem to part company – the *Filioque.* We have already seen how decisive a part this one word played in the unhappy fragmentation of Christendom. But granted that the *Filioque* is important historically, does it really matter from a theological point of view? Many people today – not excluding many Orthodox – find the whole dispute so technical and obscure that they are tempted to dismiss it as utterly trivial. From the viewpoint of traditional Orthodox theology there can be but one rejoinder to this: technical and obscure it undoubtedly is, like most questions of Trinitarian theology; but it is not trivial. Since belief in the Trinity lies at the very heart of the Christian faith, a tiny difference in Trinitarian theology may well have repercussions upon every aspect of Christian

1. For the first and second of these four points, see pp. 63–9; for the third and fourth points, see pp. 20–29.

2. In the past hundred years, under the influence of 'Modernism', many Protestants have virtually abandoned the doctrines of the Trinity and the Incarnation. Thus when I speak here of Calvinists, Lutherans, and Anglicans, I have in mind those who still respect the classical Protestant formularies of the sixteenth century.

life and thought. Let us try therefore to enter more deeply into some of the issues involved in the *Filioque* dispute.

One essence in three persons. God is one and God is three: the Holy Trinity is a mystery of unity in diversity, and of diversity in unity. Father, Son, and Spirit are 'one in essence' (*homoousios*), yet each is distinguished from the other two by personal characteristics. 'The divine is indivisible in its divisions',[1] for the persons are 'united yet not confused, distinct yet not divided';[2] 'both the distinction and the union alike are paradoxical'.[3]

The distinctive characteristic of the first person of the Trinity is Fatherhood: He is unbegotten, having His source and origin solely in Himself and not in any other person. The distinctive characteristic of the second person is Sonship: although equal to the Father and coeternal with Him, He is not unbegotten or sourceless, but has His source and origin in the Father, from whom He is begotten or born from all eternity – 'before all ages', as the Creed says. The distinctive characteristic of the third person is Procession: like the Son, He has His source and origin in the Father; but His relationship to the Father is different from that of the Son, since He is not begotten but from all eternity He *proceeds* from the Father.

It is precisely at this point that the western view of the Trinity seems to conflict with that of the east. According to Roman Catholic theology – as expressed, for example, by St Augustine of Hippo (360–430) or by the Council of Florence (1438–9) – the Holy Spirit proceeds eternally from the Father and the Son (*Filioque*). This doctrine is known as the 'Double Procession' of the Spirit. Now the Greek Fathers are willing on occasion to affirm that the Spirit proceeds from the Father *through* the Son – such language is found particularly in St Gregory of Nyssa – or that He proceeds from the Father and *rests upon* the Son; but the Christian east has almost always refused to say that the Spirit proceeds *from* the Son.

But what is meant by the term 'proceed'? Unless this is

1. Gregory of Nazianzus, *Orations*, xxxi, 14.
2. John of Damascus, *On the Orthodox Faith*, 1, 8 (*P.G.* xciv, 809A).
3. Gregory of Nazianzus, *Orations*, xxv, 17.

properly understood, nothing is understood. The Church believes that Christ underwent two births, the one eternal, the other at a particular point in time: He was born of the Father 'before all ages', and born of the Virgin Mary in the days of Herod, King of Judaea, and of Augustus, Emperor of Rome. In the same way a firm distinction must be drawn between the *eternal procession* of the Holy Spirit, and the *temporal mission*, the sending of the Spirit to the world: the one concerns the relations existing from all eternity within the Godhead, the other concerns the relation of God to creation. Thus when the west says that the Spirit proceeds from the Father and the Son, and when Orthodoxy says that He proceeds from the Father alone, both sides are referring not to the outward action of the Trinity towards creation, but to certain eternal relations within the Godhead – relations which existed before ever the world was. But Orthodoxy, while disagreeing with the west over the eternal procession of the Spirit, agrees with the west in saying that, so far as the mission of the Spirit to the world is concerned, He is sent by the Son, and is indeed the 'Spirit of the Son'.

The Orthodox position is based on John xv, 26, where Christ says: 'When the Comforter has come, whom *I will send to you* from the Father – the Spirit of truth, who *proceeds from the Father* – He will bear witness to Me.' Christ sends the Spirit, but the Spirit proceeds from the Father: so the Bible teaches, and so Orthodoxy believes. What Orthodoxy does not teach, and what the Bible does not actually say, is that the Spirit proceeds from the Son.

An eternal procession from Father and Son: such is the western position. An eternal procession of the Spirit from the Father alone, a temporal mission from the Son: such was the position upheld by St Photius against the west. But Byzantine writers of the thirteenth and fourteenth centuries – most notably Gregory of Cyprus, Patriarch of Constantinople from 1283 to 1289, and Gregory Palamas – went somewhat further than Photius, in an attempt to bridge the gulf between east and west. They were willing to allow not only a temporal mission but an *eternal manifestation* of the Holy Spirit by the Son.

While Photius had spoken only of a temporal relation between Son and Spirit, they admitted an eternal relation. Yet on the essential point the two Gregories agreed with Photius: the Spirit is manifested by the Son, but does not proceed from the Son. The Spirit derives His eternal being, His personal identity, not from the Son but from the Father alone. The Father is the unique origin, source and cause of the Godhead.

Such in outline are the positions taken up by either side. Let us now consider the Orthodox objections to the western doctrine of the Double Procession. In contemporary Orthodoxy there are, in fact, two approaches to this question. The 'hawks', those who adopt a stricter view of the *Filioque* issue, follow Photius and Mark of Ephesus in regarding the doctrine of the Double Procession as a heresy that produces a fatal distortion in the western doctrine of God as Trinity. Vladimir Lossky, the chief exponent of this stricter view in the twentieth century, goes yet further than this, and argues that the imbalance in the western doctrine of the Trinity has also led to an imbalance in the doctrine of the Church; the *Filioque*, as he sees it, is closely linked to the Roman Catholic emphasis upon the Papal claims. But among modern Orthodox theologians there are also 'doves' who advocate a more lenient approach to the question. While they deplore the unilateral insertion of the *Filioque* into the text of the Creed on the part of the west, they do not consider that the Latin doctrine of the Double Procession is in itself heretical. It is, they argue, somewhat confused in its expression and potentially misleading, but it is capable of being interpreted in an Orthodox way; and so it may be accepted as a *theologoumenon*, a theological opinion, although not as a dogma.

According to the stricter group of Orthodox thinkers, the *Filioque* leads either to ditheism or to semi-Sabellianism.[1] If the Son as well as the Father is an *arche*, a principle or source of the Godhead, are there then (the stricter group asks) two independent sources, two separate principles in the Trinity?

1. Sabellius, a heretic of the second century, regarded Father, Son and Spirit not as three distinct persons, but simply as varying 'modes' or 'aspects' of the deity.

Obviously this cannot be the Latin view, for it would be tantamount to belief in two Gods, and this is something that no
Christian, either western or eastern, has ever countenanced. In
fact the Council of Florence, following Augustine, is most
careful to state that the Spirit proceeds from Father and Son
tanquam ab uno principio, 'as from one principle'.

In the view of the stricter group among the Orthodox, however, this attempt to avoid the charge of ditheism is open to
objections that are equally grave. Out of the frying-pan into
the fire: in steering clear of one heresy, the west has deviated
into another – ditheism is avoided, but the persons of the
Father and the Son are merged and confused. Orthodox theology upholds the 'monarchy' of the Father within the Trinity:
He alone is the *arche*, the source or origin of being within the
Godhead. But western theology ascribes this distinctive characteristic of the Father to the Son as well, thus fusing the two
persons into one; and what else is this but 'Sabellius reborn, or
rather some semi-Sabellian monster', as St Photius put it?[1]

Let us look more carefully at this charge of semi-Sabellianism.
The Double Procession, so it appears to many Orthodox, im-
pairs the proper balance within Trinitarian theology between
the three distinctive persons and the shared essence. What
holds the Trinity together? The Cappadocians, followed by
later Orthodox theologians, answer that there is one God because there is one Father. The other two persons trace their
origin to the Father and are defined in terms of their relation
to Him. As the sole source of being within the Trinity, the
Father constitutes in this way the principle or ground of unity
for the Godhead as a whole. But the west, in regarding not
only the Father but also the Son as the source of the Spirit,
finds its principle of unity, no longer in the *person* of the
Father, but in the *essence* which the three persons share. And
in this way, so many Orthodox feel, the persons are overshad-
owed in Latin theology by the common essence or substance.

This, according to the stricter group within Orthodoxy,
has the effect of depersonalizing the Latin doctrine of the deity.

---

1. *P.G.* cii, 289B.

God is conceived, not so much in concrete and personal terms but as an essence in which various relations are distinguished. This way of thinking about God comes to full development in Thomas Aquinas, who went so far as to identify the persons with the relations: *personae sunt ipsae relationes*.[1] Many Orthodox thinkers find this a very meagre idea of personality. The relations, they would say, are not the *persons* – they are the *personal characteristics* of Father, Son, and Holy Spirit; and (as Gregory Palamas put it) 'personal characteristics do not constitute the person, but they characterize the person'.[2] The relations, while designating the persons, in no way exhaust the mystery of each.

Latin Scholastic theology, emphasizing as it does the essence at the expense of the persons, comes near to turning God into an abstract idea. He becomes a remote and impersonal being, whose existence has to be proved by metaphysical arguments – a God of the philosophers, not the God of Abraham, Isaac, and Jacob. Orthodoxy, on the other hand, has been far less concerned than the Latin west to find philosophical proofs of God's existence: what is important is not that we should argue about the deity, but that we should have a direct and living encounter with a concrete and personal God.

Such are some of the reasons why many Orthodox regard the *Filioque* as dangerous and heretical. Filioquism confuses the persons, and destroys the proper balance between unity and diversity in the Godhead. The oneness of the deity is emphasized at the expense of His threeness; God is regarded too much in terms of abstract essence and too little in terms of specific personality.

But this is not all. The stricter group of Orthodox feel that, as a result of the *Filioque*, the Holy Spirit in western thought has become subordinated to the Son – if not in theory, then at any rate in practice. The west pays insufficient attention to the work of the Spirit in the world, in the Church, in the daily life of each person.

1. *Summa Theologica,* 1, question 40, article 2.
2. Cf. John Meyendorff, *A Study of Gregory Palamas*, pp. 214–5.

Orthodox writers also argue that these two consequences of the *Filioque* – subordination of the Holy Spirit, over-emphasis of the unity of God – have helped to bring about a distortion in the Roman Catholic doctrine of the Church. Because the role of the Spirit has been neglected in the west, the Church has come to be regarded too much as an institution of this world, governed in terms of earthly power and jurisdiction. And just as in the western doctrine of God unity was stressed at the expense of diversity, so in the western conception of the Church unity has triumphed over diversity, and the result has been too great a centralization and too great an emphasis on Papal authority.

Such in outline is the view of the Orthodox 'hawks'. But there are Orthodox 'doves' who have significant reservations about several points in this critique of the *Filioque*. First, it is only in the present century that Orthodox writers have seen a close link between the doctrine of the Double Procession and the doctrine of the Church. Anti-Latin writers of the Byzantine period do not affirm any such connection between the two. If the *Filioque* and the Papal claims are in fact so obviously and integrally connected, why have not the Orthodox been quicker to recognize this?

Secondly, it is not true to assert, in any blunt and absolute fashion, that the principle of divine unity is personal in Orthodoxy but not in Roman Catholicism; for the Latin west as well as the Greek east upholds the doctrine of the 'monarchy' of the Father. When Augustine stated that the Spirit proceeds from both Father and Son, he was careful to qualify this by insisting that the Spirit does not proceed from the Son in the same manner as He proceeds from the Father. There are two different kinds of procession. The Spirit proceeds from the Father *principaliter*, 'principally' or 'principially', states Augustine, but He proceeds from the Son only *per donum Patris*, 'through the gift of the Father'. The procession of the Spirit from the Son, that is to say, is specifically something that the Father Himself has conferred upon the Son. Just as the Son receives all things as a gift from the Father, so also it is from the Father that He receives the power to 'spirate' or 'breathe forth' the Spirit.

In this way for Augustine, as for the Cappadocians, the Father remains the 'fountainhead of the deity', the sole source and ultimate origin within the Trinity. Augustine's teaching that the Spirit proceeds from the Father and from the Son – but with the qualification that He proceeds from the Son, not 'principially' but 'through the gift of the Father' – is thus not so very different from Gregory of Nyssa's view that the Spirit proceeds from the Father through the Son. The Council of Florence, in endorsing Augustine's doctrine of Double Procession, explicitly re-emphasized the point that the spiration of the Spirit is conferred on the Son by God the Father. The contrast, then, between Orthodoxy and Rome as regards the 'monarchy' of the Father is not nearly so stark as appears at first sight.

In the third place, the claim that the west depersonalizes the Trinity, overemphasizing the unity of essence at the expense of the diversity of persons, should not be overstated. Doubtless, as a result of the debased scholasticism prevailing in the later Middle Ages and in more recent centuries, there are some in the west who treat the Trinity in an abstract and schematic fashion. It is also true that, in the early Patristic period, there is a general tendency for the Latin west to start from the unity of the divine essence and to work from that to the threeness of the persons, whereas there is a general tendency for the Greek east to argue in the opposite direction, from the threeness of the persons to the oneness of the essence. But on this level we are speaking only of general tendencies, and not of irreconcilable oppositions or of specific heresies. If pushed to extremes, the western approach leads to modalism and Sabellianism, just as the eastern approach leads to tritheism, to the notion of 'three Gods'. Yet the great and representative thinkers, in both east and west, did not push their standpoint to extremes. It is false to claim that Augustine neglects the personal character of the Trinity, even though he is hesitant about applying the word *persona* to God; and there are certainly theologians in the medieval west, such as Richard of St Victor (died 1173), who affirm a 'social' doctrine of the Trinity that is spelt out in terms of reciprocal personal love.

For all these reasons there is today a school of Orthodox theologians who believe that the divergence between east and west over the *Filioque*, while by no means unimportant, is not as fundamental as Lossky and his disciples maintain. The Roman Catholic understanding of the person and work of the Holy Spirit, so this second group of Orthodox theologians conclude, is not basically different from that of the Christian east; and so we may hope that in the present-day dialogue between Orthodox and Roman Catholics an understanding will eventually be reached on this thorny question.

THE HUMAN PERSON: OUR CREATION, OUR VOCATION, OUR FAILURE

'You have made us for Yourself, and our hearts are restless until they rest in You.'[1] Humans were made for fellowship with God: this is the first and primary affirmation in the Christian doctrine of the human person. But humans, made for fellowship with God, everywhere repudiate that fellowship: this is the second fact which all Christian anthropology takes into account. Humans were made for fellowship with God: in the language of the Church, God created Adam according to His image and likeness, and set him in Paradise.[2] Humans everywhere repudiate that fellowship: in the language of the Church, Adam fell, and his fall – his 'original sin' – has affected all humankind.

The Creation of the Human Person. 'And God said, let Us make man according to Our image and likeness' (Genesis i, 26). God speaks in the plural: 'Let *Us* make man.' The creation of the human person, so the Greek Fathers continually emphasized, was an act of all three persons in the Trinity, and therefore the image and likeness of God must always be thought of

1. Augustine, *Confessions*, 1, i.
2. The opening chapters of Genesis are of course concerned with certain *religious* truths, and are not to be taken as literal history. Fifteen centuries before modern Biblical criticism, Greek Fathers were already interpreting the Creation and Paradise stories symbolically rather than literally.

as a *Trinitarian* image and likeness. We shall find that this is a point of vital importance.

Image and Likeness. According to most of the Greek Fathers, the terms *image* and *likeness* do not mean exactly the same thing. 'The expression *according to the image*,' wrote John of Damascus, 'indicates rationality and freedom, while the expression *according to the likeness* indicates assimilation to God through virtue.'[1] The image, or to use the Greek term the *icon*, of God signifies our human free will, our reason, our sense of moral responsibility – everything, in short, which marks us out from the animal creation and makes each of us a *person*. But the image means more than that. It means that we are God's 'offspring' (Acts xvii, 28), His kin; it means that between us and Him there is a point of contact and similarity. The gulf between creature and Creator is not impassable, for because we are in God's image we can know God and have communion with Him. And if we make proper use of this faculty for communion with God, then we will become 'like' God, we will acquire the divine likeness; in the words of John Damascene, we will be 'assimilated to God through virtue'. To acquire the likeness is to be deified, it is to become a 'second god', a 'god by grace'. 'I said, *you are gods*, and all of you sons of the Most High' (Psalm lxxxi, 6; cf. John x, 34–5).[2]

The image denotes the powers with which each one of us is endowed by God from the first moment of our existence; the likeness is not an endowment which we possess from the start, but a goal at which we must aim, something which we can only acquire by degrees. However sinful we may be, we never lose the image; but the likeness depends upon our moral choice, upon our 'virtue', and so it is destroyed by sin.

Humans at their first creation were therefore perfect, not so much in an actual as in a potential sense. Endowed with the image from the start, they were called to acquire the likeness by their own efforts (assisted of course by the grace of God).

1. *On the Orthodox Faith*, 11, 12 (*P.G.* xciv, 920B).

2. In quotations from the Psalms, the numbering of the Septuagint is followed. Some versions of the Bible reckon this Psalm as lxxxii.

Adam began in a state of innocence and simplicity. 'He was a child, not yet having his understanding perfected,' wrote Irenaeus. 'It was necessary that he should grow and so come to his perfection.'[1] God set Adam on the right path, but Adam had in front of him a long road to traverse in order to reach his final goal.

This picture of Adam before the fall is somewhat different from that presented by Augustine and generally accepted in the west since his time. According to Augustine, humans in Paradise were endowed from the start with all possible wisdom and knowledge: theirs was a realized, and in no sense potential, perfection. The dynamic conception of Irenaeus clearly fits more easily with modern theories of evolution than does the more static conception of Augustine; but both were speaking as theologians, not as scientists, so that in neither case do their views stand or fall with any particular scientific hypothesis.

The west has often associated the image of God with the human soul or intellect. While many Orthodox have done the same, others would say that since the human person is a single unified whole, the image of God embraces the entire person, body as well as soul. 'When God is said to have made the human person according to His image,' wrote Michael Choniates (died c.1222), 'the word person means neither the soul by itself nor the body by itself, but the two together.'[2] The fact that humans have a body, so Gregory Palamas argued, makes them not lower but higher than the angels. True, the angels are 'pure' spirit, whereas human nature is 'mixed' – material as well as intellectual; but this means that our human nature is more complete than the angelic and endowed with richer potentialities. The human person is a microcosm, a bridge and point of meeting for the whole of God's creation.

Orthodox religious thought lays the utmost emphasis on the image of God in the human person. Each of us is a 'living theology', and because we are God's icon, we can find God by looking within our own heart, by 'returning within ourselves':

1. *Demonstration of the Apostolic Preaching*, 12.
2. *P.G.* cl, 1361C.

'The kingdom of God is within you' (Luke xvii, 21). 'Know yourselves,' said St Antony of Egypt. '. . . He who knows himself, knows God.'[1] 'If you are pure,' wrote St Isaac the Syrian (late seventh century), 'heaven is within you; within yourself you will see the angels and the Lord of the angels.'[2] And of St Pachomius it is recorded: 'In the purity of his heart he saw the invisible God as in a mirror.'[3]

Because she or he is an icon of God, each member of the human race, even the most sinful, is infinitely precious in God's sight. 'When you see your brother or sister,' said Clement of Alexandria, 'you see God.'[4] And Evagrius taught: 'After God, we must count everyone as God Himself.'[5] This respect for every human being is visibly expressed in Orthodox worship, when the priest censes not only the icons but the members of the congregation, saluting the image of God in each person. 'The best icon of God is the human person.'[6]

Grace and Free Will. As we have seen, the fact that the human person is in God's image means among other things that we possess free will. God wanted sons and daughters, not slaves. The Orthodox Church rejects any doctrine of grace which might seem to infringe upon human freedom. To describe the relation between the grace of God and human freedom, Orthodoxy uses the term co-operation or synergy (*synergeia*); in Paul's words: 'We are fellow-workers (*synergoi*) with God' (1 Corinthians iii, 9). If we are to achieve full fellowship with God, we cannot do so without God's help, yet we must also play our own part: we humans as well as God must make our contribution to the common work, although what God does is of immeasurably greater importance than what we do. 'The incorporation of humans into Christ and our

1. *Letter* 3 (in the Greek and Latin collections, 6).
2. Quoted in P. Evdokimov, *L'Orthodoxie*, p. 88.
3. *First Greek Life*, 22.
4. *Stromateis*, 1, xix (94, 5).
5. *On Prayer*, 123 (*P.G.* lxxix, 1193C).
6 P. Evdokimov, *L'Orthodoxie*, p. 218.

union with God require the co-operation of two unequal, but equally necessary forces: divine grace and human will.'[1] The supreme example of synergy is the Mother of God.[2]

The west, since the time of Augustine and the Pelagian controversy, has discussed this question of grace and free will in somewhat different terms; and many brought up in the Augustinian tradition – particularly Calvinists – have viewed the Orthodox idea of 'synergy' with some suspicion. Does it not ascribe too much to human free will, and too little to God? Yet in reality the Orthodox teaching is very straightforward. 'Behold, I stand at the door and knock; if anyone hears my voice and opens the door, I will come in' (Revelation iii, 20). God knocks, but waits for us to open the door – He does not break it down. The grace of God invites all but compels none. In the words of John Chrysostom, 'God never draws anyone to Himself by force and violence. He wishes all to be saved, but forces no one.'[3] 'It is for God to grant His grace,' said St Cyril of Jerusalem (died 386); 'your task is to accept that grace and to guard it.'[4] But it must not be imagined that because a person accepts and guards God's grace, he thereby earns 'merit'. God's gifts are always free gifts, and we humans can never have any claims upon our Maker. But while we cannot 'merit' salvation, we must certainly work for it, since 'faith without works is dead' (James ii, 17).

The Fall: Original Sin. God gave Adam free will – the power to choose between good and evil – and it therefore rested with Adam either to accept the vocation set before him or to refuse it. He refused it. Instead of continuing along the path marked out for him by God, he turned aside and disobeyed God. Adam's fall consisted essentially in his disobedience of the will of God; he set up his own will against the divine will, and so by his own act he separated himself from God. As a result, a new form of existence appeared on earth –

1. A Monk of the Eastern Church, *Orthodox Spirituality*, p. 23.
2. See p. 258.
3. *Sermon on the words 'Saul, Saul . . .'*, 6 (*P.G.* li, 144).
4. *Catechetical Orations*, 1, 4.

that of disease and death. By turning away from God, who is immortality and life, humans put themselves in a state that was contrary to nature, and this unnatural condition led to an inevitable disintegration of their being and eventually to physical death. The consequences of Adam's disobedience extended to all his descendants. We are members one of another, as St Paul never ceased to insist, and if one member suffers the whole body suffers. In virtue of this mysterious unity of the human race, not only Adam but all humankind became subject to mortality. Nor was the disintegration which followed from the fall merely physical. Cut off from God, Adam and his descendants passed under the domination of sin and of the devil. Each new human being is born into a world where sin prevails everywhere, a world in which it is easy to do evil and hard to do good. Our will is weakened and enfeebled by what the Greeks call 'desire' and the Latins 'concupiscence'. We are all subject to these, the spiritual effects of original sin.

Thus far there is fairly close agreement between Orthodoxy, Roman Catholicism, and classic Protestantism; but beyond this point east and west do not entirely concur. Orthodoxy, holding as it does a less exalted idea of the human state before the fall, is also less severe than the west in its view of the consequences of the fall. Adam fell, not from a great height of knowledge and perfection, but from a state of undeveloped simplicity; hence he is not to be judged too harshly for his error. Certainly, as a result of the fall the human mind became so darkened, and human will-power was so impaired, that humans could no longer hope to attain to the likeness of God. Orthodox, however, do not hold that the fall deprived humanity entirely of God's grace, though they would say that after the fall grace acts on humanity from the outside, not from within. Orthodox do not say, as Calvin said, that humans after the fall were utterly depraved and incapable of good desires. They cannot agree with Augustine, when he writes that humans are under 'a harsh necessity' of committing sin, and that 'human nature was overcome by the fault into which it fell, *and so came to lack freedom*'.[1]

---

1. *On the perfection of man's righteousness*, iv (9).

FAITH AND WORSHIP

The image of God is distorted by sin, but never destroyed; in
the words of a hymn sung by Orthodox at the Funeral Service:
'I am the image of Your inexpressible glory, even though I
bear the wounds of sin.' And because we still retain the image
of God, we still retain free will, although sin restricts its scope.
Even after the fall, God 'takes not away from humans the
power to will – to will to obey or not to obey Him'.[1] Faithful
to the idea of synergy, Orthodoxy repudiates any interpretation
of the fall which allows no room for human freedom.

Most Orthodox theologians reject the idea of 'original
guilt', put forward by Augustine and still accepted (albeit in
a mitigated form) by the Roman Catholic Church. Humans
(Orthodox usually teach) automatically inherit Adam's corruption and mortality, but not his guilt: they are only guilty in
so far as by their own free choice they imitate Adam. Many
western Christians used to believe that whatever a person
does in the fallen and unredeemed state, since it is tainted by
original guilt, cannot possibly be pleasing to God: 'Works
before Justification,' says the thirteenth of the Thirty-Nine
Articles of the Church of England, '. . . are not pleasant to
God . . . but have the nature of sin.' Orthodox would hesitate
to say this. And Orthodox have never held (as Augustine and
many others in the west have done) that unbaptized babies,
because tainted with original guilt, are consigned by the just
God to the everlasting flames of hell.[2] The Orthodox picture
of fallen humanity is far less sombre than the Augustinian or
Calvinist view.

But although Orthodox maintain that humans after the fall

1. Dositheus, *Confession*, Decree iii. Compare Decree xiv.
2. Thomas Aquinas, in his discussion of the fall, on the whole followed
Augustine, and in particular retained the idea of original guilt; but as regards
unbaptized babies, he maintained that they go not to Hell but to Limbo – a
view now generally accepted by Roman theologians. So far as I can discover,
Orthodox writers do not make use of the idea of Limbo.

It should be noted that an Augustinian view of the fall is found from time to
time in Orthodox theological literature; but this is usually the result of western
influence. The *Orthodox Confession* by Peter of Moghila is, as one might
expect, strongly Augustinian; on the other hand the *Confession* of Dositheus is
free from Augustinianism.

still possessed free will and were still capable of good actions, yet they certainly agree with the west in believing that human sin had set up between humanity and God a barrier which humanity by its own efforts could never break down. Sin blocked the path to union with God. Since we could not come to God, He came to us.

JESUS CHRIST

The Incarnation is an act of God's *philanthropia*, of His loving-kindness towards humankind. Several eastern writers, looking at the Incarnation from this point of view, have argued that even if humans had never fallen, God in His love for humanity would still have become human: the Incarnation must be seen as part of the eternal purpose of God, and not simply as an answer to the fall. Such was the view of Maximus the Confessor and of Isaac the Syrian; such has also been the view of certain western writers, most notably Duns Scotus (1265–1308).

But because the human race fell, the Incarnation is not only an act of love but an act of salvation. Jesus Christ, by uniting humankind and God in His own person, reopened for us humans the path to union with God. In His own person Christ showed what the true 'likeness of God' is, and through His redeeming and victorious sacrifice He set that likeness once again within our reach. Christ, the Second Adam, came to earth and reversed the effects of the first Adam's disobedience.

The essential elements in the Orthodox doctrine of Christ have already been outlined in Chapter 2: true God and true man, one person in two natures, without separation and without confusion: a single person, but endowed with two wills and two energies.

True God and true man; as Bishop Theophan the Recluse put it: 'Behind the veil of Christ's flesh, Christians behold the Triune God.' These words bring us face to face with what is perhaps the most striking feature in the Orthodox approach to the Incarnate Christ: an overwhelming sense of His *divine glory*. There are two moments in Christ's life when this divine glory was made especially manifest: the Transfiguration, when on Mount Tabor the uncreated light of His Godhead shone visibly through the garments of His flesh; and the Resurrection, when the tomb burst open under the pressure of divine life, and Christ returned triumphant from the dead. In Orthodox worship and spirituality tremendous emphasis is placed on both these events. In the Byzantine calendar the Transfiguration is reckoned as one of the Twelve Great Feasts, and enjoys a far greater prominence in the Church's year than it possesses in the west; and we have already seen the central place which the uncreated light of Tabor holds in the Orthodox doctrine of mystical prayer. As for the Resurrection, its spirit fills the whole life of the Orthodox Church:

> Through all the vicissitudes of her history the Greek Church has been enabled to preserve something of the very spirit of the first age of Christianity. Her liturgy still enshrines that element of sheer joy in the Resurrection of the Lord that we find in so many of the early Christian writings.[1]

> The theme of the Resurrection of Christ binds together all theological concepts and realities in eastern Christianity and unites them in a harmonious whole.[2]

Yet it would be wrong to think of Orthodoxy simply as the cult of Christ's divine glory, of His Transfiguration and Resurrection, and nothing more. However great their devotion to the divine glory of Our Lord, Orthodox do not overlook His humanity. Consider for example the Orthodox love of the Holy Land: nothing could exceed the vivid reverence of devout Orthodox believers for the exact places where the Incarnate Christ lived as a man, where as a man He ate, taught, suffered, and died. Nor does the sense of Resurrection joy lead Orthodoxy to minimize the importance of the Cross. Representations of the Crucifixion are no less prominent in Orthodox than in non-Orthodox churches, while the veneration of the Cross is more developed in Byzantine than in Latin worship.

One must therefore reject as misleading the common asser-

1. P. Hammond, *The Waters of Marah*, p. 20.

2. O. Rousseau, 'Incarnation et anthropologie en orient et en occident', in *Irénikon*, vol. xxvi (1953), p. 373.

tion that the east concentrates on the Risen Christ, the west on Christ Crucified. If we are going to draw a contrast, it would be more exact to say that east and west think of the Crucifixion in slightly different ways. The Orthodox attitude to the Crucifixion is best seen in the hymns sung on Good Friday, such as the following:

> He who clothes Himself with light as with a garment,
>   Stood naked at the judgement.
> On His cheek He received blows
>   From the hands which He had formed.
> The lawless multitude nailed to the Cross
>   The Lord of glory.

The Orthodox Church on Good Friday thinks not simply of Christ's human pain and suffering by itself, but rather of the contrast between His outward humiliation and His inward glory. Orthodox see not just the *suffering humanity* of Christ, but a *suffering God*:

> Today is hanged upon the tree
>   He who hanged the earth in the midst of the waters.
> A crown of thorns crowns Him
>   Who is the king of the angels.
> He is wrapped about with the purple of mockery
>   Who wraps the heaven in clouds.

Behind the veil of Christ's bleeding and broken flesh, Orthodox still discern the Triune God. Even Golgotha is a theophany; even on Good Friday the Church sounds a note of Resurrection joy:

> We worship Your Passion, O Christ:
> Show us also Your glorious Resurrection!

> I magnify Your sufferings,
> I praise Your burial and Your Resurrection,
>   Shouting: Lord, glory to You!

The Crucifixion is not separated from the Resurrection, for both are but a single action. Calvary is seen always in the light of the empty tomb; the Cross is an emblem of victory. When Orthodox think of Christ Crucified, they think not only of His suffering and desolation; they think of Him as Christ the Victor, Christ the King, reigning in triumph from the Tree:

The Lord came into the world and dwelt among humans that He might destroy the tyranny of the Devil and set humans free. On the Tree He triumphed over the powers which opposed Him, when the sun was darkened and the earth was shaken, when the graves were opened and the bodies of the saints arose. By death He destroyed death, and brought to nought him who had the power of death.[1]

Christ is our victorious king, not in spite of the Crucifixion, but because of it: 'I call Him king, because I see Him crucified.'[2]

Such is the spirit in which Orthodox Christians regard Christ's death upon the Cross. Between this approach to the Crucifixion and that of the medieval and post-medieval west, there are of course many points of contact; yet in the western approach there are also certain things which make Orthodox feel uneasy. The west, so it seems to them, tends to think of the Crucifixion in isolation, separating it too sharply from the Resurrection. As a result the vision of Christ as a suffering God is in practice replaced by the picture of Christ's suffering humanity: the western worshipper, when he meditates upon the Cross, is encouraged all too often to feel an emotional sympathy with the Man of Sorrows, rather than to adore the victorious and triumphant king. Orthodox feel thoroughly at home in the language of the great Latin hymn by Venantius Fortunatus (530–609), *Pange lingua*, which hails the Cross as an emblem of victory:

> Sing, my tongue, the glorious battle,
>   Sing the ending of the fray;
> Now above the Cross, our trophy,
>   Sound the loud triumphal lay:
> Tell how Christ, the world's redeemer,
>   As a victim won the day.

1. From the First Exorcism before Holy Baptism.
2. John Chrysostom, *Second Sermon on the Cross and the Robber*, 3 (*P.G.* xlix, 413).

They feel equally at home in that other hymn by Fortunatus, *Vexilla regis*:

> Fulfilled is all that David told
> In true prophetic song of old:
> Among the nations God, said he,
> Hath reigned and triumphed from the Tree.

But Orthodox feel less happy about compositions of the later Middle Ages such as *Stabat Mater*:

> For His people's sins, in anguish,
> There she saw the victim languish,
>   Bleed in torments, bleed and die:
> Saw the Lord's anointed taken;
> Saw her Child in death forsaken;
>   Heard His last expiring cry.

It is significant that *Stabat Mater*, in the course of its sixty lines, makes not a single reference to the Resurrection.

Where Orthodoxy sees chiefly Christ the Victor, the late medieval and post-medieval west sees chiefly Christ the Victim. While Orthodoxy interprets the Crucifixion primarily as an act of triumphant victory over the powers of evil, the west – particularly since the time of Anselm of Canterbury (?1033–1109) – has tended rather to think of the Cross in penal and juridical terms, as an act of satisfaction or substitution designed to propitiate the wrath of an angry Father.

Yet these contrasts must not be pressed too far. Eastern writers, as well as western, have applied juridical and penal language to the Crucifixion; western writers, as well as eastern, have never ceased to think of Good Friday as a moment of victory. In the west from the 1930s onwards there has been a revival of the Patristic idea of *Christus Victor*, alike in theology, in spirituality, and in art; and Orthodox are naturally very happy that this should be so.

THE HOLY SPIRIT

In their activity among humans the second and the third persons of the Trinity are complementary and reciprocal. Christ's work of redemption cannot be considered apart from the Holy Spirit's work of sanctification. The Word took flesh, said Athanasius, that we might receive the Spirit:[1] from one point of view, the whole 'aim' of the Incarnation is the sending of the Spirit at Pentecost.

The Orthodox Church lays great stress upon the work of the Holy Spirit. As we have seen, one of the reasons why Orthodox have objected to the *Filioque* is because they have seen in it a tendency to subordinate and neglect the Spirit. St Seraphim of Sarov briefly described the whole purpose of the Christian life as nothing else than the acquisition of the Holy Spirit, saying at the beginning of his conversation with Motovilov:

> Prayer, fasting, vigils, and all other Christian practices, however good they may be in themselves, certainly do not constitute the aim of our Christian life: they are but the indispensable means of attaining that aim. *For the true aim of the Christian life is the acquisition of the Holy Spirit of God.* As for fasts, vigils, prayer, and almsgiving, and other good works done in the name of Christ, they are only the means of acquiring the Holy Spirit of God. Note well that it is only good works done in the name of Christ that bring us the fruits of the Spirit.

'This definition,' Vladimir Lossky has commented, 'while it may at first sight appear oversimplified, sums up the whole spiritual tradition of the Orthodox Church.'[2] As St Pachomius' disciple Theodore said, 'What is greater than to possess the Holy Spirit?'[3]

In the next chapter we shall have occasion to note the place of the Spirit in the Orthodox doctrine of the Church; and in later chapters something will be said of the Holy Spirit in Orthodox worship. In every sacramental action of the Church, and most notably at the climax of the Eucharistic Prayer, the Spirit is solemnly invoked. In his private prayers at the start of each day, and Orthodox Christian places himself under the protection of the Spirit, saying these words:

> O heavenly King, O Comforter, the Spirit of Truth, everywhere

---

1. *On the Incarnation and against the Arians*, 8 (*P.G.* xxvi, 996c).
2. *The Mystical Theology of the Eastern Church*, p. 196.
3. *First Greek Life* of Pachomius, 135.

present and filling all things, the treasury of blessings and giver of life, come and abide in us. Cleanse us from all impurity, and of Your goodness save our souls.[1]

'PARTAKERS OF THE DIVINE NATURE'

The aim of the Christian life, which Seraphim described as the acquisition of the Holy Spirit of God, can equally well be defined in terms of *deification*. Basil described the human person as a creature who has received the order to become a god; and Athanasius, as we know, said that God became human that we humans might become god. 'In My kingdom, said Christ, I shall be God with you as gods.'[2] Such, according to the teaching of the Orthodox Church, is the final goal at which every Christian must aim: to become god, to attain *theosis*, 'deification' or 'divinization'. For Orthodoxy our salvation and redemption mean our deification.

Behind the doctrine of deification there lies the idea of the human person made according to the image and likeness of God the Holy Trinity. 'May they all be one,' Christ prayed at the Last Supper; 'as You, Father, are in Me and I in You, so also may they be in Us' (John xvii, 21). Just as the three persons of the Trinity 'dwell' in one another in an unceasing movement of love, so we humans, made in the image of the Trinity, are called to 'dwell' in the Trinitarian God. Christ prays that we may share in the life of the Trinity, in the movement of love which passes between the divine persons; He prays that we may be taken up into the Godhead. The saints, as Maximus the Confessor put it, are those who express the Holy Trinity in themselves. This idea of a personal and organic union between God and humans – God dwelling in us, and we in Him – is a constant theme in St John's Gospel; it is also a constant theme in the Epistles of St Paul, who sees the Christian life above all else as a life 'in Christ'. The same idea recurs in the famous text of 2 Peter: 'Through these promises you may become

1. This same prayer is used at the beginning of most liturgical services.
2. Canon for Matins of Holy Thursday, Ode 4, Troparion 3.

partakers of the divine nature' (i,4). It is important to keep this New Testament background in mind. The Orthodox doctrine of deification, so far from being unscriptural (as is sometimes thought), has a solid Biblical basis, not only in 2 Peter, but in Paul and the Fourth Gospel.

The idea of deification must always be understood in the light of the distinction between God's essence and His energies. Union with God means union with the divine energies, not the divine essence: the Orthodox Church, while speaking of deification and union, rejects all forms of pantheism.

Closely related to this is another point of equal importance. The mystical union between God and humans is a true union, yet in this union Creator and creature do not become fused into a single being. Unlike the eastern religions which teach that humans are swallowed up in the deity, Orthodox mystical theology has always insisted that we humans, however closely linked to God, retain our full personal integrity. The human person, when deified, remains distinct (though not separate) from God. The mystery of the Trinity is a mystery of unity *in diversity*, and those who express the Trinity in themselves do not sacrifice their personal characteristics. When St Maximus wrote 'God and those who are worthy of God have one and the same energy',[1] he did not mean that the saints lose their free will, but that when deified they voluntarily and in love conform their will to the will of God. Nor does the human person, when it 'becomes god', cease to be human: 'We remain creatures while becoming god by grace, as Christ remained God when becoming man by the Incarnation.'[2] The human being does not become God *by nature*, but is merely a 'created god', a god *by grace* or *by status*.

Deification is something that involves the body. Since the human person is a unity of body and soul, and since the Incarnate Christ has saved and redeemed the whole person, it follows that 'our body is deified at the same time as our soul'.[3] In that divine likeness which we humans are called to realize in our-

1. *Ambigua* (*P.G.* xci, 1076c).
2. V. Lossky, *The Mystical Theology of the Eastern Church*, p. 87.
3. Maximus, *Gnostic Centuries*, 11, 88 (*P.G.* xc, 1168a).

selves, the body has its place. 'Your body is a temple of the Holy Spirit,' wrote St Paul (1 Corinthians vi, 19). 'Therefore, my brothers and sisters, I beseech you by God's mercy to offer your bodies as a living sacrifice to God' (Romans xii, 1). The full deification of the body must wait, however, until the Last Day, for in this present life the glory of the saints is as a rule an inward splendour, a splendour of the soul alone; but when the righteous rise from the dead and are clothed with a spiritual body, then their sanctity will be outwardly manifest. 'At the day of Resurrection the glory of the Holy Spirit *comes out from within*, decking and covering the bodies of the saints – the glory which they had before, but hidden within their souls. What a person has now, the same then comes forth externally *in the body*'.[1] The bodies of the saints will be outwardly transfigured by divine light, as Christ's body was transfigured on Mount Tabor. 'We must look forward also to the springtime of the body.'[2]

But even in this present life some saints have experienced the firstfruits of this visible and bodily glorification. St Seraphim is the best known, but by no means the only, instance of this. When Arsenius the Great was praying, his disciples saw him 'just like a fire';[3] and of another Desert Father it is recorded, 'Just as Moses received the image of the glory of Adam, when his face was glorified, so the face of Abba Pambo shone like lightning, and he was as a king seated on his throne.'[4] In the words of Gregory Palamas, 'If in the age to

1. *Homilies of Macarius*, v, 9. It is this transfigured 'Resurrection body' which the icon painter attempts symbolically to depict. Hence, while preserving the distinctive personal traits in a saint's physiognomy, he deliberately avoids making a realistic and 'photographic' portrait. To paint people exactly as they now appear is to paint them still in their fallen state, in their 'earthy', not their 'heavenly' body.

2. Minucius Felix (? late second century), *Octavius*, 34. Because of our reverence for the human body and our belief in the body's ultimate resurrection, in the Orthodox Church we do not permit cremation. Unfortunately this prohibition, which is based on profound theological principles, is sometimes disregarded.

3. *Apophthegmata* (*P.G.* lxv), Arsenius 27.

4. *Apophthegmata* (*P.G.* lxv), Pambo 12. Compare *Apophthegmata*, Sisoes

come the body will share with the soul in unspeakable blessings, it is certain that it must share in them, so far as possible,
even now.'[1]

Because Orthodox are convinced that the body is sanctified
and transfigured together with the soul, they have an immense
reverence for the relics of the saints. Like Roman Catholics,
they believe that the grace of God present in the saints' bodies
during life remains active in their relics when they have died,
and that God uses these relics as a channel of divine power and
an instrument of healing. In some cases the bodies of saints
have been miraculously preserved from corruption, but even
where this has not happened, Orthodox show just as great a
veneration towards their bones. This reverence for relics is not
the fruit of ignorance and superstition, but springs from a
highly developed theology of the body.

Not only our human body but the whole of the material
creation will eventually be transfigured: 'Then I saw a new
heaven *and a new earth*; for the first heaven and the first earth
had passed away' (Revelation xxi, 1). Redeemed humankind is
not to be snatched away from the rest of creation, but creation
is to be saved and glorified along with us humans (icons, as we
have seen, are the firstfruits of this redemption of matter).[2]
'The created universe waits with eager expectation for God's
children to be revealed . . . for the universe itself will be set free

---

14 and Silvanus 12. Epiphanius, in his *Life* of Sergius of Radonezh, states that
the saint's body shone with glory after death.

It is sometimes said, and with a certain truth, that bodily transfiguration by
divine light corresponds, among Orthodox saints, to the receiving of the stig-
mata among western saints. We must not, however, draw too absolute a contrast
in this matter. Instances of bodily glorification are found in the west, for
example, in the case of an Englishwoman, Evelyn Underhill (1875–1941): a
friend records how on one occasion her face could be seen transfigured with
light (the whole account recalls St Seraphim: see *the Letters of Evelyn Underhill*,
edited by Charles Williams [London 1943], p. 37). Similarly, in the east stigma-
tization is not unknown: in a Coptic life of St Macarius of Egypt, it is said
that a cherub appeared to him, 'took the measure of his chest', and 'crucified
him on the earth'.

1. *The Tome of the Holy Mountain* (*P.G.* cl, 1233C).
2. See p. 34.

from its bondage to corruption and will enter into the liberty and splendour of the children of God. We know that until now the whole created universe has been groaning in the pangs of childbirth' (Romans viii, 19–22). This idea of *cosmic redemption* is based, like the Orthodox doctrine of the human body and the Orthodox doctrine of icons, upon a right understanding of the Incarnation: Christ took flesh – something from the material order – and so has made possible the redemption and metamorphosis of *all* creation – not merely the immaterial, but the physical.

This sense of the intrinsic sacredness of the earth – created good by God, corrupted through the fall, but redeemed with us in Christ – has caused leading Orthodox in recent years to feel an increasing concern about the pollution of the environment. The present ecological crisis caused particular distress to the late Ecumenical Patriarch Dimitrios. In his Christmas message for 1988 he insisted, 'Let us consider ourselves, each one according to his or her position, to be *personally responsible* for the world, entrusted into our hands by God. Whatever the Son of God has assumed and made His body by His Incarnation should not perish. But it should become a eucharistic offering to the Creator, a life-giving bread, partaken in justice and love with others, a hymn of peace for all creatures of God.'

In 1989 Patriarch Dimitrios issued a special encyclical, calling on everyone to show a 'eucharistic and ascetic spirit', and designating 1 September – the beginning of the ecclesiastical year in the Orthodox Church – as a 'day for the protection of the environment', to be observed (he hoped) not only by Orthodox but by other Christians as well.[1] In the words of St Silouan of Mount Athos, 'The heart that has learnt to love has pity for all creation.' It is our human privilege, not to exploit the world selfishly, but to cherish it with loving sensitivity and, as cosmic priests, to offer the creation back to the Creator in thanksgiving.

1. See the booklet *Orthodoxy and the Ecological Crisis*, issued in 1990 by the Ecumenical Patriarchate in association with the World Wide Fund for Nature (World Conservation Centre, Avenue du Mont Blanc, CH-1196 Gland, Switzerland).

Such talk of deification and union, of the transfiguration of the body and of cosmic redemption, may sound very remote from the experience of ordinary Christians; but anyone who draws such a conclusion has entirely misunderstood the Orthodox conception of *theosis*. To prevent misinterpretation, six points must be made.

First, deification is not something reserved for a few select initiates, but something intended for all alike. The Orthodox Church believes that it is the normal goal for *every* Christian without exception. Certainly, we shall only be fully deified at the Last Day; but for each of us the process of divinization must begin here and now in this present life. It is true that in this present life very few indeed attain full mystical union with God. But every true Christian tries to love God and to fulfil His commandments; and so long as we sincerely seek to do that, then however weak our attempts may be and however often we may fall, we are already in some degree deified.

Secondly, the fact that a person is being deified does not mean that she or he ceases to be conscious of sin. On the contrary, deification always presupposes a continued act of repentance. A saint may be well advanced in the way of holiness, yet he or she does not therefore cease to employ the words of the Jesus Prayer, 'Lord Jesus Christ, Son of God, *have mercy on me a sinner*'. St Silouan of Mount Athos used to say to himself, 'Keep your mind in hell and despair not'; other Orthodox saints have repeated the words 'All will be saved, and I alone will be condemned'. Orthodox mystical theology is a theology of glory and of transfiguration, but it is also a theology of penitence.

In the third place, there is nothing esoteric or extraordinary about the methods which we must follow in order to be deified. If someone asks 'How can I become god?' the answer is very simple: go to church, receive the sacraments regularly, pray to God 'in spirit and in truth', read the Gospels, follow the commandments. The last of these items – 'follow the commandments' – must never be forgotten. Orthodoxy, no less than western Christianity, firmly rejects the kind of mysticism that seeks to dispense with moral rules.

Fourthly, deification is not a solitary but a 'social' process. We have said that deification means 'following the commandments'; and these commandments were briefly described by Christ as love of God and love of neighbour. The two forms of love are inseparable. A person can love his neighbour as himself only if he loves God above all; and a person cannot love God if he does not love his fellow humans (1 John iv, 20). Thus there is nothing selfish about deification; for only if he loves his neighbour can a person be deified. 'From our neighbour is life and from our neighbour is death,' said Antony of Egypt. 'If we win our neighbour we win God, but if we cause our neighbour to stumble we sin against Christ.'[1] Humans, made in the image of the Trinity, can only realize the divine likeness if they live a common life such as the Blessed Trinity lives: as the three persons of the Godhead 'dwell' in one another, so we must 'dwell' in our fellow humans, living not for ourselves alone, but in and for others. 'If it were possible for me to find a leper,' said one of the Desert Fathers, 'and to give him my body and to take his, I would gladly do it. For this is perfect love.'[2] Such is the true nature of *theosis*.

Fifthly, love of God and of our fellow humans must be practical: Orthodoxy rejects all forms of Quietism, all types of love which do not issue in action. Deification, while it includes the heights of mystical experience, has also a very prosaic and down-to-earth aspect. When we think of deification, we must think of the Hesychasts praying in silence and of St Seraphim with his face transfigured; but we must think also of St Basil caring for the sick in the hospital at Caesarea, of St John the Almsgiver helping the poor at Alexandria, of St Sergius in his filthy clothing, working as a peasant in the kitchen garden to provide the guests of the monastery with food. These are not two different ways, but one.

Finally, deification presupposes life in the Church, life in the sacraments. *Theosis* according to the likeness of the Trinity involves a common life, and it is only within the fellowship of

1. *Apophthegmata* (*P.G.* lxv), Antony 9.
2. ibid., Agatho 26.

the Church that this common life of coinherence can be properly realized. Church and sacraments are the means appointed by God whereby we may acquire the sanctifying Spirit and be transformed into the divine likeness.

CHAPTER 12

The Church of God

> Christ loved the Church, and gave Himself up for it.
>
> *Ephesians v, 25*

> The Church is one and the same with the Lord – His Body,
> of His flesh and of His bones. The Church is the living vine,
> nourished by Him and growing in Him. Never think of the
> Church apart from the Lord Jesus Christ, from the Father
> and Holy Spirit.
>
> *St John of Kronstadt*

GOD AND HIS CHURCH

An Orthodox Christian is vividly conscious of belonging to a community. 'We know that when any of us falls,' wrote Khomiakov, 'he falls alone; but no one is saved alone. He is saved in the Church, as a member of it and in union with all its other members.'[1]

Some of the differences between the Orthodox doctrine of the Church and those of western Christians will have become apparent in the first part of this book. Unlike Protestantism, Orthodoxy insists upon the hierarchical structure of the Church, upon the Apostolic Succession, the episcopate, and the priesthood; it asks the saints for their prayers and intercedes for the departed. Thus far Rome and Orthodoxy agree – but where Rome thinks in terms of the supremacy and the universal jurisdiction of the Pope, Orthodoxy thinks in terms of the five Patriarchs and of the Ecumenical Council; where Rome stresses Papal infallibility, Orthodox stress the infallibility of the Church as a whole. Doubtless neither side is entirely fair to the other, but to Orthodox it often seems that Rome envisages the Church too much in terms of earthly power and organization,

1. G. Khomiakov 'The Church is One', section 9.

while to Roman Catholics it often seems that the more spiritual and mystical doctrine of the Church held by Orthodoxy is vague, incoherent, and incomplete. Orthodox would answer that they do not neglect the earthly organization of the Church, but have many strict and minute rules, as anyone who reads the Canons can quickly discover.

Yet the Orthodox idea of the Church is certainly spiritual and mystical in this sense, that Orthodox theology never treats the earthly aspect of the Church in isolation, but thinks always of the Church in Christ and the Holy Spirit. All Orthodox thinking about the Church starts with the special relationship which exists between the Church and God. Three phrases can be used to describe this relation: the Church is (1) the Image of the Holy Trinity, (2) the Body of Christ, (3) a continued Pentecost. The Orthodox doctrine of the Church is Trinitarian, Christological, and 'pneumatological'.

(1) *The Image of the Holy Trinity*. Just as each person is made according to the image of the Trinitarian God, so the Church as a whole is an icon of God the Trinity, reproducing on earth the mystery of unity in diversity. In the Trinity the three are one God, yet each is fully personal; in the Church a multitude of human persons is united in one, yet each preserves her or his personal diversity unimpaired. The mutual indwelling of the persons of the Trinity is paralleled by the coinherence of the members of the Church. In the Church there is no conflict between freedom and authority; in the Church there is unity, but no totalitarianism. When Orthodox apply the word 'Catholic' to the Church, they have in mind (among other things) this living miracle of the unity of many persons in one.

This conception of the Church as an icon of the Trinity has many further applications. 'Unity in diversity' – just as each person of the Trinity is autonomous, so the Church is made up of a number of independent autocephalous Churches; just as in the Trinity the three persons are equal, so in the Church no one bishop can claim to wield an absolute power over all the rest; yet, just as in the Trinity the Father enjoys pre-eminence as source and fountainhead of the deity, so within the Church the Pope is 'first among equals'.

This idea of the Church as an icon of the Trinity also helps us to understand the Orthodox emphasis upon councils. A council is an expression of the Trinitarian nature of the Church. The mystery of unity in diversity according to the image of the Trinity can be seen in action, as the many bishops assembled in council freely reach a common mind under the guidance of the Spirit.

(2) *The Body of Christ*. 'We, who are many, are one body in Christ' (Romans xii, 5). Between Christ and the Church there is the closest possible bond: in the famous phrase of Ignatius, 'where Christ is, there is the Catholic Church'.[1] The Church is the extension of the Incarnation, the place where the Incarnation perpetuates itself. The Church, the Greek theologian Christos Androutsos has written, is 'the centre and organ of Christ's redeeming work . . . it is nothing else than the continuation and extension of His prophetic, priestly, and kingly power . . . The Church and its Founder are inextricably bound together . . . The Church is Christ with us.'[2] Christ did not leave the Church when He ascended into heaven: 'Lo! I am with you always, even to the end of the world,' He promised (Matthew xxviii, 20), 'for where two or three are gathered together in My name, there am I in the midst of them'. It is only too easy to fall into the mistake of speaking of Christ as absent:

> And still the Holy Church is here
> Although her Lord is gone.[3]

But how can we say that Christ 'is gone', when He has promised us His perpetual presence?

The unity between Christ and His Church is effected above all through the sacraments. At Baptism, the new Christian is buried and raised with Christ; at the Eucharist the members of

1. *To the Smyrnaeans*, viii, 2.
2. *Dogmatic Theology* (Athens 1907), pp. 262–5 (in Greek).
3. From a hymn by J. M. Neale.

Christ's Body the Church receive His Body in the sacrament. The Eucharist, by uniting the members of the Church to Christ, at the same time unites them to one another: 'We, who are many, are one loaf, one body; for we all partake of the one loaf' (I Corinthians x, 17). The Eucharist creates the unity of the Church. The Church (as Ignatius saw) is a Eucharistic society, a sacramental organism which exists – and exists in its fullness – wherever the Eucharist is celebrated. It is no coincidence that the term 'Body of Christ' should mean both the Church and the sacrament; and that the phrase *communio sanctorum* in the Apostles' Creed should mean both 'the communion of the holy people' (communion of saints) and 'the communion of the holy things' (communion in the sacraments).

The Church must be thought of primarily in sacramental terms. Its outward organization, however important, is secondary to its sacramental life.

(3) *A continued Pentecost.* It is easy to lay such emphasis on the Church as the Body of Christ that the role of the Holy Spirit is forgotten. But, as we have said, in their work among humans Son and Spirit are complementary to one another, and this is as true in the doctrine of the Church as it is elsewhere. While Ignatius said 'where Christ is, there is the Catholic Church,' Irenaeus wrote with equal truth 'where the Church is, there is the Spirit, and where the Spirit is, there is the Church'.[1] The Church, precisely because it is the Body of Christ, is also the temple and dwelling place of the Spirit.

The Holy Spirit is a Spirit of freedom. The Holy Spirit not only unites us but also ensures our infinite diversity in the Church: at Pentecost the tongues of fire were 'cloven' or divided, descending *separately* upon each one of those present. The gift of the Spirit is a gift to the Church, but it is at the same time a personal gift, appropriated by each in her or his own way. 'There are diversities of gifts, but the same Spirit' (I Corinthians xii, 4). Life in the Church does not mean the

---

1. *Against the Heresies* III, xxiv, 1.

ironing out of human variety, nor the imposition of a rigid and uniform pattern upon all alike, but the exact opposite. The saints, so far from displaying a drab monotony, have developed the most vivid and distinctive personalities. It is not holiness but evil which is dull.

Such in brief is the relation between the Church and God. This Church – the icon of the Trinity, the Body of Christ, the fullness of the Spirit – is both *visible* and *invisible*, *divine* and *human*. It is visible, for it is composed of specific congregations, worshipping here on earth; it is invisible, for it also includes the saints and the angels. It is human, for its earthly members are sinners; it is divine, for it is the Body of Christ. There is no separation between the visible and the invisible, between (to use western terminology) the Church militant and the Church triumphant, for the two make up a single and continuous reality. 'The Church visible, or upon earth, lives in complete communion and unity with the whole body of the Church, of which Christ is the Head.'[1] It stands at a point of intersection between the Present Age and the Age to Come, and it lives in both Ages at once.

Orthodoxy, therefore, while using the phrase 'the Church visible and invisible', insists always that there are not two Churches, but one. As Khomiakov said:

It is only in relation to man that it is possible to recognize a division of the Church into visible and invisible; its unity is, in reality, true and absolute. Those who are alive on earth, those who have finished their earthly course, those who, like the angels, were not created for a life on earth, those in future generations who have not yet begun their earthly course, are all united together in one Church, in one and the same grace of God ... The Church, the Body of Christ, manifests forth and fulfils itself in time, without changing its essential unity or inward life of grace. And therefore, when we speak of 'the Church visible and invisible', we so speak only in relation to man.[2]

1. 'The Church is One', section 9.
2. ibid., section 1.

The Church, according to Khomiakov, is *accomplished on earth without losing its essential characteristics*. This is a cardinal point in Orthodox teaching. Orthodoxy does not believe merely in an ideal Church, invisible and heavenly. This 'ideal Church' exists visibly on earth as a concrete reality.

Yet Orthodoxy tries not to forget that there is a human element in the Church as well as a divine. The dogma of Chalcedon must be applied to the Church as well as to Christ. Just as Christ the God–Man has two natures, divine and human, so in the Church there is a synergy or co-operation between the divine and the human. Yet between Christ's humanity and that of the Church there is this obvious difference, that the one is perfect and sinless, while the other is not yet fully so. Only a part of the humanity of the Church – the saints in heaven – has attained perfection, while here on earth the Church's members often misuse their human freedom. The Church on earth exists in a state of tension: it is already the Body of Christ, and thus perfect and sinless, and yet, since its members are imperfect and sinful, it must continually become what it is.[1]

But human sin cannot affect the essential nature of the Church. We must not say that because Christians on earth sin and are imperfect, therefore the Church sins and is imperfect; for the Church, even on earth, is a thing of heaven, and cannot sin.[2] St Ephraim of Syria rightly spoke of 'the Church of the penitents, the Church of those who perish', but this Church is at the same time the icon of the Trinity. How is it that the members of the Church are sinners, and yet they belong to the communion of saints? 'The mystery of the Church consists in the very fact that *together* sinners become *something different* from what they are as individuals; this "something different" is the Body of Christ.'[3]

---

1. 'This idea of "becoming what you are" is the key to the whole eschatological teaching of the New Testament' (Gregory Dix, *The Shape of the Liturgy*, p. 247).

2. See the *Declaration on Faith and Order* made by the Orthodox Delegates at Evanston in 1954, where this point is put very clearly.

3. J. Meyendorff, 'What Holds the Church Together?', in the *Ecumenical Review*, vol. XII (1960), p. 298.

Such is the way in which Orthodoxy approaches the mystery of the Church. The Church is integrally linked with God. It is a new life according to the image of the Holy Trinity, a life in Christ and in the Holy Spirit, a life realized by participation in the sacraments. The Church is a single reality, earthly and heavenly, visible and invisible, human and divine.

THE UNITY AND INFALLIBILITY OF
THE CHURCH

'The Church is one. Its unity follows of necessity from the unity of God.'[1] So wrote Khomiakov in the opening words of his famous essay. If we take seriously the bond between God and His Church, then we must inevitably think of the Church as one, even as God is one: there is only one Christ, and so there can be only one Body of Christ. Nor is this unity merely ideal and invisible; Orthodox theology refuses to separate the 'invisible' and the 'visible Church', and therefore it refuses to say that the Church is invisibly one but visibly divided. No: the Church is one, in the sense that here on earth there is a single, visible community which alone can claim to be the one true Church. The 'undivided Church' is not merely something that existed in the past, and which we hope will exist again in the future: it is something that exists here and now. Unity is one of the essential characteristics of the Church, and since the Church on earth, despite the sinfulness of its members, retains its essential characteristics, it remains and always will remain visibly one. There can be schisms *from* the Church, but no schisms *within* the Church. And while it is undeniably true that, on a purely human level, the Church's life is grievously impoverished as a result of schisms, yet such schisms cannot affect the essential nature of the Church.

In its teaching upon the visible unity of the Church, Orthodoxy stands far closer to Roman Catholicism than to the Protestant world. But if we ask how this visible unity is maintained,

1. 'The Church is One', section 1.

Rome and the east give somewhat different answers. For Rome the unifying principle in the Church is the Pope whose jurisdiction extends over the whole body, whereas Orthodox do not believe any bishop to be endowed with universal jurisdiction. What then holds the Church together? Orthodox answer, the act of communion in the sacraments. The Orthodox theology of the Church is above all else a *theology of communion*. Each local Church is constituted, as Ignatius saw, by the congregation of the faithful, gathered round their bishop and celebrating the Eucharist; the Church universal is constituted by the communion of the heads of the local Churches, the bishops, with one another. Unity is not maintained from without by the authority of a Supreme Pontiff, but created from within by the celebration of the Eucharist. The Church is not monarchical in structure, centred round a single hierarch; it is collegial, formed by the communion of many hierarchs with one another, and of each hierarch with the members of his flock. The act of communion therefore forms the criterion for membership of the Church. An individual ceases to be a member of the Church if she or he severs communion with her or his bishop; a bishop ceases to be a member of the Church if he severs communion with his fellow bishops.

Orthodoxy, believing that the Church on earth has remained and must remain visibly one, naturally also believes itself to be that one visible Church. This is a bold claim, and to many it will seem an arrogant one; but this is to misunderstand the spirit in which it is made. Orthodox believe that they are the true Church, not on account of any personal merit, but by the grace of God. They say with St Paul, 'We are no better than pots of earthenware to contain this treasure; the sovereign power comes from God and not from us' (2 Corinthians iv, 7). But while claiming no credit for themselves, Orthodox are in all humility convinced that they have received a precious and unique gift from God; and if they pretended to others that they did not possess this gift, they would be guilty of an act of betrayal in the sight of heaven.

Orthodox writers sometimes speak as if they accepted the 'Branch Theory', once popular among High Church Anglicans.

(According to this theory, the Catholic Church is divided into several 'branches'; usually three such branches are posited, the Roman Catholic, the Anglican, and the Orthodox.) But such a view cannot be reconciled with traditional Orthodox theology. If we are going to speak in terms of 'branches', then from the Orthodox point of view the only branches which the Catholic Church can have are the local autocephalous Churches of the Orthodox communion.

Claiming as it does to be the one true Church, the Orthodox Church also believes that, if it so desired, it could by itself convene and hold another Ecumenical Council, equal in authority to the first seven. Since the separation of east and west the Orthodox (unlike the west) have never in fact chosen to summon such a council; but this does not mean that they believe themselves to lack the power to do so.

Such, then, is the Orthodox idea of the unity of the Church. Orthodoxy also teaches that *outside the Church there is no salvation*. This belief has the same basis as the Orthodox belief in the unbreakable unity of the Church: it follows from the close relation between God and His Church. 'A person cannot have God as his Father if he does not have the Church as his Mother.'[1] So wrote St Cyprian; and to him this seemed an evident truth, because he could not think of God and the Church apart from one another. God is salvation, and God's saving power is mediated to humans in His Body, the Church. '*Extra Ecclesiam nulla salus*. All the categorical strength and point of this aphorism lies in its tautology. Outside the Church there is no salvation, because *salvation is the Church*.'[2] Does it therefore follow that anyone who is not visibly within the Church is necessarily damned? Of course not; still less does it follow that everyone who is visibly within the Church is necessarily saved. As Augustine wisely remarked, 'How many sheep there are without, how many wolves within!'[3] While there is

1. *On the Unity of the Catholic Church*, 6
2. G. Florovsky, 'The Catholicity of the Church,' in *Bible, Church, Tradition*, pp. 37–8
3. *Homilies on John*, xlv, 12

no division between a 'visible' and an 'invisible Church', yet there may be members of the Church who are not visibly such, but whose membership is known to God alone. If anyone is saved, he must *in some sense* be a member of the Church; *in what sense*, we cannot always say.[1]

The Church is infallible. This again follows from the indissoluble unity between God and His Church. Christ and the Holy Spirit cannot err, and since the Church is Christ's body, since it is a continued Pentecost, it is therefore infallible. It is 'the pillar and the ground of truth' (1 Timothy iii, 15). 'When He, the Spirit of truth, has come, He will guide you into all truth' (John xvi, 13). So Christ promised at the Last Supper; and Orthodoxy believes that Christ's promise cannot fail. In the words of Dositheus: 'We believe the Catholic Church to be taught by the Holy Spirit . . . and therefore we both believe and profess as true and undoubtedly certain, that it is impossible for the Catholic Church to err, or to be at all deceived, or ever to choose falsehood instead of truth.'[2]

The Church's infallibility is expressed chiefly through Ecumenical Councils. But before we can understand what makes a council ecumenical, we must consider the place of bishops and of the laity in the Orthodox communion.

BISHOPS:
LAITY: COUNCILS

The Orthodox Church is a hierarchical Church. An essential element in its structure is the Apostolic Succession of bishops. 'The dignity of the bishop is so necessary in the Church,' wrote Dositheus, 'that without him neither the Church nor the name Christian could exist or be spoken of at all . . . He is a living image of God upon earth . . . and a fountain of all the sacraments of the Catholic Church, through which we obtain

1. On this question, see pp. 308–9.
2. *Confession*, Decree xii.

salvation.'[1] 'If any are not with the bishop,' said Cyprian, 'they are not in the Church.'[2]

At his election and consecration an Orthodox bishop is endowed with the threefold power of (1) ruling, (2) teaching, and (3) celebrating the sacraments.

(1) A bishop is appointed by God to guide and to rule the flock committed to his charge; he is a 'monarch' in his own diocese.

(2) At his consecration a bishop receives a special gift or *charisma* from the Holy Spirit, in virtue of which he acts as a teacher of the faith. This ministry of teaching the bishop performs above all at the Eucharist, when he preaches the sermon to the people; when other members of the Church – priests or laypeople – preach sermons, strictly speaking they act as the bishop's delegates. But although the bishop has a special *charisma*, it is always possible that he may fall into error and give false teaching: here as elsewhere the principle of synergy applies, and the divine element does not expel the human. The bishop remains a man, and as such he may make mistakes. The Church is infallible, but there is no such thing as personal infallibility.

(3) The bishop, as Dositheus put it, is 'the fountain of all the sacraments'. In the primitive Church the celebrant at the Eucharist was normally the bishop, and even today a priest, when he celebrates the Divine Liturgy, is really acting as the bishop's deputy.

But the Church is not only hierarchical, it is charismatic and Pentecostal. 'Quench not the Spirit. Despise not prophesyings' (1 Thessalonians v, 19–20). The Holy Spirit is poured out upon *all* God's people. There is a special ordained ministry of bishops, priests, and deacons; yet at the same time the whole people of God are prophets and priests. In the Apostolic Church, besides the institutional ministry conferred by the laying on of hands, there were other *charismata* or gifts conferred directly by the Spirit: Paul mentions 'gifts of healing', the working of miracles, 'speaking with tongues', and the like

1. *Confession*, Decree x.
2. *Letter* lxvi, 8.

(1 Corinthians xii, 28–30). In the Church of later days, these charismatic ministries have been less in evidence, but they have never been wholly extinguished. One thinks, for example, of the ministry of 'eldership', so prominent in nineteenth-century Russia; this is not imparted by a special act of ordination, but can be exercised by a layperson as well as by priest or bishop. Seraphim of Sarov and the *startsy* of Optino exercised an influence far greater than any hierarch.

This 'spiritual', non-institutional aspect of the Church's life has been particularly emphasized by certain recent theologians in the Russian emigration; but it is also stressed by Byzantine writers, most notably Symeon the New Theologian. More than once in Orthodox history the 'charismatics' have come into conflict with the hierarchy, but in the end there is no contradiction between the two elements in the Church's life: it is the same Spirit who is active in both.

We have called the bishop a ruler and monarch, but these terms are not to be understood in a harsh and impersonal sense; for in exercising his powers the bishop is guided by the Christian law of love. He is not a tyrant but a father to his flock. The Orthodox attitude to the episcopal office is well expressed in the prayer used at a consecration:

Grant, O Christ, that this man, who has been appointed a steward of the episcopal grace, may become an imitator of You, the True Shepherd, by laying down his life for Your sheep. Make him a guide to the blind, a light to those in darkness, a teacher to the unreasonable, an instructor to the foolish, a flaming torch in the world; so that having brought to perfection the souls entrusted to him in this present life, he may stand without confusion before Your judgement seat, and receive the great reward which You have prepared for those who have suffered for the preaching of Your Gospel.

The authority of the bishop is fundamentally the authority of the Church. However great the prerogatives of the bishop may be, he is not someone set up *over* the Church, but the holder of an office *in* the Church. Bishop and people are joined in an organic unity, and neither can properly be thought of apart from the other. Without bishops there can be no Orthodox people, but without Orthodox people there can be no true bishop. 'The Church,' said Cyprian, 'is the people united to the bishop, the flock clinging to its shepherd. The bishop is in the Church and the Church in the bishop. '[1]

The relation between the bishop and his flock is a mutual one. The bishop is the divinely appointed *teacher* of the faith, but the *guardian* of the faith is not the episcopate alone, but the whole people of God, bishops, clergy, and laity together. The proclamation of the truth is not the same as the stewardship of the truth: all the people are stewards of the truth, but it is the bishop's particular office to proclaim it. Infallibility belongs to the whole Church, not just to the episcopate in isolation. As the Orthodox Patriarchs said in their Letter of 1848 to Pope Pius IX:

> Among us, neither Patriarchs nor Councils could ever introduce new teaching, for the guardian of religion is the very body of the Church, that is, the people (*laos*) itself.

Commenting on this statement, Khomiakov wrote:

> The Pope is greatly mistaken in supposing that we consider the ecclesiastical hierarchy to be the guardian of dogma. The case is quite different. The unvarying constancy and the unerring truth of Christian dogma does not depend upon any hierarchical order; it is guarded by the totality, by the whole people of the Church, which is the Body of Christ.[2]

This conception of the laity and their place in the Church must be kept in mind when considering the nature of an Ecumenical Council. The laity are guardians and not teachers; therefore, although they may attend a council and take an active part in the proceedings (as Constantine and other Byzantine Emperors did), yet when the moment comes for the council to make a formal proclamation of the faith, it is the bishops alone who, in virtue of their teaching *charisma*, take the final decision.

But councils of bishops can err and be deceived. How then can one be certain that a particular gathering is truly an

1. *Letter* lxvi, 8.
2. Letter in W. J. Birkbeck, *Russia and the English Church*, p. 94.

Ecumenical Council and therefore that its decrees are infallible? Many councils have considered themselves ecumenical and have claimed to speak in the name of the whole Church, and yet the Church has rejected them as heretical: Ephesus in 449, for example, or the Iconoclast Council of Hieria in 754, or Florence in 1438–9. Yet these councils seem in no way different in outward appearance from the Ecumenical Councils. What, then, is the criterion for determining whether a council is ecumenical?

This is a more difficult question to answer than might at first appear, and though it has been much discussed by Orthodox during the past hundred years, it cannot be said that the solutions suggested are entirely satisfactory. All Orthodox know which are the seven councils that their Church accepts as ecumenical, but precisely what it is that makes a council ecumenical is not so clear. There are, so it must be admitted, certain points in the Orthodox theology of councils which remain obscure and which call for further thinking on the part of theologians. With this caution in mind, let us briefly consider the present trend of Orthodox thought on this subject.

To the question how one can know whether a council is ecumenical, Khomiakov and his school gave an answer which at first sight appears clear and straightforward: a council cannot be considered ecumenical unless its decrees are accepted by the whole Church. Florence, Hieria, and the rest, while ecumenical in outward appearance, are not truly so, precisely because they failed to secure this acceptance by the Church at large. (One might object: What about Chalcedon? It was rejected by Syria and Egypt – can we say, then, that it was 'accepted by the Church at large'?) The bishops, so Khomiakov argued, because they are the teachers of the faith, define and proclaim the truth in council; but these definitions must then be acclaimed by the whole people of God, including the laity, because it is the whole people of God that constitutes the guardian of Tradition. This emphasis on the need for councils to be received by the Church at large has been viewed with suspicion by some Orthodox theologians, both Greek and Russian, who fear that Khomiakov and his followers have endangered the prerogatives of the episcopate and 'democratized' the idea of the Church. But in a qualified and carefully guarded form, Khomiakov's view is now fairly widely accepted in contemporary Orthodox thought.

This act of acceptance, this reception of councils by the Church as a whole, must not be understood in a juridical sense:

> It does not mean that the decisions of the councils should be confirmed by a general plebiscite and that without such a plebiscite they have no force. There is no such plebiscite. But from historical experience it clearly appears that the voice of a given council has truly been the voice of the Church or that it has not: that is all.[1]

At a true Ecumenical Council the bishops recognize what the truth is and proclaim it; this proclamation is then verified by the assent of the whole Christian people, an assent which is not, as a rule, expressed formally and explicitly, but *lived*.

It is not merely the numbers or the distribution of its members which determines the ecumenicity of a council:

> An 'Ecumenical' Council is such, not because accredited representatives of all the Autocephalous Churches have taken part in it, but because it has borne witness to the faith of the Ecumenical Church.[2]

The ecumenicity of a council cannot be decided by outward criteria alone: 'Truth can have no external criterion, for it is manifest of itself and made inwardly plain.'[3] The infallibility of the Church must not be 'exteriorized', nor understood in too 'material' a sense:

> It is not the 'ecumenicity' but the truth of the councils which makes their decisions obligatory for us. We touch here upon the fundamental mystery of the Orthodox doctrine of the Church: the Church is the miracle of the presence of God among humans, beyond all formal 'criteria', all formal 'infallibility'. It is not enough to summon an 'Ecumenical Council' . . . it is also necessary that in the midst of those so assembled there be present He who said: 'I am the Way,

1. S. Bulgakov, *The Orthodox Church*, p. 89.
2. Metropolitan Seraphim, *L'Église orthodoxe*, p. 51.
3. V. Lossky, *The Mystical Theology of the Eastern Church*, p. 188.

the Truth, the Life.' Without this presence, however numerous and representative the assembly may be, it will not be in the truth. Protestants and Catholics usually fail to understand this fundamental truth of Orthodoxy: both materialize the presence of God in the Church – the one party in the *letter* of Scripture, the other in the *person* of the Pope – though they do not thereby avoid the miracle, but clothe it in a concrete form. For Orthodoxy, the sole 'criterion of truth' remains God Himself, living mysteriously in the Church, leading it in the way of the Truth.[1]

THE LIVING AND THE DEAD:
THE MOTHER OF GOD

In God and in His Church there is no division between the living and the departed, but all are one in the love of the Father. Whether we are alive or whether we are dead, as members of the Church we still belong to the same family, and still have a duty to bear one another's burdens. Therefore just as Orthodox Christians here on earth pray for one another and ask for one another's prayers, so they pray also for the faithful departed and ask the faithful departed to pray for them. Death cannot sever the bond of mutual love which links the members of the Church together.

Prayers for the Departed. 'With the saints give rest, O Christ, to the souls of Your servants, where there is neither sickness, nor sorrow, nor sighing, but life everlasting.' So the Orthodox Church prays for the faithful departed; and again:

O God of spirits and of all flesh, You have trampled down death and overthrown the devil, and given life to Your world. Give rest, O Lord, to the souls of Your departed servants, in a place of light, refreshment, and repose, whence all pain, sorrow, and sighing have fled away. Pardon every transgression which they have committed, whether by word or deed or thought.

Orthodox are convinced that Christians here on earth have a

1. J. Meyendorff, quoted by M. J. le Guillou, *Mission et unité* (Paris 1960), vol. 2, p. 313.

duty to pray for the departed, and they are confident that the dead are helped by such prayers. But precisely in what way do our prayers help the dead? What exactly is the condition of souls in the period between death and the Resurrection of the Body at the Last Day? Here Orthodox teaching is not entirely clear, and has varied somewhat at different times. In the seventeenth century a number of Orthodox writers – most notably Peter of Moghila, and Dositheus in his *Confession* – upheld the Roman Catholic doctrine of Purgatory, or something very close to it.[1] (According to the normal Roman teaching, at least in the past, souls in Purgatory undergo expiatory suffering, and so render 'satisfaction' for their sins.) Today most if not all Orthodox theologians reject the idea of Purgatory, at least in this form. The majority would be inclined to say that the faithful departed do not suffer at all. Another school holds that perhaps they suffer, but, if so, their suffering is of a purificatory but not an expiatory character; for when a person dies in the grace of God, then God freely forgives him all his sins and demands no expiatory penalties: Christ, the Lamb of God who takes away the sin of the world, is our *only* atonement and satisfaction. Yet a third group would prefer to leave the whole question entirely open: let us avoid detailed formulation about the life after death, they say, and preserve instead a reverent and agnostic reticence. When St Antony of Egypt was once worrying about divine providence, a voice came to him, saying: 'Antony, attend to yourself; for these are the judgements of God, and it is not for you to know them.'[2]

The Saints. Symeon the New Theologian describes the saints as forming a golden chain:

The Holy Trinity, pervading everyone from first to last, from head to foot, binds them all together ... The saints in each generation, joined

1. It should be remarked, however, that even in the seventeenth century there were many Orthodox who rejected the Roman teaching on Purgatory. The statements on the departed in Moghila's *Orthodox Confession* were carefully changed by Meletius Syrigos, while in later life Dositheus specifically retracted what he had written on the subject in his *Confession*.

2. *Apophthegmata* (*P.G.* lxv), Antony, 2.

to those who have gone before, and filled like them with light, become a golden chain, in which each saint is a separate link, united to the next by faith, works, and love. So in the One God they form a single chain which cannot quickly be broken.[1]

Such is the Orthodox idea of the communion of saints. This chain is a chain of mutual love and prayer; and in this loving prayer the members of the Church on earth, 'called to be saints', have their place.

In private an Orthodox Christian is free to ask for the prayers of any member of the Church, whether canonized or not. It would be perfectly normal for an Orthodox child, if orphaned, to end his evening prayers by asking for the intercessions not only of the Mother of God and the saints, but of his own mother and father. In its public worship, however, the Church usually asks the prayers only of those whom it has officially proclaimed as saints; but in exceptional circumstances a public cult may become established without any formal act of canonization. The Greek Church under the Ottoman Empire soon began to commemorate the New Martyrs in its worship, but to avoid the notice of the Turks there was usually no official act of proclamation: the cult of the New Martyrs was in most cases something that arose spontaneously under popular initiative. The same thing happened under Communism with the New Martyrs of Russia: for a long time they were honoured in secret by believers in what was then the Soviet Union, but it was only after 1988 that it became possible for the Russian Church openly to proclaim them as saints.

Reverence for the saints is closely bound up with the veneration of icons. These are placed by Orthodox not only in their churches, but in each room of their homes, and even in cars and buses. These ever-present icons act as a point of meeting between the living members of the Church and those who have gone before. Icons help Orthodox to look on the saints not as remote and legendary figures from the past, but as contemporaries and personal friends.

At Baptism an Orthodox is given the name of a saint, as a

1. *Centuries*, III, 2–4.

symbol of her or his entry into the unity of the Church which is not only the earthly Church, but also the Church in heaven. Orthodox have a special devotion to the saint whose name they bear; usually they keep an icon of their patron saint in their room and daily ask for his or her intercessions. The festival of their patron saint they keep as their *Name Day*, and to most Orthodox (as to most Roman Catholics in Continental Europe) this is a date far more important than one's birthday. In Serbia each family has its own patron saint, and on the saint's day the family as a whole observes a collective celebration known as the *Slava*.

An Orthodox Christian invokes in prayer not only the saints but the angels, and in particular her or his guardian angel. The angels 'fence us around with their intercessions and shelter us under their protecting wings of immaterial glory'.[1]

The Mother of God. Among the saints a special position belongs to the Blessed Virgin Mary, whom Orthodox reverence as the most exalted among God's creatures, 'more honoured than the cherubim and incomparably more glorious than the seraphim'.[2] Note that we have termed her 'most exalted *among God's creatures*'; Orthodox, like Roman Catholics, *venerate* or *honour* the Mother of God, but in no sense do the members of either Church regard her as a fourth person of the Trinity, nor do they assign to her the *worship* due to God alone. In Greek theology the distinction is very clearly marked: there is a special word, *latreia*, reserved for the worship of God, while for the veneration of the Virgin entirely different terms are employed (*duleia, hyperduleia, proskynesis*).

In Orthodox services Mary is often mentioned, and on each occasion she is usually given her full title: 'Our All-Holy, immaculate, most blessed and glorified Lady, Mother of God and Ever-Virgin Mary.' Here are included the three chief epithets applied to Our Lady by the Orthodox Church: *Theotokos*

1. From the Dismissal Hymn for the Feast of the Archangels (8 November).

2. From the hymn *Meet it is*, sung at the Liturgy of St John Chrysostom and at other services.

(God-bearer, Mother of God), *Aeiparthenos* (Ever-Virgin), and *Panagia* (All-Holy). The first of these titles was assigned to her by the third Ecumenical Council (Ephesus, 431), the second by the fifth Ecumenical Council (Constantinople, 553).[1] The title *Panagia*, although never a subject of dogmatic definition, is accepted and used by all Orthodox.

The appellation *Theotokos* is of particular importance, for it provides the key to the Orthodox devotion to the Virgin. We honour Mary because she is the Mother of our God. We do not venerate her in isolation, but because of her relation to Christ. Thus the reverence shown to Mary, so far from eclipsing the worship of God, has exactly the opposite effect: the more we esteem Mary, the more vivid is our awareness of the majesty of her Son, for it is precisely on account of the Son that we venerate the Mother.

We honour the Mother on account of her Son: Mariology is simply an extension of Christology. The Fathers of the Council of Ephesus insisted on calling Mary *Theotokos*, not because they desired to glorify her as an end in herself, apart from her Son, but because only by honouring Mary could they safeguard a right doctrine of Christ's person. Anyone who thinks out the implications of that great phrase, *The Word was made flesh*, cannot but feel a profound awe for her who was chosen as the instrument of so surpassing a mystery. When people refuse to honour Mary, only too often it is because they do not really believe in the Incarnation.

But Orthodox honour Mary, not only because she is *Theotokos*, but because she is *Panagia*, All-Holy. Among all God's creatures, she is the supreme example of synergy or co-operation between the purpose of the deity and human freedom. God, who always respects our liberty of choice, did not wish to become incarnate without the willing consent of His Mother. He waited for her voluntary response: 'Here am I, the

1. Belief in the Perpetual Virginity of Mary may seem at first sight contrary to Scripture, since Mark iii, 31 mentions the 'brothers' of Christ. But the reference here may be to half-brothers, born to Joseph from a previous marriage; also the word employed here in Greek can mean cousin or other close relative, as well as brother in the strict sense.

servant of the Lord; let it be as you have said' (Luke i, 38).
Mary could have refused; she was not merely passive, but an
active participant in the mystery. As Nicolas Cabasilas said:

> The Incarnation was not only the work of the Father, of His
> Power and His Spirit ... but it was also the work of the will and
> faith of the Virgin ... Just as God became incarnate voluntarily, so
> He wished that His Mother should bear Him freely and with her
> full consent.[1]

If Christ is the New Adam, Mary is the New Eve, whose
obedient submission to the will of God counterbalanced Eve's
disobedience in Paradise. 'So the knot of Eve's disobedience
was loosed through the obedience of Mary; for what Eve, a
virgin, bound by her unbelief, that Mary, a virgin, unloosed by
her faith.'[2] 'Death by Eve, life by Mary.'[3]

The Orthodox Church calls Mary 'All-Holy'; it calls her
'immaculate' or 'spotless' (in Greek, *achrantos*); and all Orthodox are agreed in believing that Our Lady was free from *actual*
sin. But was she also free from *original* sin? In other words,
does Orthodoxy agree with the Roman Catholic doctrine of the
Immaculate Conception, proclaimed as a dogma by Pope Pius
IX in 1854, according to which Mary, from the moment she was
conceived by her mother St Anne, was by God's special decree
delivered from 'all stain of original sin'? The Orthodox Church
has never in fact made any formal and definitive pronounce-
ment on the matter. In the past individual Orthodox have
made statements which, if not definitely affirming the doctrine
of the Immaculate Conception, at any rate approach close to it;
but since 1854 the great majority of Orthodox have rejected
the doctrine, for several reasons. They feel it to be unnecessary;
they feel that, at any rate as defined by the Roman Catholic
Church, it implies a false understanding of original sin; they
suspect the doctrine because it seems to separate Mary from
the rest of the descendants of Adam, putting her in a completely

1. *On the Annunciation*, 4–5, in *Patrologia Orientalis*, vol. XIX (Paris 1926),
p.488.

2. Irenaeus, *Against the Heresies*, III, xxii, 4.

3. Jerome, *Letter* xxii, 21.

different class from all the other righteous men and women of the Old Testament. From the Orthodox point of view, however, the whole question belongs to the realm of theological opinion; and if an individual Orthodox today felt impelled to believe in the Immaculate Conception, he or she could not be termed a heretic for so doing.

But Orthodoxy, while for the most part denying the doctrine of the Immaculate Conception of Mary, firmly believes in her Bodily Assumption.[1] Like the rest of humankind, Our Lady underwent physical death, but in her case the Resurrection of the Body has been anticipated: after death her body was taken up or 'assumed' into heaven and her tomb was found to be empty. She has passed beyond death and judgement, and lives already in the Age to Come. Yet she is not thereby separated from the rest of humanity, for that same bodily glory which Mary enjoys now, all of us hope one day to share.

Belief in the Assumption of the Mother of God is clearly and unambiguously affirmed in the hymns sung by the Church on 15 August, the Feast of the 'Dormition' or 'Falling Asleep'. But Orthodoxy, unlike Rome, has never proclaimed the Assumption as a dogma, nor would it ever wish to do so. The doctrines of the Trinity and the Incarnation have been proclaimed as dogmas, for they belong to the public preaching of the Church; but the glorification of Our Lady belongs to the Church's inner Tradition:

It is hard to speak and not less hard to think about the mysteries which the Church keeps in the hidden depths of her inner consciousness ... The Mother of God was never a theme of the public preaching of the Apostles; while Christ was preached on the housetops, and proclaimed for all to know in an initiatory teaching addressed to the whole world, the mystery of his Mother was revealed only to those who were within the Church ... It is not so much an object of faith as a foundation of our hope, a fruit of faith, ripened in Tradition. Let us

---

1. Immediately after the Pope proclaimed the Assumption as a dogma in 1950, a few Orthodox (by way of reaction against the Roman Catholic Church) began to express doubts about the Bodily Assumption and even explicitly to deny it; but they are certainly *not* representative of the Orthodox Church as a whole.

therefore keep silence, and let us not try to dogmatize about the supreme glory of the Mother of God.[1]

THE LAST THINGS

For the Christian there exist but two ultimate alternatives, heaven and hell. The Church awaits the final consummation of the end, which in Greek theology is termed the *apocatastasis* or 'restoration', when Christ will return in great glory to judge both the living and the dead. The final *apocatastasis* involves, as we have seen, the redemption and the glorification of matter: at the Last Day the righteous will rise from the grave and be united once more to a body – not such a body as we now possess, but one that is transfigured and 'spiritual', in which inward sanctity is made outwardly manifest. And not only our human bodies but the whole material order will be transformed: God will create a new heaven and a new earth.

But hell exists as well as heaven. In recent years many Christians – not only in the west, but at times also in the Orthodox Church – have come to feel that the idea of hell is inconsistent with belief in a loving God. But to argue thus is to display a sad and perilous confusion of thought. While it is true that God loves us with an infinite love, it is also true that He has given us free will; and since we have free will, it is possible for us to reject God. Since free will exists, hell exists; for hell is nothing else than the rejection of God. If we deny hell, we deny free will. 'No one is so good and full of pity as God,' wrote Mark the Monk or Hermit (early fifth century); 'but even He does not forgive those who do not repent.'[2] God will not force us to love Him, for love is no longer love if it is not free; how then can God reconcile to Himself those who refuse all reconciliation?

The Orthodox attitude towards the Last Judgement and hell is clearly expressed in the choice of Gospel readings at the Liturgy on three successive Sundays shortly before Lent. On

1. V. Lossky, '*Panagia*', in *The Mother of God*, edited by E. L. Mascall (London 1949), p. 35.

2. *On those who think to be justified from works*, 71 (*P.G.* lxv, 940D).

the first Sunday is read the parable of the Publican and Pharisee, on the second the parable of the Prodigal Son, stories which illustrate the immense forgiveness and mercy of God towards all sinners who repent. But in the Gospel for the third Sunday – the parable of the Sheep and the Goats – we are reminded of the other truth: that it is possible to reject God and to turn away from Him to hell. 'Then shall He say to those on the left hand, The curse of God is upon you, go from My sight into everlasting fire' (Matthew xxv, 41).

There is no terrorism in the Orthodox doctrine of God. Orthodox Christians do not cringe before Him in abject fear, but think of Him as *philanthropos*, the 'lover of humankind'. Yet they keep in mind that Christ at His Second Coming will come as *judge*.

Hell is not so much a place where God imprisons humans, as a place where humans, by misusing their free will, choose to imprison themselves. And even in hell the wicked are not deprived of the love of God, but by their own choice they experience as suffering what the saints experience as joy. 'The love of God will be an intolerable torment for those who have not acquired it within themselves.'[1]

Hell exists as a final possibility, but several of the Fathers have none the less believed that in the end all will be reconciled to God. It is heretical to say that all *must* be saved, for this is to deny free will; but it is legitimate to hope that all *may* be saved. Until the Last Day comes, we must not despair of anyone's salvation, but must long and pray for the reconciliation of all without exception. No one must be excluded from our loving intercession. 'What is a merciful heart?' asked Isaac the Syrian. 'It is a heart that burns with love for the whole of creation, for humans, for the birds, for the beasts, *for the demons*, for all creatures.'[2] Gregory of Nyssa said that Christians may legitimately hope even for the redemption of the devil.

The Bible ends upon a note of keen expectation: 'Surely I

1. V. Lossky, *The Mystical Theology of the Eastern Church*, p. 234.
2. *Mystic Treatises*, edited by A. J. Wensinck (Amsterdam, 1923), p. 341.

am coming quickly. Amen. Even so, come, Lord Jesus' (Revelation xxii, 20). In the same spirit of eager hope the first Christians used to pray, 'Let grace come and let this world pass away.'[1] From one point of view the first Christians were wrong: they imagined that the end of the world would occur almost immediately, whereas in fact two millennia have passed and still the end has not yet come. It is not for us to know the times and the seasons, and perhaps this present order will last for many millennia more. Yet from another point of view the early Church was right. For whether the end comes soon or late, it is always *imminent*, always spiritually close at hand, even though it may not be temporally close. The Day of the Lord will come 'as a thief in the night' (1 Thessalonians v, 2) at an hour when we expect it not. Christians, therefore, as in Apostolic times, today must always be prepared, waiting in constant expectation. One of the most encouraging signs of revival in contemporary Orthodoxy is the renewed awareness among many Orthodox of the Second Coming and its relevance. 'When a pastor on a visit to Russia asked what is the burning problem of the Russian Church, a priest replied without hesitation: the *Parousia*.'[2]

Yet the Second Coming is not simply an event in the future, for in the life of the Church the Age to Come has already begun to break through into this present age. For members of God's Church, the 'Last Times' are already inaugurated, since here and now Christians enjoy the firstfruits of God's Kingdom. *Even so, come, Lord Jesus*. He comes already – in the Holy Liturgy and the worship of the Church.

1. *Didache*, x, 6.
2. P. Evdokimov, *L'Orthodoxie*. p. 9 (*Parousia*: the Greek term for the Second Coming).

CHAPTER 13

Orthodox Worship, I:
The Earthly Heaven

> The church is an earthly heaven in which the heavenly God
> dwells and moves.
>
> *St Germanus, Patriarch of Constantinople (died 733)*

DOCTRINE AND WORSHIP

There is a story in the *Russian Primary Chronicle* of how
Vladimir, Prince of Kiev, while still a pagan, desired to know
which was the true religion, and therefore sent his followers
to visit the various countries of the world in turn. They went
first to the Muslim Bulgars of the Volga, but observing that
these when they prayed gazed around them like men possessed, the Russians continued on their way dissatisfied.
'There is no joy among them,' they reported to Vladimir,
'but mournfulness and a great smell; and there is nothing
good about their system.' Travelling next to Germany and
Rome, they found the worship more satisfactory, but com-
plained that here too it was without beauty. Finally they jour-
neyed to Constantinople, and here at last, as they attended
the Divine Liturgy in the great Church of the Holy Wisdom,
they discovered what they desired. 'We knew not whether
we were in heaven or on earth, for surely there is no such
splendour or beauty anywhere upon earth. We cannot describe it to you: only this we know, that God dwells there
among humans, and that their service surpasses the worship
of all other places. For we cannot forget that beauty.'

In this story can be seen several features characteristic of
Orthodox Christianity. There is first the emphasis upon divine
beauty: *we cannot forget that beauty*. It has seemed to many
that the peculiar gift of Orthodox peoples – and especially of
Byzantium and Russia – is this power of perceiving the beauty

of the spiritual world, and expressing that celestial beauty in their worship.

In the second place it is characteristic that the Russians should have said, *we knew not whether we were in heaven or on earth*. Worship, for the Orthodox Church, is nothing else than 'heaven on earth'. The Holy Liturgy is something that embraces two worlds at once, for both in heaven and on earth the Liturgy is one and the same – one altar, one sacrifice, one presence. In every place of worship, however humble its outward appearance, as the faithful gather to perform the Eucharist, they are taken up into the 'heavenly places'; in every place of worship when the Holy Sacrifice is offered, not merely the local congregation is present, but the Church universal – the saints, the angels, the Mother of God, and Christ himself. 'Now the celestial powers are present with us, and worship invisibly.'[1] *This we know, that God dwells there among humans.*

Orthodox, inspired by this vision of 'heaven on earth', have striven to make their worship in outward splendour and beauty an icon of the great Liturgy in heaven. In the year 612, on the staff of the Church of the Holy Wisdom, there were 80 priests, 150 deacons, 40 deaconesses, 70 subdeacons, 160 readers, 25 cantors, and 100 doorkeepers: this gives some faint idea of the magnificence of the service which Vladimir's envoys attended. But many who have experienced Orthodox worship under very different outward surroundings have felt, no less than those Russians from Kiev, a sense of God's presence among humans. Turn, for example, from the *Russian Primary Chronicle* to the letter of an Englishwoman, written in 1935:

This morning was so queer. A very grimy and sordid Presbyterian mission hall in a mews over a garage, where the Russians are allowed once a fortnight to have the Liturgy. A very stage property iconostasis and a few modern icons. A dirty floor to kneel on and a form along the wall . . . And in this two superb old priests and a deacon, clouds of incense, and at the Anaphora, an overwhelming supernatural impression.[2]

1. Words sung at the Great Entrance in the Liturgy of the Presanctified.
2. *The Letters of Evelyn Underhill*, p. 248.

There is yet a third characteristic of Orthodoxy which the story of Vladimir's envoys illustrates. When they wanted to discover the true faith, the Russians did not ask about moral rules or demand a reasoned statement of doctrine, but watched the different nations at prayer. The Orthodox approach to religion is fundamentally a liturgical approach, which understands doctrine in the context of divine worship: it is no coincidence that the word 'Orthodoxy' should signify alike right belief and right worship, for the two things are inseparable. It has been truly said of the Byzantines, 'Dogma with them is not only an intellectual system apprehended by the clergy and expounded to the laity, but a field of vision wherein all things on earth are seen in their relation to things in heaven, first and foremost through liturgical celebration.'[1] In the words of Georges Florovsky, 'Christianity is a liturgical religion. The Church is first of all a worshipping community. Worship comes first, doctrine and discipline second.'[2] Those who wish to know about Orthodoxy should not so much read books as follow the example of Vladimir's retinue and attend the Liturgy. As Christ said to Andrew, 'Come and see' (John i, 39).

Orthodoxy sees human beings above all else as liturgical creatures who are most truly themselves when they glorify God, and who find their perfection and self-fulfilment in worship. Into the Holy Liturgy which expresses their faith, the Orthodox peoples have poured their whole religious experience. It is the Liturgy which has inspired their best poetry, art, and music. Among Orthodox, the Liturgy has never become the preserve of the learned and the clergy, as it tended to be in the medieval west, but it has remained *popular* – the common possession of the whole Christian people:

The normal Orthodox lay worshipper, through familiarity from earliest childhood, is entirely at home in church, thoroughly conversant with the audible parts of the Holy Liturgy, and takes part with unconscious and unstudied ease in the action of the rite, to an extent only

1. George Every, *The Byzantine Patriarchate* (London 1947), p. ix.

2. 'The Elements of Liturgy in the Orthodox Catholic Church', in the periodical *One Church*, vol. XIII (New York 1959), nos. 1–2, p. 24.

shared in by the hyper-devout and ecclesiastically minded in the west.[1]

In the dark days of their history – under the Mongols, the Turks, or the Communists – it is to the Holy Liturgy that the Orthodox peoples have always turned for inspiration and new hope; nor have they turned in vain.

THE OUTWARD SETTING OF THE SERVICES:
PRIEST AND PEOPLE

The basic pattern of services is the same in the Orthodox as in the Roman Catholic Church: there is, first the *Holy Liturgy* (the Eucharist or Mass); secondly, the *Divine Office* (i.e. the two chief offices of Matins and Vespers, together with the Midnight Office, the First, Third, Sixth and Ninth Hours, and Compline);[2] and thirdly, the *Occasional Offices* – i.e. services intended for special occasions, such as Baptism, Marriage, Monastic Profession, Royal Coronation, Consecration of a Church, Burial of the Dead. In addition to these, the Orthodox Church makes use of a great variety of lesser blessings.

While in many Anglican and almost all Roman Catholic parish churches, the Eucharist is celebrated daily, in the Orthodox Church today a daily Liturgy is not usual except in cathedrals and large monasteries; in a normal parish church it is celebrated only on Sundays and feasts. But in contemporary Russia, where places of worship are few and many Christians are obliged to work on Sundays, a daily Liturgy has become the practice in many town parishes.

In its services the Orthodox Church uses the language of the people: Arabic in Antioch, Finnish in Helsinki, Japanese in Tokyo, English (when required) in London or New York. One of the first tasks of Orthodox missionaries – from Cyril and Methodius in the ninth century, to Innocent Veniaminov and

1. Austin Oakley, *The Orthodox Liturgy* (London 1958), p. 12.

2. In the Roman rite Nocturns (the equivalent of the Byzantine Midnight Office) is a part of Matins, but in the Byzantine rite the Midnight Office is a separate service. Byzantine Matins is equivalent to Matins and Lauds in the Roman rite.

Nicolas Kassatkin in the nineteenth – has always been to translate the service books into native tongues. In practice, however,
there are partial exceptions to this general principle of using
the vernacular; the Greek-speaking Churches employ, not
modern Greek, but the Greek of New Testament and Byzantine times, while the Russian Church still uses the medieval
translations in Church Slavonic. In 1906 many Russian bishops
in fact recommended that Church Slavonic be replaced more
or less generally by modern Russian, but the Bolshevik Revolution occurred before this scheme could be carried into effect.

In the Orthodox Church today, as in the early Church, all
services are sung or chanted. There is no Orthodox equivalent
to the Roman 'Low Mass' or to the Anglican 'Said Celebration'. At every Liturgy, as at every Matins and Vespers, incense
is used and the service is sung, even though there may be no
choir or congregation, but the priest and a single reader alone.
In their Church music the Greek-speaking Orthodox continue
to use the ancient Byzantine plain-chant, with its eight 'tones'.
This plain-chant the Byzantine missionaries took with them
into the Slavonic lands, but over the centuries it has become
extensively modified, and the various Slavonic Churches have
each developed their own style and tradition of ecclesiastical
music. Of these traditions the Russian is the best known and
the most immediately attractive to western ears; many consider
Russian Church music the finest in all Christendom, and alike
in Russia itself and in the emigration there are justly celebrated
Russian choirs. Until very recent times all singing in Orthodox
churches was usually done by the choir; today, a small but
increasing number of parishes in Greece, Russia, Romania,
and the diaspora are beginning to revive congregational singing
– if not throughout the service, then at any rate at special
moments such as the Creed and the Lord's Prayer.

In the Orthodox Church today, as in the early Church, singing
is unaccompanied and instrumental music is not found, except
among certain Orthodox in America – particularly the Greeks –
who are now showing a *penchant* for the organ or the harmonium.
Most Orthodox do not use hand or sanctuary bells inside the
church; but they have outside belfries, and take great delight in

ringing the bells not only before but at various moments during the service itself. Russian bell-ringing used to be particularly famous. 'Nothing,' wrote Paul of Aleppo during his visit to Moscow in 1655, 'nothing affected me so much as the united clang of all the bells on the eves of Sundays and great festivals, and at midnight before the festivals. The earth shook with their vibrations, and like thunder the drone of their voices went up to the skies.' 'They rang the brazen bells after their custom. May God not be startled at the noisy pleasantness of their sounds!'[1]

An Orthodox Church is usually more or less square in plan, with a wide central space covered by a dome. (In Russia the church dome has assumed that striking onion shape which forms so characteristic a feature of every Russian landscape.) The elongated naves and chancels, common in cathedrals and larger parish churches of the Gothic style, are not found in eastern church architecture. In the past it was not the custom to have chairs or pews in the central part of the church, although there might be benches or stalls along the walls; but sadly in recent years there has been an increasing tendency, alike in Greece and in the diaspora, to clutter the entire church with rows of seats. Yet even so it is still the normal practice for an Orthodox to stand during the greater part of the church service (non-Orthodox visitors are often astonished to see old women remaining on their feet for several hours without apparent signs of fatigue); but there are moments when the congregation can sit or kneel. Canon xx of the first Ecumenical Council forbids all kneeling on Sundays or on any of the fifty days between Easter and Pentecost, but today this rule is unfortunately not always strictly observed.

It is a remarkable thing how great a difference the presence or absence of pews can make to the whole spirit of Christian worship. There is in Orthodox worship a flexibility, an unselfconscious informality, not found among western congregations, at any rate north of the Alps. Western worshippers, ranged in their neat rows, all in their proper places, cannot move about during the service without causing a disturbance; a western

1. *The Travels of Macarius*, edited Ridding, p. 27 and p. 6.

congregation is generally expected to arrive at the beginning and to stay to the end. But in Orthodox worship people can come and go far more freely, and nobody is greatly surprised if they move about during the service. The same informality and freedom also characterizes the behaviour of the clergy: ceremonial movements are not so minutely prescribed as in the west, priestly gestures are less stylized and more natural. This informality, while it can lead at times to irreverence, is in the end a precious quality which Orthodox would be most sorry to lose. They are at home in their church – not troops on a parade ground, but children in their Father's house. Orthodox worship is often termed 'otherworldly', but could more truly be described as 'homely': it is a *family* affair. Yet behind this homeliness and informality there lies a deep sense of mystery.

In every Orthodox Church the sanctuary is divided from the rest of the interior by the *iconostasis*, a solid screen, usually of wood, covered with panel icons. In early days the chancel was separated merely by a low screen three or four feet high. Sometimes this screen was surmounted by an open series of columns supporting a horizontal beam or architrave: a screen of this kind can still be seen at St Mark's, Venice. Only in comparatively recent times – in many places not until the fifteenth or sixteenth century – was the space between these columns filled up, and the iconostasis given its present solid form. Many Orthodox liturgists today would be glad to follow St John of Kronstadt's example, and revert to a more open type of iconostasis; in a few places this has actually been done.

The iconostasis is pierced by three doors. The large door in the centre – the *Holy* or *Royal Door* – when opened affords a view through to the altar. This door is closed by double gates, behind which hangs a curtain. Outside service time, except during Easter week, the gates are kept closed and the curtain drawn. During services, at particular moments the gates are sometimes open, sometimes closed, while occasionally when the gates are closed the curtain is drawn across as well. Many Greek parishes, however, now no longer close the gates or draw the curtain at any point in the Liturgy; in a number of churches the gates have been removed altogether, while other churches have followed a course which is liturgically far more correct – keeping the gates, but removing the curtain. Of the two other doors, that on the left leads into the 'chapel' of the *Prothesis* or Preparation (here the sacred vessels are kept, and here the priest prepares the bread and the wine at the beginning of the Liturgy); that on the right leads into the *Diakonikon* (now generally used as a vestry, but originally the place where the sacred books, particularly the Book of the Gospels, were kept together with the relics). Laypeople are not allowed to go behind the iconostasis, except for a special reason such as serving at the Liturgy. The altar in an Orthodox Church – the Holy Table or Throne, as it is called – stands free of the east wall, in the centre of the sanctuary; behind the altar and against the wall is set the bishop's throne.

Orthodox churches are full of icons – on the screen, on the walls, in special shrines, or on a kind of desk where they can be venerated by the faithful. When Orthodox people enter a church, their first action will be to buy a candle, go up to an icon, cross themselves, kiss the icon, and light the candle in front of it. 'They be great offerers of candles,' commented the English merchant Richard Chancellor, visiting Russia in the reign of Elizabeth I. In the decoration of the church, the various iconographical scenes and figures are not arranged fortuitously, but according to a definite theological scheme, so that the whole edifice forms one great icon or image of the Kingdom of God. In Orthodox religious art, as in the religious art of the medieval west, there is an elaborate system of symbols, involving every part of the church building and its decoration. Icons, frescoes, and mosaics are not mere ornaments, designed to make the church 'look nice', but have a theological and liturgical function to fulfil.

The icons which fill the church serve as a point of meeting between heaven and earth. As each local congregation prays Sunday by Sunday, surrounded by the figures of Christ, the angels, and the saints, these visible images remind the faithful unceasingly of the invisible presence of the whole company of heaven at the Liturgy. The faithful can feel that the walls of the church open out upon eternity, and they are helped to realize that their Liturgy on earth is one and the same with the great Liturgy of heaven. The multitudinous icons express visibly the sense of 'heaven on earth'.

The worship of the Orthodox Church is communal and popular. Any non-Orthodox who attends Orthodox services with some frequency will quickly realize how closely the whole worshipping community, priest and people alike, are bound together into one; among other things, the absence of pews helps to create a sense of unity. Although most Orthodox congregations do not join in the singing, it should not therefore be imagined that they are taking no real part in the service; nor does the iconostasis – even in its present solid form – make the people feel cut off from the priest in the sanctuary. In any case, many of the ceremonies take place in front of the screen, in full view of the congregation.

There is in most Orthodox worship an unhurried and timeless quality, an effect produced in part by the constant repetition of *Litanies*. Either in a longer or a shorter form, the Litany recurs several times in every service of the Byzantine rite. In these Litanies, the deacon (if there is no deacon, the priest) calls the people to pray for the various needs of the Church and the world, and to each petition the choir or the people reply *Lord, have mercy – Kyrie eleison* in Greek, *Gospodi pomilui* in Russian – probably the first words in an Orthodox service which the visitor grasps. (In some Litanies the response is changed to *Grant this, O Lord*.) The congregation associate themselves with the different intercessions by making the sign of the Cross and bowing. In general the sign of the Cross is employed far more frequently by Orthodox than by western worshippers, and there is a greater freedom about the times when it is used: different worshippers cross themselves at different moments, each as he or she wishes, although there are of course occasions in the service when almost all sign themselves at the same time.

We have described Orthodox worship as timeless and unhurried. Most western people have the idea that Byzantine services, even if not literally timeless, are at any rate of an extreme and intolerable length. Certainly Orthodox functions tend to be more prolonged than their western counterparts, but we must not exaggerate. It is perfectly possible to celebrate the Byzantine Liturgy, and to preach a short sermon, in an hour and a quarter; and in 1943 the Patriarch of Constantinople laid down that in parishes under his jurisdiction the Sunday Liturgy should not last over an hour and a half. Russians on the whole take longer than Greeks over services, but in a normal Russian parish of the emigration, the Vigil Service on Saturday nights lasts no more than two hours, and often less. Monastic offices of course are more extended, and on Mount Athos at great festivals the service sometimes goes on for twelve or even fifteen hours without a break, but this is altogether exceptional.

Non-Orthodox may take heart from the fact that Orthodox are often as alarmed as they by the length of services. 'And now we are entered on our travail and anguish,' writes Paul of Aleppo in his diary as he enters Russia. 'For all their churches are empty of seats. There is not one, even for the bishop; you see the people all through the service standing like rocks, motionless or incessantly bending with their devotions. God help us for the length of their prayers and chants and Masses, for we suffered great pain, so that our very souls were tortured with fatigue and anguish.' And in the middle of Holy Week he exclaims, 'God grant us His special aid to get through the whole of this present week! As for the Muscovites, their feet must surely be of iron.'[1]

---

1. *The Travels of Macarius*, edited Ridding, p. 14 and p. 46.

CHAPTER 14

Orthodox Worship, II:
The Sacraments

> He who was visible as our Redeemer has now passed into the sacraments.
>
> *St Leo the Great*

The chief place in Christian worship belongs to the sacraments or, as they are called in Greek, the *mysteries*. 'It is called a mystery,' writes St John Chrysostom of the Eucharist, 'because what we believe is not the same as what we see, but we see one thing and believe another ... When I hear the Body of Christ mentioned, I understand what is said in one sense, the unbeliever in another.'[1] This double character, at once outward and inward, is the distinctive feature of a sacrament: the sacraments, like the Church, are both visible and invisible; in every sacrament there is the combination of an outward visible sign with an inward spiritual grace. At Baptism the Christian undergoes an outward washing in water and is at the same time cleansed inwardly from sin; at the Eucharist he or she receives what appears from the visible point of view to be bread and wine but in reality is the Body and Blood of Christ.

In most of the sacraments the Church takes material things – water, bread, wine, oil – and makes them a vehicle of the Spirit. In this way the sacraments look back to the Incarnation, when Christ took material flesh and made it a vehicle of the Spirit; and they look forward to, or rather they anticipate, the *apocatastasis* and the final redemption of matter at the Last Day. Orthodoxy rejects any attempt to diminish the materiality of the sacraments. The human person is to be seen in holistic terms, as an integral unity of soul and body, and so the sacra-

---

1. *Homilies on 1 Corinthians*, vii, 1 (*P.G.* lxi, 55).

mental worship in which we humans participate should involve to the full our bodies along with our minds. Baptism is performed by immersion; at the Eucharist leavened bread is used, not just wafers; at Confession the celebrant does not confer absolution from a distance, but lays his hand on the head of the penitent; at a funeral the coffin is customarily left open and all approach to give a last kiss to the departed – the dead body is an object of love, not of abhorrence.

The Orthodox Church speaks customarily of seven sacraments, basically the same seven as in Roman Catholic theology:

- (i)   Baptism;
- (ii)   Chrismation (equivalent to Confirmation in the west);
- (iii) The Eucharist;
- (iv)   Repentance or Confession;
- (v)   Holy Orders;
- (vi)   Marriage or Holy Matrimony;
- (vii) The Anointing of the Sick.

Only in the seventeenth century, when Latin influence was at its height, did this list become fixed and definite. Before that date Orthodox writers vary considerably as to the number of sacraments: John of Damascus speaks of two; Dionysius the Areopagite of six; Joasaph, Metropolitan of Ephesus (fifteenth century), of ten; and those Byzantine theologians who in fact speak of seven sacraments differ as to the items which they include in their list. Even today the number seven has no particular dogmatic significance for Orthodox theology, but is used primarily as a convenience in teaching.

Those who think in terms of 'seven sacraments' must be careful to guard against two misconceptions. In the first place, while all seven are true sacraments, they are not all of equal importance, but there is a certain 'hierarchy' among them. The Eucharist, for example, stands at the heart of all Christian life and experience in a way that the Anointing of the Sick does not. Among the seven, Baptism and the Eucharist occupy a special position: to use a phrase adopted by the Joint Committee of Romanian and Anglican theologians at Bucharest in

1935, these two sacraments are 'pre-eminent among the divine mysteries'.

In the second place, when we talk of 'seven sacraments', we must never isolate these seven from the many other actions in the Church which also possess a sacramental character, and which are conveniently termed *sacramentals*. Included among these sacramentals are the rites for a monastic profession, the great blessing of waters at Epiphany, the service for the burial of the dead, and the anointing of a monarch. In all these there is a combination of outward visible sign and inward spiritual grace. The Orthodox Church also employs a great number of minor blessings, and these, too, are of a sacramental nature: blessings of corn, wine, and oil; of fruits, fields, and homes; of any object or element. These lesser blessings and services are often very practical and prosaic: there are prayers for blessing a car or a railway engine, or for clearing a place of vermin.[1] Between the wider and the narrower sense of the term 'sacrament' there is no rigid division: the whole Christian life must be seen as a unity, as a single mystery or one great sacrament, whose different aspects are expressed in a great variety of acts, some performed but once in our life, others perhaps daily.

The sacraments are *personal*: they are the means whereby God's grace is appropriated to every Christian *individually*. For this reason, in most of the sacraments of the Orthodox Church, the priest mentions the Christian name of each person as he administers the sacrament. When giving Holy Communion, for example, he says: 'The servant of God . . . [name] partakes of the holy Body and Blood of Our Lord'; at the Anointing of the Sick he says: 'O Father, heal Your servant [name] from his sickness both of body and soul'; at an ordination the bishop says, 'The divine grace, which always heals what is weak and makes up what is lacking, ordains [name]'. Note how in each case the celebrant does not speak in the first

1. 'The popular religion of Eastern Europe is liturgical and ritualistic, but not wholly otherworldly. A religion that continues to propagate new forms for cursing caterpillars and for removing dead rats from the bottoms of wells can hardly be dismissed as pure mysticism' (G. Every, *The Byzantine Patriarchate*, p. 198).

person; he does not say, 'I baptize . . .', 'I anoint . . .', 'I ordain . . .'. The 'mysteries' are not our actions but the actions of God in the Church, and the true officiant is always Christ Himself. As St John Chrysostom puts it, 'The priest merely lends his tongue and provides his hand.'[1]

BAPTISM[2]

In the Orthodox Church today, as in the Church of the early centuries, the three sacraments of Christian initiation – Baptism, Confirmation, First Communion – are linked closely together. An Orthodox who becomes a member of Christ is admitted at once to the full privileges of such membership. Orthodox children are not only baptized in infancy, but confirmed in infancy, and given communion in infancy. 'Suffer the little children to come to Me, and forbid them not; for of such is the kingdom of heaven' (Matthew xix, 14).

There are two essential elements in the act of Baptism: the invocation of the Name of the Trinity, and the threefold immersion in water. The priest says, 'The servant of God [name] is baptized into the Name of the Father, Amen. And of the Son, Amen. And of the Holy Spirit, Amen.' As the name of each person in the Trinity is mentioned, the priest immerses the child in the font, either plunging it entirely under the water, or at any rate pouring water over the whole of its body. If the person to be baptized is so ill that immersion would be life endangering, then it is sufficient for water to be poured over the forehead; but otherwise immersion must not be omitted.

Many Orthodox are disturbed by the fact that western Christendom, abandoning the primitive practice of Baptism by immersion, is now content merely to pour a little water over the candidate's forehead, or even to smear some slight moisture on the forehead without pouring any water at all (regrettably this

1. *Homilies on John,* lxxxvi, 4 (*P.G.* lix, 472).
2. In this and the following sections, the sacraments are described according to the present practice in the Byzantine rite; but we must not, of course, forget the possibility, or rather the fact, of a western rite in Orthodoxy (see pp. 185–6).

is now becoming frequent in the Anglican communion). Even though some Orthodox clergy have grown careless about observing the proper practice, there is no doubt about the true Orthodox teaching: immersion is essential (except in emergencies), for if there is no immersion the correspondence between outward sign and inward meaning is lost, and the symbolism of the sacrament is overthrown. Baptism signifies a mystical burial and resurrection with Christ (Romans vi, 4–5 and Colossians ii, 12); and the outward sign of this is the plunging of the candidate into the font, followed by the emergence from the water. Sacramental symbolism therefore requires immersion or 'burial' in the waters of Baptism, and then 'resurrection' out of them once more. Baptism by infusion (when the water is merely poured over part of the body) is permitted in special cases; but Baptism by sprinkling or smearing is quite simply not real Baptism at all.

Through Baptism we receive a full forgiveness of all sin, whether original or actual; we 'put on Christ', becoming members of His Body the Church. To remind them of their Baptism, Orthodox Christians usually wear throughout life a small Cross, hung round the neck on a chain.

Baptism must normally be performed by a bishop or a priest. In cases of emergency, it can be performed by a deacon, or by any man or woman, provided they are Christian. But whereas Roman Catholic theologians hold that if necessary even a non-Christian can administer Baptism, Orthodoxy holds that this is not possible. The person who baptizes must himself have been baptized.

CHRISMATION

Immediately after Baptism, an Orthodox child is 'chrismated' or 'confirmed'. The priest takes a special ointment, the Chrism (in Greek, *myron*), and with this he anoints various parts of the child's body, marking them with the sign of the Cross: first the forehead, then the eyes, nostrils, mouth, and ears, the breast, the hands, and the feet. As he marks each he says, 'The seal of the gift of the Holy Spirit.' The child, who has been incorporated into Christ at Baptism, now receives in Chrismation the gift of the Spirit, thereby becoming a *laïkos* (layperson), a full member of the people (*laos*) of God. Chrismation is an extension of Pentecost: the same Spirit who descended on the Apostles visibly in tongues of fire now descends on the newly baptized invisibly, but with no less reality and power. Through Chrismation every member of the Church becomes a prophet, and receives a share in the royal priesthood of Christ; all Christians alike, because they are chrismated, are called to act as conscious witnesses to the Truth. 'You have an anointing (*chrisma*) from the Holy One, and know all things' (1 John ii, 20).

In the west, it is normally the bishop in person who confers Confirmation; in the east, Chrismation is administered by a priest, but the Chrism which he uses must first have been blessed by a bishop. (In modern Orthodox practice, only a bishop who is head of an autocephalous Church enjoys the right to bless the Chrism.) Thus both in east and west the bishop is involved in the second sacrament of Christian initiation: in the west directly, in the east indirectly.

Chrismation is also used as a sacrament of reconciliation. If an Orthodox apostatizes to Islam and then returns to the Church, when accepted back he or she is chrismated. Similarly if Roman Catholics become Orthodox, the Patriarchate of Constantinople and the Church of Greece usually receive them by Chrismation; but the Russian Church commonly receives them after a simple profession of faith, without chrismating them. Anglicans and other Protestants are always received by Chrismation. Sometimes converts are received by Baptism.

As soon as possible after Chrismation an Orthodox child is brought to communion. A child's earliest memories of the Church will centre on the act of receiving the Holy Gifts of Christ's Body and Blood. Communion is not something to which infants come at the age of six or seven (as in the Roman Catholic Church) or in adolescence (as in Anglicanism), but something from which they have never been excluded.

THE EUCHARIST

Today the Eucharist is celebrated in the Eastern Church according to one of four different services:

(1) *The Liturgy of St John Chrysostom* (the normal Liturgy on Sundays and weekdays).

(2) *The Liturgy of St Basil the Great* (used ten times a year; in structure it closely resembles the Liturgy of St John Chrysostom, but the central Eucharistic Prayer is much longer).

(3) *The Liturgy of St James, the Brother of the Lord* (used once a year, on St James's Day, 23 October, in Jerusalem and a few other places).

(4) *The Liturgy of the Presanctified* (used on Wednesdays and Fridays in Lent, and on the first three days of Holy Week. There is no consecration in this Liturgy, but communion is given from elements consecrated on the previous Sunday.)

In general structure the Liturgies of St John Chrysostom and St Basil are as follows:

I. THE OFFICE OF PREPARATION – the *Prothesis* or *Proskomidia*: the preparation of the bread and wine to be used at the Eucharist.

II. THE LITURGY OF THE WORD – the *Synaxis*
    A. *The Opening of the Service* – the *Enarxis*
    The Litany of Peace
    Psalm 102 (103)
    The Little Litany
    Psalm 145 (146), followed by the hymn *Only-begotten Son and Word of God*
    The Little Litany
    The Beatitudes (with special hymns or *Troparia* appointed for the day)
    B. *The Little Entrance*, followed by the special *Troparia* for the day
    The *Trisagion* – 'Holy God, Holy and Strong, Holy and Immortal, have mercy upon us' – repeated several times
    C. *Readings from Scripture*
    The *Prokimenon* – verses, usually from the Psalms
    The Epistle

Alleluia – sung nine or sometimes three times, with
verses from Scripture intercalated

The Gospel

The Sermon (often transferred to the end of the service)

D. *Intercession for the Church*

The Litany of Fervent Supplication

The Litany of the Departed

The Litany of the Catechumens, and the dismissal of
the Catechumens

III. THE EUCHARIST

A. Two short Litanies of the Faithful lead up to the *Great
Entrance*, which is then followed by the Litany of
Supplication

B. *The Kiss of Peace* and *the Creed*

C. *The Eucharistic Prayer*

Opening Dialogue

Thanksgiving – culminating in the narrative of the Last
Supper, and the words of Christ: 'This is My Body
... This is My Blood ...'

Anamnesis – the act of 'calling to mind' and offering.
The priest 'calls to mind' Christ's death, burial,
Resurrection, Ascension, and Second Coming, and
he 'offers' the Holy Gifts to God

Epiclesis – the Invocation or 'calling down' of the Spirit
on the Holy Gifts

A great Commemoration of all the members of the
Church: the Mother of God, the saints, the departed,
the living

The Litany of Supplication, followed by the Lord's
Prayer

D. The *Elevation* of the Consecrated Gifts and *Fraction*
('breaking') of the Bread

E. *Communion* of the clergy and people

F. *Conclusion* of the service: Thanksgiving and final
Blessing; distribution of the *Antidoron*

The first part of the Liturgy, the Office of Preparation, is performed privately by the priest and deacon in the chapel of the *Prothesis*. Thus the public portion of the service falls into two sections, the Synaxis (a service of hymns, prayers, and readings from Scripture) and the Eucharist proper: originally the Synaxis and the Eucharist were often held separately, but since the fourth century the two have virtually become fused into one service. The Synaxis and the Eucharist each contain a procession, known respectively as the Little and the Great Entrance. At the Little Entrance the Book of the Gospels is carried in procession round the church; at the Great Entrance the bread and wine (prepared before the beginning of the Synaxis) are brought processionally from the *Prothesis* chapel to the altar. The Little Entrance corresponds to the Introit in the western rite (originally the Little Entrance marked the beginning of the public part of the service, but at present it is preceded by various Litanies and Psalms); the Great Entrance corresponds broadly, although not exactly, to the western Offertory Procession. Synaxis and Eucharist alike have a clearly marked climax: in the Synaxis, the reading of the Gospel; in the Eucharist, the *Epiclesis* of the Holy Spirit.

The belief of the Orthodox Church concerning the Eucharist is made quite clear during the course of the Eucharistic Prayer. The priest reads the opening part of the Thanksgiving in a low voice (in some places it is now recited aloud), until he comes to the words of Christ at the Last Supper: 'Take, eat, This is My Body . . .' 'Drink of it, all of you, This is My Blood . . .'; these words are always read in a loud voice, in the full hearing of the congregation. In a low voice once more, the priest recites the *Anamnesis*:

Commemorating the Cross, the Tomb, the Resurrection on the third day, the Ascension into Heaven, the Enthronement at the right hand, and the second and glorious Coming again.

He continues aloud:

Your own from Your own we offer You, in all and for all.

Then comes the *Epiclesis*, as a rule read secretly, but sometimes in full hearing of the congregation:

Send down Your Holy Spirit upon us and upon these gifts here set forth:

And make this bread the Precious Body of Your Christ,
And what is in this cup, the Precious Blood of Your Christ,
Changing them by Your Holy Spirit. Amen, Amen, Amen.[1]

Priest and deacon immediately make a deep bow or prostrate themselves before the Holy Gifts, which have now been consecrated.

It will be evident that the 'moment of consecration' is understood somewhat differently by the Orthodox and the Roman Catholic Churches. According to medieval Latin theology, the consecration is effected by the Words of Institution: 'This is My Body . . .' 'This is My Blood . . .'. According to Orthodox theology, the act of consecration is not complete until the end of the *Epiclesis*, and worship of the Holy Gifts before this point is condemned by the Orthodox Church as 'artolatry' (bread worship). Orthodox, however, do not teach that consecration is effected *solely* by the *Epiclesis*, nor do they regard the Words of Institution as incidental and unimportant. On the contrary, they look upon the entire Eucharistic Prayer as forming a single and indivisible whole, so that the three main sections of the prayer – Thanksgiving, *Anamnesis*, *Epiclesis* – all form an integral part of the one act of consecration. But this of course means that if we are to single out a 'moment of consecration', such a moment cannot come until the *Amen* of the *Epiclesis*.

The Presence of Christ in the Eucharist. As the words of the *Epiclesis* make abundantly plain, the Orthodox Church believes that after consecration the bread and wine become in very truth the Body and Blood of Christ: they are not mere symbols, but the reality. But while Orthodoxy has always insisted on the *reality* of the change, it has never attempted to explain the *manner* of the change: the Eucharistic Prayer in the Liturgy simply uses the neutral term *metaballo*, to 'turn about', 'change', or 'alter'. It is true that in the seventeenth century

1. The *Anamnesis* and *Epiclesis*, as quoted here, are from the Liturgy of St John Chrysostom. In the Liturgy of St Basil they are slightly different.

not only individual Orthodox writers, but Orthodox councils such as that of Jerusalem in 1672, made use of the Latin term 'transubstantiation' (in Greek, *metousiosis*), together with the Scholastic distinction between substance and accidents.[1] But at the same time the Fathers of Jerusalem were careful to add that the use of these terms does not constitute an explanation of the manner of the change, since this is a mystery and must always remain incomprehensible.[2] Yet despite this disclaimer, many Orthodox felt that Jerusalem had committed itself too unreservedly to the terminology of Latin Scholasticism, and it is significant that when in 1838 the Russian Church issued a translation of the Acts of Jerusalem, while retaining the word transubstantiation, it carefully paraphrased the rest of the passage in such a way that the technical terms substance and accidents were not employed.[3]

Today a few Orthodox writers still use the word transubstantiation, but they insist on two points: first, there are many other words which can with equal legitimacy be used to describe the consecration, and, among them all, the term transubstantiation enjoys no unique or decisive authority; secondly, its use does not commit theologians to the acceptance of Aristotelian philosophical concepts. The general position of Orthodoxy in the whole matter is clearly summed up in the *Longer Catechism*, written by St Philaret, Metropolitan of

1. In medieval philosophy a distinction is drawn between the substance or essence (i.e. that which constitutes a thing, which makes it what it is), and the accidents or qualities that belong to a substance (i.e. everything that can be perceived by the senses – size, weight, shape, colour, taste, smell, and so on). A substance is something existing by itself (*ens per se*), an accident can only exist by inhering in something else (*ens in alio*).

Applying this distinction to the Eucharist, we arrive at the doctrine of Transubstantiation. According to this doctrine, at the moment of consecration in the Mass there is a change of substance, but the accidents continue to exist as before: the substances of bread and wine are changed into those of the Body and Blood of Christ, but the accidents of bread and wine – i.e. the qualities of colour, taste, smell, and so forth – continue miraculously to exist and to be perceptible to the senses.

2. Doubtless most Roman Catholics would say the same.

3. This is an interesting example of the way in which the Church is 'selective' in its acceptance of the decrees of local councils (see above, pp. 202–3).

Moscow (1782–1867), and authorized by the Russian Church in 1839:

QUESTION: How are we to understand the word transubstantiation?
ANSWER: ... The word transubstantiation is not to be taken to define the manner in which the bread and wine are changed into the Body and Blood of the Lord; for this none can understand but God; but only thus much is signified, that the bread truly, really, and substantially becomes the very true Body of the Lord, and the wine the very Blood of the Lord.[1]

And the Catechism continues with a quotation from John of Damascus:

If you enquire how this happens, it is enough for you to learn that it is through the Holy Spirit ... we know nothing more than this, that the word of God is true, active, and omnipotent, but in its manner of operation unsearchable.[2]

In every Orthodox parish church, the Blessed Sacrament is normally reserved, most often in a tabernacle on the altar, although there is no strict rule as to the place of reservation. Orthodox, however, do not hold services of public devotion before the reserved sacrament, nor do they have any equivalent to the Roman Catholic functions of Exposition and Benediction. The sacrament is reserved so that communion can be given to the sick, but not for other purposes. The priest blesses the people with the sacrament during the course of the Liturgy, but never outside it. The Eucharist is essentially a meal, and so the significance of the consecrated elements becomes distorted if they are used outside the context of eating and drinking.

The Eucharist as a sacrifice. The Orthodox Church believes the Eucharist to be a sacrifice; and here again the basic Orthodox teaching is set forth clearly in the text of the Liturgy itself. 'Your own from Your own we offer You, in all and for all.' (1) We offer *Your own from Your own*. At the Eucharist the

1. English translation in R. W. Blackmore, *The Doctrine of the Russian Church* (London 1845), p. 92.
2. *On the Orthodox Faith*, IV, 13 (*P.G.* xciv, 1145A).

sacrifice offered is Christ Himself. Our offering of bread and wine is taken up into Christ's self-offering, and so is transformed into His Body and Blood. (2) The offering is *Your own* in a second way: not only is Christ the sacrifice that is offered, but He is also, in the true and deep sense, the one who performs the act of offering. He is both victim and priest, both offering and offerer. As the celebrant says to Christ in the prayer before the Great Entrance, 'You are the one who offers and the one who is offered.' (3) We offer *to You*. The Eucharist, according to the Council of Constantinople held in 1156–7, is offered to the Trinity. It is offered, that is to say, not just by Christ to God the Father, but by Christ to all three persons of the Godhead – by Christ to Himself, together with the Father and the Spirit. Thus if we ask, *What* is the sacrifice of the Eucharist? *By whom* is it offered? *To whom* is it offered? – in each case the answer is *Christ* (although in the third instance we need to add that, when Christ receives the sacrifice, He does this in union with the other two members of the Trinity, for the Godhead is undivided). (4) We offer *for all*: according to Orthodox theology, the Eucharist is a propitiatory sacrifice (in Greek, *thysia hilastirios*), offered on behalf of both the living and the dead.

In the Eucharist, then, the sacrifice which we offer is the sacrifice of Christ. But what does this mean? Theologians have held and continue to hold many different theories on this subject. Some of these theories the Church has rejected as inadequate, but it has never formally committed itself to any particular explanation of the Eucharistic sacrifice. Nicolas Cabasilas sums up the standard Orthodox position as follows:

First, the sacrifice is not a mere figure or symbol but a true sacrifice; secondly, it is not the bread that is sacrificed, but the very Body of Christ; thirdly, the Lamb of God was sacrificed once only, for all time ... The sacrifice at the Eucharist consists, not in the real and bloody immolation of the Lamb, but in the transformation of the bread into the sacrificed Lamb.[1]

The Eucharist is not a bare commemoration nor an imaginary

1. *Commentary on the Divine Liturgy*, 32.

representation of Christ's sacrifice, but the true sacrifice itself; yet on the other hand it is not a new sacrifice, nor a repetition of the sacrifice on Calvary, since the Lamb was sacrificed 'once only, for all time'. The events of Christ's sacrifice – the Incarnation, the Last Supper, the Crucifixion, the Resurrection, the Ascension[1] – are not repeated in the Eucharist, but they are *made present*. 'During the Liturgy, through its divine power, we are projected to the point where eternity cuts across time, and at this point we become true *contemporaries* with the events which we commemorate.'[2] 'All the holy suppers of the Church are nothing else than one eternal and unique Supper, that of Christ in the Upper Room. The same divine act both takes place at a specific moment in history, and is offered always in the sacrament.'[3]

Holy Communion. In the Orthodox Church the laity as well as the clergy always receive communion 'under both kinds'. Communion is given to the laity in a spoon, containing a small piece of the Holy Bread together with a portion of the Wine; it is received standing. Orthodoxy insists on a strict fast before communion, and nothing can be eaten or drunk after waking in the morning.[4] Many Orthodox at the present day receive communion infrequently – perhaps only three or four times a year – not from any disrespect towards the sacrament, but because they have been taught from childhood to approach only after lengthy and careful preparation. During recent years, however, frequent communion – in some parishes, on every Sunday – has become more widespread, alike in Greece, Russia, Romania and the west. This is a welcome return to the practice of the early Christians.

1. Note that Christ's sacrifice includes many things besides His death: this is a most important point in Patristic and Orthodox teaching.

2. P. Evdokimov, *L'Orthodoxie*, p. 241.

3. ibid., p. 208.

4. 'You know that those who invite the Emperor to their house, first clean their home. So you, if you want to bring God into your bodily home for the illumination of your life, must first sanctify your body by fasting' (from the *Hundred Chapters* of Gennadius). In cases of sickness or genuine necessity, a confessor can grant dispensations from this communion fast.

After the final blessing with which the Liturgy ends, the people come up to receive a little piece of bread, called the *Antidoron*, which is blessed but not consecrated, although taken (in part at any rate) from the same loaf as the bread used in the consecration. In most Orthodox parishes non-Orthodox present at the Liturgy are permitted – and indeed, encouraged – to receive the *Antidoron*, as an expression of Christian fellowship and love.

REPENTANCE

Orthodox children receive communion from infancy. Once they are old enough to know the difference between right and wrong and to understand what sin is – probably aged about six or seven – they may be taken to receive another sacrament: Repentance, Penitence, or Confession (in Greek, *metanoia* or *exomologisis*). Through this sacrament sins committed after Baptism are forgiven and the sinner is reconciled to the Church: hence it is often called a 'Second Baptism'. The sacrament acts at the same time as a cure for the healing of the soul, since the priest gives not only absolution but spiritual advice. Since all sin is sin not only against God but against our neighbour, against the community, Confession and penitential discipline in the early Church were a public affair; but for many centuries alike in eastern and western Christendom Confession has taken the form of a private 'conference' between priest and penitent alone. The priest is strictly forbidden to reveal to any third party what he has learnt in Confession.

In Orthodoxy confessions are heard, not in a closed confessional with a grille separating confessor and penitent, but in any convenient part of the church, usually in the open immediately in front of the iconostasis; sometimes priest and penitent stand behind a screen, or there may be a special room in the church set apart for confessions. Whereas in the west the priest sits and the penitent kneels, in the Orthodox Church they both stand (or sometimes they both sit). The penitent often faces a desk on which are placed the Cross and an icon of the Saviour or the Book of the Gospels; the priest stands slightly to one side. This outward arrangement emphasizes that in Confession it is not the priest but God who is the judge, while the priest is only a witness and God's minister. This point is also stressed in words which, in the Russian practice, the priest says to the penitent at the beginning:

Behold, my child, *Christ stands here invisibly and receives your confession*. Therefore do not be ashamed or afraid; conceal nothing from me, but tell me without hesitation everything that you have done, and so you shall have pardon from Our Lord Jesus Christ. See, His holy icon is before us: and *I am merely a witness*, bearing testimony before Him of all the things which you have to say to me. But if you conceal anything from me, you shall have greater sin. Take care, therefore, lest having come to a physician's you depart unhealed.

After this the priest listens to the Confession and if necessary asks questions, and then gives advice. After confessing everything, the penitent kneels or bows his or her head, and the priest, placing his stole (*epitrachilion*) on the penitent's head and then laying his hand upon the stole, says the prayer of absolution. In the Greek books the formula of absolution is deprecative (i.e. in the third person, 'May God forgive . . .'), whereas in the Slavonic books it is indicative (i.e. in the first person, 'I forgive . . .'). The usual Greek formula runs:

Whatever you have said to my humble person, and whatever you have failed to say, whether through ignorance or forgetfulness, whatever it may be, may God forgive you in this world and the next . . . Have no further anxiety; go in peace.

In Slavonic there is this formula:

May Our Lord and God, Jesus Christ, through the grace and bounties of His love towards mankind, forgive you, my child [name], all your transgressions. And I, an unworthy priest, through the power given me by Him, forgive and absolve you from all your sins.

This form, using the word 'I', was originally introduced into Orthodox service books under Latin influence by Peter of Moghila in the Ukraine, and was adopted by the Russian Church in the eighteenth century. Many Orthodox deplore this departure from the traditional sacramental practice of the

Christian east, for in no other case does the priest speak in the first person singular.

The priest may, if he thinks it advisable, impose a penance (*epitimion*), but this is not an essential part of the sacrament and is very often omitted. Many Orthodox have a special 'spiritual father', not necessarily their parish priest, to whom they go regularly for Confession and spiritual advice.[1] There is in Orthodoxy no strict rule laying down how often one should go to Confession; the Russians tend to go more often than the Greeks do. Where infrequent communion prevails – for example, four or five times a year – the faithful may be expected to go to Confession before each communion; but in circles where frequent communion has been re-established, the priest does not necessarily expect a Confession to be made before every communion.

HOLY ORDERS

There are three 'Major Orders' in the Orthodox Church, Bishop, Priest, and Deacon; and two 'Minor Orders', Subdeacon and Reader (once there were other Minor Orders, but at present all except these two have fallen largely into disuse). Ordinations to the Major Orders always occur during the course of the Liturgy, and must always be done individually (the Byzantine rite, unlike the Roman, lays down that no more than one deacon, one priest, and one bishop can be ordained at any single Liturgy). Only a bishop has power to ordain,[2] and the consecration of a new bishop must be performed by three or at least two bishops, never by one alone: since the episcopate is 'collegial' in character, an episcopal consecration is carried

1. In the Orthodox Church guidance is given, not only by an ordained priest, but often by an unordained monk or by a nun; less commonly, members of the non-monastic laity, both men and women, may act as 'spiritual fathers' or 'spiritual mothers'. In such cases, they listen to the penitent's Confession, give counsel and, acting in God's name, they assure the penitent of divine forgiveness; but they are not considered to administer sacramental absolution in the strict canonical sense.

2. In cases of necessity an Archimandrite or Archpriest, acting as the bishop's delegate, can ordain a Reader.

out by a 'college' of bishops. An ordination, while performed
by the bishop, also requires the consent of the *whole* people of
God; and so at a particular point in the service the assembled
congregation acclaim the ordination by shouting '*Axios!*' ('He
is worthy!').[1]

Orthodox priests are divided into two distinct groups, the
'white' or married clergy, and the 'black' or monastic. Ordin-
ands must make up their mind before ordination to which
group they wish to belong, for it is a strict rule that no one can
marry after he has been ordained to a Major Order. Those
who wish to marry must therefore do so before they are made
deacon. Those who do not wish to marry are normally expected
to become monks prior to their ordination; but in the Orthodox
Church today there are now a number of celibate clergy who
have not taken formal monastic vows. These celibate priests,
however, cannot afterwards change their minds and decide to
get married. If a priest's wife dies, he cannot marry again.

In the past the parochial clergy were almost invariably married men, but today it is now quite common for a monk-priest
to be put in charge of a parish. Since the sixth or seventh
century the bishop has been required to be celibate, and from
at least the fourteenth century onwards he has had to be in
monastic vows; a widower, however, can be made a bishop if
he receives monastic profession. Such is the state of monasticism in many parts of the Orthodox Church today that it is not
always easy to find suitable candidates for the episcopate, and
a growing number of Orthodox consider that the limitation of
bishops to the monastic clergy is no longer desirable under
modern conditions. Yet perhaps the solution is not to change
the present rule that bishops must be monks, but to reinvigor-
ate the monastic life itself.

In the early Church the bishop was often elected by the
people of the diocese, clergy and laity together. In Orthodoxy

1. What happens if they shout '*Anaxios!*' ('He is unworthy!')? This is not
very clear. On several occasions in Constantinople or Greece during the present
century the congregation has in fact expressed its disapproval in this way,
although without effect. But some would claim that, at any rate in theory, if
the laity expresses its dissent, the ordination or consecration cannot take place.

today it is usually the Governing Synod in each autocephalous Church which appoints bishops to vacant sees; but in some Churches – Antioch, for example, and Cyprus – a modified system of popular election still exists. The Moscow Council of 1917–18 laid down that henceforward bishops in the Russian Church should be elected by the clergy and laity of the diocese; this ruling is followed by the Paris group of Russians and by the OCA in America, but in the Soviet Union under Communism such election was for obvious reasons impossible. Now that religion is free once more in Russia, the Moscow decision of 1917–18 could surely be applied, although as yet this has not been done.

In the Orthodox Church the diaconate is in principle a permanent office, not just a stepping-stone on the way to the priesthood, and there are many Orthodox deacons who have no expectation of advancing to any higher rank. For the full celebration of the Divine Liturgy a deacon is required, and so every parish ought if possible to have a deacon of its own (who may of course have a full-time secular job); but in practice deacons have now become a rarity in some areas. There is a pressing need in contemporary Orthodoxy for the diaconal ministry to be rethought and reinvigorated.

What is the attitude in the present-day Orthodox world towards the burning issue of the ordination of women? Orthodoxy certainly accepts that women can be ordained to the first of the Major Orders, the diaconate. In the ancient Church women served as female deacons; and although in the west these deaconesses seem usually to have been regarded as a 'lay' rather than an 'ordained' ministry, in the Christian east they were blessed with the same prayers and according to exactly the same rite as male deacons, so there are sound reasons to place them on the same sacramental level. They helped in particular at the Baptism of adult women, and also did pastoral work among the female members of the congregation, although they do not seem to have preached or assisted in the administration of holy communion. The order of deaconesses has never been abolished in the Orthodox Church, but from the sixth or seventh century it fell increasingly into disuse, finally disappearing around the eleventh century. Many Orthodox today wish to see the female diaconate revived, as a matter of urgent priority.

If women can be ordained to the diaconate, can they also be ordained to the priesthood? The great majority of Orthodox consider that this is impossible. They appeal primarily to the unvarying practice of the Church over the past two millennia. If Christ had wished women to be priests, so they argue, He would have taught His Apostles accordingly, and the latter would have obeyed. The ordination of women to the priesthood lacks all basis in Scripture and Tradition, and after two thousand years we have no right to innovate in a matter of such importance. A few Orthodox theologians also use the 'symbolic' or 'iconic' arguments that are advanced by certain Roman Catholics: the priest at the Eucharist represents Christ, and since Christ was male, the priest should likewise be male. But other Orthodox, while opposed to women priests, find this 'iconic' argument unconvincing, and prefer to invoke simply the appeal to Tradition.

There is, however, a small but growing minority within Orthodoxy which feels strongly that the whole question has yet to receive from Orthodox bishops and theologians the rigorous, searching examination that it requires. Only a very few Orthodox, as yet, would say that they are definitely in favour of ordaining women here and now to the priesthood. But there is a much larger group that finds the arguments that have so far been advanced, whether against or in favour of such ordination, to be deeply inadequate. They believe that there exists today an imperative need for Orthodox to reflect on a whole range of basic topics: What is a priest? How can we reactivate the rich diversity of ministries that was to be found in the early Church? How far do our existing views about the ministry appropriate respectively to woman and to man spring from our inherited cultural stereotypes rather than from genuinely theological principles? On the spiritual level, what significance should we attach to the sexual differentiation and complementarity between women and men? There is a mystery here that we have hardly begun to explore.

If we Orthodox are to investigate this mystery with greater

courage and imagination, then certainly it cannot be done by Orthodox men on their own. The voice of Orthodox women needs to be heard in our Church life, in a way that has not so far happened. Fortunately they are now beginning to play a much more active role in Orthodoxy. In the theological schools of Greece and Russia, for example, there is a rapidly increasing number of women students, while in the USA there are active and vocal associations of priests' wives. All this is surely to be welcomed: for if Orthodoxy is to bear creative witness in the twenty-first century, it needs to use to the utmost the gifts of its women as well as of its men.

MARRIAGE

The Trinitarian mystery of unity in diversity applies not only to the doctrine of the Church but to the doctrine of marriage. Humans are made in the image of the Trinity, and except in special cases they are not intended by God to live alone, but in a family. And just as God blessed the first family, commanding Adam and Eve to be fruitful and multiply, so the Church today gives its blessing to the union of man and woman. Marriage is not only a state of nature but a state of grace. Married life, no less than the life of a monk, is a special vocation, requiring a particular gift or *charisma* from the Holy Spirit; and this gift is conferred in the sacrament of Holy Matrimony.

The Marriage Service is divided into two parts, formerly held separately but now celebrated in immediate succession: the preliminary *Office of Betrothal*, and the *Office of Crowning*, which constitutes the sacrament proper. At the Betrothal service the chief ceremony is the blessing and exchange of rings; this is an outward token that the two partners join in marriage of their own free will and consent, for without free consent on both sides there can be no sacrament of Christian marriage. The second part of the service culminates in the ceremony of coronation: on the heads of the bridegroom and bride the priest places crowns, made among the Greeks of leaves and flowers, but among the Russians of silver or gold. This, the outward and visible sign of the sacrament, signifies the special grace which the couple receive from the Holy Spirit, before they set out to found a new family or domestic Church. The crowns are crowns of joy, but they are also crowns of martyrdom, since every true marriage involves self-sacrifice on both sides. At the end of the service the newly married couple drink from the same cup of wine, which recalls the miracle at the marriage feast of Cana in Galilee: this common cup is a symbol of the fact that henceforward they will share a common life with one another.

The Orthodox Church permits divorce and remarriage, quoting as its authority the text of Matthew xix, 9, where Our Lord says: 'If a man divorces his wife, *for any cause other than unchastity*, and marries another, he commits adultery.' Since Christ, according to the Matthaean account, allowed an exception to His general ruling about the indissolubility of marriage, the Orthodox Church also is willing to allow exceptions. Certainly Orthodoxy regards the marriage bond as in principle lifelong and indissoluble, and it sees the breakdown of marriage as a tragedy due to human weakness and sin. But while condemning the sin, the Church still desires to help suffering humans and to allow them a second chance. When, therefore, a marriage has entirely ceased to be a reality, the Orthodox Church does not insist on the preservation of a legal fiction. Divorce is seen as an exceptional but unavoidable concession to our human brokenness, living as we do in a fallen world. Yet although assisting men and women to rise again after a fall, the Orthodox Church knows that a second alliance cannot have exactly the same character as the first; and so in the service for a second marriage several of the joyful ceremonies are omitted, and replaced by penitential prayers. In practice, however, this second marriage service is scarcely ever used.

Orthodox Canon Law, while permitting a second or even a third marriage, absolutely forbids a fourth. In theory the Canons only permit divorce in cases of adultery, but in practice it is granted for other reasons as well.

From the point of view of Orthodox theology a divorce granted by the State in the civil courts is not sufficient. Remarriage in church is only possible if the Church authorities have themselves granted a divorce.

Sexual intercourse is a gift from God, but a gift given for use between man and woman only within the sacrament of marriage. The Orthodox Church for this reason cannot approve of sexual intercourse outside marriage, even when a couple has the firm intention of eventually getting married; the marriage blessing is not to be anticipated. Still less can the Church give its approval to sexual unions between persons of the same sex. But in all specific cases of homosexuality we should of course seek to show the utmost pastoral sensitivity and generous compassion. 'A brother who had committed a sin was driven out from the church by the priest. But Abba Bessarion rose up and went out with him, saying: "I too am a sinner".'[1]

Concerning contraceptives and other forms of birth control, differing opinions exist within the Orthodox Church. In the past birth control was in general strongly condemned, but today a less strict view is coming to prevail, not only in the west but in traditional Orthodox countries. Many Orthodox theologians and spiritual fathers consider that the responsible use of contraception within marriage is not in itself sinful. In their view, the question of how many children a couple should have, and at what intervals, is best decided by the partners themselves, according to the guidance of their own consciences.

Abortion, on the other hand, is unambiguously condemned in Orthodox moral teaching. We do not have the right to destroy human life.

THE ANOINTING OF THE SICK

This sacrament – known in Greek as *evchelaion*, 'the oil of prayer' – is described by St James: 'Is any sick among you? Let him send for the presbyters of the Church, and let them pray over him, anointing him with oil in the name of the Lord. The prayer offered in faith will save the sick person and the Lord will raise him from his bed; and he will be forgiven any sins he has committed' (James v, 14–15). The sacrament, as this passage indicates, has a double purpose: not only bodily

1. *Apophthegmata* (*P.G.* lxv), Bessarion 7.

healing but the forgiveness of sins. The two things go together, for the human being is a unity of body and soul and there can therefore be no sharp and rigid distinction between bodily and spiritual ills. Orthodoxy does not of course believe that the Anointing is invariably followed by a recovery of health; the sacraments are not magic. Sometimes, indeed, the *evchelaion* does indeed assist the patient's physical recovery, but in other cases it serves as a preparation for death. 'This sacrament', remarks Sergius Bulgakov, 'has two faces: one turns towards healing, the other towards the liberation from illness by death.'[1]

The sacrament of Anointing has never been regarded by the Orthodox Church as 'Extreme Unction', intended only for the dying, but it is available for all who suffer from any physical or mental illness. In many Orthodox parishes and monasteries it is the custom to celebrate the *evchelaion* in church on Wednesday evening or Thursday morning during Holy Week, and everyone present is invited to approach for anointing, whether physically ill or not; for, even if we do not require healing of the body, we are all of us in need of healing for our soul. All too often in Orthodoxy the Anointing of the Sick has become a forgotten sacrament: we Orthodox need to make far greater use of it.

1. Sergius Bulgakov, *The Orthodox Church*, p. 135.

CHAPTER 15

Orthodox Worship, III:
Feasts, Fasts, and Private Prayer

The true aim of prayer is to enter into conversation with
God. It is not restricted to certain hours of the day. A
Christian has to feel himself personally in the presence of
God. The goal of prayer is precisely to be with God always.

Fr Georges Florovsky

THE CHRISTIAN YEAR

If anyone wishes to recite or to follow the public services of
the Church of England, then (in theory, at any rate) two volumes will be sufficient – the Bible and the Book of Common
Prayer (or the Alternative Service Book); similarly in the
Roman Catholic Church only two books are required – the
Missal and the Breviary; but in the Orthodox Church, such is
the complexity of the services that a small library of some
nineteen or twenty substantial tomes will be needed. 'On a
moderate computation,' remarked J. M. Neale of the Orthodox
Service Books, 'these volumes together comprise 5,000 closely
printed quarto pages, in double columns.'[1] Yet these books, at
first sight so unwieldy, are one of the greatest treasures of the
Orthodox Church.

In these twenty volumes are contained the services for the
Christian year – that annual sequence of feasts and fasts which
commemorates the Incarnation and its fulfilment in the Church.
The ecclesiastical calendar begins on 1 September. Pre-
eminent among all festivals is Easter, the Feast of Feasts, which
stands in a class by itself. Next in importance come the *Twelve
Great Feasts*, usually reckoned as follows:

The Nativity of the Mother of God (8 September)

1. *Hymns of the Eastern Church*, third edition (London 1866), p. 52.

The Exaltation (or Raising Up) of the Honoured and Life-
giving Cross (14 September)

The Entry of the Mother of God into the Temple
(21 November)

The Nativity of Christ (Christmas) (25 December)

The Baptism of Christ in the Jordan (Theophany or
Epiphany) (6 January)

The Meeting of Our Lord (The Presentation of Christ in
the Temple; western 'Candlemas') (2 February)

The Annunciation of the Mother of God (western 'Lady
Day') (25 March)

The Entry of Our Lord into Jerusalem (Palm Sunday) (one
week before Easter)

The Ascension of Our Lord Jesus Christ (40 days after
Easter)

Pentecost (known in the west as Whit Sunday, but in the
east as Trinity Sunday) (50 days after Easter)

The Transfiguration of Christ (6 August)

The Falling Asleep of the Mother of God (the Dormition)
(15 August)

Thus three of the Twelve Great Feasts depend on the date of
Easter and are 'movable'; the rest are 'fixed'. Seven are feasts
of the Lord, and five are feasts of the Mother of God.[1]

There are also a large number of other festivals, of varying
importance. Among the more prominent are:

The Circumcision of Christ (1 January)
The Three Great Hierarchs (30 January)
The Nativity of St John the Baptist (24 June)
St Peter and St Paul (29 June)
The Beheading of St John the Baptist (29 August)
The Protecting Veil of the Mother of God (1 October)
St Nicolas the Wonderworker (6 December)
All Saints (First Sunday after Pentecost)

---

1. The Meeting (2 February) is sometimes reckoned as a feast of the Lord,
in which case there are eight feasts of the Lord, and four of the Mother of
God.

But besides feasts there are fasts. The Orthodox Church, regarding the human person as a unity of soul and body, has always insisted that the body must be trained and disciplined as well as the soul. 'Fasting and self-control are the first virtue, the mother, root, source, and foundation of all good.'[1] There are four main periods of fasting during the year:

   (i)   *The Great Fast* (Lent) – begins seven weeks before Easter.
   (ii) *The Fast of the Apostles* – starts on the Monday eight days after Pentecost, and ends on 28 June, the eve of the Feast of Saints Peter and Paul; in length varies between one and six weeks.
   (iii) *The Dormition Fast* – lasts two weeks, from 1 to 14 August.
   (iv) *The Christmas Fast* – lasts forty days, from 15 November to 24 December.

In addition to these four chief periods, all Wednesdays and Fridays – and in some monasteries Mondays as well – are fast days (except between Christmas and Epiphany, during Easter week, and during the week after Pentecost). The Exaltation of the Cross, the Beheading of St John the Baptist, and the eve of Epiphany are also fasts.

The rules of fasting in the Orthodox Church are of a rigour which will astonish and appal many western Christians. On most days in Great Lent and Holy Week, for example, not only is meat forbidden, but also fish and all animal products (lard, eggs, butter, milk, cheese), together with wine and oil. In practice, however, many Orthodox – particularly in the western world – find that under the conditions of modern life it is no longer practicable to follow exactly the traditional rules, devised with a very different outward situation in mind; and so certain dispensations are granted. Yet even so Great Lent – especially the first week and Holy Week itself – is still, for devout Orthodox, a period of genuine austerity and serious physical

1. Kallistos and Ignatios Xanthopoulos, in *The Philokalia*, vol. 4 (Athens 1961), p. 232.

hardship. When all relaxations and dispensations are taken into account, it remains true that Orthodox Christians in the twentieth century – laity as well as monks – fast with a severity for which there is no parallel in western Christendom, except perhaps in the strictest Religious Orders.

Different moments in the year are marked by special ceremonies: the great blessing of waters at Theophany (often performed out of doors, beside a river or on the sea shore); the blessing of fruits at the Transfiguration; the solemn exaltation and adoration of the Cross on 14 September; the service of forgiveness on the Sunday immediately before Lent, when clergy and people kneel one by one before each other, and ask one another's forgiveness. But naturally it is during Holy Week that the most moving and impressive moments in Orthodox worship occur, as day by day and hour by hour the Church enters into the Passion of the Lord. Holy Week reaches its climax, first in the procession of the *Epitaphion* (the figure of the Dead Christ laid out for burial) on the evening of Good Friday, and then in the exultant Matins of the Resurrection at Easter midnight. None can be present at this midnight service without being caught up in the sense of universal joy. Christ has released the world from its ancient bondage and its former terrors, and the whole Church rejoices triumphantly in His victory over darkness and death.

Before we leave the subject of the Church's year, something must be said about the vexed question of the *calendar*. Up to the end of the First World War, all Orthodox still used the Old Style or Julian Calendar, which is at present thirteen days behind the New or Gregorian Calendar, followed in the west. In 1923, an Inter-Orthodox Congress was held in Constantinople, attended by some, but by no means all, of the Orthodox Churches; and this gathering decided to introduce a revision of the Julian Calendar, corresponding for all practical purposes to the New or Gregorian Calendar. The change to the New Style was introduced in Constantinople and Greece in March 1924, but it proved highly controversial and was not adopted everywhere. At present the Revised Julian Calendar is followed by

Constantinople, Alexandria, Antioch, Romania, Bulgaria, Cyprus and Greece; but Jerusalem, Russia, Serbia, Georgia and Poland, together with the Holy Mountain of Athos, continue to follow the Old Style or unrevised Julian reckoning.[1] This results in a difficult and confusing situation which one hopes will shortly be brought to an end. At present the Greeks (outside Athos and Jerusalem) keep Christmas at the same time as the west, on 25 December (New Style), while the Russians keep it thirteen days later, on 7 January (New Style); the Greeks keep Epiphany on 6 January, the Russians on 19 January; and so on. But practically the whole Orthodox Church observes Easter at the same time, taking no account of the Revised Julian Calendar and reckoning the equinox according to the Old Style. This means that in practice Orthodox Easter sometimes coincides with the western date, and is sometimes one or five – occasionally four – weeks later. The Church of Finland and a few parishes in the western world always keep Easter on the western date.

The reform in the calendar aroused lively opposition, particularly in Greece, where groups of 'Old Calendarists' or *Palaioimerologitai* broke with the official New Calendar Church and set up a separate organization of their own. In the 1930s and 1940s, although persecuted by the Greek civil authorities, they commanded a substantial following, with their own bishops and monasteries, together with some 800 parishes and perhaps as many as a million sympathizers. But more recently they have split into a number of rival groups and lost most of their influence. There are also Old Calendarists in Cyprus and Romania. The monks of Athos, while adhering to the Old Style, have for the most part maintained communion with the Patriarch of Constantinople and the official Church of Greece. The Old Calendarists see the change in the calendar as the first in a long series of innovations which, so they believe, have corrupted the mainstream Orthodox Churches in the present century. In their view, what is at stake is not just a technical

1. But some parishes in the Orthodox Church of Poland use the New Style; so also do many parishes under Moscow in the diaspora. The New Style is also used by the OCA.

matter of thirteen days, but the purity of the Orthodox faith. They object in particular to the initiatives taken by the Ecumenical Patriarch and others towards reunion with western Christendom.

PERSONAL PRAYER

Alongside public liturgical prayer, there is also personal prayer in the home – the daily prayers recited morning and evening before the icons, either by the whole family together or by each member individually. For these daily prayers there exist special Manuals. Most of the material in them, however, is taken directly from the service books employed in public worship, so that even when alone we are still praying *with the Church*, using the words that are also being spoken in countless parish churches and monasteries. 'Personal prayer is possible only in the context of the community. Nobody is a Christian by himself, but only as a member of the body. Even in solitude, "in the chamber", a Christian prays as a member of the redeemed community, of the Church. And it is in the Church that he learns his devotional practice.'[1] Naturally the Manuals are only intended as a general guide, and all are at liberty also to pray spontaneously in their own words.

By way of example let us take two prayers from the Manual, the first a prayer for the beginning of the day, written by Philaret, Metropolitan of Moscow, perhaps based on a western model:

O Lord, grant me to greet the coming day in peace. Help me in all things to rely upon Your holy will. In every hour of the day reveal Your will to me. Bless my dealings with all who surround me. Teach me to treat all that comes to me throughout the day with peace of soul, and with firm conviction that Your will governs all. In all my deeds and words guide my thoughts and feelings. In unforeseen events let me not forget that all are sent by You. Teach me to act firmly and wisely, without embittering and embarrassing others. Give me strength to bear the fatigue of the coming day with all that it shall

1. G. Florovsky, *Prayer Private and Corporate* ('Ologos' publications, Saint Louis), p. 3.

bring. Direct my will, teach me to pray, pray You Yourself in me. Amen.

And these are a few clauses from the general intercession with which the night prayers close:

Forgive, O Lord, lover of all, those who hate and wrong us. Reward our benefactors. Grant to our brothers and sisters and friends all that they ask for their salvation and eternal life. Visit and heal the sick. Free the prisoners. Guide those at sea. Travel with those who travel . . . On those who charge us in our unworthiness to pray for them, have mercy according to Your great mercy. Remember, O Lord, our departed parents and brothers and sisters and give them rest where shines the light of Your face . . .

There is one type of private prayer, widely used in the west since the time of the Counter-Reformation, which has never been a feature of Orthodox spirituality – the formal 'Meditation', made according to a 'Method' – the Ignatian, the Sulpician, the Salesian, or some other. Orthodox are encouraged to read the Bible or the Fathers slowly and thoughtfully; but such an exercise, while regarded as altogether excellent, is not considered to constitute *prayer*, nor has it been systematized and reduced to a 'Method'. Each is urged to read in the way that he or she finds most helpful.

But while Orthodox do not practise discursive Meditation, there is another type of personal prayer which has for many centuries played an extraordinarily important part in the life of Orthodoxy – the Jesus Prayer: *Lord Jesus Christ, Son of God, have mercy on me.* Since it is sometimes said that Orthodox do not pay sufficient attention to the person of the Incarnate Christ, it is worth pointing out that this – surely the most classic of all Orthodox prayers – is essentially a Christocentric prayer, a prayer addressed to and concentrated upon the Lord Jesus. Those brought up in the tradition of the Jesus Prayer are never allowed for one moment to forget the centrality of the Incarnation.

As a help in reciting this prayer many Orthodox use a chaplet or prayer-rope, differing somewhat in structure from the western rosary; an Orthodox prayer-rope is usually made of wool or twine, so that unlike a string of beads it makes no noise.

The Jesus Prayer is a prayer of marvellous versatility. It is a prayer for beginners, but equally a prayer that leads to the deepest mysteries of the contemplative life. It can be used by anyone, at any time, in any place: standing in queues, walking, travelling on buses or trains; when at work; when unable to sleep at night; at times of special anxiety when it is impossible to concentrate upon other kinds of prayer. But while of course every Christian can use the Prayer at odd moments in this way, it is a different matter to recite it more or less continually and to use the physical exercises which have become associated with it. Orthodox spiritual writers insist that those who use the Jesus Prayer systematically should, if possible, place themselves under the guidance of an experienced director and do nothing on their own initiative.

For some there comes a time when the Jesus Prayer 'enters into the heart', so that it is no longer recited by a deliberate effort, but recites itself spontaneously, continuing even when a person talks or writes, present in his dreams, waking him up in the morning. In the words of St Isaac the Syrian:

When the Spirit takes its dwelling-place in someone, he does not cease to pray, because the Spirit will constantly pray in him. Then, neither when he sleeps, nor when he is awake, will prayer be cut off from his soul; but when he eats and when he drinks, when he lies down or when he does any work, even when he is immersed in sleep, the perfumes of prayer will breathe in his heart spontaneously.[1]

Orthodox believe that the power of God is present in the Name of Jesus, so that the invocation of this Divine Name acts as an effective sign of God's action, endowed with sacramental grace. 'The Name of Jesus, present in the human heart, communicates to it the power of deification ... Shining through the heart, the light of the Name of Jesus illuminates all the universe.'[2]

Alike to those who recite it continually and to those who

---

1. *Mystic Treatises*, edited by Wensinck, p. 174.
2. S. Bulgakov, *The Orthodox Church*, pp. 170-1.

only employ it occasionally, the Jesus Prayer proves a great source of reassurance and joy. To quote the Pilgrim:

And that is how I go about now, and ceaselessly repeat the Jesus Prayer, which is more precious and sweet to me than anything in the world. At times I do as much as forty-three or forty-four miles a day, and do not feel that I am walking at all. I am aware only of the fact that I am saying my Prayer. When the bitter cold pierces me, I begin to say my Prayer more earnestly, and I quickly become warm all over. When hunger begins to overcome me, I call more often on the Name of Jesus, and I forget my wish for food. When I fall ill and get rheumatism in my back and legs, I fix my thoughts on the Prayer, and do not notice the pain. If anyone harms me I have only to think, 'How sweet is the Jesus Prayer!' and the injury and the anger alike pass away and I forget it all ... I thank God that I now understand the meaning of those words I heard in the Epistle – *Pray without ceasing* (1 Thessalonians v,17).[1]

1. *The Way of a Pilgrim*, R. M. French, pp. 17–18.

CHAPTER 16

The Orthodox Church and the Reunion of Christians

On the heights of their spiritual lives have not the saints passed beyond the walls that separate us, *walls which*, according to the grand saying of Metropolitan Platon of Kiev, *do not mount up as far as heaven?*

Metropolitan Evlogy

Unity is something already given and something we must attain to.

Fr Sergius Bulgakov

The highest and most promising 'ecumenical virtue' is patience.

Fr Georges Florovsky

'ONE HOLY CATHOLIC CHURCH': WHAT DO WE MEAN?

The Orthodox Church in all humility believes itself to be the 'one, holy, Catholic and Apostolic Church', of which the Creed speaks: such is the fundamental conviction which guides Orthodox in their relations with other Christians. There are divisions among Christians, but the Church itself is not divided nor can it ever be.

It may seem that this exclusive claim on the Orthodox side precludes any serious 'ecumenical dialogue' between Orthodox and other Christians, and any constructive work by Orthodox for reunion. And yet it would be wrong to draw such a conclusion: for, paradoxically enough, over the past seventy years there have been a large number of encouraging and fruitful contacts. Although enormous obstacles still remain, there has also been real progress towards a reconciliation.

If Orthodox claim to constitute the one true Church, what

then do they consider to be the status of those Christians who do not belong to their communion? Different Orthodox would answer in different ways, for although nearly all Orthodox are agreed in their fundamental teaching concerning the Church, they do not entirely agree concerning the practical consequences which follow from this teaching. There is first a more moderate group, which includes most of those Orthodox who have had close personal contact with other Christians. This group holds that, while it is true to say that Orthodoxy is the Church, it is false to conclude from this that those who are not Orthodox cannot possibly belong to the Church. Many people may be members of the Church who are not visibly so; invisible bonds may exist despite an outward separation. The Spirit of God blows where it chooses and, as Irenaeus said, where the Spirit is, there is the Church. We know where the Church is but we cannot be sure where it is not. This means, as Khomiakov insists, that we must refrain from passing judgement on non-Orthodox Christians:

Inasmuch as the earthly and visible Church is not the fullness and completeness of the whole Church which the Lord appointed to appear at the final judgement of all creation, she acts and knows only within her own limits ... She does not judge the rest of humankind, and only looks upon those as excluded, that is to say, not belonging to her, who exclude themselves. The rest of humankind, whether alien from the Church, *or united to her by ties which God has not willed to reveal to her*, she leaves to the judgement of the great day.[1]

There is only one Church, but there are many different ways of being related to this one Church, and many different ways of being separated from it. Some non-Orthodox are very close indeed to Orthodoxy, others less so; some are friendly to the Orthodox Church, others indifferent or hostile. By God's grace the Orthodox Church possesses the fullness of truth (so its members are bound to believe), but there are other Christian communions which possess to a greater or lesser degree a genuine measure of Orthodoxy. All these facts must be taken into account: one cannot simply say that all non-Orthodox are out-

1. *The Church is One*, section 2 (italics not in the original).

side the Church, and leave it at that; one cannot treat other Christians as if they stood on the same level as unbelievers.

Such is the view of the more moderate party. But there also exists in the Orthodox Church a more rigorous group, who hold that since Orthodoxy is the Church, anyone who is not Orthodox cannot be a member of the Church. Thus Metropolitan Antony Khrapovitsky, the first head of the Russian Orthodox Church Outside Russia and one of the most distinguished of modern Russian theologians, wrote in his *Catechism*:

QUESTION: Is it possible to admit that a split within the Church or among the Churches could ever take place?

ANSWER: Never. Heretics and schismatics have from time to time fallen away from the one indivisible Church, and, by so doing, *they ceased to be members of the Church*, but the Church itself can never lose its unity according to Christ's promise.[1]

Of course (so this stricter group add) divine grace may well be active among many non-Orthodox, and if they are sincere in their love of God, then we may be sure that God will have mercy upon them; but they cannot, in their present state, be termed members of the Church. Workers for Christian unity who do not often encounter this rigorist school should not forget that such opinions are held today by Orthodox of great holiness and loving compassion.

Because they believe their Church to be the true Church, Orthodox can have but one ultimate desire: the reconciliation of all Christians to Orthodoxy. Yet it must not be thought that Orthodox demand the subjection of other Christians to a particular centre of power and jurisdiction. In the words of Sergius Bulgakov, 'Orthodoxy does not desire the submission of any person or group; it wishes to make each one understand.'[2] The Orthodox Church is a family of sister Churches, decentralized in structure, which means that separated communities can be integrated into Orthodoxy without forfeiting their internal autonomy. Orthodoxy desires unity-in-diversity, not uniformity; harmony-in-freedom, not absorption. There is room in the

1. Italics not in the original.
2. Sergius Bulgakov, *The Orthodox Church*, p. 214.

Orthodox Church for many different cultural patterns, for many different ways of worship, and even for many different systems of outward organization.

Yet there is one field in which diversity cannot be permitted. Orthodoxy insists upon unity in matters of faith. *Before there can be reunion among Christians, there must first be full agreement in faith*: this is a basic principle for Orthodox in all their ecumenical relations. It is unity in faith that matters, not organizational unity; and to secure unity of organization at the price of a compromise in dogma is like throwing away the kernel of a nut and keeping the shell. Orthodox are not willing to take part in a 'minimal' reunion scheme, which secures agreement on a few points and leaves everything else to private judgement. There can be only one basis for union – the *fullness* of the faith. But at the same time, as we have insisted earlier, there is a vital distinction between Tradition and traditions, between the essential faith and theological opinions. We seek unity in faith, not in opinions and customs.

This basic principle – no reunion without unity in the faith – has an important corollary: *until unity in the faith has been achieved, there can be no communion in the sacraments*. Communion at the Lord's Table (most Orthodox believe) cannot be used as a means to secure unity in the faith, but must come as the consequence and crown of a unity already attained. Orthodoxy rejects the concept of '*inter*communion' between separated Christian bodies, and admits no form of sacramental fellowship short of full communion. Either Churches are in communion with one another, or they are not: there can be no half-way house. It is often thought that the Anglican and the Old Catholic Churches are in communion with the Orthodox Church, but this is not in fact the case. Despite our deep sorrow that we cannot share in communion with other Christians – Anglicans and Old Catholics, Roman Catholics and Protestants – we Orthodox believe that there are serious doctrinal difficulties which must first be resolved before sacramental fellowship can be possible.

Such is the basic Orthodox standpoint concerning intercommunion, but in practice it is qualified in various ways. Orthodoxy is not altogether monolithic over this delicate matter. There is a small but significant minority of Orthodox who feel that the official position of their Church on the sharing of the sacraments is far too rigid. They are convinced that, with the current progress towards Christian unity, a much more open policy should be adopted, as has happened in the last thirty years both in Roman Catholicism and in Anglicanism. Most Orthodox disagree with this more liberal approach, but they would perhaps allow occasional exceptions to the general prohibition, not so much for 'ecumenical' as for personal and pastoral reasons. Virtually all Orthodox Churches permit what is termed 'economic' intercommunion,[1] whereby non-Orthodox Christians, when cut off from the ministrations of their own Church, may be allowed – with special permission – to receive communion from an Orthodox priest. But does the reverse hold true? Can isolated Orthodox, with no parish of their own near at hand – and this is frequently the situation in the west – approach non-Orthodox for communion? Most Orthodox authorities answer: no, this is not possible. But in fact it happens, in some instances with the tacit or even explicit blessing of an Orthodox bishop. There is also the question of mixed marriages, a human situation in which separation before the altar is bound to be particularly wounding: here again some measure of intercommunion across Church boundaries is occasionally permitted, although by no means regularly so. The great majority of Orthodox insist, however, that despite flexibility in special cases the basic principle still holds good: unity in faith should precede communion in the sacraments.

ORTHODOX RELATIONS WITH OTHER COMMUNIONS: OPPORTUNITIES AND PROBLEMS

The Non-Chalcedonian Churches. When thinking about reunion, Eastern Orthodox look primarily not to the west but to their neighbours in the east, the Oriental Orthodox. The Copts and the other Non-Chalcedonians stand closer to us, alike in

1. In Orthodox canon law, the term 'economy' signifies a departure from the rules of the Church, so as to assist the salvation of particular persons.

historical experience, in doctrine and in spirituality, than does any Christian confession in the west. Of all the current dialogues in which the Orthodox Church is engaged, it is that with the Non-Chalcedonians which is proving the most fruitful and by far the most likely to result in practical action within the immediate future.

Unofficial consultations were held in Aarhus (Denmark) in 1964 and in Bristol (England) in 1967, attended by leading theologians from the two sides; there were further meetings in Geneva (1970) and Addis Ababa (1971). The results were unexpectedly positive. It became clear that on the basic question which had led historically to the division – the doctrine of the person of Christ – there is in fact no real disagreement. The divergence, it was stated in Aarhus, lies only on the level of phraseology. The delegates concluded, 'We recognize in each other the one Orthodox faith of the Church . . . On the essence of the Christological dogma we found ourselves in full agreement.' In the words of the Bristol consultation, 'Some of us affirm two natures, wills and energies hypostatically united in the one Lord Jesus Christ. Some of us affirm one united divine-human nature, will and energy in the same Christ. But both sides speak of a union without confusion, without change, without divisions, without separation.[1] The four adverbs belong to our common tradition. Both affirm the dynamic permanence of the Godhead and the Manhood, with all their natural properties and faculties, in the one Christ.'

These four unofficial conversations during 1964–71 were followed up by the convening of an official Joint Commission representing the two Church families: this met in Geneva in 1985, at Amba Bishoy Monastery in Egypt in 1989, and again in Geneva in 1990. The doctrinal agreements reached at the unofficial consultations were reaffirmed, and it was recommended that each side should now revoke all anathemas and condemnations issued in the past against the other. Difficulties still remain, for not everyone on the two sides is equally posi-

1. Here the Bristol consultation is using the language of the Council of Chalcedon (451): see above, p. 26.

tive about the dialogue: there are some in Greece, for example, who continue to regard the Oriental Orthodox as 'Monophysite heretics', just as there are some Non-Chalcedonians who continue to regard Chalcedon and the Tome of Leo as 'Nestorian'. But the official view of both the Orthodox and the Non-Chalcedonians was clearly expressed at the 1989 meeting: 'As two families of Orthodox Churches long out of communion with each other, we now pray and trust in God to *restore that communion* on the basis of the apostolic faith of the undivided Church of the first centuries which we confess in our common creed.' May this full restoration of sacramental communion soon be an accomplished fact!

The Church of the East. If there has been such hopeful progress in relations with the Non-Chalcedonians, could there not be a similar healing of the ancient division between the Orthodox and the Church of the East (the Assyrians)? The separation occurred for historical rather than doctrinal reasons – more through lack of mutual contact than because of direct theological controversy (although there is of course the problem of the Council of Ephesus [431] and the title *Theotokos*).[1] Has not the moment come for a reconciliation? The difficulty is that the Assyrians are now much reduced in numbers, for they suffered tragically at the hands of the Turks in massacres during 1915–18. Scattered abroad, or else – if they are still in their homelands in Iraq and Iran – living under many restrictions, they lack theological spokesmen. In fact a partial reunion between the Church of the East and the Orthodox took place in 1898, when Mar Yonan of Urmia and much of his flock were received into communion with the Russian Church.[2] The

1. See above, p. 25.

2. On this, see the fascinating book by J. F. Coakley, *The Church of the East and the Church of England: A History of the Archbishop of Canterbury's Assyrian Mission* (Oxford 1992), especially pp. 218–33. When visiting the Russian convent at Spring Valley near New York in 1960, I had the pleasure of meeting a survivor from the union of 1898, likewise called Mar Yonan. Originally a married priest, he had become bishop after the death of his wife. When I asked the nuns how old he was, I was told, 'He says he's 102, but his children say he must be *much* older than that!'

Assyrians seem on this occasion to have found no difficulty in accepting the *Theotokos*. No doubt political factors played a part in 1898; but a century later could there not now be a fresh act of union, free from secular pressures?

The Roman Catholic Church. Among western Christians, it is the Anglicans with whom Orthodoxy has enjoyed the most cordial relationship during the last hundred years, but it is the Roman Catholics with whom we have by far the more in common. There are of course doctrinal and canonical issues which need to be clarified between Orthodoxy and Rome: above all the *Filioque* and the Papal claims, to which some Orthodox would add Purgatory and the Immaculate Conception; Roman Catholics for their part sometimes call in question the Orthodox practice over divorce, and the Palamite distinction between the essence and the energies of God. Less explicit, but perhaps equally important, are the differences in theological mentality and method: Orthodox often feel that Latin scholastic theology makes too much use of legal concepts, and relies too heavily on rational categories and syllogistic argumentation, while the Latins for their part have frequently found the more mystical approach of Orthodoxy too vague and ill-defined. Beyond the differences in doctrine and theological method, there are also psychological barriers which must never be overlooked. During the present century, within the memory of many persons still alive, Catholics and Orthodox have confronted each other in Poland, Czechoslovakia, Croatia and Ukraine, undergoing violence and even death at each other's hands; and these bitter conflicts continue in the 1990s.

Yet, when full allowance has been made for all this, it remains true that there is a vast area of common ground that the two sides share. We both believe in God as Trinity, in Jesus Christ as God incarnate; we both accept the Eucharist as the true Body and Blood of the Saviour; we have a common devotion to the Mother of God and the saints, and we both pray for the faithful departed. Orthodox can acknowledge with gratitude the eirenic initiatives of such pioneers on the Roman Catholic side as Andrei Sheptytsky (1865–1944), Greek Catholic Metropolitan of L'vov (Ukraine), and Dom Lambert Beauduin (1873–1960), who in 1925 founded the 'Monastery of Union' at Amay-sur-Meuse (it moved to Chevetogne in 1939). This is a 'double rite' community in which the members worship according to both the Latin and the Byzantine rites. It has many Orthodox visitors and friends, and issues a valuable periodical, *Irénikon*. Orthodox theology has also benefited immeasurably from the renewal of Patristic studies within the Roman Catholic Church, through the work of such scholars as Henri de Lubac, Jean Daniélou and Hans Urs von Balthasar.

The changes brought about in the Roman Catholic Church at the Second Vatican Council (1962–5) have made possible a gradual *rapprochement* between Rome and Orthodoxy at the official level. In January 1964 Pope Paul VI and Patriarch Athenagoras held a historic meeting at Jerusalem – the first occasion on which a Pope and an Ecumenical Patriarch had met face to face since the Council of Florence (1438–9). On 7 December 1965 the anathemas of 1054 were solemnly revoked at simultaneous ceremonies, in Rome by the Vatican Council and in Constantinople by the Holy Synod. This was only a symbolical gesture, for it did not in itself re-establish communion between the two sides. But the value of symbolical gestures in restoring mutual trust should not be underestimated.

In 1980 the inaugural meeting of the Joint International Commission for theological dialogue between Orthodoxy and Rome was held on the Greek islands of Patmos and Rhodes, and during 1982–8 the Commission produced three important agreed texts, covering the Church, the sacraments and the apostolic succession. Without dealing directly with the *Filioque* or the Papal claims, these two documents provide a solid basis for a future discussion of these two disputed issues. Unfortunately, since the late 1980s the Commission has run into difficulties because of the growing tensions between the Orthodox and the Eastern Catholics in Ukraine and elsewhere, and several meetings have had to be cancelled. Although the dialogue has not been broken off, its immediate future is problematic. Clearly, discussions are still at an early stage.

The crucial issue between Orthodoxy and Rome is certainly

the understanding of the Papal ministry within the Church. We Orthodox cannot accept the definitions of the First Vatican Council, promulgated in 1870, concerning the infallibility and the supreme universal jurisdiction of the Pope. These definitions were emphatically reaffirmed by the Second Vatican Council, but at the same time Vatican II placed the Papal claims within a new context by insisting also upon the collegiality of the bishops. Orthodoxy recognizes that, in the early centuries of the Church, Rome was pre-eminent in its steadfast witness to the true faith; but we do not believe that, in his teaching ministry, the Pope possesses a special charisma or gift of grace that is not granted to his fellow bishops. We recognize him as first – but only as first among equals. He is the elder brother, not the supreme ruler. We do not consider that, in the first ten centuries of the Church, the Pope possessed direct and immediate power of jurisdiction in the Christian east, and so we find it impossible to grant such power to him today.

To Roman Catholic ears all this may sound negative and unhelpful. So, instead of saying what Orthodox will *not* accept, let us ask in positive terms what the nature of Papal primacy is from an Orthodox viewpoint. Surely we Orthodox should be willing to assign to the Pope, in a reunited Christendom, not just an honorary seniority but an all-embracing apostolic care. We should be willing to assign to him the right, not only to accept appeals from the whole Christian world, but even to take the initiative in seeking ways of healing when crisis and conflict arise anywhere among Christians. We envisage that on such occasions the Pope would act, not in isolation, but always in close co-operation with his brother bishops. We would wish to see his ministry spelt out in pastoral rather than juridical terms. He would encourage rather than compel, consult rather than coerce.

In 1024 Patriarch Eustathius of Constantinople suggested to Pope John XIX the following formula, differentiating between the primacy of Rome and that of the Ecumenical Patriarchate: 'Let the Church of Constantinople be called and accounted universal in her own sphere, as Rome is throughout the world."[1] Might not the Orthodox/Roman Catholic Joint Commission take this as a basis for discussion at some future meeting?

The Old Catholics. Although the origins of the Old Catholic Church go back to the early eighteenth century, it assumed its present form only in the 1870s and 1880s, when it was joined by an appreciable number of Roman Catholics who felt unable to accept the decisions of Vatican I concerning the Papacy. The Old Catholics, appealing as they do to the faith of the ancient undivided Church, without later Papal accretions, have naturally looked with sympathy to the Christian east. Important conferences between the Old Catholics and the Orthodox (attended also by the Anglicans) were held at Bonn in 1874 and 1875. Here, and at a further Orthodox–Old Catholic meeting at Bonn in 1931, the two sides found themselves very close in their viewpoint. A joint theological commission representing the two Churches on an international basis, at its meetings during 1975–87, reached a detailed and comprehensive agreement on the Trinity, Christology, the doctrine of the Church, and the sacraments. In spite of this, no concrete steps have yet been taken to establish visible unity. From the Orthodox viewpoint a complicating factor is the relationship of full communion that has existed since 1931 between the Old Catholics and the Anglicans. Thus the question of Old Catholic/Orthodox union cannot be settled in isolation; only if the Orthodox Church also comes to an understanding with Anglicanism can it implement its agreement with the Old Catholics.

The Anglican Communion. There has been an international Orthodox–Lutheran dialogue since 1981 and an international Orthodox–Reformed dialogue since 1988, while in 1992 preparations began for an Orthodox–Methodist dialogue. Far more important for the Orthodox, however, is their long-standing relationship with the Anglicans. Ever since the early seventeenth century there have always been Anglicans for whom the Reformation settlement under Queen Elizabeth I represented

---

1. Raoul Glaber, *Historiarum libri quinque* iv, 1 (*Patrologia Latina* cxlii, 671A).

no more than an interim arrangement, and who appealed, like the Old Catholics, to the General Councils, the Fathers, and the Tradition of the undivided Church. One thinks of Bishop John Pearson (1613–86) with his plea, 'Search how it was in the beginning; go to the fountainhead; look to antiquity.' Or of Bishop Thomas Ken (1637–1711), the Non-Juror, who said, 'I die in the Holy, Catholic and Apostolic Faith, professed by the whole Church, before the disunion of East and West.' This appeal to antiquity has led many Anglicans to look with sympathy and interest at the Orthodox Church, and equally it has led many Orthodox to look with interest and sympathy at Anglicanism. As a result of pioneer work by Anglicans such as William Palmer (1811–79),[1] J. M. Neale (1818–66), and W. J. Birkbeck (1859–1916), firm bonds of Anglo-Orthodox solidarity were established by the end of the nineteenth century.

On the initiative more particularly of Neale, the Eastern Church Association was founded in Britain in 1863. Now known as the Anglican and Eastern Churches Association, this issues a periodical, *Eastern Churches News Letter*, and fosters contact between Anglicans and the Christian east through pilgrimages and meetings. A more recent society, the Fellowship of St Alban and St Sergius, founded in 1928 as an offshoot of the Student Christian Movement, pursues similar aims. It issues a substantial journal, *Sobornost*. Its annual conference was attended in the past by such leading Orthodox theologians as Bulgakov, Lossky and Florovsky, and on the Anglican side by Archbishop Michael Ramsey (1904–88), a staunch although not uncritical admirer of the Orthodox; and it continues to be a forum where the cause of Christian unity is advanced through the forging of close personal friendships.[2]

Important official conferences were held between the Anglican and the Orthodox Churches in London in 1930 and 1931, and in Bucharest in 1935. This last represents in many ways the high point in Anglican–Orthodox *rapprochement*. At the

1. Received into the Roman Catholic Church in 1855.
2. See Nicolas and Militza Zernov, *The Fellowship of St Alban and St Sergius: A Historical Memoir* (Oxford 1979).

end of the meeting the delegates stated, 'A solid basis has been prepared whereby full dogmatic agreement may be affirmed between the Orthodox and Anglican communions.'[1] In retrospect these words appear over-optimistic, and the conference held at Moscow in 1956 between the Church of England and the Russian Church – which had not been represented at the meetings in the 1930s – was noticeably more cautious.[2]

During the inter-war period the Orthodox devoted considerable attention to the question of Anglican Orders. After the condemnation of Anglican ordinations by Pope Leo XIII in 1896 in his encyclical *Apostolicae Curae*, many Anglicans hoped to counterbalance this by persuading the Orthodox Church to recognize the validity of their priesthood and episcopate. In 1922 the Ecumenical Patriarch Meletios IV (Metaxakis) issued a declaration stating that Anglican Orders 'possess the same validity as those of the Roman, Old Catholic and Armenian Churches possess, inasmuch as all essentials are found in them which are held indispensable from the Orthodox point of view'.[3] Positive statements in similar terms were issued by the Churches of Jerusalem (1923), Cyprus (1923), Alexandria (1930), and Romania (1936). None of these Churches, however, seems actually to have given practical effect to these acts of recognition. Anglican clergy entering Orthodoxy, if called to serve in the Orthodox priesthood, have always been reordained, whereas in the case of Roman Catholic clergy who become Orthodox there is usually no such reordination.

Since the war, no other Orthodox Church has made a favourable declaration about Anglican Orders. In 1948 the Moscow Patriarchate came to a negative conclusion, stating, 'The Orthodox Church cannot agree to recognize the rightness of Anglican teaching on the sacraments in general, and on the sacrament of Holy Order in particular; and so it cannot recognize the validity of Anglican ordinations.' But a hope was extended for the

1. E. R. Hardy (ed.), *Orthodox Statements on Anglican Orders* (London/Oxford 1946), p. 35.

2. See H. M. Waddams (ed.), *Anglo-Russian Theological Conference: Moscow, July 1956* (London 1958).

3. Hardy, *Orthodox Statements on Anglican Orders*, p. 2.

future: were the Anglican Church formally to endorse a confession of faith that the Orthodox Church could acknowledge as fully Orthodox, then the question could be reopened and a recognition might perhaps be possible.[1]

It is significant that, in this declaration, the Moscow Patriarchate declines to treat the question of valid orders in isolation, but insists on placing the issue within the context of the *total faith* of the Anglican Church. For Orthodoxy, the validity of ordinations does not depend simply on the fulfilment of certain technical conditions (external possession of the apostolic succession; correct form, matter and intention). The Orthodox also ask: What is the general sacramental teaching of the Christian body in question? What does it believe concerning the inner meaning of the apostolic succession and the priesthood? How does it understand the eucharistic presence and sacrifice? Only when these questions have been answered can a decision be made about the validity or otherwise of ordinations. To isolate the problem of valid orders is to go up a blind alley. Realizing this, Anglicans and Orthodox in their discussions from the 1950s onwards have left the question of valid orders largely to one side, and have concentrated on more substantive and central themes of doctrinal belief.

An official theological dialogue, involving all the Orthodox Churches and the whole Anglican communion, was started in 1973. Despite a crisis in the talks during 1977–8, due to the ordination of women priests in several Anglican Churches, the dialogue still continues. Two agreed statements have been produced, in Moscow (1976) and in Dublin (1984). These contain admirable paragraphs on, for example, Scripture and Tradition, councils, the communion of saints, and icons. But it must be confessed that these two statements have so far remained no more than agreements on paper, and have had disappointingly little effect on the life of the two Churches as a whole. Often it seems that the Anglican–Orthodox dialogue is being carried on in a vacuum.

1. Paul B. Anderson (ed.), *Major Portions of the Proceedings of the Conference of Heads and Representatives of Autocephalous Orthodox Churches . . . 8–18 July 1948* (Paris 1952), p. 239.

From the Orthodox point of view, the main obstacle to closer relations with the Anglican communion is the comprehensiveness of Anglicanism, the extreme ambiguity of Anglican formularies, the wide variety of interpretations which these formularies permit. There are individual Anglicans whose faith is virtually indistinguishable from that of an Orthodox; but there are others within the Anglican communion, on the extreme liberal wing, who openly repudiate fundamental elements in the doctrinal and moral teaching of Christianity. It is this bewildering variety within Anglicanism that makes Anglican–Orthodox relations at once so hopeful and yet so elusive.

The closeness of certain individual Anglicans to the Orthodox faith is evident in two remarkable pamphlets, *Orthodoxy and the Conversion of England*, by Derwas Chitty,[1] and *Anglicanism and Orthodoxy* by H. A. Hodges. Both authors were active and influential members of the Fellowship of St Alban and St Sergius. 'The ecumenical problem', Professor Hodges concludes, is to be seen 'as the problem of bringing back the West . . . to a sound mind and a healthy life, and that means to Orthodoxy . . . The Orthodox faith, that faith to which the Orthodox fathers bear witness and of which the Orthodox Church is the abiding custodian, is the Christian faith in its true and essential form.'[2] But how representative of Anglicanism are these two authors? The Orthodox Church, however deep its longing for reunion, cannot enter into closer relations with the Anglican communion until Anglicans themselves are clearer about their own beliefs. The words of General Alexander Kireev (1832–1910) are as true today as they were at the start of this century: 'We Easterners sincerely desire to come to an understanding with the great Anglican Church; but this happy result cannot be obtained . . . unless the Anglican Church itself becomes homogeneous and the doctrines of its different constitutive parts become identical.'[3]

1. Originally published in 1947; new edition by Edward Every (The Anglo-Orthodox Society: Colchester 1990).

2. *Anglicanism and Orthodoxy* (London 1955), pp. 46–7.

3. Olga Novikoff (ed.), *Le Général Alexandre Kiréeff et l'ancien-catholicisme* (Berne 1911), p. 224.

The World Council of Churches. At the beginning of each celebration of the Divine Liturgy, Orthodox Christians pray 'for the peace of the whole world . . . and the unity of everyone'. Another Orthodox prayer states, 'O Christ, You have bound Your Apostles in a union of love, and have bound us Your believing servants to You with the same bond: grant us in all sincerity to fulfil Your commandments and to love one another . . .'. This commitment to unity and mutual love has led many Orthodox to participate actively in the World Council of Churches (WCC) and in other expressions of the Ecumenical Movement. But the attitude of Orthodoxy towards ecumenism remains ambivalent. Although at present almost all the Orthodox Churches are full members of the WCC, within each local Church there are some who feel strongly that any such membership compromises the claim of Orthodoxy to be the one true Church of Christ. In the opinion of this minority – which is large enough to be significant – it would be best for the Orthodox to withdraw altogether from the World Council, or at least to participate only as observers.

From the beginning of the twentieth century the Ecumenical Patriarchate has shown a special concern for Christian reconciliation. At his accession in 1902, Patriarch Joachim III sent an encyclical letter to all the autocephalous Orthodox Churches, asking in particular for their opinion on relations with other Christian bodies. In January 1920 the Ecumenical Patriarchate followed this up with a bold and prophetic letter addressed 'To all the Churches of Christ, wherever they may be', urging closer co-operation among separated Christians, and suggesting a 'League of Churches', parallel to the newly founded League of Nations. Many of the ideas in this letter anticipate subsequent developments in the WCC. Constantinople, along with several of the other Orthodox Churches, was represented at the Faith and Order Conferences at Lausanne in 1927 and at Edinburgh in 1937. The Ecumenical Patriarchate also participated in the first Assembly of the WCC at Amsterdam in 1948, and has been a consistent supporter of the work of the WCC ever since.

A very different attitude towards the WCC was expressed

by the Moscow Conference, held in the same year (1948). 'The aims of the Ecumenical Movement', the delegates bluntly stated, 'as expressed in the formation of the "World Council of Churches" . . . do not correspond to the ideal of Christianity or to the aims of the Church of Christ, as understood by the Orthodox Church.'[1] All participation in the WCC was therefore condemned. While there were theological reasons for this stance, the international tensions at that time – the 'Cold War' was then at its height – have also to be taken into account. But in 1961 the Moscow Patriarchate applied for membership of the WCC and was accepted; and this opened the way for other Orthodox Churches in the Communist world to become members as well. Since then the representation of the Orthodox at WCC gatherings has been much fuller and more representative.

Yet, although participating in the WCC, the Orthodox have often found their membership problematic. At several early meetings they felt unable to sign the main resolutions, and submitted separate declarations; particularly important is the declaration made by the Orthodox delegates at Evanston in 1954. Since 1961 the Orthodox have ceased to make separate statements, but some would like to see a return to the earlier practice. The Orthodox have regularly found themselves outvoted by the Protestant majority, and have had to insist that doctrinal questions cannot be decided simply by majority vote. They have also regretted the lack of consideration given by many WCC assemblies to prayer and spirituality. Orthodox spokesmen object to what they see as the undue 'horizontalism' of the WCC in recent years, with an over-emphasis on social and economic issues at the expense of serious theological discussion. They have regularly sought to recall the primary aim of the WCC, which is to be a meeting-place between Church bodies which are seeking the *restoration of Christian unity* on the basis of *doctrinal agreement*.

For the Orthodox, it is crucially important that the WCC, in the official definition of its basis, affirms, 'The World

1. Anderson, *Major Portions of the Proceedings*, p. 240.

Council of Churches is a fellowship of Churches which confess the Lord Jesus Christ as God and Saviour and therefore seek to fulfil together their common calling to the glory of the one God, Father, Son and Holy Spirit.' If this clear expression of faith in the divinity of Christ and the Trinitarian nature of God were to be in any way diminished, that would make it difficult for the Orthodox to continue as full members.

Another foundation document, of particular significance to Orthodoxy, is the Toronto statement adopted by the central committee of the WCC in 1950, which carefully lays down, 'Membership of the World Council does not imply acceptance of a specific doctrine concerning the nature of Church unity . . . Membership does not imply that each Church must regard the other member Churches as Churches in the true and full sense of the word.' This makes it possible for Orthodox to belong to the WCC without thereby repudiating their belief that Orthodoxy is the one true Church, which alone holds the fullness of the faith. Those Orthodox who are opposed to membership of the WCC argue that to participate in the Ecumenical Movement is to fall into the 'pan-heresy of ecumenism', according to which all Christian confessions stand on an equal footing. But, in the light of the Toronto statement, it is patently obvious that membership of the WCC need not imply anything of the kind. Orthodox representatives at WCC gatherings have in fact repeatedly insisted – often to the exasperation of others present – upon the Orthodox claim to be the true Church, one and unique.

Orthodox participation in the WCC is a factor of cardinal importance for the Ecumenical Movement: it is the presence of Orthodox – and, to a lesser degree, of Old Catholics and Anglicans – which prevents the World Council of Churches from appearing to be simply a pan-Protestant alliance and nothing more. But the Ecumenical Movement in turn is important for Orthodoxy: it has helped to force the various Orthodox Churches out of their comparative isolation, making them meet one another and enter into a living contact with non-Orthodox Christians. We Orthodox are there, not simply to bear witness to what we ourselves believe, but also to listen to what others have to say.

LEARNING FROM ONE ANOTHER

Khomiakov, seeking to describe the Orthodox attitude to other Christians, in one of his letters makes use of a parable. A master departed, leaving his teaching to his three disciples. The eldest faithfully repeated what his master had taught him, changing nothing. Of the other two, one added to the teaching, the other took away from it. At his return the master, without being angry with anyone, said to the two younger, 'Thank your eldest brother; without him you would not have preserved the truth which I handed over to you.' Then he said to the eldest brother, 'Thank your younger brothers; without them you would not have understood the truth which I entrusted to you.'

Orthodox in all humility see themselves as in the position of the eldest brother. They believe that by God's grace they have been enabled to preserve the true faith unimpaired, 'neither adding anything, nor taking anything away'. They claim a living continuity with the ancient Church, with the Tradition of the Apostles and the Fathers, and they believe that in a divided and bewildered Christendom it is their duty to bear witness to this continuing Tradition that, although unchanging, is always young, alive and new. Today in the west there are many, both on the Catholic and on the Protestant side, who are trying to shake themselves free of the 'crystallizations and fossilizations of the sixteenth century', and who desire to 'get behind the Reformation and the Middle Ages'. There are also many western Christians who, reacting against an extreme liberalism that doubts all the basic teachings of the Bible, are seeking to recover a firm doctrinal standpoint which none the less avoids rigid fundamentalism. It is precisely here that the Orthodox can help. Orthodoxy stands outside the circle of ideas in which western Christians have moved for the past eight centuries; it has undergone no scholastic revolution, no Reformation and Counter-Reformation, but still lives in that older Tradition of the Fathers which so many in the west now desire to recover. This, then, is the ecumenical role of Orthodoxy: to question the accepted formulae of the Latin west, of the Middle Ages and the Reformation. At the same time Orthodoxy, which bases itself not upon the exterior letter of Scripture but upon the way in which Scripture has been experienced and lived by the Church throughout the ages, can offer a middle path between fundamentalist literalism and the semi-agnosticism of the extreme liberals.

And yet, if we Orthodox are to fulfil this role properly, we must understand our own Tradition better than we have done in the past; and it is the west in its turn which can help us to do this. We Orthodox must thank our younger brothers, for through contact with Christians of the west we are being enabled to acquire a new vision of Orthodoxy.

The two sides are only just beginning to discover one another, and each has much to learn. Just as in the past the separation of east and west has proved a great tragedy for both parties and a cause of grievous mutual improverishment, so today the renewal of contact between east and west is already proving a source of mutual enrichment. The west, with its critical standards, with its Biblical and Patristic scholarship, can enable Orthodox to understand the historical background of Scripture in new ways and to read the Fathers with increased accuracy and discrimination. The Orthodox in turn can bring western Christians to a renewed awareness of the inner meaning of Tradition, assisting them to look on the Fathers as a living reality. (The Romanian edition of the *Philokalia* shows how profitably western critical standards and traditional Orthodox spirituality can be combined.) As Orthodox Christians strive to recover frequent communion, the example of their western sisters and brothers acts as an encouragement to them; many western Christians in turn have found their own prayer and worship incomparably deepened by an acquaintance with Orthodox icons, the Jesus Prayer and the Byzantine Liturgy. Over the past seventy years the persecuted Orthodox Church in Russia and elsewhere has served as a reminder to the west of the central significance of martyrdom, and has constituted a living testimony to the value of creative suffering. Now that the Orthodox Churches in former Communist lands find themselves in a pluralist situation – and now that the Church of

Greece has to confront an ever-increasing secularization – western experience will surely help the Orthodox to tackle the problems of Christian life within a post-Constantinian industrialized society.

We have everything to gain by continuing to talk to each other.

Further Reading

THE EARLY CHURCH AND BYZANTIUM

Alexander Schmemann provides a lively sketch, from an Orthodox perspective, in *The Historical Road of Eastern Orthodoxy* (New York 1963). St Vladimir's Seminary Press is planning a multi-volume Orthodox history of the Church; a high standard is set by the first two volumes to appear: John Meyendorff, *Imperial Unity and Christian Divisions: The Church 450–680 A.D.* (New York 1989); Aristeides Papadakis and John Meyendorff, *The Christian East and the Rise of the Papacy: The Church 1071–1453 A.D.* (New York 1994). J. M. Hussey, *The Orthodox Church in the Byzantine Empire* (Oxford 1986), is a sound overall survey, although giving little attention to the lives of the saints and to the religion of the people. George Ostrogorsky, *History of the Byzantine State* (second ed., Oxford 1968), remains the best general history. On the Church's charitable work, see Demetrios J. Constantelos, *Byzantine Philanthropy and Social Welfare* (new ed., New Rochelle 1991).

Patristic and Byzantine Theology. John Meyendorff, *Byzantine Theology: Historical Trends and Doctrinal Themes* (New York 1974), is the best general introduction; compare also Jaroslav Pelikan, *The Christian Tradition: A History of the Development of Doctrine*, vols. 1–2 (Chicago 1971–4). For a classic treatment by one of the outstanding twentieth-century Orthodox theologians, see the three volumes by Georges Florovsky, *The Eastern Fathers of the Fourth Century*; *The Byzantine Fathers of the Fifth Century*; and *The Byzantine Fathers of the Sixth to Eighth Centuries*, in *The Collected Works*, vols. 7–9 (Vaduz/Belmont 1987), but unfortunately these are totally lacking in references and footnotes. On Christology, consult John Meyendorff, *Christ in Eastern Christian Thought* (New York 1975): a good presentation, but he underestimates

Dionysius. Andrew Louth, *The Origins of the Christian Mystical Tradition: From Plato to Denys* (Oxford 1981), is excellent.

On individual Fathers, the following can be recommended:

Jean Daniélou and Herbert Musurillo, *From Glory to Glory: Texts from Gregory of Nyssa's Mystical Writings* (London 1962).

Andrew Louth, *Denys the Areopagite* (London 1989).

Lars Thunberg, *Microcosm and Mediator: The Theological Anthropology of Maximus the Confessor* (new ed., Chicago 1995); to be supplemented by the same author's more popular treatment, *Man and Cosmos: the Vision of St Maximus the Confessor* (New York 1985), and by Andrew Louth, *Maximus the Confessor* (London 1996).

For the writings of St Symeon the New Theologian, see *The Discourses*, tr. C. J. deCatanzaro (The Classics of Western Spirituality: New York 1980); *The Practical and Theological Chapters and the Three Theological Discourses*, tr. Paul McGuckin (Cistercian Studies 41: Kalamazoo 1982); *Hymns of Divine Love*, tr. George A. Maloney (Denville, no date). The most reliable presentations of Symeon are Basil Krivocheine, *In the Light of Christ: St Symeon the New Theologian* (New York 1987), and H. J. M. Turner, *St Symeon the New Theologian and Spiritual Fatherhood* (Leiden 1990). George A. Maloney, *The Mystic of Fire and Light: St Symeon the New Theologian* (Denville 1975), is readable but more superficial.

Extracts from St Gregory Palamas, *The Triads*, have been translated by Nicholas Gendle (The Classics of Western Spirituality: New York 1983). A brief but comprehensive account of Hesychasm is provided by John Meyendorff, *St Gregory Palamas and Orthodox Spirituality* (New York 1974); his major work, *A Study of Gregory Palamas* (London 1964), still remains fundamental.

The Oriental Orthodox Churches. For a full and well-documented account, see S. H. Moffett, *A History of Christianity in Asia,* vol. I: *Beginnings to 1500* (San Francisco 1992). Aziz S. Atiya, *A History of Eastern Christianity* (second ed., Millwood 1980), covers both the early and the modern periods.

W. H. C. Frend, *The Rise of the Monophysite Movement* (Cambridge 1972), is a detailed historical treatment. Karekin Sarkissian (now Patriarch-Catholicos of Etchmiadzin), *The Council of Chalcedon and the Armenian Church* (London 1967), shows how the rejection of Chalcedon by the Non-Chalcedonians was determined mainly by non-theological factors. Compare also Paulos Gregorios, William H. Lazareth and Nikos A. Nissiotis, *Does Chalcedon Divide or Unite?* (Geneva 1981). On Syriac spirituality, see Robert Murray, *Symbols of Church and Kingdom: A Study in Early Syriac Tradition* (Cambridge 1975), and Sebastian Brock, *The Syriac Fathers on Prayer and the Spiritual Life* (Cistercian Studies 101: Kalamazoo 1987). On the Copts, consult Otto F. A. Meinardus, *Christian Egypt: Faith and Life* (Cairo 1970). *The Ascetical Homilies of St Isaac the Syrian*, tr. Dana Miller (Holy Transfiguration Monastery, Boston 1984), takes account of the Greek translation as well as the Syriac original; see also *Isaac of Nineveh, 'The Second Part'*, Chapters IV–XLI, tr. Sebastian Brock (Corpus Scriptorum Christianorum Orientalium 555: Louvain 1995).

The Schism between East and West. For a well-documented factual narrative, better on history than on theology, read Steven Runciman, *The Eastern Schism* (Oxford 1955), covering the period up to 1204; compare also Francis Dvornik, *Byzantium and the Roman Primacy* (second ed., New York 1979). R. W. Southern, *Western Society and the Church in the Middle Ages* (Pelican History of the Church, vol. 2: Harmondsworth 1970, reprinted in Penguin 1990), pp. 53–90, is brief but perceptive, although it says nothing about Photius. The classic study on Photius is still Francis Dvornik, *The Photian Schism: History and Legend* (Cambridge 1948). On the *Filioque* in the ninth century, see Richard Haugh, *Photius and the Carolingians: The Trinitarian Controversy* (Belmont 1973), which is well argued but less eirenic than Dvornik. For a reassessment of the *Filioque* question, see Lukas Vischer (ed.), *Spirit of God, Spirit of Christ* (Geneva 1981). Joseph Gill, *The Council of Florence* (Cambridge 1959), is full and scholarly on the historical side, but curiously insensitive to Orthodox theological concerns. For a far-seeing analysis of the underlying issues by a sympathetic Roman Catholic, see Yves M.-J. Congar, *After Nine Hundred Years* (New York 1959); for a more severe estimate by an Orthodox, see the books of Philip Sherrard, *The Greek East and the Latin West* (London 1959) and *Church, Papacy and Schism* (London 1978).

THE TURKISH PERIOD

The finest general survey in English, although making only limited use of the Greek sources, is Steven Runciman, *The Great Church in Captivity: A Study of the Patriarchate of Constantinople from the Eve of the Turkish Conquest to the Greek War of Independence* (Cambridge 1968). Theodore H. Papadopoullos, *Studies and Documents relating to the History of the Greek Church and People under Turkish Domination* (Brussels 1952), is more technical. On Orthodox and Roman Catholics, see Charles A. Frazee, *Catholics and Sultans: The Church and the Ottoman Empire, 1453–1923* (Cambridge 1983), and Timothy Ware, *Eustratios Argenti: A Study of the Greek Church under Turkish Rule* (Oxford 1964). George A. Maloney, *A History of Orthodox Theology since 1453* (Belmont 1976), is a pioneering study, not always accurate in detail, covering Slavs and Romanians as well as Greeks.

The correspondence between the Lutherans and Patriarch Jeremias II is translated by George Mastrantonis, *Augsburg and Constantinople* (Brookline 1982). Colin Davey, *Pioneer for Unity* (London 1987), is highly informative about Kritopoulos. For the *Confession* of Peter of Moghila, as revised at Jassy, see J. J. Overbeck (ed.), *The Orthodox Confession of the Catholic and Apostolic Eastern Church* (London 1898); for the *Confession* of Dositheus (and of Lukaris), see J. N. W. B. Robertson (ed.), *The Acts and Decrees of the Synod of Jerusalem* (London 1899); for the negotiations between the Orthodox and the Non-Jurors, see George Williams, *The Orthodox Church of the East in the Eighteenth Century* (London 1868). G. P. Henderson, *The Revival of Greek Thought 1620–1830* (Edinburgh/London 1971), is concerned more with philosophy than with theology.

On spiritual life during the Turcocratia, see the studies by Constantine Cavarnos in the useful series 'Modern Orthodox Saints': *St. Cosmas Aitolos* (Belmont 1971); *St. Macarios of Corinth* (Belmont 1972); *St. Nicodemos the Hagiorite* (Belmont 1974). Nomikos Michael Vaporis has translated the sermons of St Kosmas in *Father Kosmas the Apostle of the Poor* (Brookline 1977). For the personal teaching of St Nicodemus of the Holy Mountain, see his work *A Handbook of Spiritual Counsel*, tr. Peter A. Chamberas (The Classics of Western Spirituality: New York 1989). Accounts of the *neomartyres*, often by eyewitnesses, are given in Leonidas J. Papadopoulos and Georgia Lizardos (tr.), *New Martyrs of the Turkish Yoke* (Seattle 1985).

MODERN GREECE

On events leading to the grant of autocephaly by the Ecumenical Patriarchate, see Charles A. Frazee, *The Orthodox Church and Independent Greece* (Cambridge 1969). Peter Hammond, *The Waters of Marah* (London 1956), provides a moving and beautifully written, if at times idealized, picture of the Greek Church in the late 1940s. Mario Rinvolucri, *Anatomy of a Church: Greek Orthodoxy Today* (London 1966), indicates the steady encroachments of secularization. For more recent developments, consult Kallistos Ware, 'The Church: A Time of Transition', in Richard Clogg (ed.), *Greece in the 1980s* (London 1983), pp. 208–30.

The Greek Diaspora.   Theodore E. Dowling and Edwin W. Fletcher, *Hellenism in England* (London 1915), is interesting, but incomplete and often inexact. Theodore Saloutos, *The Greeks in the United States* (Cambridge, Massachusetts 1964), is much more thorough. See also George Papaioannou, *The Odyssey of Hellenism in America* (Thessaloniki 1985), and Charles C. Moskos, *Greek Americans: Struggle and Success* (second ed., New Brunswick 1989).

RUSSIA

Georges Florovsky, *Ways of Russian Theology*, in *The Collected*

Works, vols. 5–6 (Belmont/Vaduz 1979, 1987), is fundamental, albeit sometimes partisan. On the early period, see John Fennell, *A History of the Russian Church to 1448* (London 1995). G. P. Fedotov, *A Treasury of Russian Spirituality* (London 1950), contains a good selection of primary texts. *The Russian Religious Mind*, by the same author (2 vols., Cambridge, Massachusetts 1946, 1966), covering the tenth to the fifteenth centuries, is partially outdated, yet still important. Dimitri Obolensky, *The Byzantine Commonwealth: Eastern Europe, 500–1453* (London 1971), is excellent on the conversion of the Slavs (as on many other matters). John Meyendorff, in *Byzantium and the Rise of Russia* (Cambridge 1981), writes authoritatively on the fourteenth century. On the monastic tradition, see Sergius Bolshakoff, *Russian Mystics* (Cistercian Studies 26: Kalamazoo 1977); Muriel Heppell (tr.), *The Paterik of the Kievan Caves Monastery* (Harvard 1989); Pierre Kovalevsky, *St Sergius and Russian Spirituality* (New York 1976). For a Ukrainian Orthodox interpretation, see Ivan Wlasowsky, *Outline History of the Ukrainian Orthodox Church*, vol. 1, *988–1596* (Bound Brook, New Jersey 1956). For a more detailed discussion by a Ukrainian Catholic, consult Sophia Senyk, *A History of the Church in Ukraine*, vol. I: *To the End of the Thirteenth Century* (Orientalia Christiana Analecta 243: Rome 1993).

On the seventeenth-century disputes involving Patriarch Nikon, see Paul Meyendorff, *Russia, Ritual, and Reform* (New York 1991). The outward organization of the Church in the Synodal period is well covered by Gregory L. Freeze, *The Russian Levites: Parish Clergy in the Eighteenth Century* (Cambridge, Massachusetts 1977), and *The Parish Clergy in Nineteenth-Century Russia: Crisis, Reform, Counter-Reform* (Princeton 1983). On the inner life, see Nadejda Gorodetsky's sensitive studies, *Saint Tikhon Zadonsky: Inspirer of Dostoevsky* (London 1951), and *The Humiliated Christ in Modern Russian Thought* (London 1938).

On St Paissy Velichkovsky, read his own autobiography, tr. J. M. E. Featherstone, *The Life of Paisij Velyčkovs'kyj* (Harvard 1989), along with other source material contained in Fr Seraphim (Rose), *Blessed Paisius Velichkovsky* (St Herman of

Alaska Brotherhood, Platina 1976); cf. Sergii Chetverikov, *Starets Paisii Velichkovskii* (Belmont 1980). On St Paissy's Romanian links, see Bishop Seraphim Joantă, *Romania: Its Hesychast Tradition and Culture* (Wildwood 1992). A striking, although personal, account of St Seraphim of Sarov is provided by Iulia de Beausobre, *Flame in the Snow* (London 1945); for a more factual treatment, see Valentine Zander, *St Seraphim of Sarov* (London 1975). *The Way of a Pilgrim*, the anonymous apologia for the Jesus Prayer, has been translated by, among others, R. M. French (London 1954). On the Optino *startsy*, see Macarius, *Russian Letters of Direction 1834–1860*, ed. Iulia de Beausobre (London 1944), and John B. Dunlop, *Staretz Amvrosy: Model for Dostoevsky's Staretz Zossima* (Belmont 1972). On women's monasticism in the nineteenth century, see Brenda Meehan, *Holy Women of Russia* (San Francisco 1993). For extracts from St John of Kronstadt's *My Life in Christ*, arranged thematically, see W. Jardine Grisbrooke (ed.), *Spiritual Counsels of Father John of Kronstadt* (London 1967); cf. Bishop Alexander (Semenoff-Tian-Chansky), *Father John of Kronstadt: A Life* (London ?1978).

Nicolas Zernov, *The Russian Religious Renaissance of the Twentieth Century* (London 1963), is based in part on personal contacts with leading members in the renewal movement. There is a good selection of material in Alexander Schmemann (ed.), *Ultimate Questions: An Anthology of Modern Russian Religious Thought* (New York 1965). For a good account of one of the most original Russian theologians at the start of the century, see Robert Slesinski, *Pavel Florensky: A Metaphysics of Love* (New York 1984). On the Church situation immediately before the Revolution, consult John Shelton Curtiss, *Church and State in Russia: The Last Years of the Empire 1900–1917* (New York 1940), and James W. Cunningham, *A Vanquished Hope: The Movement for Church Renewal in Russia 1905–1906* (New York 1981).

The Church under and after Communism. The best of older accounts are Walter Kolarz, *Religion in the Soviet Union* (London 1961), and Nikita Struve, *Christians in Contemporary Russia* (London 1967). Dimitry Pospielovsky, *The*

Russian Church under the Soviet Regime 1917–1982 (2 vols., New York 1984), although thorough, is one-sided in its treatment of the Russian emigration. Jane Ellis, *The Russian Orthodox Church: A Contemporary History* (London 1986), covering the period of 1965–85, is balanced and objective, yet deeply concerned. Among the many books on Solzhenitsyn, Olivier Clément, *The Spirit of Solzhenitsyn* (London 1976), has the advantage of being written by a distinguished Orthodox thinker. For recent changes, see Jane Ellis, *The Russian Orthodox Church: Triumphalism and Defensiveness* (Oxford/London 1996); Nathaniel Davis, *A Long Walk to Church: A Contemporary History of Russian Orthodoxy* (Boulder 1995). On Fr Men, see Elizabeth Roberts and Ann Shukman, *Christianity for the Twenty-First Century: The Life and Work of Alexander Men* (London 1996). The persecution and revival of Eastern-rite Catholicism are recounted by Serge Keleher, *Passion and Resurrection – The Greek Catholic Church in Soviet Ukraine, 1939–1989* (L'viv 1993).

Russian Missions. For a sound overview, including also the Greeks, see James J. Stamoolis, *Eastern Orthodox Mission Theology Today* (Maryknoll 1986). On the Alaskan mission, see Paul D. Garrett, *St Innocent Apostle to America* (New York 1979), and the well-chosen anthology of Michael Oleksa, *Alaskan Missionary Spirituality* (New York 1987).

The Russian Emigration. For a general picture, consult Marc Raeff, *Russia Abroad: A Cultural History of the Russian Emigration, 1919–1939* (New York/Oxford 1990). On Russian religious movements in Paris, see Donald A. Lowrie, *St Sergius in Paris: The Orthodox Theological Institute* (London 1954); Aidan Nichols, *Theology in the Russian Diaspora: Church, Fathers, Eucharist in Nikolai Afanas'ev (1893–1966)* (Cambridge 1989): an important study; James Pain and Nicolas Zernov (ed.), *A Bulgakov Anthology* (London 1976); Nicolas Berdyaev, *Dream and Reality: An Essay in Autobiography* (London 1950). For the experiences of a married Russian parish priest, see Alexander Elchaninov, *The Diary of a Russian Priest* (London 1967) – excellent as an informal introduction to Orthodox pastoral theology. Sergei Hackel, *Pearl of Great*

Price: The Life of Mother Maria Skobtsova (1891–1945) (London 1981), recounts the life of a Russian nun who protected Jews in occupied Paris during the Second World War and died in the gas chambers of Ravensbrück. On the Russians (and others) in the USA, consult Constance J. Tarasar (ed.), *Orthodox America 1794–1976* (New York 1975); for Russian Orthodoxy in dialogue with American culture, see Anthony Ugolnik, *The Illuminating Icon* (Grand Rapids 1989). Andrew Blane (ed.), *Georges Florovsky: Russian Intellectual and Orthodox Churchman* (New York 1993), is full of interest.

ORTHODOX THEOLOGY

General Studies. Vladimir Lossky, *The Mystical Theology of the Eastern Church* (London 1957), is most valuable and deserves frequent re-reading. See also Lossky's other books, *The Vision of God* (London 1963) and *In the Image and Likeness of God* (New York 1974). Kallistos Ware, *The Orthodox Way* (London 1979), covers many of the same themes in a simpler way. The *Dogmatics* of Dumitru Staniloae has begun to appear in English under the title *The Experience of God* (Brookline 1994).

Biblical Theology. Not a field in which twentieth-century Orthodox have excelled, although some useful contributions have begun to appear, such as Veselin Kesich, *The Gospel Image of Christ* (new ed., New York 1992), and John Breck, *Spirit of Truth: the Holy Spirit in Johannine Tradition*, vol. 1 (New York 1991). Georges Florovsky, *Bible, Church, Tradition: An Eastern Orthodox View*, in *The Collected Works*, vol. 1 (Belmont 1972), is a masterly summary of the basic guidelines.

The Church. Alexis Khomiakov's essay, 'The Church is One', in W. J. Birkbeck, *Russia and the English Church* (London 1895), is an impressive statement of the unity between the earthly and the heavenly Church. Sergius Bulgakov, *The Orthodox Church* (London 1935), is helpful on the interdependence of hierarchy and laity and on the reception of Church councils. Florovsky's essay, 'The Catholicity of the Church', in *Bible, Church, Tradition*, pp. 37–55, says more in nineteen pages than most authors do in several volumes. On 'eucharistic ecclesiology', see the eloquent but overstated presentation by Nicolas Afanassieff, 'The Church which presides in love', in John Meyendorff (ed.), *The Primacy of Peter* (new ed., New York 1992), but this makes too sharp a contrast between 'eucharistic' and 'universal' ecclesiology. Important correctives are provided by John D. Zizioulas (now Metropolitan of Pergamon), *Being as Communion: Studies in Personhood and the Church* (London/New York 1985). For a Romanian approach, see Dumitru Staniloae, *Theology and the Church* (New York 1980). John H. Erickson, *The Challenge of our Past* (New York 1991), and Archbishop Peter (l'Huillier), *The Church of the Ancient Councils: The Disciplinary Work of the First Four Ecumenical Councils* (New York 1996), are useful introductions to Orthodox Canon Law.

The Theology of Creation and the Ecological Crisis. Paulos Mar Gregorios, *The Human Presence: Ecology and the Age of the Spirit* (new ed., New York 1987), includes many references to the Greek Fathers. Philip Sherrard, *The Rape of Man and Nature: An Enquiry into the Origins and Consequences of Modern Science* (Ipswich 1987), is powerfully argued but unduly negative about modern science.

Human Nature, Sexuality, Marriage. On the distinctive gifts of woman, see Paul Evdokimov, *Woman and the Salvation of the World* (New York 1994). Christos Yannaras, *The Freedom of Morality* (New York 1984), is a courageous and controversial reassessment of Orthodox teaching on asceticism and sexuality; compare Philip Sherrard, *Christianity and Eros* (London 1976). Panayiotis Nellas, *Deification in Christ: Orthodox Perspectives on the Nature of the Human Person* (New York 1987), deals in particular with the image of God and the fall. On the theology of marriage, see the challenging discussion by Paul Evdokimov, *The Sacrament of Love: The Nuptial Mystery in the Light of Orthodox Tradition* (New York 1985), and the more factual treatment by John Meyendorff, *Marriage: An Orthodox Perspective* (second ed., New York 1975); both include the marriage service.

Sacramental Theology. Among Alexander Schmemann's many works in this field, *For the Life of the World: Sacraments* *and Orthodoxy* (New York 1973) is especially valuable. See also *Introduction to Liturgical Theology* (London 1966); *Great Lent* (New York 1969); *Of Water and the Spirit* (New York 1974) (on Baptism); and his last work, published posthumously, *The Eucharist: Sacrament of the Kingdom* (New York 1988). The older study by 'A Monk of the Eastern Church' (Lev Gillet), *Orthodox Spirituality* (new ed., London 1978), is simple yet profound. The finest Byzantine treatment is by St Nicolas Cabasilas, *The Life in Christ*, tr. C. J. deCatanzaro (New York 1984). Archimandrite Vasileios, *Hymn of Entry: Liturgy and Life in the Orthodox Church* (New York 1984), by a contemporary abbot on the Holy Mountain, shows how all things find their unity in the Eucharist.

On Confession, see V. Palachkovsky, *Sin in the Orthodox Church* (New York, no date), and John Chryssavgis, *Repentance and Confession in the Orthodox Church* (Brookline 1990). On the priesthood, consult Joseph J. Allen, *The Ministry of the Church: the Image of Pastoral Care* (New York 1986). For two Orthodox discussions of the ordination of women as priests – the first opposed, the second tentatively in favour – see Thomas Hopko (ed.), *Women and the Priesthood* (New York 1983), and Elisabeth Behr-Sigel, *The Ministry of Women in the Church* (Redondo Beach 1991). On sacramental healing, see Stanley S. Harakas, *Health and Medicine in the Eastern Orthodox Tradition* (New York 1990).

LITURGICAL WORSHIP

For a translation of the Divine Liturgy in 'traditional' language, see *Service Books of the Orthodox Church*, ed. Bishop Herman of Philadelphia (2 vols., St Tikhon's, South Canaan 1984); in 'contemporary' English, see *The Order of the Divine and Holy Liturgy* (Brookline 1987). Hugh Wybrew, *The Orthodox Liturgy* (London 1989), is clear and helpful on the history of the rite; for more detailed study, use Hans-Joachim Schultz, *The Byzantine Liturgy* (New York 1986). A full and authoritative history of the Liturgy is being written by Robert E. Taft: see *The Great Entrance* and *The Diptychs* (Orientalia Christiana

Analecta 200, 238: Rome 1975, 1991). 'A Monk of the Eastern Church', *Serve the Lord with Gladness* (New York 1990), contains short but beautifully expressed meditations on the Liturgy. For the classic Byzantine interpretation, see St Nicolas Cabasilas, *A Commentary on the Divine Liturgy*, tr. J. M. Hussey and P. A. McNulty (new ed., London 1978).

Service Book of the Holy Orthodox-Catholic Apostolic Church, tr. Isabel Florence Hapgood (second ed., New York 1922), is a comprehensive collection of material, prepared with the blessing of St Tikhon of Moscow while Russian Archbishop in America, and still widely used by English-speaking Orthodox. *The Liturgikon: the Book of Divine Services for the Priest and Deacon* (Englewood 1989), issued by the Antiochian Archdiocese in the USA, is superior to Hapgood in translation and arrangement. Full texts for Christmas, Epiphany and seven of the other Great Feasts are contained in *The Festal Menaion*, tr. Mother Mary and Archimandrite Kallistos Ware (London 1969). For Lenten services, see *The Lenten Triodion* (London 1978), by the same translators; for the Paschal season, see *The Pentecostarion* (Holy Transfiguration Monastery, Boston 1990). 'A Monk of the Eastern Church', *The Year of Grace of the Lord* (New York 1980), comments on the Scripture readings for Sundays and Great Feasts throughout the liturgical year, while Metropolitan Anthony (Bloom), *Meditations on a Theme: A Spiritual Journey* (London/Oxford 1972), deals particularly with the Gospels in the pre-Lenten period.

On Vespers and the Presanctified Liturgy, read N. D. Uspensky, *Evening Worship in the Orthodox Church* (New York 1985). On Church music the primary study is still Egon Wellesz, *A History of Byzantine Music and Hymnography* (second ed., Oxford 1961); compare Johann von Gardner, *Russian Church Singing*, vol. 1, *Orthodox Worship and Hymnography* (New York 1980).

For the daily prayers used at home, see *A Manual of Eastern Orthodox Prayers* (The Fellowship of St Alban and St Sergius, London 1945) (also includes the rite of Confession); *Prayer Book* (Holy Trinity Monastery, Jordanville: revised ed., Jordanville 1986); *Daily Prayers for Orthodox Christians*, ed. N. M. Vaporis (Brookline 1986).

INNER PRAYER

Many of the basic texts are to be found in *The Philokalia*: see
the new translation (from the Greek) by G. E. H. Palmer, Philip
Sherrard and Kallistos Ware, vols. i–iv (London 1979–95: one
vol. to follow). There is an earlier translation (from the Russian
text of St Theophan) of selected portions, by E. Kadloubovsky
and G. E. H. Palmer, in 2 vols.: *Writings from the Philokalia on
Prayer of the Heart* (London 1951); *Early Fathers from the
Philokalia* (London 1954). Igumen Chariton of Valamo, *The
Art of Prayer: An Orthodox Anthology* (London 1966), consist-
ing mainly of extracts from St Theophan the Recluse and St
Ignaty Brianchaninov, is easier than *The Philokalia* and might
serve as an introduction to it. For a modern writer from Orthodox Finland in the 'Philokalic' tradition, see Tito Colliander,
The Way of the Ascetics (new ed., London/Oxford 1983).

The best 'initiation' into the Jesus Prayer is 'A Monk of the
Eastern Church', *The Jesus Prayer* (new ed., New York 1987).
Irénée Hausherr, *The Name of Jesus* (Cistercian Studies 44:
Kalamazoo 1978), is learned but at times perverse. On the
practical use of the Prayer, see Kallistos Ware, *The Power of
the Name: The Jesus Prayer in Orthodox Spirituality* (Fairacres
Publication 43: new ed., Oxford 1986).

MONASTICISM

Derwas J. Chitty, *The Desert a City* (Oxford 1966), on the
early history of monasticism in Egypt and Palestine, is the
work of an expert who loved the Judaean wilderness. Peter
Brown, *The Body and Society: Men, Women and Sexual Renun-
ciation in Early Christianity* (London 1989), is a brilliant analysis of the wider cultural context. Primary sources include St
Athanasius, *The Life of Antony*, tr. R. C. Gregg (The Classics
of Western Spirituality: New York 1980); *The Sayings of the
Desert Fathers. The Alphabetical Collection*, tr. Sister Benedicta
Ward (new ed., London/Oxford 1981) (the *Apophthegmata* –
particularly important); *The Ascetic Writings of St Basil*, tr.
W. K. Lowther Clarke (London 1925); Cyril of Scythopolis,

Lives of the Monks of Palestine, tr. R. M. Price (Cistercian Studies 114; Kalamazoo 1991); St John Climacus, *The Ladder of Divine Ascent*, tr. Colm Luibheid and Norman Russell (The Classics of Western Spirituality: New York 1982). N. F. Robinson, *Monasticism in the Orthodox Churches* (London 1916), includes the monastic profession rites. On the ministry of the 'elder', the *geron* or *starets*, see Irénée Hausherr, *Spiritual Direction in the Early Christian East* (Cistercian Studies 116: Kalamazoo 1990).

Mount Athos. The best introduction, emphasizing the inner ideal of the monk, is Philip Sherrard, *Athos: The Holy Mountain* (London 1982). Emmanuel Amand de Mendieta, *Mount Athos: The Garden of the Panaghia* (Berlin 1972), is good on the historical side, while R. M. Dawkins, *The Monks of Athos* (London 1936), recounts many of the monastic traditions concerning icons and miracles. For the life and writings of St Silouan, see the book by his disciple Archimandrite Sophrony, *Saint Silouan the Athonite* (Tolleshunt Knights 1991).

ICONS

On the theology and spirituality of the icon and its place in worship, the three best studies available in English are Leonid Ouspensky and Vladimir Lossky, *The Meaning of Icons* (new ed., New York 1982); Leonid Ouspensky, *Theology of the Icon* (new ed., 2 vols., New York 1992); and Paul Evdokimov, *The Art of the Icon: A Theology of Beauty* (Redondo Beach 1990). For a simpler introduction, see Michel Quenot, *The Icon: Window on the Kingdom* (London 1992), or John Baggley, *Doors of Perception – icons and their spiritual significance* (London/Oxford 1987). On the practical techniques of icon painting, see Egon Sendler, *The Icon: Image of the Invisible* (Redondo Beach 1988).

On the Iconoclast controversy, consult Jaroslav Pelikan, *Imago Dei: The Byzantine Apologia for Icons* (New Haven 1990). For the primary sources, see St John of Damascus, *On the Divine Images*, tr. David Anderson (New York 1980); St Theodore the Studite, *On the Holy Icons*, tr. Catharine P. Roth

(New York 1981). The decisions of the 787 Council are translated in Daniel J. Sahas, *Icon and Logos: Sources in Eighth-Century Iconoclasm* (Toronto 1986). Gervase Mathew, *Byzantine Aesthetics* (London 1963), is fascinating but often obscure. For the urgent relevance of the icon in our desacralized society, see Philip Sherrard, *The Sacred in Life and Art* (Ipswich 1990).

REUNION

Dictionary of the Ecumenical Movement, ed. Nicholas Lossky and others (Geneva/Grand Rapids 1991), contains many articles by Orthodox or about Orthodoxy. The involvement of the Orthodox Church in reunion schemes from the fifteenth century onwards is described by Georges Florovsky and Nicolas Zernov in *A History of the Ecumenical Movement 1517–1948*, ed. Ruth Rouse and Stephen Charles Neill (3rd ed., Geneva 1986). For a fuller version of Florovsky's text, see his *Collected Works*, vols. 2 and 4 (Belmont 1974, 1975); cf. also vols. 13–14 (Vaduz/Belmont 1989). Methodios Fouyas, *Orthodoxy, Roman Catholicism, and Anglicanism* (London 1972), contains abundant documentation, but would be more illuminating if fuller allowance were made for the historical and cultural setting. On Orthodox relations with Rome, see Edward Kilmartin, *Toward Reunion: The Roman Catholic and the Orthodox Churches* (New York 1979), and Robert Barringer (ed.), *Rome and Constantinople: Essays in the Dialogue of Love* (Brookline 1984). For documentation, see E. J. Stormon (ed.), *Towards the Healing of Schism: The Sees of Rome and Constantinople* (New York 1987). On relations with Anglicanism, see William Palmer, *Notes on a Visit to the Russian Church in the Years 1840, 1841*, ed. Cardinal Newman (London 1882), a vivid personal narrative of an exploratory journey; W. J. Birkbeck, *Russia and the English Church* (London 1895), containing the important Khomiakov–Palmer correspondence; J. A. Douglas, *The Relations of the Anglican Churches with the Eastern-Orthodox* (London 1921), which discusses the question of intercommunion; V. T. Istavridis, *Orthodoxy and Anglicanism* (London 1966), a useful summary; *Anglican–Orthodox Dialogue: The Dublin Agreed Statement 1984* (London 1984), also including the Moscow Agreed Statement (1976) and the Athens Report (1978) on the ordination of women priests. On Orthodoxy and the World Council of Churches, see Gennadios Limouris, *Orthodox Visions of Ecumenism: Statements, Messages, and Reports on the Ecumenical Movement 1902–1992* (Geneva 1994).

BIBLIOGRAPHIES: WORKS OF REFERENCE

Only books in English are listed above. For further bibliography consult:

Byzantine Christianity: Hans-Georg Beck, *Kirche und Theologische Literatur im Byzantinischen Reich* (Munich 1959); J. M. Hussey (ed.), *The Cambridge Medieval History*, vol. 4, parts 1–2, *The Byzantine Empire* (Cambridge 1966–7); Alexander P. Kazhdan (ed.), *The Oxford Dictionary of Byzantium* (3 vols., New York/Oxford 1991).

The Copts: Aziz S. Atiya (ed.), *The Coptic Encyclopedia* (8 vols., New York 1991).

The Turkish period: Gerhard Podskalsky, *Griechische Theologie in der Zeit der Türkenherrschaft 1453–1821* (Munich 1988).

Modern Greece: Mary Jo Clogg and Richard Clogg, *Greece* (World Bibliographical Series, vol. 17: Oxford 1981).

The twelve-volume Greek work published by A. Martinos, *Thriskevtiki kai Ithiki Enkyklopaideia* (Athens 1962–8), although uneven, is a mine of information. The later volumes of the *Dictionnaire de Spiritualité* (17 vols., Paris 1933–95) contain excellent articles on Eastern Christendom.

For facts and figures on contemporary Orthodoxy, consult Ronald G. Roberson, *The Eastern Christian Churches: A Brief Survey* (Pontifical Oriental Institute: 5th ed., Rome 1995). For the names and addresses of Orthodox bishops, see Nikolaus Wyrwoll (ed.), *Orthodoxia 1994–1995* (Ostkirchliches Institut, Regensburg 1994).

Index

John the Evangelist, St 21, 231
John, Archbishop of Finland 133
John of Kronstadt, St 121–2, 239,
 270
John Tzimisces, Emperor 41
John II, Metropolitan of
 Russia 18
John VIII, Emperor of
 Byzantium 70–71
John VIII, Pope 56
John XIX, Pope 316
Jordanville 183
Joseph, Metropolitan of
 Petrograd 154
Joseph of the New Skete, Fr 130,
 131
Joseph of Volokalamsk, St 104–7,
 109
Julian Calendar 301–3
Justinian, Emperor 38, 41, 44
Justinian, Patriarch of
 Romania 167–8

Karlovtsy Synod 153, 175–6
Karmiris, I. 140
Kartashev, A. 124, 178
Kazan, Academy of 122–3
Ken, Bishop 318
kenosis 80, 84
Kenya 133, 189–90
Khazars 73
Khodre, Metropolitan
 George 134
Khomiakov, A. 1–2, 43, 51, 120,
 123–4, 239, 243–5, 251–3, 308,
 325
Khrushchev 157
Kiev 78–82, 94, 102, 103, 117
Kireev, A. 321
Kireyevsky, I. 121
Kleronomia 128
kneeling 269
Kollyvades 99–100
Kontoglou, P. 142
Korea 189
Kosmas the Aetolian, St 101
Kovalevsky, E. (Bishop Jean de St-
 Denys) 186

Krasnov-Levitin, A. 158
Kritopoulos *see* Metrophanes
 Kritopoulos
Kroug, Gregory 179
Kulikovo, Battle of 82, 84
Kyrill, Metropolitan of
 Smolensk 164

laity 251–3
 as theologians 48
 in brotherhoods 95
language in worship 74, 77, 179,
 184, 267–8
Last Day 233, 261–2
Lausanne, Treaty of 127
Lavra, the Great 39
League of Militant Atheists 147
Lebanon 134
Lenin 125
Leo III, Emperor 31
Leo V, Emperor 31
Leo the Great, St 26, 28, 274, 313
Leo III, Pope 45, 51
Leo IX, Pope 58
Leo XIII, Pope 203, 319
Leonid of Optino, Fr 120
Leontius of Neapolis 32, 36n.
Lev (Gillet), Archimandrite 180,
 222n.
Liddon, H. P. 102
Light, the Divine 66–9, 119,
 234n.
Limbo 224n.
Lintula 133
Litanies 272
Little Entrance 280
Little Russia 94
 see Ukraine; Kiev
liturgical approach of
 Orthodoxy 264–7
Liturgies, the four different 280
Liturgy, the Divine 14n.
 see Eucharist
Liturgy and personal
 devotion 303
Liturgy and Tradition 204
'Living Church' 150–51, 153, 197
London 172–3

Lossky, N.   179
Lossky, V.   37n., 68n., 140, 149n.,
   179, 191n., 195, 208n., 213,
   218, 230, 232n., 253n., 260,
   262n., 318
Louis of France, St   82
Loyola *see* Ignatius Loyola
Lubac, H. de   315
Lucas Notaras   71
Lukaris *see* Cyril Lukaris
Luke, Bishop of Vladimir   80
Lutheranism   93–4, 317

Macarius of Alexandria, St   38
Macarius of Egypt, St   38, 64–5,
   67, 233n., 234n.
Macarius (Glukharev)   123
Macarius (Notaras), St   100
Macarius of Optino, St   120–1
Macarius, Travels of see Paul of
   Aleppo
Macedonia   169
Makarios III, Archbishop of
   Cyprus   89, 136
Maksim, Patriarch of
   Bulgaria   170
man, doctrine of *see* personhood
Marcian, Emperor   25
Maria (Skobtsova), Mother   336
Mark of Ephesus, St   71, 203,
   213
Mark the Hermit, St   261
marriage   294–6
   of clergy   51, 95, 139, 291
   of bishops   150, 291
   mixed marriages   311
Martin of Tours, St   81
martyrdom   14–15, 148, 188, 191
   and monastic life   37
   and marriage   295
Mary the Mother of God   25, 99,
   222, 257–61
matter, Orthodox doctrine of
   33–4, 234–5, 261, 274
Matthopoulos, E.   142
Mau Mau   190
Maximos, Bishop of
   Pittsburgh   183

Maximus, Bishop of
   Serpukhov   154
Maximus the Confessor, St   63,
   64, 68n., 207, 225, 231, 232
Maximus the Greek, St   107–8,
   109
Meditation, 'methods of'   304
Meletios IV, Patriarch of
   Constantinople   319
Meletius Syrigos   97, 255n.
Men, A.   163
Mensbrugghe *see* Alexis
'merit'   222
Methodists   317
Methodius, St   5, 73–6
Metousiosis see Transubstantiation
Metrophanes Kritopoulos   98,
   203
Metropolitans   16, 27
Meyendorff, J.   179, 244n., 254n.
Michael III of Constantinople   46
Michael VIII of
   Constantinople   61–2
Michael Cerularius   58–9, 203
Michael Choniates   220
Milan, 'Edict' of   18–19
millet system   89
Minucius Felix   233n.
missionary work   73–4, 83–4, 88,
   122–3, 187–90
Mitrophan of Sarai   83
Moghila *see* Peter of Moghila
Mohammed the Prophet   29
   see Islam
Mohammed II, Sultan   88
Moldavia   76
moment of consecration at
   Eucharist   283
'Monarchy' of the Father   214,
   216
monasticism
   in Byzantium   36–40
   in Russia   79–80, 104–6, 115,
   118
   in Orthodoxy today   129–32,
   133, 134, 135, 136, 143, 162,
   168, 169, 170, 180, 183, 191
Mongols   81–3